Praise for *Causal Inference in Python*

Causal inference is one of the most important approaches for modern data scientists, but there's still a big gap between theory and applications. Matheus has written the best book yet to teach you how to go from toy models to state-of-the-art methods that work on real data and solve important, practical problems. I'm excited to finally have the perfect resource to recommend that clearly explains the latest approaches and provides detailed code and examples for those who learn by doing.

—*Sean J. Taylor, Chief Scientist at Motif Analytics*

The analyst who avoids answering all causal questions is limiting themselves greatly, and the analyst who answers them carelessly is asking for trouble. Facure's book is an accessible introduction to causal inference, focusing on the tools and contexts most familiar to the Python data analytics community

—*Nick Huntington-Klein, Professor of Economics and author of*
The Effect: An Introduction to Research Design and Causality

Causal inference tools play a major role in guiding decision-making. In this engaging book, Matheus Facure provides a clear introduction to these tools, paying particular attention to how to use them in practice. The business applications and detailed Python code will help you get the job done.

—*Pedro H. C. Sant'Anna, Emory University*
and Causal Solutions

Causal Inference in Python
Applying Causal Inference in the Tech Industry

Matheus Facure

Beijing · Boston · Farnham · Sebastopol · Tokyo

Causal Inference in Python

by Matheus Facure

Published by O'Reilly Media, Inc., 1005 Gravenstein Highway North, Sebastopol, CA 95472.

O'Reilly books may be purchased for educational, business, or sales promotional use. Online editions are also available for most titles (*http://oreilly.com*). For more information, contact our corporate/institutional sales department: 800-998-9938 or *corporate@oreilly.com*.

Acquisitions Editor: Nicole Butterfield
Development Editor: Virginia Wilson
Production Editor: Katherine Tozer
Copyeditor: Kim Cofer
Proofreader: James Fraleigh

Indexer: Sue Klefstad
Interior Designer: David Futato
Cover Designer: Karen Montgomery
Illustrator: Kate Dullea

July 2023:   First Edition

Revision History for the First Edition
2023-07-14:   First Release

See *http://oreilly.com/catalog/errata.csp?isbn=9781098140250* for release details.

978-1-098-14025-0

[LSI]

Table of Contents

Part II. Adjusting for Bias

Part III.   Effect Heterogeneity and Personalization

Part IV.   Panel Data

Part V. Alternative Experimental Designs

Preface

Picture yourself as a new data scientist who's just starting out in a fast-growing and promising startup. Although you haven't mastered machine learning, you feel pretty confident about your skills. You've completed dozens of online courses on the subject and even gotten a few good ranks in prediction competitions. You are now ready to apply all that knowledge to the real world and you can't wait for it. Life is good.

Then, your team leader comes with a graph that looks something like this:

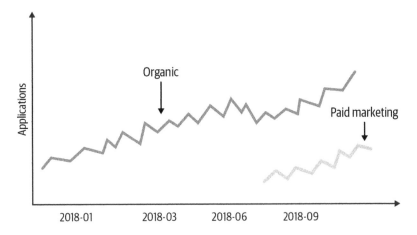

And an accompanying question: "Hey, we want you to figure out how many additional customers paid marketing is really bringing us. When we turned it on, we definitely saw some customers coming from the paid marketing channel, but it looks like we also had a drop in organic applications. We think *some of the customers from paid marketing would have come to us even without paid marketing*." Well…you were expecting a challenge, but this?! How could you know what would have happened without paid marketing? I guess you could compare the total number of applications, organic and paid, before and after turning on the marketing campaign. But in a fast growing and dynamic company, how would you know that nothing else changes when they launch the campaign (see Figure P-1)?

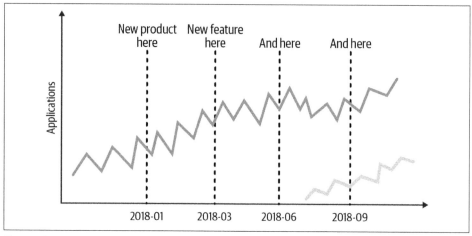

Figure P-1. Fast-growing company with an ever-changing product

Changing gears a bit (or not at all), place yourself in the shoes of a brilliant risk analyst. You were just hired by a lending company and your first task is to perfect its credit risk model. The goal is to have a good automated decision-making system that assesses the customers' credit worthiness (underwrites them) and decides how much credit the company can lend them. Needless to say, errors in this system are incredibly expensive, especially if the given credit line is high.

A key component of this automated decision making is understanding the impact more credit lines have on the likelihood of customers defaulting. Can they manage a huge chunk of credit and pay it back or will they go down a spiral of overspending and unmanageable debt? To model this behavior, you start by plotting credit average default rates by given credit lines. To your surprise, the data displays this unexpected pattern:

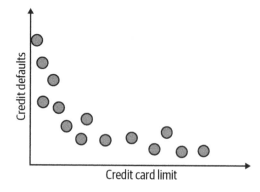

The relationship between credit and defaults seems to be negative. How come giving more credit results in lower chances of defaults? Rightfully suspicious, you go talk to other analysts in an attempt to understand this. It turns out the answer is very simple: to no one's surprise, the lending company gives more credit to customers that have lower chances of defaulting. So, it is not the case that high lines reduce default risk, but rather, the other way around. Lower risk increases the credit lines. That explains it, but you still haven't solved the initial problem: how to model the relationship between credit risk and credit lines with this data. Surely you don't want your system to think more lines implies lower chances of default. Also, naively randomizing lines in an A/B test just to see what happens is pretty much off the table, due to the high cost of wrong credit decisions.

What both of these problems have in common is that you need to know the impact of changing something that you can control (marketing budget and credit limit) on some business outcome you wish to influence (customer applications and default risk). Impact or effect estimation has been the pillar of modern science for centuries, but only recently have we made huge progress in systematizing the tools of this trade into the field that is coming to be known as *causal inference*. Additionally, advancements in machine learning and a general desire to automate and inform decision-making processes with data has brought causal inference into the industry and public institutions. Still, the causal inference toolkit is not yet widely known by decision makers or data scientists.

Hoping to change that, I wrote *Causal Inference for the Brave and True*, an online book that covers the traditional tools and recent developments from causal inference, all with open source Python software, in a rigorous, yet lighthearted way. Now, I'm taking that one step further, reviewing all that content from an industry perspective, with updated examples and, hopefully, more intuitive explanations. My goal is for this book to be a starting point for whatever question you have about making decisions with data.

Prerequisites

This book is an introduction to causal inference in Python, but it is not an introductory book in general. It's introductory because I'll focus on application, rather than rigorous proofs and theorems of causal inference; additionally, when forced to choose, I'll opt for a simpler and intuitive explanation, rather than a complete and complex one.

It is not introductory in general because I'll assume some prior knowledge about machine learning, statistics, and programming in Python. It is not too advanced either, but I will be throwing in some terms that you should know beforehand.

For example, here is a piece of text that might appear:

> The first thing you have to deal with is the fact that continuous variables have $P(T = t) = 0$ everywhere. That's because the probability is the area under the density and the area of a single point is always zero. A way around this is to use the conditional density $f(T|X)$ instead of the conditional probability $P(T = t|X)$.

I won't provide much explanation on what a density is and why it is different from a probability. Here is another example, this time about machine learning:

> Alternatively, you can use machine learning models to estimate the propensity score. But you have to be more careful. First, you must ensure that your ML model outputs a calibrated probability prediction. Second, you need to use out-of-fold predictions to avoid bias due to overfitting.

Here, I won't explain what a machine learning model is, nor what it means for it to have calibrated predictions, what overfitting is, or out-of-fold prediction. Since those are fairly basic data science concepts, I'll expect you to know them from the start.

In fact, here is a list of things I recommend you know before reading this book:

- Basic knowledge of Python, including the most commonly used data scientist libraries: pandas, NumPy, Matplotlib, scikit-learn. I come from an economics background, so you don't have to worry about me using very fancy code. Just make sure you know the basics pretty well.
- Knowledge of basic statistical concepts, like distributions, probability, hypothesis testing, regression, noise, expected values, standard deviation, and independence. Chapter 2 will include a statistical review, in case you need a refresher.
- Knowledge of basic data science concepts, like machine learning model, cross-validation, overfitting, and some of the most used machine learning models (gradient boosting, decision trees, linear regression, logistic regression).
- Knowledge of high school math, such as functions, logarithms, roots, matrices, and vectors, and some college-level math, such as derivatives and integrals.

The main audience of this book is data scientists working in the industry. If you fit this description, there is a pretty good chance that you cover the prerequisites that I've mentioned. Also, keep in mind that this is a broad audience, with very diverse skill sets. For this reason, I might include some notes, paragraphs, or sections that are meant for the most advanced reader. So don't worry if you don't understand every single line in this book. You'll still be able to extract a lot from it. And maybe you'll come back for a second read once you've mastered some of the basics.

Outline

Part I covers the basics concepts on causal inference. Chapter 1 introduces the key concepts of causal inference as you use them to reason about the effect of cutting prices. Chapter 2 talks about the importance of A/B testing (or randomized control trial) not only as an instrument for decision making, but as the gold standard you will use to benchmark the other causal inference tools. This will also be a great opportunity to review some statistical concepts. Chapter 3 is mostly theoretical, covering causal identification and graphical models, a powerful method for (literally) drawing your assumptions about the causal process and reasoning about what you need to do in order to untangle association from causation. After finishing Part I, you should have the basic foundation to think in terms of causal inference.

In Part II you'll be introduced to two of the workhorses for untangling causation from correlation: linear regression and propensity weighting. Chapter 4 covers linear regression, but not from a perspective that most data scientists are familiar with. Rather, you'll learn about an important bias removal technique: orthogonalization. Chapter 5 covers propensity score and doubly robust estimation.

Part III takes what you saw in Part II and adds machine learning and big data to the mix. You'll look into causal inference as a tool for personalized decision making. Through the eyes of a food delivery service, you'll try to understand which customers should be given discount coupons to capture their loyalty and which customers don't need that extra incentive. In Chapter 6, you'll enter the world of heterogeneous treatment effects. Chapter 7 goes into some of the recent developments in the intersection between machine learning and causal inference. In this chapter, you'll learn methods like the T-, X-, and S-learners and Double/Debiased Machine Learning, all in the context of treatment personalization.

Part IV adds the time dimension to causal inference. In some situations, you'll have records of the same customers or markets across multiple time periods, which builds up to what is called a *panel dataset*. You'll learn how to leverage panels to uncover the true impact of paid marketing, even without being able to randomize who gets to see your advertisements. Chapter 8 will walk you through difference-in-differences, including some of the recent developments in this literature. Chapter 9 will cover synthetic control (and variations of it), also in the context of understanding the impact of marketing campaigns.

Finally, Part V dives into alternative experiment designs, for when randomization is off the table. Chapter 10 will cover geo-experiments, where the goal is to find regions to treat and regions to serve as controls, and switchback experiments, for when you have very few units of analysis and wish to figure out the treatment effect by turning the treatment on and off for the same unit. Chapter 11 dives into experiments with noncompliance and introduces you to instrumental variables (IV). It also briefly covers discontinuity design.

Conventions Used in This Book

The following typographical conventions are used in this book:

Italic
:   Indicates new terms, URLs, email addresses, filenames, and file extensions.

`Constant width`
:   Used for program listings, as well as within paragraphs to refer to program elements such as variable or function names, databases, data types, environment variables, statements, and keywords.

`Constant width bold`
:   Shows commands or other text that should be typed literally by the user.

`Constant width italic`
:   Shows text that should be replaced with user-supplied values or by values determined by context.

This element signifies a tip or suggestion.

This element signifies a general note.

This element indicates a warning or caution.

Using Code Examples

Supplemental material (code examples, exercises, etc.) is available for download at *https://github.com/matheusfacure/causal-inference-in-python-code*.

If you have a technical question or a problem using the code examples, please email *support@oreilly.com*.

This book is here to help you get your job done. In general, if example code is offered with this book, you may use it in your programs and documentation. You do not need to contact us for permission unless you're reproducing a significant portion of the code. For example, writing a program that uses several chunks of code from this book does not require permission. Selling or distributing examples from O'Reilly books does require permission. Answering a question by citing this book and quoting example code does not require permission. Incorporating a significant amount of example code from this book into your product's documentation does require permission.

We appreciate, but generally do not require, attribution. An attribution usually includes the title, author, publisher, and ISBN. For example: "*Causal Inference in Python* by Matheus Facure (O'Reilly). Copyright 2023 Matheus Facure Alves, 978-1-098-14025-0."

If you feel your use of code examples falls outside fair use or the permission given above, feel free to contact us at *permissions@oreilly.com*.

O'Reilly Online Learning

For more than 40 years, *O'Reilly Media* has provided technology and business training, knowledge, and insight to help companies succeed.

Our unique network of experts and innovators share their knowledge and expertise through books, articles, and our online learning platform. O'Reilly's online learning platform gives you on-demand access to live training courses, in-depth learning paths, interactive coding environments, and a vast collection of text and video from O'Reilly and 200+ other publishers. For more information, visit *https://oreilly.com*.

How to Contact Us

Please address comments and questions concerning this book to the publisher:

O'Reilly Media, Inc.
1005 Gravenstein Highway North
Sebastopol, CA 95472
800-889-8969 (in the United States or Canada)
707-829-7019 (international or local)
707-829-0104 (fax)
support@oreilly.com
https://www.oreilly.com/about/contact.html

We have a web page for this book, where we list errata, examples, and any additional information. You can access this page at *https://oreil.ly/causal-inference-in-python*.

For news and information about our books and courses, visit *https://oreilly.com*.

Find us on LinkedIn: *https://linkedin.com/company/oreilly-media*.

Follow us on Twitter: *https://twitter.com/oreillymedia*.

Watch us on YouTube: *https://youtube.com/oreillymedia*.

Acknowledgments

First, I would like to express my gratitude to my amazing editor, Virginia Wilson. I am grateful for all the feedback and patience you have shown me. Without you, this book would not have been written. I am also thankful for Nicole Butterfield and the entire team at O'Reilly for supporting my first work and putting so much trust in me. Also, a special thanks to Danny Elfanbaum, who helped me out a lot with technical issues during the writing process.

I am indebted to all the technical reviewers who dedicated their precious time to review this book. Thank you, Laurence Wong, for the very detailed comments and for suggesting important additions to the book. Thank you, Adrian Keister, for your thorough review, incredibly pertinent critiques, for trying out the code and making very relevant suggestions on how to make it clearer. The book has greatly improved thanks to your feedback. Jorge Reyes, thanks for leaving no stone unturned and spotting very hard-to-find mistakes in the technical notation, for all the relevant questions you made, and for all the kind compliments. Thank you, Roni Kobrosly, for your comments on how to make the book more accessible and engaging. Thank you, Subhasish Misra, for the helpful feedback, especially on Chapter 5. Shawhin Talebi, I appreciate the suggestions you have made on very pertinent topics to add to the book.

Thank you to all those who provided me with more content-specific feedback. Thank you, Guilherme Jardim Duarte, for all your help with all things related to Pearlian causality, especially in reviewing Chapter 3. Many thanks to Henrique Lopes and Juliano Garcia for your review on the intersection between causal inference and business applications. Chapters 4, 6, and 7 were greatly improved with your feedback. Raphael Bruce, I'm very grateful for your honest and precise feedback on Chapter 4. Thank you, Luis Moneda, for your expertise, for all our great talks about causality, and for helping me review Chapter 1. Thank you, Denis Reis, for the review of Chapter 2. Statistics is a tricky subject, and having you as a reviewer took a lot of anxiety off my shoulders.

Writing about a technical topic can sometimes be a solitary endeavor, which is why I feel incredibly fortunate for all the support I got from such amazing and respected professionals: Sean J. Taylor, Pedro H. C. Sant'Anna, Nick C. Huntington-Klein,

Carlos Cinelli, Joshua Angrist and Scott Cunningham. Without your kind feedback, I would have likely given up long ago.

It is a blessing to work in a field that has such helpful and solicitous researchers. I am deeply grateful to Kaspar Wüthrich, for your patience with my synthetic control questions and for reviewing the section on synthetic control t-test. Jinglong Zhao, I greatly appreciate your work on nontraditional experiment design. Thanks for helping me with the questions I had with synthetic control and switchback experiment design. Peter Hull, thanks for always surprising me with the intricacies of linear regression.

Thank you to all the great academics I've interacted with, who have made me think more clearly about causality: Pedro H. C. Sant'Anna, Carlos Cinelli, Nick C. Huntington-Klein, and Peter Hull. I'm also grateful for my friends and colleagues from Nubank, who I can always count on to discuss and propose the most interesting and challenging causal inference problems: Arthur Goes, Nilo Kruchelski, Pedro Igor, Tatyana Zabanova, Diandra Kubo, Pedro Bairão, Fernanda Leal, Murilo Nicolau, Mariana Sanches, Victor Dalla, Euclides Filho, Guilherme Peixoto, Silvano Filho, Alexandre Floriano, Ana Ortega, Hector Lira, Lucas Estevam, Risk Slangen, and André Segalla.

Edigar Antonio Lutero Alves, thanks for reading this book and providing your critical and accurate feedback. You have always been an amazing father and a role model.

Elis Jordão Stropa, thank you for staying by my side and supporting my crazy ideas and projects. Thank you for your patience with me while this book was being written at the same time Francisco came into the world. You are a great wife and a great mother.

PART I

Fundamentals

CHAPTER 1

Introduction to Causal Inference

In this first chapter I'll introduce you to a lot of the fundamental concepts of causal inference as well as its main challenges and uses. Here, you will learn a lot of jargon that will be used in the rest of the book. Also, I want you to always keep in mind why you need causal inference and what you can do with it. This chapter will not be about coding, but about very important first concepts of causal inference.

What Is Causal Inference?

Causality is something you might know as a dangerous epistemological terrain you must avoid going into. Your statistics teacher might have said over and over again that "association is not causation" and that confusing the two would cast you to academic ostracism or, at the very least, be severely frowned upon. But you see, that is the thing: *sometimes, association is causation.*

We humans know this all too well, since, apparently, we've been primed to take association for causation. When you decide not to drink that fourth glass of wine, you correctly inferred that it would mess you up on the next day. You are drawing from past experience: from nights when you drank too much and woke up with a headache; from nights you took just one glass of wine, or none at all, and nothing happened. You've learned that there is something more to the association between drinking and hangovers. You've inferred causality out of it.

On the flip side, there is some truth to your stats teacher's warnings. Causation is a slippery thing. When I was a kid, I ate calamari doré twice and both times it ended terribly, which led me to conclude I was allergic to squid (and clam, octopus, and any other type of sea invertebrate). It took me more than 20 years to try it again. When I did, it was not only delicious, but it also caused me no harm. In this case, I had confused association with causation. This was a harmless confusion, as it only deprived me of delicious seafood for some years, but mistaking association for causation can have much more severe consequences. If you invest in the stock market, you've probably been through a situation where you decided to put money in just before a steep increase in prices, or to withdraw just before everything collapsed. This likely tempted you to think you could time the market. If you managed to ignore that temptation, good for you. But many fall for it, thinking that their intuition is causally linked to the erratic movements of stocks. In some situations, this belief leads to riskier and riskier bets until, eventually, almost everything is lost.

In a nutshell, association is when two quantities or random variables move together, whereas causality is when change in one variable causes change in another. For example, you could associate the number of Nobel Prizes a country has with the per-capita consumption of chocolate, but even though these variables might move together, it would be foolish to think one causes the other. It's easy to see why association doesn't imply causation, but equating the two is a whole different matter. *Causal inference is the science of inferring causation from association and understanding when and why they differ.*

Why We Do Causal Inference

Causal inference can be done for the sole purpose of understanding reality. But there is often a normative component to it. The reason you've inferred that too much drinking causes headaches is that you want to change your drinking habits to avoid the pain. The company you work for wants to know if marketing costs cause growth in revenues because, if they do, managers can use it as a leverage to increase profits. Generally speaking, *you want to know cause-and-effect relationships so that you can intervene on the cause to bring upon a desired effect.* If you take causal inference to the industry, it becomes mostly a branch of the decision-making sciences.

Since this book is mostly industry focused, it will cover the part of causal inference that is preoccupied with understanding the impact of interventions. What would happen if you used another price instead of this price you're currently asking for your merchandise? What would happen if you switch from this low-sugar diet you're on to that low-fat diet? What will happen to the bank's margins if it increases the customers' credit line? Should the government give tablets to every kid in school to boost their reading test score or should it build an old-fashioned library? Is marrying good for your personal finances or are married couples wealthier just because wealthy people are more likely to attract a partner in the first place? These questions are all practical. They stem from a desire to change something in your business or in your life so that you can be better off.

Machine Learning and Causal Inference

If you take a deeper look at the types of questions you want to answer with causal inference, you will see they are mostly of the "what if" type. I'm sorry to be the one that says it, but machine learning (ML) is just awful at those types of questions.

ML is very good at answering prediction questions. As Ajay Agrawal, Joshua Gans, and Avi Goldfarb put it in the book *Prediction Machines* (Harvard Business Review Press), "the new wave of artificial intelligence does not actually bring us intelligence but instead a critical component of intelligence—prediction." You can do all sorts of beautiful things with machine learning. The only requirement is to frame your problems as prediction ones. Want to translate from English to Portuguese? Then build an ML model that predicts Portuguese sentences when given English sentences. Want to recognize faces? Then create an ML model that predicts the presence of a face in a subsection of a picture.

However, ML is not a panacea. It can perform wonders under rigid boundaries and still fail miserably if its data deviates a little from what the model is accustomed to. To give another example from *Prediction Machines*, "in many industries, low prices are associated with low sales. For example, in the hotel industry, prices are low outside the tourist season, and prices are high when demand is highest and hotels are full. Given that data, a naive prediction might suggest that increasing the price would lead to more rooms sold."

Machine learning uses associations between variables to predict one from the other. It will work incredibly well as long as you don't change the variables it is using to make predictions. This completely defeats the purpose of using predictive ML for most decision making that involves interventions.

The fact that most data scientists know a lot of ML but not much about causal inference leads to an abundance of ML models being deployed where they are not useful for the task at hand. One of the main goals of companies is to *increase* sales or usage. Yet, an ML model that just predicts sales is oftentimes useless—if not harmful—for this purpose. This model might even conclude something nonsensical, as in the example where high volumes of sales are associated with high prices. Yet, you'd be surprised by how many companies implement predictive ML models when the goal they have in mind has nothing to do with predictions.

This does not mean that ML is completely useless for causal inference. It just means that, when naively applied, it often does more harm than good. But if you approach ML from a different angle, as a toolbox of powerful models rather than purely predictive machines, you'll start to see how they can connect to the goals of causal inference. In Part III I'll show what you need to watch out for when mixing ML and causal inference and how to repurpose common ML algorithms, like decision trees and gradient boosting, to do causal inference.

Association and Causation

Intuitively, you kind of know why association is not causation. If someone tells you that top-notch consulting causes your business to improve, you are bound to raise an eyebrow. How can you know if the consulting firm is actually causing business to improve or if it is just that only flourishing businesses have the luxury to hire those services?

To make things a bit more tangible, put yourself in the shoes of an online marketplace company. Small and medium-sized businesses use your online platform to advertise and sell their products. These businesses have complete autonomy in stuff like setting prices and when to have sales. But it is in the best interest of your company that these businesses flourish and prosper. So, you decide to help them by giving guidance on how, if, and when to set up a sales campaign where they announce a temporary price drop to consumers. To do that, the first thing you need to know is the *impact of lowering prices on units sold*. If the gains from selling more compensate for the loss of selling cheaper, sales will be a good idea. If you hadn't already noticed, this is a causal question. You need to answer how many additional units a business would have sold had they lowered prices compared to not doing anything.

Needless to say, this is a complicated question; maybe too complicated for the beginning of this book. Different businesses operate within your platform. Some sell food; some sell clothes. Some sell fertilizers and agricultural products. As a result, price cuts might have different impacts depending on the type of business. For instance, it might be a good idea for a clothing business to announce lower prices one week prior to Father's Day. Yet, a similar price drop for an agribusiness will probably do very little. So, let's simplify the problem a bit. Let's focus your attention on only one type of business: those that sell kids' toys. Also, let's focus your attention on one period of the year: December, before Christmas. For now, you'll just try to answer how cutting prices during these periods increases sales so you can pass this information along to the businesses operating in the kids' toy industry, allowing them to make better decisions.

To decide if sales is a good idea, you can leverage information from multiple kids' toys businesses. This data is stored in a pandas data frame for you to access. Here are the first few rows for you to get a sense of what you are dealing with:

	store	weeks_to_xmas	avg_week_sales	is_on_sale	weekly_amount_sold
0	1	3	12.98	1	219.60
1	1	2	12.98	1	184.70
2	1	1	12.98	1	145.75
3	1	0	12.98	0	102.45
4	2	3	19.92	0	103.22
5	2	2	19.92	0	53.73

The first column is the store's unique identifier (ID). You have weekly data for each store in the month of December. You also have information about the size of each business in terms of average products sold per week during that year. A boolean column (0 or 1) flags the business as having a sale at the time. The last column shows the average weekly sales of that store during that week.

Unit of Analysis

The unit of analysis in a causal inference study is usually the thing you wish to intervene on (treat). In most cases, the unit of analysis will be people, as when you want to know the effect of a new product on customer retention. But it is not uncommon to have other types of units. For instance, in this chapter's example, the unit of analysis is business. In this same example, you could also try to answer *when* is the best moment to have sales, in which case the unit of analysis would be a time period (week, in this case).

The Treatment and the Outcome

Now that you have some data to look at, it's time to learn our first bit of technicality. Let's call T_i the treatment for unit i:

$$T_i = \begin{cases} 1 \text{ if unit } i \text{ received the treatment} \\ 0 \text{ otherwise} \end{cases}$$

The treatment here doesn't need to be medicine or anything from the medical field. Instead, it is just a term I'll use to denote some intervention for which I want to know the effect of. In this case, the treatment is simply a price drop for one of the businesses inside your online platform, represented by the column is_on_sale.

Treatment Notation

In some texts and later on in this book, you'll sometimes see D instead of T to denote the treatment. D will avoid much confusion when you have a time dimension to your causal problems.

Additionally, I'll be referring to weekly_amount_sold (the variable that I want to influence here) as the *outcome*. I'll represent the outcome for unit i with Y_i. With these two new concepts, I can restate the goal of causal inference as the process of learning the impact T has on Y. In our example, this amounts to figuring out the effect of is_on_sale on weekly_amount_sold.

The Fundamental Problem of Causal Inference

Here is where things get interesting. The *fundamental problem of causal inference* is that you can never observe the same unit with and without treatment. It is as if you have two diverging roads and can only know what lies ahead of the one taken. To fully appreciate this issue, let's go back to our example and plot the outcome by the treatment, that is, `weekly_amount_sold` by `is_on_sale`. You can immediately see that the stores that dropped their price sell a lot more (see Figure 1-1).

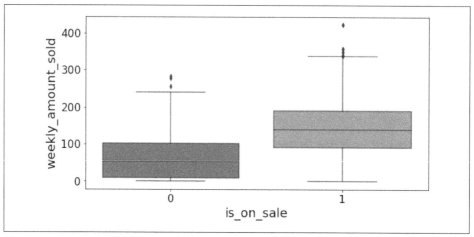

Figure 1-1. Amount sold per week during sales (1) and without sales (0)

This also matches our intuition about how the world works: people buy more when prices are low and sales (usually) means lower prices. This is very nice, as causal inference goes hand in hand with expert knowledge. But you shouldn't be too careless. It is probably the case that giving and advertising discounts will make customers buy more. But this much more? From the plot in Figure 1-1, it looks like the amount sold is about 150 units higher, on average, when a sale is going on than otherwise. This sounds suspiciously high, since the range of units sold when there is no sale is about 0 to 50. If you scratch your brains a bit, you can start to see that you might be mistaking association for causation. Maybe it is the case that only larger businesses, which are the ones that sell the most anyway, can afford to do aggressive price drops. Maybe businesses have sales closer to Christmas and that's when customers buy the most anyway.

The point is, you would only be certain about the true effect of price cuts on units sold if you could observe the same business (unit), at the same time, with and without sales going on. Only if you compare these two counterfactual situations will you be sure about the effect of price drops. However, as discussed earlier, the fundamental problem of causal inference is that you simply can't do that. Instead, you'll need to come up with something else.

Causal Models

You can reason about all these problems intuitively, but if you want to go beyond simple intuition, you need some formal notation. This will be our everyday language to speak about causality. Think of it as the common tongue we will use with fellow practitioners of the arts of causal inference.

A *causal model* is a series of assignment mechanisms denoted by ←. In these mechanisms, I'll use u to denote variables outside the model, meaning I am not making a statement about how they are generated. All the others are variables I care very much about and are hence included in the model. Finally, there are functions f that map one variable to another. Take the following causal model as an example:

$$T \leftarrow f_t(u_t)$$
$$Y \leftarrow f_y(T, u_y)$$

With the first equation, I'm saying that u_t, a set of variables I'm not explicitly modeling (also called exogenous variables), causes the treatment T via the function f_t. Next, T alongside another set of variables u_y (which I'm also choosing not to model) jointly causes the outcome Y via the function f_y. u_y is in this last equation to say that the outcome is not determined by the treatment alone. Some other variables also play a role in it, even if I'm choosing not to model them. Bringing this to the sales example, it would mean that `weekly_amount_sold` is caused by the treatment `is_on_sale` and other factors that are not specified, represented as u. The point of u is to account for all the variation in the variables caused by it that are not already accounted for by the variables included in the model—also called endogenous variables. In our example, I could say that price drops are caused by factors—could be business size, could be something else—that are not inside the model:

$$IsOnSales \leftarrow f_t(u_t)$$
$$AmountSold \leftarrow f_y(IsOnSales, u_y)$$

I'm using ← instead of = to explicitly state the nonreversibility of causality. With the equals sign, $Y = T + X$ is equivalent to $T = Y - X$, but I don't want to say that T causing Y is equivalent to Y causing T. Having said that, I'll often refrain from using ← just because it's a bit cumbersome. Just keep in mind that, due to nonreversibility of cause and effects, unlike with traditional algebra, you can't simply throw things around the equal sign when dealing with causal models.

If you want to explicitly model more variables, you can take them out of u and account for them in the model. For example, remember how I said that the large difference you are seeing between price cuts and no price cuts could be because larger businesses can engage in more aggressive sales? In the previous model, *BusinessSize* is not explicitly included in the model. Instead, its impact gets relegated to the side, with everything else in *u*. But I could model it explicitly:

$$BusinessSize \leftarrow f_s(u_s)$$

$$IsOnSales \leftarrow f_t(BusinessSize, u_t)$$

$$AmountSold \leftarrow f_y(IsOnSales, BusinessSize, u_y)$$

To include this extra endogenous variable, first, I'm adding another equation to represent how that variable came to be. Next, I'm taking *BusinessSize* out of u_t. That is, I'm no longer treating it as a variable outside the model. I'm explicitly saying that *BusinessSize* causes *IsOnSales* (along with some other external factors that I'm still choosing not to model). This is just a formal way of encoding the beliefs that bigger businesses are more likely to cut prices. Finally, I can also add *BusinessSize* to the last equation. This encodes the belief that bigger businesses also sell more. In other words, *BusinessSize* is a common cause to both the treatment *IsOnSales* and the outcome *AmountSold*.

Since this way of modeling is probably new to you, it's useful to link it to something perhaps more familiar. If you come from economics or statistics, you might be used to another way of modeling the same problem:

$$AmountSold_i = \alpha + \beta_1 IsOnSales_i + \beta_2 BusinessSize_i + e_i$$

It looks very different at first, but closer inspection will reveal how the preceding model is very similar to the one you saw earlier. First, notice how it is just replacing the final equation in that previous model and opening up the f_y function, stating explicitly that endogenous variables *IsOnSales* and *BusinessSize* are linearly and additively combined to form the outcome *AmountSold*. In this sense, this *linear model* assumes more than the one you saw earlier. You can say that it imposes a functional form to how the variables relate to each other. Second, you are not saying anything about how the independent (endogenous) variables—*IsOnSales* and *BusinessSize*—come to be. Finally, this model uses the equals sign, instead of the assignment operator, but we already agreed not to stress too much about that.

Interventions

The reason I'm taking my time to talk about causal models is because, once you have one, you can start to tinker with it in the hopes of answering a causal question. The formal term for this is *intervention*. For example, you could take that very simple causal model and force everyone to take the treatment t_0. This will eliminate the natural causes of T, replacing them by a single constant:

$$T \leftarrow t_0$$
$$Y \leftarrow f_y(T, u_y)$$

This is done as a thought experiment to answer the question "what would happen to the outcome Y if I were to set the treatment to t_0?" You don't actually have to intervene on the treatment (although you could and will, but later). In the causal inference literature, you can refer to these interventions with a $do(.)$ operator. If you want to reason about what would happen if you intervene on T, you could write $do(T = t_0)$.

Expectations

I'll use a lot of expectations and conditional expectations from now on. You can think about expectations as the population value that the average is trying to estimate. $E[X]$ denotes the (marginal) expected values of the random variable X. It can be approximated by the sample average of X. $E[Y \mid X = x]$ denotes the expected value of Y when $X = x$. This can be approximated by the average of Y when $X = x$.

The $do(.)$ operator also gives you a first glance at why association is different from causation. I have already argued how high sales volume for a business having a sale, $E[AmountSold \mid IsOnSales = 1]$, could overestimate the average sales volume a business would have had if it made a price cut, $E[AmountSold \mid do(IsOnSales = 1)]$. In the first case, you are looking at businesses that chose to cut prices, which are probably bigger businesses. In contrast, the latter quantity, $E[AmountSold \mid do(IsOnSales = 1)]$, refers to what would've happened if you forced every business to engage in sales, not just the big ones. Importantly, in general,

$$E[AmountSold \mid IsOnSales = 1] \neq E[AmountSold \mid do(IsOnSales = 1)]$$

One way to think about the difference between the two is in terms of selection and intervention. When you condition on sales, you are measuring the amount sold on a selected subsample of business that actually cut prices. When you condition on the intervention $do(IsOnSales)$, you are forcing every business to cut prices and then measuring the amount sold on the entire sample (see Figure 1-2).

$do(.)$ is used to define causal quantities that are not always recoverable from observed data. In the previous example, you can't observe $do(IsOnSales = 1)$ for every business, since you didn't force them to do sales. $do(.)$ is most useful as a theoretical concept that you can use to explicitly state the causal quantity you are after. Since it is not directly observable, a lot of causal inference is about eliminating it from theoretical expression—a process called *identification*.

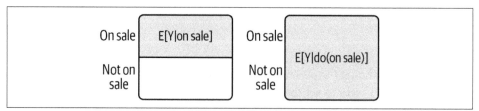

Figure 1-2. Selection filters the sample based on the treatment; intervention forces the treatment on the entire sample

Individual Treatment Effect

The *do(.)* operator also allows you to express the *individual treatment effect*, or the impact of the treatment on the outcome for an individual unit *i*. You can write it as the difference between two interventions:

$$\tau_i = Y_i|do(T = t_1) - Y_i|do(T = t_0)$$

In words, you would read this as "the effect, τ_i, of going from treatment t_0 to t_1 for unit *i* is the difference in the outcome of that unit under t_1 compared to t_0". You could use this to reason about our problem of figuring out the effect of flipping *IsOnSales* from 0 to 1 in *AmountSold*:

$$\tau_i = AmountSold_i|do(IsOnSales = 1) - AmountSold_i|do(IsOnSales = 0)$$

Due to the fundamental problem of causal inference, you can only observe one term of the preceding equation. So, even though you can theoretically express that quantity, it doesn't necessarily mean you can recover it from data.

Potential Outcomes

The other thing you can define with the *do(.)* operator is perhaps the coolest and most widely used concept in causal inference—counterfactual or *potential outcomes*:

$$Y_{ti} = Y_i|do(T_i = t)$$

You should read this as "unit *i*'s outcome would be *Y* if its treatment is set to *t*." Sometimes, I'll use function notation to define potential outcomes, since subscripts can quickly become too crowded:

$$Y_{ti} = Y(t)_i$$

When talking about a binary treatment (treated or not treated), I'll denote Y_{0i} as the potential outcome for unit i without the treatment and Y_{1i} as the potential outcome for *the same* unit i with the treatment. I'll also refer to one potential outcome as factual, meaning I can observe it, and the other one as counterfactual, meaning it cannot be observed. For example, if unit i is treated, I get to see what happens to it under the treatment; that is, I get to see Y_{1i}, which I'll call the factual potential outcome. In contrast, I can't see what would happen if, instead, unit i wasn't treated. That is, I can't see Y_{0i}, since it is counterfactual:

$$Y_i = \begin{cases} Y_{1i} \text{ if unit } i \text{ received the treatment} \\ Y_{0i} \text{ otherwise} \end{cases}$$

You might also find the same thing written as follows:

$$Y_i = T_i Y_{1i} + (1 - T_i) Y_{0i} = Y_{0i} + (Y_{1i} - Y_{0i}) T_i$$

Back to our example, you can write $AmountSold_{0i}$ to denote the amount business i would have sold had it not done any price cut and $AmountSold_{1i}$, the amount it would have sold had it done sales. You can also define the effect in terms of these potential outcomes:

$$\tau_i = Y_{1i} - Y_{0i}$$

Assumptions

Throughout this book, you'll see that causal inference is always accompanied by assumptions. Assumptions are statements you make when expressing a belief about how the data was generated. The catch is that they usually can't be verified with the data; that's why you need to assume them. Assumptions are not always easy to spot, so I'll do my best to make them transparent.

Consistency and Stable Unit Treatment Values

In the previous equations, there are two hidden assumptions. The first assumption implies that the potential outcome is consistent with the treatment: $Y_i(t) = Y$ when $T_i = t$. In other words, there are no hidden multiple versions of the treatment beyond the ones specified with T. This assumption can be violated if the treatment comes in multiple dosages, but you are only accounting for two of them; for example, if you care about the effect of discount coupons on sales and you treat it as being binary—customers received a coupon or not—but in reality you tried multiple discount values. Inconsistency can also happen when the treatment is ill defined. Imagine, for example, trying to figure out the effect of receiving help from a financial planner in one's finances. What does "help" mean here? Is it a one-time consultation? Is it regular advice and goal tracking? Bundling up all those flavors of financial advice into a single category also violates the consistency assumption.

A second assumption that is implied is that of no interference, or stable unit of treatment value (SUTVA). That is, the effect of one unit is not influenced by the treatment of other units: $Y_i(T_i) = Y_i(T_1, T_2, \ldots, T_i, \ldots, T_n)$. This assumption can be violated if there are spillovers or network effects. For example, if you want to know the effect of vaccines on preventing a contagious illness, vaccinating one person will make other people close to her less likely to catch this illness, even if they themselves did not get the treatment. Violations of this assumption usually cause us to think that the effect is lower than it is. With spillover, control units get some treatment effect, which in turn causes treatment and control to differ less sharply than if there was no interference.

Violations

Fortunately, you can often deal with violations on both assumptions. To fix violations of consistency, you have to include all versions of the treatment in your analysis. To deal with spillovers, you can expand the definition of a treatment effect to include the effect that comes from other units and use more flexible models to estimate those effects.

Causal Quantities of Interest

Once you've learned the concept of a potential outcome, you can restate the fundamental problem of causal inference: *you can never know the individual treatment effect because you only observe one of the potential outcomes.* But not all is lost. With all these new concepts, you are ready to make some progress in working around this fundamental problem. Even though you can never know the individual effects, τ_i, there are other interesting causal quantities that you can learn from data. For instance, let's define *average treatment effect* (ATE) as follows:

$$ATE = E[\tau_i],$$

or

$$ATE = E[Y_{1i} - Y_{0i}],$$

or even

$$ATE = E[Y|do(T = 1)] - E[Y|do(T = 0)],$$

The average treatment effect represents the impact the treatment T would have on average. Some units will be more impacted by it, some less, and you can never know the individual impact on a unit. Additionally, if you wanted to estimate the ATE from data, you could replace the expectation with sample averages:

$$\frac{1}{N}\Sigma_{i=0}^{N}\tau_i$$

or

$$\frac{1}{N}\Sigma_{i=0}^{N}\left(Y_{1i} - Y_{0i}\right)$$

Of course, in reality, due to the fundamental problem of causal inference, you can't actually do that, as only one of the potential outcomes will be observed for each unit. For now, don't worry too much about how you would go about estimating that quantity. You'll learn it soon enough. Just focus on understanding how to define this causal quantity in terms of potential outcomes and why you want to estimate them.

Another group effect of interest is the *average treatment effect on the treated* (ATT):

$$ATT = E\left[Y_{1i} - Y_{0i}|T = 1\right]$$

This is the impact of the treatment on the units that got the treatment. For example, if you did an offline marketing campaign in a city and you want to know how many extra customers this campaign brought you in that city, this would be the ATT: the effect of marketing on the city where the campaign was implemented. Here, it's important to notice how both potential outcomes are defined for the same treatment. In the case of the ATT, since you are conditioning on the treated, Y_{0i} is always unobserved, but nonetheless well defined.

Finally, you have *conditional average treatment effects* (CATE),

$$CATE = E\left[Y_{1i} - Y_{0i}|X = x\right],$$

which is the effect in a group defined by the variables X. For example, you might want to know the effect of an email on customers that are older than 45 years and on those that are younger than that. Conditional average treatment effect is invaluable for personalization, since it allows you to know which type of unit responds better to an intervention.

You can also define the previous quantities when the treatment is continuous. In this case, you replace the difference with a partial derivative:

$$\frac{\partial}{\partial t} E[Y_i]$$

This might seem fancy, but it's just a way to say how much you expect $E[Y_i]$ to change given a small increase in the treatment.

Causal Quantities: An Example

Let's see how you can define these quantities in our business problem. First, notice that you can never know the effect price cuts (having sales) have on an individual business, as that would require you to see both potential outcomes, $AmountSold_{0i}$ and $AmountSold_{1i}$, at the same time. But you could instead focus your attention on something that is possible to estimate, like the average impact of price cuts on amount sold:

$$ATE = E[AmountSold_{1i} - AmountSold_{0i}],$$

how the business that engaged in price cuts increased its sales:

$$ATT = E[AmountSold_{1i} - AmountSold_{0i} | IsOnSales = 1],$$

or the impact of having sales during the week of Christmas:

$$CATE = E[AmountSold_{1i} - AmountSold_{0i} | weeksToXmas = 0]$$

Now, I know you can't see both potential outcomes, but just for the sake of argument and to make things a lot more tangible, let's suppose you could. Pretend for a moment that the causal inference deity is pleased with the many statistical battles you fought and has rewarded you with godlike powers to see the potential alternative universes, one where each outcome is realized. With that power, say you collect data on six businesses, three of which were having sales and three of which weren't.

In the following table i is the unit identifier, y is the observed outcome, $y0$ and $y1$ are the potential outcomes under the control and treatment, respectively, t is the treatment indicator, and x is the covariate that marks time until Christmas. Remember that being on sale is the treatment and amount sold is the outcome. Let's also say that, for two of these businesses, you gathered data one week prior to Christmas, which is denoted by $x = 1$, while the other observations are from the same week as Christmas:

i	y0	y1	t	x	y	te
0	1	200	220	0	0	200	20
1	2	120	140	0	0	120	20
2	3	300	400	0	1	300	100
3	4	450	500	1	0	500	50
4	5	600	600	1	0	600	0
5	6	600	800	1	1	800	200

With your godly powers, you can see both $AmountSold_0$ and $AmountSold_1$. This makes calculating all the causal quantities we've discussed earlier incredibly easy. For instance, the ATE here would be the mean of the last column, that is, of the treatment effect:

$$ATE = (20 + 20 + 100 + 50 + 0 + 200)/6 = 65$$

This would mean that sales increase the amount sold, on average, by 65 units. As for the ATT, it would just be the mean of the last column when $T = 1$:

$$ATT = (50 + 0 + 200)/3 = 83.33$$

In other words, for the business that chose to cut prices (where treated), lowered prices increased the amount sold, on average, by 83.33 units. Finally, the average effect conditioned on being one week prior to Christmas ($x = 1$) is simply the average of the effect for units 3 and 6:

$$CATE(x = 1) = (100 + 200)/2 = 150$$

And the average effect on Christmas week is the average treatment effect when $x = 0$:

$$CATE(x = 0) = (20 + 20 + 50 + 0)/4 = 22.5$$

meaning that business benefited from price cuts much more one week prior to Christmas (150 units), compared to price cuts in the same week as Christmas (increase of 22.5 units). Hence, stores that cut prices earlier benefited more from it than those that did it later.

Now that you have a better understanding about the causal quantities you are usually interested in (ATE, ATT, and CATE), it's time to leave Fantasy Island and head back to the real world. Here things are brutal and the data you actually have is much harder to work with. Here, you can only see one potential outcome, which hides the individual treatment effect:

i	y0	y1	t	x	y	te
0	1	200.0	NaN	0	0	200	NaN
1	2	120.0	NaN	0	0	120	NaN
2	3	300.0	NaN	0	1	300	NaN
3	4	NaN	500.0	1	0	500	NaN
4	5	NaN	600.0	1	0	600	NaN
5	6	NaN	800.0	1	1	800	NaN

Missing Data Problem

One way to see causal inference is as a missing data problem. To infer the causal quantities of interest, you must impute the missing potential outcomes.

You might look at this and ponder "This is certainly not ideal, but can't I just take the mean of the treated and compare it to the mean of the untreated? In other words, can't I just do $\text{ATE} = (500 + 600 + 800)/3 - (200 + 120 + 300)/3 = 426.67$?" No! You've just committed the gravest sin of mistaking association for causation!

Notice how different the results are. The ATE you calculated earlier was less than 100 and now you are saying it is something above 400. The issue here is that the businesses that engaged in sales are different from those that didn't. In fact, those that did would probably have sold more regardless of price cut. To see this, just go back to when you could see both potential outcomes. Then, Y_0 for the treated units are much higher than that of the untreated units. This difference in Y_0 between treated groups makes it much harder to uncover the treatment effect by simply comparing both groups.

Although comparing means is not the smartest of ideas, I think that your intuition is in the right place. It's time to apply the new concepts that you've just learned to refine this intuition and finally understand why association is not causation. It's time to face the main enemy of causal inference.

Bias

To get right to the point, *bias is what makes association different from causation.* The fact that what you estimate from data doesn't match the causal quantities you want to recover is the whole issue. Fortunately, this can easily be understood with some intuition. Let's recap our business example. When confronted with the claim that cutting prices increases the amount sold by a business, you can question it by saying that those businesses that did sales would probably have sold more anyway, even with no price cuts. Maybe this is because they are bigger and can afford to do more aggressive sales. In other words, it is the case that treated businesses (businesses having sales) are not comparable with untreated businesses (not having sales).

To give a more formal argument, you can translate this intuition using potential outcome notation. First, to estimate the ATE, you need to estimate what would have happened to the treated had they not been treated, $E[Y_0|T = 1]$, and what would have happened to the untreated, had they been treated, $E[Y_1|T = 0]$. When you compare the average outcome between treated and untreated, you are essentially using $E[Y|T = 0]$ to estimate $E[Y_0]$ and $E[Y|T = 1]$ to estimate $E[Y_1]$. In other words, you are estimating the $E[Y|T = t]$ hoping to recover $E[Y_t]$. If they don't match, an estimator that recovers $E[Y|T = t]$, like the average outcome for those that got treatment t, will be a biased estimator of $E[Y_t]$.

Technical Definition

You can say that an estimator is biased if it differs from the parameter it is trying to estimate. $Bias = E[\hat{\beta} - \beta]$, where $\hat{\beta}$ is the estimate and β the thing it is trying to estimate—the estimand. For example, an estimator for the average treatment effect is biased if it's systematically under- or overestimating the true ATE.

Back to intuition, you can even leverage your understanding of how the world works to go even further. You can say that, probably, Y_0 of the treated business is bigger than Y_0 of the untreated business. That is because businesses that can afford to engage in price cuts tend to sell more regardless of those cuts. Let this sink in for a moment. It takes some time to get used to talking about potential outcomes, as it involves reasoning about things that would have happened but didn't. Read this paragraph over again and make sure you understand it.

The Bias Equation

Now that you understand why a sample average may differ from the average potential outcome it seeks to estimate, let's take a closer look at why differences in averages generally do not recover the ATE. This section may be a bit technical, so feel free to skip to the next one if you're not a fan of math equations.

In the sales example, the association between the treatment and the outcome is measured by $E[Y|T = 1] - E[Y|T = 0]$. This is the average amount sold for the business having sales minus the average amount sold for those that are not having sales. On the other hand, causation is measured by $E[Y_1 - Y_0]$ (which is shorthand for $E[Y|do(t = 1)] - E[Y|do(t = 0)]$).

To understand why and how they differ, let's replace the observed outcomes with the potential outcomes in the association measure $E[Y|T = 1] - E[Y|T = 0]$. For the treated, the observed outcome is Y_1, and for the untreated, it is Y_0:

$$E[Y|T = 1] - E[Y|T = 0] = E[Y_1|T = 1] - E[Y_0|T = 0]$$

Now let's add and subtract $E[Y_0|T = 1]$, which is a counterfactual outcome that tells us what would have happened to the outcome of the treated had they not received the treatment:

$$E[Y|T = 1] - E[Y|T = 0] = E[Y_1|T = 1] - E[Y_0|T = 0] + E[Y_0|T = 1] - E[Y_0|T = 1]$$

Finally, you can reorder the terms and merge some expectations:

$$E[Y|T = 1] - E[Y|T = 0] = \underbrace{E[Y_1 - Y_0|T = 1]}_{ATT} + \underbrace{\{E[Y_0|T = 1] - E[Y_0|T = 0]\}}_{BIAS}$$

This simple piece of math encompasses all the problems you'll encounter in causal questions. To better understand it, let's break it down into some of its implications. First, this equation tells us why association is not causation. As you can see, association is equal to the treatment effect on the treated plus a bias term. *The bias is given by how the treated and control group differ regardless of the treatment*, which is expressed by the difference in Y_0. You can now explain why you may be suspicious when someone tells us that price cuts boost the amount sold by such a high number. In this sales example, you believe that $E[Y_0|T = 0] < E[Y_0|T = 1]$, meaning that businesses that can afford to do price cuts tend to sell more, regardless of whether or not they are having a sale.

Why does this happen? That's an issue for Chapter 3, where you'll examine confounding. For now, you can think of bias arising because many things you can't observe are changing together with the treatment. As a result, the treated and untreated businesses differ in more ways than just whether or not they are having a sale. They also differ in size, location, the week they choose to have a sale, management style, the cities they are located in, and many other factors. To determine how much price cuts increase the amount sold, you would need businesses with and without sales to be, on average, similar to each other. In other words, *treated and control units would have to be exchangeable*.

A Glass of Wine a Day Keeps the Doctor Away

A popular belief is that wine, in moderation, is good for your health. The argument is that Mediterranean cultures, like Italian and Spanish, are famous for drinking a glass of wine every day and also display high longevity.

You should be suspicious about this claim. To attribute the extended lifespan to wine, those who drink and those who don't would need to be exchangeable, and we know they are not. For instance, Italy and Spain both have generous healthcare systems and comparatively elevated Human Development Indexes. In technical terms, $E[Lifespan_0 \mid WineDrinking = 1] > E[Lifespan_0 \mid WineDrinking = 0]$, so bias might be clouding the true causal effect.

A Visual Guide to Bias

You don't have to only use math and intuition to talk about exchangeability. In our example, you can even check that they are not exchangeable by plotting the relationship in outcome by variables for the different treatment groups. If you plot the outcome (`weekly_amount_sold`) by business size, as measured by `avg_week_sales`, and color each plot by the treatment, `is_on_sale`, you can see that the treated—business having sales—are more concentrated to the right of the plot, meaning that they are usually bigger businesses. That is, treated and untreated are not balanced.

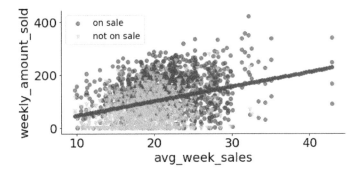

This is very strong evidence that your hypothesis $E[Y_0 \mid T = 1] > E[Y_0 \mid T = 0]$ was correct. There is an upward bias, as both the number of businesses with price cuts ($T = 1$) and the outcome of those businesses, had they not done any sale (Y_0 for those businesses), would go up with business size.

If you've ever heard about Simpson's Paradox, this bias is like a less extreme version of it. In Simpson's Paradox, the relationship between two variables is initially positive, but, once you adjust for a third variable, it becomes negative. In our case, bias is not so extreme as to flip the sign of the association (see Figure 1-3). Here, you start with a situation where the association between price cuts and amount sold is too high and controlling for a third variable reduces the size of that association. If you zoom in inside businesses of the same size, the relationship between price cuts and amount sold decreases, but remains positive.

Figure 1-3. How bias relates to Simpson's Paradox

Once again, this is so important that I think it is worth going over it again, now with some images. They are not realistic, but they do a good job of explaining the issue with bias. Let's suppose you have a variable indicating the size of the business. If you plot the amount sold against size, you'll see an increasing trend, where the bigger the size, the more the business sells. Next, you color the dots according to the treatment: white dots are businesses that cut their prices and black dots are businesses that didn't do that. If you simply compare the average amount sold between treated and untreated business, this is what you'll get:

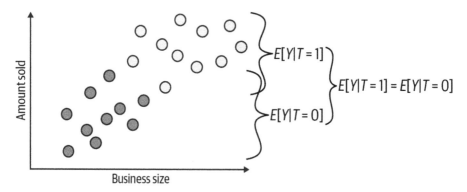

Notice how the difference in amount sold between the two groups can (and probably does) have two causes:

1. The treatment effect. The increase in the amount sold, which is caused by the price cut.

2. The business size. Bigger businesses are able both to sell more and do more price cuts. This source of difference between the treated and untreated is *not* due to the price cut.

The challenge in causal inference is untangling both causes.

Contrast this with what you would see if you add both potential outcomes to the picture (counterfactual outcomes are denoted as triangles). The individual treatment effect is the difference between the unit's outcome and another theoretical outcome that the same unit would have if it got the alternative treatment. The average treatment effect you would like to estimate is the average difference between the potential outcomes for each individual unit, $Y_1 - Y_0$. These individual differences are much smaller than the difference you saw in the previous plot, between treated and untreated groups. The reason for this is bias, which is depicted in the right plot:

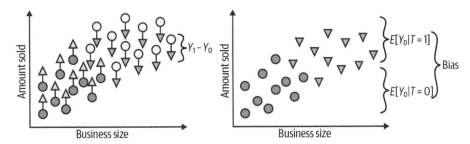

You can represent the bias by setting everyone to not receive the treatment. In this case, you are only left with the Y_0 potential outcome. Then, you can see how the treated and untreated groups differ on those potential outcomes under no treatment. If they do, something other than the treatment is causing the treated and untreated to be different. This is precisely the bias I've been talking about. It is what shadows the true treatment effect.

Identifying the Treatment Effect

Now that you understand the problem, it's time to look at the (or at least one) solution. Identification is the first step in any causal inference analysis. You'll see much more of it in Chapter 3, but for now, it's worth knowing what it is. Remember that you can't observe the causal quantities, since only one potential outcome is observable. You can't directly estimate something like $E[Y_1 - Y_0]$, since you can't observe this difference for any data point. But perhaps you can find some other quantity, which is observable, and can be used to recover the causal quantity you care about. This is the process of identification: *figuring out how to recover causal quantities from observable data*. For instance, if, by some sort of miracle, $E[Y|T = t]$ managed to recover

$E[Y_t]$ (identify $E[Y_t]$), you would be able to get $E[Y_1 - Y_0]$ by simply estimating $E[Y|T = 1] - E[Y|T = 0]$. This can be done by estimating the average outcome for the treated and untreated, which are both observed quantities.

See Also

In the past decade (2010–2020), an entire body of knowledge on causal identification was popularized by Judea Pearl and his team, as an attempt to unify the causal inference language. I use some of that language in this chapter—although probably an heretical version of it—and I'll cover more about it in Chapter 3. If you want to learn more about it, a short yet really cool paper to check out is "Causal Inference and Data Fusion in Econometrics," by Paul Hünermund and Elias Bareinboim.

You can also see identification as the process of getting rid of bias. Using potential outcomes, you can also say what would be necessary to make association equal to causation. *If* $E[Y_0|T = 0] = E[Y_0|T = 1]$, *then, association IS CAUSATION!* Understanding this is not just remembering the equation. There is a strong intuitive argument here. To say that $E[Y_0|T = 0] = E[Y_0|T = 1]$ is to say that treatment and control group are comparable regardless of the treatment. Mathematically, the bias term would vanish, leaving only the effect on the treated:

$$E[Y|T = 1] - E[Y|T = 0] = E[Y_1 - Y_0|T = 1] = ATT$$

Also, if the treated and the untreated respond similarly to the treatment, that is, $E[Y_1 - Y_0|T = 1] = E[Y_1 - Y_0|T = 0]$, then (pay close attention), *difference in means BECOMES the average causal effect*:

$$E[Y|T = 1] - E[Y|T = 0] = ATT = ATE = E[Y_1 - Y_0]$$

Despite the seemingly fancy-schmancy math here, all it's saying is that *once you make treated and control group interchangeable*, expressing the causal effect in terms of observable quantities in the data becomes trivial. Applying this to our example, if businesses that do and don't cut prices are similar to each other—that is, exchangeable—then, the difference in amount sold between the ones having sales and those not having sales can be entirely attributed to the price cut.

The Independence Assumption

This exchangeability is the key assumption in causal inference. Since it's so important, different scientists found different ways to state it. I'll start with one way, probably the most common, which is the *independence assumption*. Here, I'll say that the potential outcomes are independent of the treatment: $(Y_0, Y_1) \perp T$.

This independence means that $E[Y_0|T] = E[Y_0]$, or, in other words, that the treatment gives you no information about the potential outcomes. The fact that a unit was treated doesn't mean it would have a lower or higher outcome, had it not been treated (Y_0). This is just another way of saying that $E[Y_0|T = 1] = E[Y_0|T = 0]$. In our business example, it simply means that you wouldn't be able to tell apart the businesses that chose to engage in sales from those that didn't, had they all not done any sales. Except for the treatment and its effect on the outcome, they would be similar to each other. Similarly, $E[Y_1|T] = E[Y_1]$ means that you also wouldn't be able to tell them apart, had they all engaged in sales. Simply put, it means that treated and untreated groups are comparable and indistinguishable, regardless of whether they all received the treatment or not.

Identification with Randomization

Here, you are treating independence as an assumption. That is, you know you need to make associations equal to causation, but you have yet to learn how to make this condition hold. Recall that a causal inference problem is often broken down into two steps:

1. Identification, where you figure out how to express the causal quantity of interest in terms of observable data.
2. Estimation, where you actually use data to estimate the causal quantity identified earlier.

To illustrate this process with a very simple example, let's suppose that you can randomize the treatment. I know I said earlier that in the online marketplace you work for, businesses had full autonomy on setting prices, but you can still find a way to randomize the treatment *IsOnSales*. For instance, let's say that you negotiate with the businesses the right to force them to cut prices, but the marketplace will pay for the price difference you've forced. OK, so suppose you now have a way to randomize sales, so what? This is a huge deal, actually!

First, randomization ties the treatment assignment to a coin flip, so variations in it become completely unrelated to any other factors in the causal mechanism:

$$IsOnSales \leftarrow rand(t)$$
$$AmountSold \leftarrow f_y\big(IsOnSales, u_y\big)$$

Under randomization u_t vanished from our model since the assignment mechanism of the treatment became fully known. Moreover, since the treatment is random, it becomes independent from anything, including the potential outcomes. Randomization pretty much forces independence to hold.

To make this crystal clear, let's see how randomization pretty much annihilates bias, starting before the treatment assignment. The first image shows the world of potential outcomes (triangles) yet to be realized. This is depicted by the image on the left:

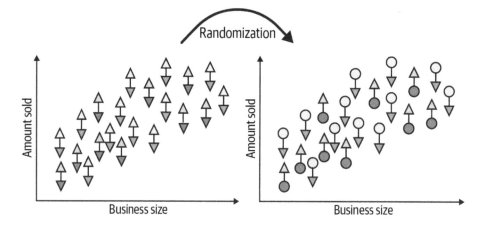

Then, at random, the treatment materializes one or the other potential outcome.

Randomized Versus Observational

In causal inference, we use the term *randomized* to talk about data where the treatment was randomized or when the assignment mechanism is fully known and nondeterministic. In contrast to that, the term *observational* is used to describe data where you can see who got what treatment, but you don't know how that treatment was assigned.

Next, let's get rid of the clutter, removing the unrealized potential outcomes (triangles). Now you can compare the treated to the untreated:

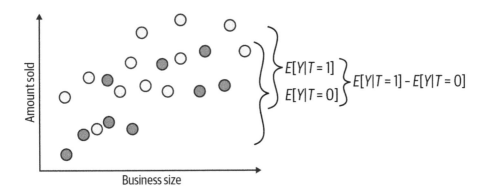

In this case, the difference in the outcome between treated and untreated *is* the average causal effect. This happens because there is no other source of difference between them other than the treatment itself. Therefore, all the differences you see must be attributed to the treatment. Or, simply put, there is no bias. If you set everyone to not receive the treatment so that you only observe the Y_0s, you would find no difference between the treated and untreated groups:

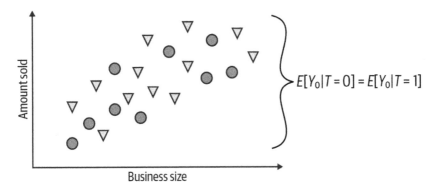

This is what the herculean task of causal identification is all about. It's about finding clever ways of removing bias and making the treated and the untreated comparable so that all the difference you see can be attributed to the treatment effect. Importantly, *identification is only possible if you know (or are willing to assume) something about the data-generating process. Usually, how the treatment was distributed or assigned.* This is why I said earlier that data alone cannot answer causal questions. Sure, data is important for estimating the causal effect. But, besides data, you'll always require a statement about how the data—specifically, the treatment—came to be. You get that statement using your expert knowledge or by intervening in the world, influencing the treatment and observing how the outcome changes in response.

An Incredible Membership Program

A big online retailer implemented a membership program, where members pay an extra fee to have access to more discounts, faster deliveries, return fee waiver, and amazing customer service. To understand the impact of the program, the company rolled it out to a random sample of the customers, which could opt in for paying the fee to get the membership benefits. After a while, they saw that customers in the membership program were much more profitable than those in the control group. Customers not only bought from the company, but they also spent less time with customer service. Should we then say that the membership program was a huge success in increasing sales and decreasing time spent serving customers?

Not really. Although the eligibility to the program was randomized, the random chunk that could opt in still self-selected into the program. In other words, randomization of program eligibility ensures that people who were able to get the program are comparable to those that weren't. But, out of the eligible, only a fraction choose to participate. This choice was not random. Probably, only the more engaged customers chose to participate, while the casual ones dropped out. So, even though eligibility to the program was randomized, participation in the program was not. The result is that those that participated are not comparable to those that didn't.

If you think about it, out of the eligible customers, the ones that actually chose to participate probably opted in for the program precisely because they already spent a lot in the online company, which made the extra discounts something worth paying for. This would imply that $E[Revenues_0 | OptIn = 1] > E[Revenues_0 | OptIn = 0]$, meaning those customers that opted in probably generated more revenues regardless of the program.

Ultimately, causal inference is about figuring out how the world works, stripped of all delusions and misinterpretations. And now that you understand this, you can move forward to mastering some of the most powerful methods to remove bias, the instruments of the brave and true, to identify the causal effect.

Key Ideas

You've learned the mathematical language that we'll use to talk about causal inference in the rest of this book. Importantly, you've learned the definition of potential outcome as the outcome you would observe for a unit had that unit taken a specific treatment $T = t$:

$$Y_{ti} = Y_i | do(T_i = t)$$

Potential outcomes were very useful in understanding why association is different from causation. Namely, when treated and untreated are different due to reasons other than the treatment, $E[Y_0|T=1] \neq E[Y_0|T=0]$, and the comparison between both groups will not yield the true causal effect, but a biased estimate. We also used potential outcomes to see what we would need to make association equal to causation:

$$\left(Y_0, Y_1\right) \perp T$$

When treated and control groups are interchangeable or comparable, like when we randomize the treatment, a simple comparison between the outcome of the treated and untreated groups will yield the treatment effect:

$$E[Y_1 - Y_0] = E[Y|T=1] - E[Y|T=0]$$

You also started to understand some of the key assumptions that you need to make when doing causal inference. For instance, in order to not have any bias when estimating the treatment effect, you assumed independence between the treatment assignment and the potential outcomes, $T \perp Y_t$.

You've also assumed that the treatment of one unit does not influence the outcome of another unit (SUTVA) and that all the versions of the treatment were accounted for (if $Y_i(t) = Y$, then $T_i = t$), when you defined the outcome Y as a switch function between the potential outcomes:

$$Y_i = \left(1 - T_i\right)Y_{0i} + T_i Y_{1i}$$

In general, it is always good to keep in mind that causal inference always requires assumptions. You need assumptions to go from the causal quantity you wish to know to the statistical estimator that can recover that quantity for you.

CHAPTER 2

Randomized Experiments and Stats Review

Now that you know the basics about causality, its time to talk about the inference part in causal inference. This chapter will first recap some concepts from the previous chapter in the context of randomized experiments. Randomized experiments are the gold standard for causal inference, so it is really important that you understand what makes them special. Even when randomization is not an option, having it as an ideal to strive for will be immensely helpful when thinking about causality.

Next, I'll use randomized experiments to review some important statistical concepts and tools, such as error, confidence interval, hypothesis tests, power, and sample size calculations. If you know about all of this, I'll make it clear when the review will start so you can skip it.

Brute-Force Independence with Randomization

In the previous chapter, you saw why and how association is different from causation. You also saw what is required to make association equal to causation:

$$E[Y|T=1] - E[Y|T=0] = \underbrace{E[Y_1 - Y_0|T=1]}_{ATT} + \underbrace{\{E[Y_0|T=1] - E[Y_0|T=0]\}}_{BIAS}$$

To recap, association can be described as the sum of two components: the average treatment effect on the treated and the bias. The measured association is only fully attributed to causation if the bias component is zero. There will be no bias if $E[Y_t|T=0] = E[Y_t|T=1]$. In other words, association will be causation if the treated and control are equal or comparable, except for their treatment. Or, in slightly more technical terms, when the potential outcomes of the treated are equal to the potential outcomes of the untreated, at least in expectations. Remember that potential outcome Y_{ti} is the outcome you would see had unit i received treatment t.

In Chapter 1, I also briefly touched on how to equate association and causation in the case that the potential outcomes are independent from the treatment:

$$(Y_0, Y_1) \perp T.$$

Importantly, I'm *not* talking about the independence between the treatment and the outcome. If that were the case, the treatment would have no impact on the outcome for you to measure. For example, let's say that the treatment is a new feature in your company's app and the outcome is time spent in that app. Saying that *Feature* $\perp$ *TimeSpent* means that time spent in the app is the same in both treated and untreated groups. In other words, the new feature has simply no effect.

Instead, what you want is for the *potential outcomes* to be independent of the treatment. There is an important distinction here. Saying that $Y_1 \perp T$ means that the outcome that would have been observed had the subjects received the treatment is independent of whether they actually received it or not. Analogously, $Y_0 \perp T$ indicates that the outcome that would have been observed if the subjects were untreated does not depend on the actual treatment assignment. In summary, the outcome Y that was actually observed still depends on the treatments actually assigned.

Another simpler way of putting this is that the independence assumption implies that treatment and control groups are comparable. Or that knowing the treatment assignment doesn't give me any information about the baseline potential outcome, Y_0. Consequently, $(Y_0, Y_1) \perp T$ means that the treatment is the only thing that causes difference in outcome between treatment and control:

$$E[Y_0 | T = 0] = E[Y_0 | T = 1] = E[Y_0]$$

and

$$E[Y_1 | T = 0] = E[Y_1 | T = 1] = E[Y_1]$$

which, as you've seen, allows a simple comparison between treated and control averages to identify the ATE:

$$E[Y | T = 1] - E[Y | T = 0] = E[Y_1 - Y_0] = ATE$$

Although independence is nothing more than an assumption, you can make it a lot more plausible if you randomize the treatment T. By doing so, you are tying the treatment assignment to the flip of a coin; that is, a random mechanism completely known to us. This coin doesn't have to be fair. You could assign the treatment to just 10% of the subjects, 1%, or even less. As long as the assignment mechanism is random, you can get the right conditions to identify the treatment effect.

By randomizing the treatment, you ensure that the treated and control group are roughly (in expectation) comparable. The only systematic difference between them is the treatment itself, which allows you to attribute any difference in the outcome to that treatment. Essentially, randomization brute-forces your way toward independence between the treatment and the *potential* outcomes.

Let's now take all this math and go over an example so you can see that it is actually quite simple. In the following section, I'll use randomized control trials (RCT) in order to understand the impact of cross-sell emails.

An A/B Testing Example

A common strategy among companies is to have a cheap or even free product that isn't profitable, but serves as the doorway to attracting new customers. Once the company has those customers, it can then cross-sell other products that are more profitable. Let's suppose you work for a coffee delivery company. Your main product is a low-cost monthly subscription that allows the customers to have high-quality and curated coffee delivered to them weekly. Beyond this basic and low-cost subscription, your company provides a more premium one, with brewing perks and the world's finest coffee, like that from local producers in the small town of Divinolandia, Brazil. This is by far your most profitable service, and therefore your goal is to increase its sales to the users who have already subscribed for your low-cost, entry product. For that, your company has a marketing team that tries to sell the premium coffee delivery subscription to its customers. They do this mainly through cross-sell emails. As the causal inference expert, your goal is to understand how effective those emails are.

When you look into the existing data (nonrandomized) to answer this question, you can clearly see that customers who received an email were more likely to buy the premium subscription. In technical terms, when a customer buys the product you are trying to sell, you can say they converted. So, you can say that the customers who received an email converted more:

$$E[Conversion|Email = 1] > E[Conversion|Email = 0]$$

Unfortunately, you also discover that the marketing team tends to send emails for the customers who they thought were more likely to convert in the first place. It is not entirely clear how they did this. Maybe they looked for customers who interacted the most with the company, or those who answered positively in a satisfaction survey. Regardless, this is very strong evidence that

$$E\big[Conversion_0 \big| Email = 1\big] > E\big[Conversion_0 \big| Email = 0\big].$$

In other words, customers who were actually sent the email would convert in greater numbers than other customers, even if no email was sent at all. As a result, a simple comparison in means is a biased estimator of the true causal effect of the cross-sell email. To solve that, you need to make the treated and untreated comparable: $E[Y_0 | T = 1] = E[Y_0 | T = 0]$, which can be done by randomly assigning the emails. If you manage to do that, the treated and untreated will have, on average, the same conversion, except for the treatment they receive. So, suppose you did just that. You selected three random samples from your customer base. To one of them, you didn't send any emails. To the other, you sent a large and beautifully written email about the premium subscription. To the last sample, you sent a short and to-the-point email about the premium subscription. After some time collecting data, you have something that looks like this:

```
In [1]: import pandas as pd # for data manipulation
        import numpy as np # for numerical computation

        data = pd.read_csv("./data/cross_sell_email.csv")
        data
```

	gender	cross_sell_email	age	conversion
0	0	short	15	0
1	1	short	27	0
...	...	...	...	...
321	1	no_email	16	0
322	1	long	24	1

323 rows × 4 columns

You can see that you have 323 observations. It's not exactly big data, but something you can work with.

Simulated Versus Real-World Data

When teaching about causal inference, it is very helpful to use simulated data. First, because causal inference is always accompanied by a statement about how the data was generated. Simulation allows me to talk about this assignment mechanism without any uncertainty. Second, causal inference involves counterfactual quantities that I can choose to show in order to give a better explanation of what is going on. However, so that the data doesn't look too artificial, I often take real-world data and transform it to fit the example I'm trying to give. For instance, this example takes data from the paper "A Randomized Assessment of Online Learning" (2016), by William T. Alpert et al., and transforms it to look like cross-sell email data.

To estimate the causal effect, you can simply compute the average conversion for each of the treatment groups:

```
In [2]: (data
         .groupby(["cross_sell_email"])
         .mean())
```

cross_sell_email	gender	age	conversion
long	0.550459	21.752294	0.055046
no_email	0.542553	20.489362	0.042553
short	0.633333	20.991667	0.125000

Yup. It's really that simple. You can see that the group assigned to no email had a conversion rate of 4.2%, while the groups assigned to the long and short email had a conversion rate of 5.5% and a whopping 12.5%, respectively. Therefore, the ATEs, measured as the difference between each treated group and the control group, $ATE = E[Y|T = t] - E[Y|T = 0]$, where 1.3 and 8.3 percentage points increase for the long and short email, respectively. Interestingly, sending an email that is short and to the point seems better than an elaborated one.

The beauty of RCTs is that you no longer have to worry if the marketing team somehow targeted customers who were likely to convert or, for that matter, you don't have to worry that the customers from the distinct treatment groups are different in any systematic way, other than the treatment they received. By design, the random experiment is made to wipe out those differences, making $(Y_0, Y_1) \perp T$, at least in theory.

In practice, a good sanity check to see if the randomization was done right (or if you are looking at the correct data) is to check if the treated are equal to the untreated in pretreatment variables. For example, you have data on gender and age and you can see whether these two characteristics are balanced across treatment groups.

When you look at age, treatment groups seem very much alike, but there seems to be a difference in gender (*woman* = 1, *man* = 0). It seems that the group that received the short email had 63% men, compared to 54% in the control group and 55% in the group that got the long email. This is somewhat unsettling, as the treatment group in which you found the highest impact also appears to be different from the other groups. So, even if independence should hold in theory in RCTs, it does not necessarily hold in practice. It could be that the large effect you saw for the short email was due to the fact that, for whatever reason, $E[Y_0|man] > E[Y_0|woman]$.

There isn't a clear consensus on how to evaluate balance, but one very simple suggestion is to check the normalized differences between the treatment groups:

$$\frac{\hat{\mu}_{tr} - \hat{\mu}_{co}}{\sqrt{(\hat{\sigma}_{tr}^2 + \hat{\sigma}_{co}^2)/2}},$$

where $\hat{\mu}$, $\hat{\sigma}^2$ are the sample mean and variance, respectively. Since there are three treatment groups in your example, you can just compute this difference with respect to the control group:

```
In [3]: X = ["gender", "age"]

        mu = data.groupby("cross_sell_email")[X].mean()
        var = data.groupby("cross_sell_email")[X].var()

        norm_diff = ((mu - mu.loc["no_email"])/
                     np.sqrt((var + var.loc["no_email"])/2))

        norm_diff
```

	gender	age
cross_sell_email		
long	0.015802	0.221423
no_email	0.000000	0.000000
short	0.184341	0.087370

If this difference is too small or too large, you should be worried. Unfortunately, there isn't a clear threshold for how much difference is too much, but 0.5 seems to be a good rule of thumb. In this example, you don't have any difference that is that high, but it does seem that the group that got the short email has a large difference in gender, while the group that got the long email has a large difference in age.

See Also

For a more in-depth discussion of this topic, check out section 14.2 of the book *Causal Inference for Statistics, Social, and Biomedical Sciences: An Introduction*, by Guido W. Imbens and Donald B. Rubin (Cambridge University Press).

If the preceding formula seems a bit magic right now, don't worry. It will become clearer once you go over the statistical review part of this chapter. For now, I just want to draw your attention to what happens with a small dataset. Even under randomization, it could be that, by chance, one group is different from another. In large samples, this difference tends to disappear. It also brings forth the issue of how much difference is enough for you to conclude that the treatments are indeed effective and not just due to chance, which is something I'll address shortly.

The Ideal Experiment

Randomized experiments or randomized controlled trials are the most reliable way to get causal effects. It's a straightforward technique and absurdly convincing. It is so powerful that most countries have it as a requirement for showing the effectiveness of new drugs. Think of it this way: if you could, RCT would be all you would ever do to uncover causality. A well-designed RCT is the dream of any scientist and decision maker.

Unfortunately, they tend to be either very expensive—both in money, but more importantly, in time—or just plain unethical. Sometimes, you simply can't control the assignment mechanism. Imagine yourself as a physician trying to estimate the effect of smoking during pregnancy on baby weight at birth. You can't simply force a random portion of moms to smoke during pregnancy. Or say you work for a big bank, and you need to estimate the impact of the credit line on customer churn. It would be too expensive to give random credit lines to your customers. Or say you want to understand the impact of increasing the minimum wage on unemployment. You can't simply assign countries to have one or another minimum wage. Moreover, as you will see in Chapter 3, there are some situations (selection biased ones) where not even RCTs can save you.

Still, I would like you to think about random experiments beyond a tool for uncovering causal effects. Rather, the goal here is to use it as a benchmark. Whenever you do causal inference without RCTs, you should always ask yourself what would be the perfect experiment to answer your question. Even if that ideal experiment is not feasible, it serves as a valuable benchmark. It often sheds some light on how you can discover the causal effect even without such an experiment.

The Most Dangerous Equation

Now that you understand the value of an experiment, it's time to review what it means to not have infinite data. Causal inference is a two-step process. RCTs are invaluable in helping with identification, but if the sample size of an experiment is small, you'll struggle with the second step: inference. To understand this, it's worth reviewing some statistical concepts and tools. If you are already familiar with them, feel free to skip to the next chapter.

In his famous article of 2007, Howard Wainer writes about very dangerous equations:

> "Some equations are dangerous if you know them, and others are dangerous if you do not. The first category may pose danger because the secrets within its bounds open doors behind which lies terrible peril. The obvious winner in this is Einstein's iconic equation $E = MC^2$, for it provides a measure of the enormous energy hidden within ordinary matter. [...] Instead I am interested in equations that unleash their danger not when we know about them, but rather when we do not. Kept close at hand, these equations allow us to understand things clearly, but their absence leaves us dangerously ignorant."

The equation he talks about is Moivre's equation:

$$SE = \frac{\sigma}{\sqrt{n}}$$

where SE is the standard error of the mean, σ is the standard deviation, and n is the sample size. This math is definitely something you should master, so let's get to it.

To see why not knowing this equation is very dangerous, let's look at some education data. I've compiled data on ENEM scores (Brazilian standardized high school scores, similar to SATs) from different schools over a three-year period. I've also cleaned the data to keep only the information relevant to you in this section.

If you look at the top-performing school, something catches the eye—those schools have a reasonably small number of students:

```
In [4]: df = pd.read_csv("data/enem_scores.csv")
        df.sort_values(by="avg_score", ascending=False).head(10)
```

	year	school_id	number_of_students	avg_score
16670	2007	33062633	68	82.97
16796	2007	33065403	172	82.04
...	...	...	...	...
14636	2007	31311723	222	79.41
17318	2007	33087679	210	79.38

Looking at it from another angle, you can separate only the 1% of top schools and study them. What are they like? Perhaps you can learn something from the best and replicate it elsewhere. And sure enough, if you look at the top 1% of schools, you'll figure out they have, on average, fewer students:

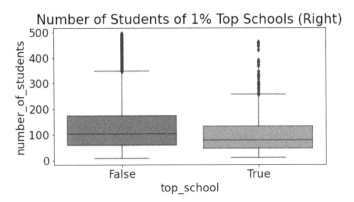

One natural conclusion is that small schools lead to higher academic performance. This makes intuitive sense, since we believe that fewer students per teacher allows the teacher to give focused attention to each student. But what does this have to do with Moivre's equation? And why is it dangerous?

Well, it becomes dangerous once people start to make important and expensive decisions based on this information. In his article, Howard continues:

> In the 1990s, it became popular to champion reductions in the size of schools. Numerous philanthropic organizations and government agencies funded the division of larger schools because students at small schools are overrepresented in groups with high test scores.

What people forgot to do was to also look at the bottom 1% of schools: they also have very few students!

What you see in Figure 2-1 is precisely what's expected according to Moivre's equation. As the number of students grows, the average score becomes more and more precise. Schools with very few students (low sample size) can have very high and low scores simply due to chance. This is less likely to occur in large schools. Moivre's equation talks about a fundamental fact regarding the reality of information and records in the form of data: it is always imprecise. The question then becomes: how imprecise? And what can you do to take those inaccuracies into account?

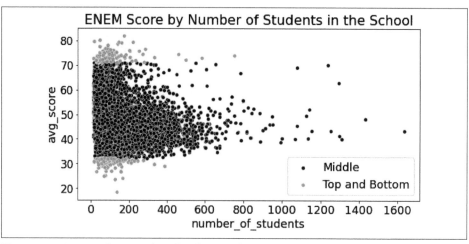

Figure 2-1. A typical triangular plot showing how variance decreases with sample size

One way to quantify our uncertainty is the *variance of our estimates*. Variance tells you how much observation deviates from its central (expected) value. As Moivre's equation indicates, this uncertainty shrinks as the amount of data you observe increases. This makes sense, right? If you see many students performing excellently at a school, you can be more confident that this is indeed a good school. However, if you see a school with only 10 students and 8 of them perform well, you need to be more suspicious. By chance, it could be that the school got some above-average students.

The beautiful triangular plot you see in Figure 2-1 tells precisely this story. It shows you how your estimate of the school performance has a huge variance when the sample size is small. It also indicates that variance shrinks as the sample size increases. This is true for the average score in a school, but it is also true about any summary statistics you might have, including the ATE you often want to estimate. Back to our cross-sell email application, if you had thousands of customers in each treatment group, instead of hundreds, you would be much more confident that the difference in conversion you saw between treated and control groups are not simply due to chance.

Random and Systematic Error

Another way to think about this uncertainty in the data is to *contrast systematic error with random error*. Systematic errors are consistent biases that affect all measurements in the same way, while random errors are unpredictable fluctuations in data due to chance. Systematic error, or bias, doesn't diminish as you gather more data, as it pushes all measurements to the same direction, away from the quantity you want to estimate. In contrast, random error decreases as the sample size increases, as seen in Moivre's equation. Statistics is the science that deals with these imprecisions due to random error, so they don't catch you off-guard. It's a way to take uncertainty into account.

The Standard Error of Our Estimates

Since this is just a review of statistics, I'll take the liberty to go a bit faster. If you are not familiar with distributions, variance, and standard errors, please read on, but keep in mind that you might need some additional resources. I suggest you google any MIT course on introduction to statistics. They are usually quite good and you can watch them for free on YouTube.

In "The Most Dangerous Equation" on page 38, you estimated the average treatment effect $E[Y_1 - Y_0]$ as the difference in the means between the treated and the untreated $E[Y|T=1] - E[Y|T=0]$. Specifically, you figured out the ATE for two types of cross-sell emails on conversion. You then saw that the short email had a very impressive lift, of more than 8 percentage points, while the long email had a smaller impact, of just 1.3 percentage points increase. But there is still a lingering question: are those effects large enough so you can be confident they are not due to chance? In technical terms, do you know if they are statistically significant?

To do so, you first need to estimate the *SE*, according to the equation I've shown earlier. *n* is pretty easy to get. You just need the `len` of each treatment. Or, you can use pandas `groupby` followed by a `size` aggregation:

```
In [5]: data = pd.read_csv("./data/cross_sell_email.csv")

        short_email = data.query("cross_sell_email=='short'")["conversion"]
        long_email = data.query("cross_sell_email=='long'")["conversion"]
        email = data.query("cross_sell_email!='no_email'")["conversion"]
        no_email = data.query("cross_sell_email=='no_email'")["conversion"]

        data.groupby("cross_sell_email").size()

Out[5]: cross_sell_email
        long        109
        no_email     94
```

```
short          120
dtype: int64
```

To get the estimate for the standard deviation, you can apply the following equation:

$$\hat{\sigma} = \sqrt{\frac{1}{N-1}\Sigma_{i=0}^{N}(x-\bar{x})^2}$$

where $\bar{x}$ is the mean of x.

Hats

In this book, I'll use hats to denote the sample estimate of parameters and predictions.

Fortunately for you, most programming software already implements this. In pandas, you can use the method std (*https://oreil.ly/kCUZc*). Putting it all together, you have the following function for the standard error:

```
In [6]: def se(y: pd.Series):
            return y.std() / np.sqrt(len(y))

        print("SE for Long Email:", se(long_email))
        print("SE for Short Email:", se(short_email))


Out[6]: SE for Long Email: 0.021946024609185506
        SE for Short Email: 0.030316953129541618
```

Knowing this formula is incredibly handy (we'll come back to it multiple times, trust me), but know that pandas also has a built-in method for calculating the standard error, .sem() (as in standard error of the mean):

```
In [7]: print("SE for Long Email:", long_email.sem())
        print("SE for Short Email:", short_email.sem())


Out[7]: SE for Long Email: 0.021946024609185506
        SE for Short Email: 0.030316953129541618
```

Confidence Intervals

The standard error of your estimate is a measure of confidence. You need to go into turbulent and polemical statistical waters to understand precisely what it means. For one view of statistics, the frequentist view, we would say that our data is nothing more than a manifestation of an underlying data-generating process. This process is abstract and ideal. It is governed by true parameters that are unchanging but also unknown to us. In the context of cross-sell email, if you could run multiple experiments and calculate the conversion rate for each of them, they would fall around the true underlying conversion rate, even though not being exactly equal to it. This is very much like Plato's writing on the Forms:

> Each [of the essential forms] manifests itself in a great variety of combinations, with actions, with material things, and with one another, and each seems to be many.

To understand this, let's suppose you have the true abstract distribution of conversion for the short cross-sell email. Because conversion is either zero or one, it follows a Bernoulli distribution and let's say that the probability of success in this distribution is 0.08. That is, whenever a customer receives the short email, it has an 8% chance of converting. Next, let's pretend you can run 10,000 experiments. On each one, you collect a sample of 100 customers, send them the short email and observe the average conversion, giving you a total of 10,000 conversion rates. The 10,000 conversion rates from those experiments will be distributed around the true mean of 0.08 (see Figure 2-2). Some experiments will have a conversion rate lower than the true one, and some will be higher, but the mean of the 10,000 conversion rate will be pretty close to the true mean.

List Comprehension

I tend to use a lot of list comprehension instead of for loops whenever I want to apply a function to every item in a sequence. A list comprehension is just a syntactic sugar for a mapping for loop:

```
table_2 = []
for n in range(11):
    table_2.append(n*2)


table_2 = [n*2 for n in range(11)]
```

```
In [8]: n = 100
        conv_rate = 0.08

        def run_experiment():
            return np.random.binomial(1, conv_rate, size=n)

        np.random.seed(42)

        experiments = [run_experiment().mean() for _ in range(10000)]
```

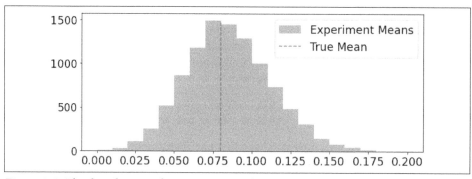

Figure 2-2. The distribution of conversion rate (average conversion) of 10,000 experiments, each with 100 units

This is to say that you can never be sure that the mean of your experiment matches the true platonic and ideal mean. However, *with the standard error, you can create an interval that will contain the true mean in 95% of the experiments you run.*

In real life, you don't have the luxury of simulating the same experiment with multiple datasets. You often only have one. But you can draw from the idea of simulating multiple experiments to construct a *confidence interval*. Confidence intervals come with a probability attached to them. The most common one is 95%. This probability tells you that if you were to run multiple experiments and construct the 95% confidence interval in each one of them, the true mean would fall inside the interval 95% of the time.

To calculate the confidence interval, you'll use what is perhaps the most mind-blowing result in statistics: the Central Limit Theorem. Take a closer look at the distribution of conversion rates you've just plotted. Now, remember that conversion is either zero or one and hence follows a Bernoulli distribution. If you plot this Bernoulli distribution in a histogram, it will have a huge bar at 0 and small bar at 1, since the success rate is only 8%. This looks nothing like a normal distribution, right?

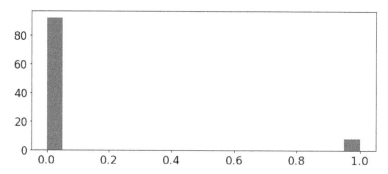

This is where that mind-blowing result comes into play. Even though the distribution of the data is not normally distributed (like in the conversion case, which follows a Bernoulli distribution), the *average of the data is always normally distributed*. If you collect data on conversion multiple times and calculate the average conversion each time, those averages will follow a normal distribution. This is very neat, because normal distribution is well known and you can do all sorts of interesting things with it. For example, for the purpose of calculating the confidence interval, you can leverage knowledge from statistical theory that 95% of the mass of a normal distribution falls between 2 standard deviations (see Figure 2-3) above and below the mean (technically, 1.96, but 2 is a good approximation that is easier to remember).

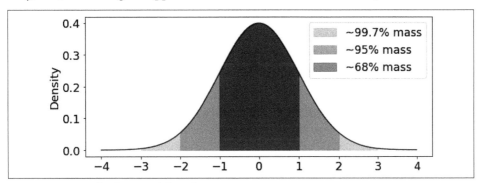

Figure 2-3. Standard normal distribution

Back to your cross-sell experiments, you now know that the conversion rate would follow a normal distribution, if you could run multiple similar experiments. The best estimate you have for the mean of that (unknown) distribution is the mean from your small experiment. Moreover, the standard error serves as your estimate of the standard deviation of that unknown distribution for the sample mean. So, if you multiply the standard error by 2 and add and subtract it from the mean of your experiments, you will construct a 95% confidence interval for the true mean:

```
In [9]: exp_se = short_email.sem()
        exp_mu = short_email.mean()
        ci = (exp_mu - 2 * exp_se, exp_mu + 2 * exp_se)
        print("95% CI for Short Email: ", ci)


Out[9]: 95% CI for Short Email:  (0.06436609374091676, 0.18563390625908324)
```

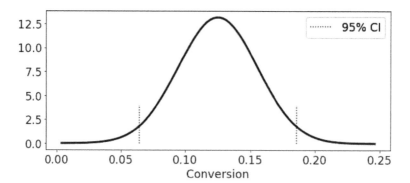

Of course, you don't need to restrict yourself to the 95% confidence interval. If you want to be more careful you could generate the 99% interval instead. You just need to multiply the standard deviation by the factor that will contain 99% of the mass of a normal distribution.

To find that factor, you can use the `ppf` function from `scipy`. This function gives you the inverse of cumulative distribution function (CDF) of a standard normal distribution. For example, `ppf(0.5)` will return 0.0, saying that 50% of the mass of the standard normal distribution is below 0.0. So, for any significance level α, the factor you need to multiply the SE by in order to get a $1 - \alpha$ confidence interval is given by $|ppf((1 - \alpha)/2)|$:

```
In [10]: from scipy import stats

         z = np.abs(stats.norm.ppf((1-.99)/2))
         print(z)
         ci = (exp_mu - z * exp_se, exp_mu + z * exp_se)
         ci


Out[10]: 2.5758293035489004


Out[10]: (0.04690870373460816, 0.20309129626539185)


In [11]: stats.norm.ppf((1-.99)/2)


Out[11]: -2.5758293035489004
```

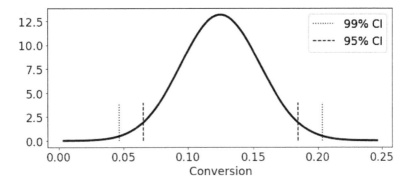

That is for the short email. You could also show the 95% CI for the conversion rate associated with the other treatment groups:

```
In [12]: def ci(y: pd.Series):
             return (y.mean() - 2 * y.sem(), y.mean() + 2 * y.sem())

         print("95% CI for Short Email:", ci(short_email))
         print("95% CI for Long Email:", ci(long_email))
         print("95% CI for No Email:", ci(no_email))


Out[12]: 95% CI for Short Email: (0.06436609374091676, 0.18563390625908324)
         95% CI for Long Email: (0.01115382234126202, 0.09893792077800403)
         95% CI for No Email: (0.0006919679286838468, 0.08441441505003955)
```

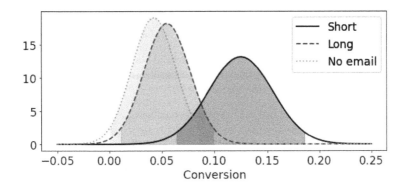

Here, you can see that the 95% CI of the three groups overlap with each other. If they didn't, you would be able to conclude that the difference in conversion between the groups is not simply by chance. In other words, you would be able to say that sending a cross-sell email causes a statistically significant difference in conversion rates. But since the intervals do overlap, you can't say that. At least not yet. Importantly, over-lapping confidence intervals is not enough to say that the difference between the groups is not statistically significant, however, if they didn't overlap, that would mean they are statistically different. In other words, nonoverlapping confidence intervals is conservative evidence for statistical significance.

To recap, confidence intervals are a way to place uncertainty around your estimates. The smaller the sample size, the larger the standard error, and hence, the wider the confidence interval. Since they are super easy to compute, lack of confidence intervals signals either some bad intentions or simply lack of knowledge, which is equally concerning. Finally, you should always be suspicious of measurements without any uncertainty metric.

PRACTICAL EXAMPLE

The Effectiveness of COVID-19 Vaccines

Randomized control trials are incredibly important for the pharmaceutical industry. Perhaps the most widely known examples are the tests conducted to determine the effectiveness of COVID-19 vaccines, given the tremendous impact those had on almost everyone on the planet. Here is the result section from the study *Efficacy and Safety of the mRNA-1273 SARS-CoV-2 Vaccine*, published in 2020:

> The trial enrolled 30,420 volunteers who were randomly assigned in a 1:1 ratio to receive either vaccine or placebo (15,210 participants in each group). More than 96% of participants received both injections, and 2.2% had evidence (serologic, virologic, or both) of SARS-CoV-2 infection at baseline. Symptomatic COVID-19 illness was confirmed in 185 participants in the placebo group (56.5 per 1,000 person-years; 95% confidence interval (CI), 48.7 to 65.3) and in 11 participants in the mRNA-1273 group (3.3 per 1,000 person-years; 95% CI, 1.7 to 6.0); vaccine efficacy was 94.1% (95% CI, 89.3 to 96.8%; P<0.001).

Here is my take on how to interpret these results in the light of the concepts you've been learning. Keep in mind that I'm no health expert and my commentary is purely about the statistical and causal inference concepts.

First, they defined the treatment and control (placebo) groups, saying that the treatment was randomly assigned, which ensures independence of the treatment from the potential outcomes. This would allow them to identify the causal effect of the vaccine from statistical the quantities $E[Y \mid T = 0]$ and $E[Y \mid T = 1]$. Next, they define the outcome as being the presence of symptomatic COVID-19 per 1,000 person-years. Finally, they report the 95% CI for the estimate of $E[Y \mid T = 0]$ and $E[Y \mid T = 1]$ as being 48.7 to 65.3 and 1.7 to 6.0, respectively. This tells you that symptomatic COVID-19 was detected far less in those with the vaccine, compared to those that got the placebo. They report the efficacy of the vaccine, $E[Y \mid T = 0]/E[Y \mid T = 1]$, as well as the 95% confidence interval around it, 89.3 to 96.8%.

One final word of caution here. Confidence intervals are trickier to interpret than at first glance. For instance, I *shouldn't* say that a particular 95% confidence interval contains the true mean with 95% chance. In frequentist statistics, the population mean is regarded as a true population constant. This constant is either inside or outside a particular confidence interval. In other words, a specific confidence interval either contains or doesn't contain the true mean. If it does, the chance of containing it would be 100%, not 95%. If it doesn't, the chance would be 0%. Instead, in confidence intervals, the 95% refers to the frequency that such confidence intervals, computed in many studies, contains the true mean. The 95% is our confidence in the algorithm used to calculate the 95% CI, not on the particular interval itself.

Now, having said that, as an economist (statisticians, please look away now), I think this purism is not very useful. In practice, you will see people saying that the particular confidence interval contains the true mean 95% of the time. Although wrong, this is not very harmful, as it still places a visual degree of uncertainty in your estimates. What I mean by this is that I would rather you have a confidence interval around your estimate and interpret it wrong than avoid the confidence interval in fear of misinterpretation. I don't care if you say they contain the true mean 95% of the time. Just, please, never forget to place them around your estimates; otherwise, you will look silly.

Credible Intervals

If you really want to attach a probability statement to a parameter estimate being inside an interval, you should check Bayesian credible intervals. However, from my experience, in most situations (especially when the sample size is relatively large) they tend to yield something similar to the frequentists confidence interval. This is also why I tend to be more forgiving of misinterpretation of the confidence interval.

Hypothesis Testing

Another way to incorporate uncertainty is to state a hypothesis test: is the difference in means between two groups statistically different from zero (or any other value)? To answer these types of questions, you need to recall that the sum or difference of two independent normal distributions is also a normal distribution. The resulting mean will be the sum or difference between the two distributions, while the variance will always be the sum of the variances:

$$N\left(\mu_1, \sigma_1^2\right) - N\left(\mu_2, \sigma_2^2\right) = N\left(\mu_1 - \mu_2, \sigma_1^2 + \sigma_2^2\right)$$

$$N\left(\mu_1, \sigma_1^2\right) + N\left(\mu_2, \sigma_2^2\right) = N\left(\mu_1 + \mu_2, \sigma_1^2 + \sigma_2^2\right)$$

If you don't remember, it's OK. You can always use code and simulated data to check it for yourself:

```
In [13]: import seaborn as sns
         from matplotlib import pyplot as plt

         np.random.seed(123)

         n1 = np.random.normal(4, 3, 30000)
         n2 = np.random.normal(1, 4, 30000)
         n_diff = n2 - n1

         plt.figure(figsize=(10,4))
         sns.distplot(n1, hist=False, label="$N(4,3^2)$")
         sns.distplot(n2, hist=False, label="$N(1,4^2)$")
         sns.distplot(n_diff, hist=False,
                     label=f"$N(-3, 5^2) = N(1,4^2) - (4,3^2)$")
         plt.legend();
```

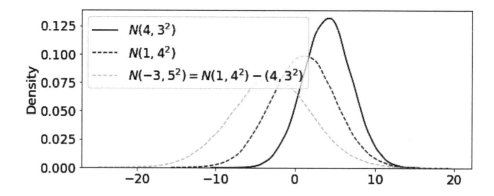

If you take two groups, each with a distribution attached to it, and subtract one from the other, you'll end up with a third distribution. The mean of this final distribution will be the difference in the means, and the standard deviation will be the square root of the sum of the variances. Since you are talking about the distributions of experiment averages, you can think about the standard deviation of these as the standard error of the mean:

$$\mu_{diff} = \mu_1 - \mu_2$$

$$SE_{diff} = \sqrt{SE_1^2 + SE_2^2}$$

You can use this idea in the problem of comparing the conversion from your cross-sell email experiment. If you take the estimated distribution of two groups—let's say, the short email and the no email group—and subtract one from the other, you get the distribution of the difference. With this distribution, you can easily construct a 95% confidence interval for the difference in means:

```
In [14]: diff_mu = short_email.mean() - no_email.mean()
         diff_se = np.sqrt(no_email.sem()**2 + short_email.sem()**2)

         ci = (diff_mu - 1.96*diff_se, diff_mu + 1.96*diff_se)
         print(f"95% CI for the difference (short email - no email):\n{ci}")


Out[14]: 95% CI for the difference (short email - no email):
         (0.01023980847439844, 0.15465380854687816)
```

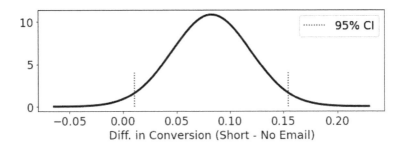

Null Hypothesis

With this interval, you can answer questions about what is called a *null hypothesis*. For example, you can state the hypothesis that there is no difference in conversion rate between a short email and no email at all. You'll usually use H_0 to talk about the null hypothesis:

$$H_0: Conversion_{no\_email} = Conversion_{short\_email}$$

Once you have this hypothesis, it's time to ask yourself, "Is it likely that I would observe such a difference if the null hypothesis were true?" You'll look at the data and see if it conforms to your null hypothesis. If it doesn't, you'll say that seeing such data would be too weird, if the null hypothesis were true, and hence you should reject it. One way to do this is with the confidence intervals you have just constructed.

Notice how the preceding 95% confidence interval does not contain zero. Also, recall that this is the CI of the difference between conversion rates. Since the null hypothesis states that this difference is zero, but you can see that the confidence interval is entirely outside zero, you can say that the probability of seeing such a result would be too low, if the null hypothesis were true. Hence, you can reject the null hypothesis with 95% confidence.

Significance Level

The significance level, α, is the chance of rejecting the null when it is true—committing a Type I error. Significance is set prior to gathering or analyzing the data. To achieve a certain significance level, say, 5%, you would construct a $1 - \alpha$ confidence interval, say 95%, around your estimate during the analysis.

Of course you can also formulate other null hypotheses, besides the one that states no difference at all. For example, let's say there is some cost to sending emails, which is very realistic. Even if there is no significant monetary cost, if you send too many emails to customers, eventually they will flag you as spammers, which will shut down this communication channel with them, leading to lower sales in the future. Under this situation, perhaps the marketing team is only willing to roll out the cross-sell email if the lift in conversion rate is higher than 1%. Then, you can state the null hypothesis as follows: "the difference in conversion rate is 1%." To test this hypothesis, all you need to do is shift the confidence interval by subtracting 1% from the difference in means:

```
In [15]: # shifting the CI
         diff_mu_shifted =  short_email.mean() - no_email.mean() - 0.01
         diff_se = np.sqrt(no_email.sem()**2 + short_email.sem()**2)

         ci = (diff_mu_shifted - 1.96*diff_se, diff_mu_shifted + 1.96*diff_se)
         print(f"95% CI 1% difference between (short email - no email):\n{ci}")

Out[15]: 95% CI 1% difference between (short email - no email):
         (0.00023980847439844521, 0.14465380854687815)
```

Since this 95% CI is also above zero, you can also reject this other null hypothesis. However, now the 95% CI is very close to zero, meaning you would not be able to reject the null hypothesis of the effect being equal to something like 2%, at least not with a 95% confidence.

Noninferiority Testing

In this book, most null hypotheses will be stated as an equality (usually to zero). This type of null is motivated by the desire to treat only if an effect is found to be significantly different from zero. However, in some situations, you want to act only if a treatment effect is equal to zero. Consider, for instance, the case where you want to shut down a marketing campaign. You only want to do that if its effect is negligible (or not high enough to compensate its costs). In these situations, *you want to state the null in terms of a parameter being different from some value.*

That's because not being able to reject a null like $H_0 = 0$ is not the same thing as accepting it as true. This is known as the famous adage that "absence of evidence is not evidence of absence." The $H_0 = 0$ could be rejected simply because the sample size is too small, yielding a large confidence interval. This, however, doesn't point in the direction of it being true.

To work around this issue, statisticians created noninferiority testing, which is a way to test for a treatment being equal to another (or having a zero treatment effect). The basic idea is to see if the confidence interval contains zero, while also making sure it is small enough.

Test Statistic

Besides confidence intervals, sometimes it is useful to think about rejecting the null hypothesis in terms of a *test statistic*. These statistics are often constructed such that higher values point toward rejection of the null. One of the most commonly used test statistics is the t-statistic. It can be defined by normalizing the distribution that gives rise to the confidence interval:

$$t_\Delta = \frac{\mu_\Delta - H_0}{SE_\Delta} = \frac{(\mu_1 - \mu_2) - H_0}{\sqrt{\sigma_1^2/n_1 + \sigma_2^2/n_2}},$$

where H_0 is the value defined by your null hypothesis.

Notice how the numerator is simply the difference between the observed average difference and the null hypothesis. If the null were true, the expected value of this numerator would be zero: $E[\mu_\Delta - H_0] = 0$. The denominator is simply the standard error, which normalizes the statistic to have unit variance. It ensures that t_Δ follows a standard normal distribution—$N(0, 1)$—if the null is true. Since t_Δ is centered around zero under the null, values above or below the 1.96 would be extremely unlikely (appear less than 95% of the time). This means you can also reject the null hypothesis if you see such an extreme t-statistics. In our running example, the statistics associated with H_0 of no effect is greater than 2, meaning you can reject it at a 95% confidence level:

```
In [16]: t_stat = (diff_mu - 0) / diff_se
         t_stat
```

```
Out[16]: 2.2379512318715364
```

Additionally, since t-statistic is normally distributed under the null, you can use it to easily compute p-values.

T Versus Normal

Technically speaking using the normal distribution here is not accurate. Instead, you should use the T distribution with degrees of freedom equal to the sample size minus the number of parameters you've estimated (2, since you are comparing two means). However, with samples above 100, the distinction between the two is of little practical importance.

p-values

Previously, I've said that there is less than a 5% chance you would observe such an extreme difference if the conversion of customers that received no email and short email were the same. But can you precisely estimate what that chance is? How likely are you to observe such an extreme value? Enter p-values!

Like with confidence intervals (and most frequentist statistics, as a matter of fact), the true definition of p-values can be very confusing. So, to not take any risks, I'll copy the definition from Wikipedia: "the p-value is the probability of obtaining test results at least as extreme as the results actually observed during the test, assuming that the null hypothesis is correct."

To put it more succinctly, the p-value is the probability of seeing such data, if the null hypothesis were true (see Figure 2-4). It measures how unlikely that measurement you are seeing is, considering that the null hypothesis is true. Naturally, this often gets confused with the probability of the null hypothesis being true. Note the difference here. The p-value is *not* $P(H_0 | data)$, but rather $P(data | H_0)$.

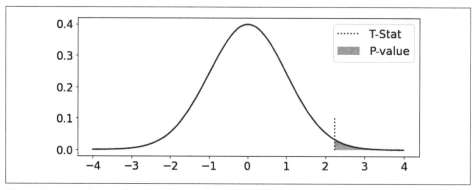

Figure 2-4. p-value is the probability of seeing a extreme statistic, given that the null hypothesis is true

To get the p-value, all you need to do is compute the area under the standard normal distribution before the test-statistic for a one-sided null hypothesis ("the difference is greater than x" or "the difference is smaller than x") and multiply the result by 2 for a two-sided null hypothesis ("the difference is x"):

```
In [17]: print("p-value:", (1 - stats.norm.cdf(t_stat))*2)


Out[17]: P-value: 0.025224235562152142
```

The p-value is interesting because it frees you from having to specify a confidence level, like 95% or 99%. But, if you wish to report one, from the p-value, you know precisely at which confidence your test will pass or fail. For instance, with a p-value of 0.025, you'll have significance up to the 2.5% level. So, while the 95% CI for the difference will not contain zero, the 99% CI will. This p-value also means that there is only a 2.5% chance of observing this extreme test statistic, if the difference was truly zero.

PRACTICAL EXAMPLE

Face-to-Face Versus Online Learning

Besides the direct impact of the virus, the 2020 pandemic brought other important issues with it. Chief among those was the fact that kids could not go to school, so learning was taken to the online environment for as much as two years. It's hard to estimate the generational impact this will have, since the decision to come back from the online environment to a face-to-face one was not randomized. In Brazil, for example, public schools took longer to open up, compared to private schools.

However, although certainly not trivial, one can design an experiment to test the impact of online versus face-to-face learning, as Figlio, Rush, and Yin did in "Is It Live or Is It Internet? Experimental Estimates of the Effects of Online Instruction on Student Learning" (2013). Here is the abstract:

> Students in a large introductory microeconomics course at a major research university were randomly assigned to live lectures versus watching these same lectures in an internet setting, where all other factors (e.g., instruction, supplemental materials) were the same. Counter to the conclusions drawn by a recent U.S. Department of Education meta-analysis of nonexperimental analyses of internet instruction in higher education, we find modest evidence that live-only instruction dominates internet instruction. These results are particularly strong for Hispanic students, male students, and lower-achieving students. We also provide suggestions for future experimentation in other settings.

Notice that this study was conducted at a university in the US; it's hard to say those results will generalize to basic education and to other countries. In technical terms, we say that the study has internal validity, as treatment and control groups are comparable due to randomization. But this study might not have external validity in terms of generalizing its results to other settings, since the people in it were not a random sample of the population, but rather economics students from a US university.

Power

So far, you've been looking into these statistical concepts from the perspective of a data analyst who's been presented with the data from an existing test. You are treating the data as given. But what if you are asked to design an experiment, instead of just reading one that was already designed? In this case, you need to decide the sample you would like to have for each variant. For example, what if you haven't yet run the cross-sell email experiment, but, instead, need to decide how many customers you should send the long email and how many, the short email and no email at all? From this perspective, the goal is to have a big enough sample so that you can correctly reject the null hypothesis of no effect, if it is indeed false. *The probability that a test correctly rejects the null hypothesis is called the power of the test.* It's not only a useful concept if you want to figure out the sample size you need for an experiment, but also for detecting issues in poorly run experiments.

Power is closely related to statistical significance. While α is the chance of rejecting the null hypothesis when it is actually true, power $(1 - \beta)$ is the chance of rejecting the null when it is false. In some sense, power is also defined in terms of α as in order to correctly reject the null, you need to specify how much evidence you need for rejection.

Recall how the 95% confidence interval means that 95% of the experiments will contain the true parameter you are trying to estimate. This also means that 5% of them won't, which will cause you to falsely reject the null hypothesis 5% of the time. With $\alpha = 0.05$, you need δ, the difference between the parameter estimate and the null hypothesis, to be at least $1.96SE$ away from zero in order to conclude that it is statistically significant. That's because $\delta - 1.96SE$ is the lower end of the 95% confidence interval.

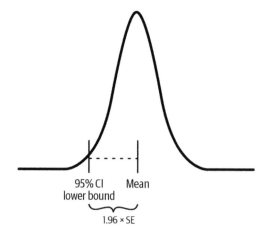

OK, so you need $\delta - 1.96SE > 0$ to claim the result as significant. But how likely are you to see this significant difference? This is where you need to think about power. Power is the chance of correctly rejecting the null, or $1 - \beta$, with β being the probability of not rejecting the null when it is false (probability of false negative). The industry standard for power is 80%, meaning that you'll only have a 20% ($\beta = 0.2$) chance of not rejecting the null, when it is indeed false. To achieve 80% power, you need to reject the null hypothesis 80% of the time when it is false. Since rejecting the null means that $\delta - 1.96SE > 0$, you need to get this big difference 80% of the time. In other words, you need to get the lower end of the 95% CI above zero, 80% of the time.

What is striking (or not) is that the lower end of the 95% confidence interval also follows a normal distribution. Just like the distribution of the sample average, the distribution of the lower end of the 95% CI has variance equal to the SE, but now the mean is $\delta - 1.96SE$. It is just the distribution of the sample average, shifted by $1.96SE$. Therefore, in order to have $\delta - 1.96SE > 0$ 80% of the time (80% power), you need the difference to be $1.96 + 0.84SE$ away from zero: 1.96 to give you the 95% CI and 0.84 so that the lower end of that interval falls above zero 80% of the time.

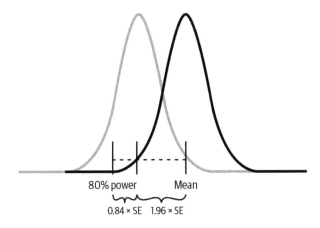

```
In [18]: stats.norm.cdf(0.84)
```

```
Out[18]: 0.7995458067395503
```

Sample Size Calculation

Another way to look at this is to realize that δ—the difference between the null hypothesis and the observed estimate—must be detectable if the null is false. With $\alpha = 5\%$ and $1 - \beta = 80\%$, the detectable effect is given by $2.8SE = (1.96SE + 0.84SE)$. So, if you want to craft a cross-sell email experiment where you want to detect a 1% difference, you must have a sample size that gives you at least $1\% = 2.8SE$. If you open up the *SE* formula for the difference, you have $SE_\Delta = \sqrt{SE_1^2 + SE_2^2}$. But recall that you are now speaking from the perspective of an analyst who has not seen the experiment, but is actually trying to design it. In this case, you don't have the *SE* of the treated group, but you can assume that the variance in both treated and control will be the same and hence $SE_\Delta = \sqrt{2SE^2} = \sqrt{2\sigma^2/n} = \sigma\sqrt{2/n}$. Plugging this in the detectable difference, you end up with a pretty simple formula for determining the sample size of each variant in a test if you want 80% power and 95% significance:

$$\delta = 2.8\sigma\sqrt{2/n}$$

$$n = 2 * 2.8^2\sigma^2/\delta^2 \approx 16\sigma^2/\delta^2$$

where δ is the detectable difference and I've rounded $2 * 2.8^2$ to be conservative. Applying this formula to your data, using the variance of the control group as our best guess for σ^2, you end up with the following required sample size:

```
In [19]: np.ceil(16 * no_email.std()**2/0.01)
```

```
Out[19]: 66.0
```

```
In [20]: data.groupby("cross_sell_email").size()
```

```
Out[20]: cross_sell_email
         long        109
         no_email     94
         short       120
         dtype: int64
```

This is of course invaluable in terms of experiment design, but is also good news for the cross-sell experiment we currently have. In it, we have more than 100 samples for both treatment groups and 94 samples for the control, which indicates a properly powered test.

See Also

This very simple way of calculating sample size was taken from "A/B Testing Intuition Busters: Common Misunderstandings in Online Controlled Experiments" (2022), by Ron Kohavi et al. This sample size formula is only one of the many very interesting and useful things presented in the article, so I definitely recommend you check it out.

Key Ideas

The idea of this chapter was to link causal identification with estimation (and also review some important statistical concepts). Recall that the goal of causal inference is to learn about causal quantities from data. The first step in the process is identification, where you use key assumptions to go from unobservable causal quantities to observable statistical quantities you can estimate from data.

For example, the ATE is a causal quantity; it is defined by the unobservable potential outcomes $ATE = E[Y_1 - Y_0]$. To identify the ATE, you use the independence assumption, $T \perp (Y_0, Y_1)$, which allows you to write it in terms of observable quantities, $E[Y \mid T = 1]$, and $E[Y \mid T = 0]$. That is, under the independence assumption:

$$E[Y_1 - Y_0] = E[Y \mid T = 1] - E[Y \mid T = 0]$$

You also saw how you could use randomized control trials (RCTs) to make this assumption more plausible. If you randomize the treatment, you are brute-forcing it to be independent from the potential outcomes Y_t.

But identification is just the first step in causal inference. Once you are able to write the causal quantities in terms of statistical quantities, you still need to estimate those statistical quantities. For instance, even though you can write the ATE in terms of $E[Y \mid T = 1]$ and $E[Y \mid T = 0]$, you still need to estimate them.

The second part of this chapter covered statistical concepts used in that estimation process. Specifically, you learned about the standard error:

$$SE = \sigma / \sqrt{n},$$

and how to use it to place confidence intervals around an estimate μ:

$$\hat{\mu} \pm z^* SE,$$

where z is the value between which lies $\alpha\%$ of the mass of a normal distribution.

You also learned how to construct a confidence interval for a difference in averages between two groups, which boiled down to summing the variances for those groups and finding a standard error for the difference:

$$SE_{diff} = \sqrt{SE_1^2 + SE_2^2}$$

Finally, you learned about power and how it can be used to calculate the sample size for an experiment you wish to run. Specifically, for 95% confidence and 80% power, you could simplify the sample size formula to:

$$N = 16 * \sigma^2 / \delta$$

where σ^2 is the variance of the outcome and δ is the detectable difference.

CHAPTER 3

Graphical Causal Models

In Chapter 1 you saw how causal inference can be broken down into two problems: identification and estimation. In this chapter, you'll dive deeper into the identification part, which is arguably the most challenging one. This chapter is mostly theoretical, as you will be playing with graphical models without necessarily estimating their parameters with data. Don't let this fool you. Identification is the heart of causal inference, so learning its theory is fundamental for tackling causal problems in real life. In this chapter, you will:

- Get an introduction to graphical models, where you will learn what a graphical model for causality is, how associations flow in a graph, and how to query a graph using off-the-shelf software.
- Revisit the concept of identification through the lens of graphical models.
- Learn about two very common sources of bias that hinder identification, their causal graph structure, and what you can do about them.

Thinking About Causality

Have you ever noticed how those cooks in YouTube videos are excellent at describing food? "Reduce the sauce until it reaches a velvety consistency." If you are just learning to cook, you have no idea what this even means. Just give me the time I should leave this thing on the stove, will you! With causality, it's the same thing. Suppose you walk into a bar and hear folks discussing causality (probably a bar next to an economics department). In that case, you will hear them say how the confounding of income made it challenging to identify the effect of immigration on that neighborhood unemployment rate, so they had to use an instrumental variable. And by now, you might not understand what they are talking about. That's OK. You've only scratched the surface when it comes to understanding the language of causal inference. You've learned a bit about counterfactual outcomes and biases; enough so you could understand the key issue causal inference is trying to solve. Enough to appreciate what's going on behind the most powerful tool of causal inference: randomized controlled trials. But this tool won't always be available or simply won't work (as you'll soon see in "Selection Bias" on page 83). As you encounter more challenging causal inference problems, you'll also need a broader understanding of the causal inference language, so you can properly understand what you are facing and how to deal with it.

A well-articulated language allows you to think clearly. This chapter is about broadening your causal inference vocabulary. You can think of graphical models as one of the fundamental languages of causality. They are a powerful way of structuring a causal inference problem and making identification assumptions explicit, or even visual. Graphical models will allow you to make your thoughts transparent to others and to yourself.

Structural Causal Model

Some scientists use the term *structural causal model* (SCM) to refer to a unifying language of causal inference. These models are composed of graphs and causal equations. Here, I'll mostly focus on the graph aspect of SCMs.

As a starting point into the fantastic world of graphs, let's take our previous example of estimating the impact of emails on conversion. In that example, the treatment T is cross-sell email and the outcome Y is if a customer converted to a new product or not:

```
In [1]: import pandas as pd
        import numpy as np

        data = pd.read_csv("./data/cross_sell_email.csv")
        data
```

	gender	cross_sell_email	age	conversion
0	0	short	15	0
1	1	short	27	0
2	1	long	17	0
...	...	...	...	...
320	0	no_email	15	0
321	1	no_email	16	0
322	1	long	24	1

Let's also recall from the previous chapter that, in this problem, T is randomized. Hence, you can say that the treatment is independent from the potential outcomes, $(Y_0, Y_1) \perp T$, which makes association equal to causation:

$$E[Y_1 - Y_0] = E[Y|T = 1] - E[Y|T = 0]$$

Importantly, there is absolutely no way of telling that the independence assumption holds just by looking at the data. You can only say that it does because you have information about the treatment assignment mechanism. That is, you know that emails were randomized.

Visualizing Causal Relationships

You can encode this knowledge in a graph, which captures your beliefs about what causes what. In this simple example, let's say you believe that cross-sell emails cause conversion. You also believe that the other variables you measured, age and gender, also cause conversion. Moreover, you can also add variables you didn't measure to the graph. We usually denote them by the letter U, since they are unobserved. There are probably many unobserved variables that cause conversion (like customer income, social background), and age (how your product appeals to different demographics, the city the company is operating in). But since you don't measure them, you can bundle everything into a U node that represents all those unmeasured variables. Finally, you can add a randomization node pointing to T, representing your knowledge of the fact that the cross-sell email was randomized.

DAG

You might find people referring to causal graphs as *DAGs*. The acronym stands for directed acyclic graph. The directed part tells you that the edges have a direction, as opposed to undirected graphs, like a social network, for example. The acyclic part tells you that the graph has no loops or cycles. Causal graphs are usually directed and acyclic because causality is nonreversible.

To add those beliefs of yours to a graph and literally see them, you can use `graphviz`:

```
In [2]: import graphviz as gr

        g_cross_sell = gr.Digraph()

        g_cross_sell.edge("U", "conversion")
        g_cross_sell.edge("U", "age")
        g_cross_sell.edge("U", "gender")

        g_cross_sell.edge("rnd", "cross_sell_email")
```

```
g_cross_sell.edge("cross_sell_email", "conversion")
g_cross_sell.edge("age", "conversion")
g_cross_sell.edge("gender", "conversion")

g_cross_sell
```

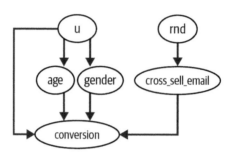

Each node in the graph is a random variable. You can use arrows, or edges, to show if a variable causes another. In this graphical model, you are saying that email causes conversion, that U causes age, conversion, and gender, and so on and so forth. This language of graphical models will help you clarify your thinking about causality, as it makes your beliefs about how the world works explicit. If you are pondering how impractical this is—after all, there is no way you are going to encode all the hundreds of variables that are commonly present in today's data applications—rest assured you won't need to. In practice, you can radically simplify things, by bundling up nodes, while also keeping the general causal story you are trying to convey. For example, you can take the preceding graph and bundle the observable variables into an X node. Since they both are caused by U and cause conversion, your causal story remains intact by joining them.

Also, when you are representing variables that have been randomized or intervened on, you can just remove all incoming arrows from it:

```
In [3]: # rankdir:LR layers the graph from left to right
        g_cross_sell = gr.Digraph(graph_attr={"rankdir": "LR"})

        g_cross_sell.edge("U", "conversion")
        g_cross_sell.edge("U", "X")

        g_cross_sell.edge("cross_sell_email", "conversion")
        g_cross_sell.edge("X", "conversion")

        g_cross_sell
```

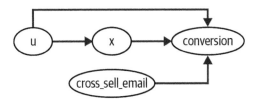

What is interesting to realize here is that perhaps the most important information in a DAG is actually what is *not* in it: an edge missing from one variable to another means there is an assumption of no direct causal link between the two. For example, in the preceding graph, you are assuming that nothing causes both the treatment and the outcome.

Just like with every language you learn, you are probably looking into this and thinking it doesn't all make complete sense. That's normal. I could just throw at you a bunch of rules and best practices to represent causal relationships between variables in a graph. But that is probably the least efficient way of learning. Instead, my plan is to simply expose you to lots and lots of examples. With time, you will get the hang of it. For now, I just want you to keep in mind that graphs are a very powerful tool for understanding why association isn't causation.

Are Consultants Worth It?

To see the power of DAGs, let's consider a more interesting example, where the treatment is not randomized. Let's suppose you are the manager of a company contemplating the decision of whether to bring in some top-notch consultants. You know that they are expensive, but you also know that they have expert knowledge from working with the best companies in the business. To make things more complicated, you are not sure if the top-notch consultants will improve your business or if it is just the case that only very profitable businesses can afford those consultants, which is why their presence correlates with strong business performance. It would be awesome if someone had randomized the presence of consultants, as this would make answering the question trivial. But of course you don't have that luxury, so you will have to come up with something else. As you can probably see by now, this is a problem of untangling causation from association. To understand it, you can encode your beliefs about its causal mechanisms in a graph:

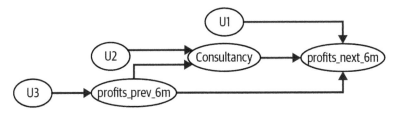

Notice how I've added U nodes to each of these variables to represent the fact that there are other things we can't measure causing them. Since graphs usually represent random variables, it is expected that a random component will cause all the variables, which is what those Us represent. However, they won't add anything to the causal story I'm going to tell, so I might just as well omit them:

Here, I'm saying that the past performance of a company causes the company to hire a top-notch consultant. If the company is doing great, it can afford to pay the expensive service. If the company is not doing so great, it can't. Hence, past performance (measured here by past profits) is what determines the odds of a company hiring a consultant. Remember that this relationship is not necessarily deterministic. I'm just saying that companies that are doing well are *more likely* to hire top-notch consultants.

Not only that, companies that did well in the past 6 months are very likely to also do well in the next 6 months. Of course, this doesn't always happen, but, on average, it does, which is why you also have an edge from past performance to future performance. Finally, I've added an edge from consultancy to the firm's future performance. Your goal is to know the strengths of this connection. This is the causal relationship you care about. Does consultancy actually cause company performance to increase?

Answering this question is not straightforward because there are two sources of association between consultancy and future performance. One is causal and the other is not. To understand and untangle them, you first need to take a quick look at how association flows in causal graphs.

Crash Course in Graphical Models

Schools offer whole semesters on graphical models. By all means, if you want to go deep in graphical models, it will be very beneficial for your understanding of causal inference. But, for the purpose of this book, it is just (utterly) important that *you understand what kind of independence and conditional independence assumptions a graphical model entails*. As you'll see, associations flow through a graphical model as water flows through a stream. You can stop this flow or enable it, depending on how you treat the variables in the graph. To understand this, let's examine some common graphical structures and examples. They will be pretty straightforward, but they are the sufficient building blocks to understand everything about the flow of association, independence, and conditional independence on graphical models.

Chains

First, look at this very simple graph. It's called a chain. Here T causes M, which causes Y. You can sometimes refer to the intermediary node as a mediator, because it mediates the relationship between T and Y:

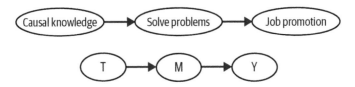

In this first graph, although causation only flows in the direction of the arrows, association flows both ways. To give a more concrete example, let's say that knowing about causal inference improves your problem-solving skills, and problem solving increases your chances of getting a promotion. So causal knowledge causes your problem-solving skills to increase, which in turn causes you to get a job promotion. You can say here that job promotion is dependent on causal knowledge. The greater the causal expertise, the greater your chances of getting a promotion. Also, the greater your chances of promotion, the greater your chance of having causal knowledge. Otherwise, it would be difficult to get a promotion. In other words, job promotion is associated with causal inference expertise the same way that causal inference expertise is associated with job promotion, even though only one of the directions is causal. When two variables are associated with each other, you can say they are dependent or not independent:

$$T \not\perp Y$$

Now, let's hold the intermediary variable fixed. You could do that by looking only at people with the same M, or problem-solving skills in our example. Formally, you can say you are conditioning on M. In this case, the dependence is blocked. So, T and Y are independent given M. You can write this mathematically as:

$$T \perp Y | M$$

To indicate that we are conditioning on a node, I'll shade it:

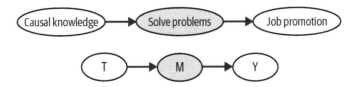

To see what this means in our example, think about conditioning on people's problem-solving skills. If you look at a bunch of people with the same problem-solving skills, knowing which ones are good at causal inference doesn't give any further information about their chances of getting a job promotion. In mathematical terms:

$$E[Promotion|Solve\ problems, Causal\ knowledge] = E[Promotion|Solve\ problems]$$

The inverse is also true; once I know how good you are at solving problems, knowing about your job promotion status gives me no further information about how likely you are to know causal inference.

As a general rule, if you have a chain like in the preceding graph, association flowing in the path from T to Y is blocked when you condition on an intermediary variable M. Or:

$$T \not\perp Y$$

but

$$T \perp Y|M$$

Forks

Moving on, let's consider a fork structure. In this structure, you have a common cause: the same variable causes two other variables down the graph. In forks, association flows backward through the arrows:

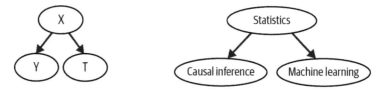

For example, let's say your knowledge of statistics causes you to know more about causal inference and about machine learning. However, knowing causal inference doesn't help you with machine learning and vice versa, so there is no edge between those variables.

This graph is telling you that if you don't know someone's level of statistical knowledge, then knowing that they are good at causal inference makes it more likely that they are also good at machine learning, even if causal inference doesn't help you with machine learning. That is because even if you don't know someone's level of statistical knowledge, you can infer it from their causal inference knowledge. If they are good at causal inference, they are probably good at statistics, making it more likely that they are also good at machine learning. The variables at the tip of a fork move together even if they don't cause each other, simply because they are both caused by the same thing. In the causal inference literature, when we have a common cause between a treatment and the outcome, we call that common cause a *confounder*.

The fork structure is so important in causal inference that it deserves another example. Do you know how tech recruiters sometimes ask you to solve problems that you'll probably never find in the job you are applying for? Like when they ask you to invert a binary tree or count duplicate elements in Python? Well, they are essentially leveraging the fact that association flows through a fork structure in the following graph:

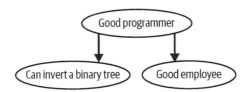

The recruiter knows that good programmers tend to be top performers. But when they interview you, they don't know if you are a good programmer or not. So they ask you a question that you'll only be able to answer if you are. That question doesn't have to be about a problem that you'll encounter in the job you are applying for. It just signals whether you are a good programmer or not. If you can answer the question, you will likely be a good programmer, which means you will also likely be a good employee.

Now, let's say that the recruiter already knows that you are a good programmer. Maybe they know you from previous companies or you have an impressive degree. In this case, knowing whether or not you can answer the application process questions gives no further information on whether you will be a good employee or not. In technical terms, you can say that answering the question and being a good employee are independent, once you condition on being a good programmer.

More generally, if you have a fork structure, two variables that share a common cause are dependent, but independent when you condition on the common cause. Or:

$$T \not\perp Y$$

but

$$T \perp Y | X$$

Immorality or Collider

The only structure missing is the immorality (and yes, this is a technical term). An *immorality* is when two nodes share a child, but there is no direct relationship between them. Another way of saying this is that two variables share a common effect. This common effect is often referred to as a *collider*, since two arrows collide at it:

In an immorality, the two parent nodes are independent of each other. But they become dependent if you condition on the common effect. For example, consider that there are two ways to get a job promotion. You can either be good at statistics or flatter your boss. If I don't condition on your job promotion, that is, I don't know if you will or won't get it, then your level of statistics and flattering are independent. In other words, knowing how good you are at statistics tells me nothing about how good you are at flattering your boss. On the other hand, if you did get a job promotion, suddenly, knowing your level of statistics tells me about your flattering level. If you are bad at statistics and did get a promotion, you will likely be good at flattering your boss. Otherwise, it will be very unlikely for you to get a promotion. Conversely, if you are good at statistics, it is more likely that you are bad at flattering, as being good at statistics already explains your promotion. This phenomenon is sometimes called *explaining away*, because one cause already explains the effect, making the other cause less likely.

As a general rule, conditioning on a collider opens the association path, making the variables dependent. Not conditioning on it leaves it closed. Or:

$$T \perp Y$$

and

$$T \not\perp Y | X$$

Importantly, you can open the same dependence path if instead of conditioning on the collider, you condition on a effect (direct or not) of the collider. Continuing with our example, let's now say that getting a job promotion massively increases your salary, which gives you the next graph:

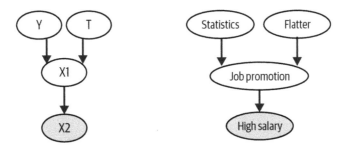

In this graph, even if you don't condition on the collider, but condition on a cause of it, the causes of the collider become dependent. For instance, even if I don't know about your promotion, but I do know about your massive salary, your knowledge about statistics and boss flattering become dependent: having one makes it less likely that you also have the other.

The Flow of Association Cheat Sheet

Knowing these three structures—chains, forks, and immoralities—you can derive an even more general rule about independence and the flow of association in a graph.

A path is blocked if and only if:

1. It contains a non-collider that has been conditioned on.
2. It contains a collider that has not been conditioned on and has no descendants that have been conditioned on.

Figure 3-1 is a cheat sheet about how dependence flows in a graph.

If these rules seem a bit opaque or hard to grasp, now is a good time for me to tell you that, thankfully, you can use off-the-shelf algorithms to check if two variables in a graph are associated with each other or if they are independent. To tie everything you learned together, let's go over a final example so I can show you how to code it up.

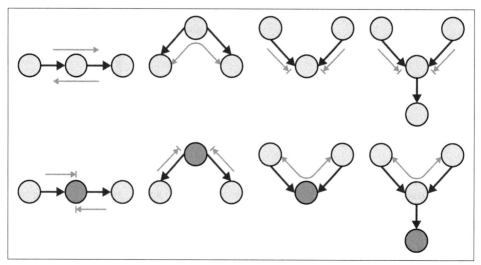

Figure 3-1. Cheat sheet about how dependence flows in a graph

Querying a Graph in Python

Take the following graph:

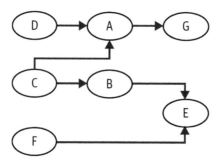

In a moment, you'll input this graph to a Python library that will make answering questions about it pretty easy. But before you do that, as an exercise to internalize the concepts you've just learned, try to answer the following questions on your own:

- Are D and C dependent?
- Are D and C dependent given A?
- Are D and C dependent given G?
- Are A and B dependent?
- Are A and B dependent given C?

- Are G and F dependent?
- Are G and F dependent given E?

Now, to see if you got them right, you can input that graph into a DiGraph, from networkx. networkx is a library to handle graphical models and has a bunch of handy algorithms that will help you inspect this graph:

```
In [4]: import networkx as nx

        model = nx.DiGraph([
            ("C", "A"),
            ("C", "B"),
            ("D", "A"),
            ("B", "E"),
            ("F", "E"),
            ("A", "G"),
        ])
```

As a starter, let's take D and C. They form the immorality structure you saw earlier, with A being a collider. From the rule about independence in an immorality structure, you know that D and C are independent. You also know that if you condition on the collider A, association starts to flow between them. The method d_separated tells you if association flows between two variables in the graph (d-separation is another way of expressing the independence between two variables in a graph). To condition on a variable, you can add it to the observed set. For example, to check if D and C are dependent given A, you can use d_separated and pass the fourth argument z={"A"}:

```
In [5]: print("Are D and C dependent?")
        print(not(nx.d_separated(model, {"D"}, {"C"}, {})))

        print("Are D and C dependent given A?")
        print(not(nx.d_separated(model, {"D"}, {"C"}, {"A"})))

        print("Are D and C dependent given G?")
        print(not(nx.d_separated(model, {"D"}, {"C"}, {"G"})))

Out[5]: Are D and C dependent?
        False
        Are D and C dependent given A?
        True
        Are D and C dependent given G?
        True
```

Next, notice that D, A, and G form a chain. You know that association flows in a chain, so D is not independent from G. However, if you condition on the intermediary variable A, you block the flow of association:

```
In [6]: print("Are G and D dependent?")
        print(not(nx.d_separated(model, {"G"}, {"D"}, {})))

        print("Are G and D dependent given A?")
        print(not(nx.d_separated(model, {"G"}, {"D"}, {"A"})))

Out[6]: Are G and D dependent?
        True
        Are G and D dependent given A?
        False
```

The last structure you need to review is the fork. You can see that A, B, and C form a fork, with C being a common cause of A and B. You know that association flows through a fork, so A and B are not independent. However, if you condition on the common cause, the path of association is blocked:

```
In [7]: print("Are A and B dependent?")
        print(not(nx.d_separated(model, {"A"}, {"B"}, {})))

        print("Are A and B dependent given C?")
        print(not(nx.d_separated(model, {"A"}, {"B"}, {"C"})))

Out[7]: Are A and B dependent?
        True
        Are A and B dependent given C?
        False
```

Finally, let's put everything together and talk about G and F. Does association flow between them? Let's start at G. You know that association flows between G and E, since they are in a fork. However, association stops at the collider E, which means that G and F are independent. Yet if you condition on E, association starts to flow through the collider and the path opens, connecting G and F:

```
In [8]: print("Are G and F dependent?")
        print(not(nx.d_separated(model, {"G"}, {"F"}, {})))

        print("Are G and F dependent given E?")
        print(not(nx.d_separated(model, {"G"}, {"F"}, {"E"})))

Out[8]: Are G and F dependent?
        False
        Are G and F dependent given E?
        True
```

This is great. Not only did you learn the three basics structures in graphs, you also saw how to use off-the-shelf algorithms to check for independences in the graph. But what does this have to do with causal inference? It's time to go back to the problem we were exploring at the beginning of the chapter. Recall that we were trying to understand the impact of hiring expensive, top-notch consultants on business performance, which we depicted as the following graph:

You can use your newly acquired skills to see why association is not causation in this graph. Notice that you have a fork structure in this graph. Therefore, there are two flows of association between consultancy and company's future performance: a direct causal path and a noncausal path that is confounded by a common cause. This latter one is referred to as a *backdoor path*. The presence of a confounding backdoor path in this graph demonstrates that the observed association between consultancy and company performance cannot be solely attributed to a causal relationship.

Understanding how associations flow in a graph through noncausal paths will allow you to be much more precise when talking about the difference between association and causation. For this reason, it pays to revisit the concept of identification, now under the new light of graphical models.

Identification Revisited

So far, in the absence of randomization, the argument I've been using to explain why it is so hard to find the causal effect is that treated and untreated are not comparable to each other. For example, companies that hire consultants usually have better past performance than those that don't hire expensive consultants. This results in the sort of bias you've seen before:

$$E[Y|T=1] - E[Y|T=0] = \underbrace{E[Y_1 - Y_0|T=1]}_{ATT} + \underbrace{\{E[Y_0|T=1] - E[Y_0|T=0]\}}_{BIAS}$$

Now that you've learned about causal graphs, you can be more precise about the nature of that bias and, more importantly, you can understand what you can do to make it go away. Identification is intimately related to independence in a graphical model. If you have a graph that depicts the causal relationship between the treatment, the outcome, and other relevant variables, you can think about identification as the process of isolating the causal relationship between the treatment and the outcome in that graph. During the identification phase, you will essentially close all undesirable flows of association.

Take the consultancy graph. As you saw earlier, there are two association paths between the treatment and the outcome, but only one of them is causal. You can check for bias by creating a causal graph that is just like the original one, but with the causal relationship removed. If treatment and outcome are still connected in this graph, it must be due to a noncausal path, which indicates the presence of bias:

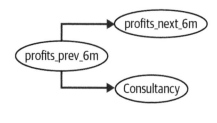

```
In [9]: consultancy_model_severed = nx.DiGraph([
            ("profits_prev_6m", "profits_next_6m"),
            ("profits_prev_6m", "consultancy"),
        #   ("consultancy", "profits_next_6m"), # causal relationship removed
        ])

        not(nx.d_separated(consultancy_model_severed,
                        {"consultancy"}, {"profits_next_6m"}, {}))

Out[9]: True
```

These noncausal flows of association are referred to as *backdoor paths*. To identify the causal relationship between T and Y, you need to close them so that only the causal path one remains. In the consultancy example, you know that conditioning on the common cause, the company's past performance, closes that path:

CIA and the Adjustment Formula

You just saw that conditioning on `profits_prev_6m` blocks the noncausal association flow between the treatment, consultancy, and the outcome—the company's future performance. As a result, if you look at a group of companies with similar past performance and, inside that group, compare the future performance of those that hired consultants with those that didn't, the difference can be entirely attributed to the consultants. This makes intuitive sense, right? The difference in future performance between the treated (companies that hired consultants) and the untreated is 1) due to the treatment itself and 2) due to the fact that companies that hire consultants tend to be doing well to begin with. If you just compare treated and untreated companies that are doing equally well, the second source of difference disappears.

Of course, like with everything in causal inference, you are making an assumption here. Specifically, you are assuming that all sources of noncausal association between the treated and the outcome is due to the common causes you can measure and condition on. This is very much like the independence assumption you saw earlier, but in its weaker form:

$$(Y_0, Y_1) \perp T \mid X$$

This *conditional independence assumption* (CIA) states that, if you compare units (i.e.,companies) with the same level of covariates X, their potential outcomes will be, on average, the same. Another way of saying this is that treatment seems *as if it were randomized*, if you look at units with the same values of covariate X.

CIA Names

The CIA permeates a lot of causal inference research and it goes by many names, like ignorability, exogeneity, or exchangeability.

The CIA also motivates a very simple way to identify the causal effect from observable quantities in the data. If treatment looks as good as random within groups of X, all you need to do is compare treated and untreated inside each of the X defined groups and average the result using the size of the group as weights:

$$ATE = E_X[E[Y \mid T = 1] - E[Y \mid T = 0]]$$

$$ATE = \sum_x \{(E[Y \mid T = 1, X = x] - E[Y \mid T = 0, X = x])P(X = x)\}$$
$$= \sum_x \{E[Y \mid T = 1, X = x]P(X = x) - E[Y \mid T = 0, X = x]P(X = x)\}$$

This is called the *adjustment formula* or conditionality principle. It says that, if you condition on or control for X, the average treatment effect can be identified as the weighted average of in-group differences between treated and control. Again, if conditioning on X blocks the flow of association through the noncausal paths in the graph, a causal quantity, like the ATE, becomes identifiable, meaning that you can compute it from observable data. The process of closing backdoor paths by adjusting for confounders gets the incredibly creative name of *backdoor adjustment*.

Positivity Assumption

The adjustment formula also highlights the importance of positivity. Since you are averaging the difference between treatment and outcome over X, you must ensure that, for all groups of X, there are some units in the treatment and some in the control, otherwise the difference is undefined. More formally, you can say that the conditional probability of the treatment needs to be strictly positive and below 1: $1 > P(T|X) > 0$. Identification is still possible when positivity is violated, but it will require you to make dangerous extrapolations.

Positivity Names

Since the positivity assumption is also very popular in causal inference, it too goes by many names, like common support or overlap.

An Identification Example with Data

Since this might be getting a bit abstract, let's see how it all plays out with some data. To keep our example, let's say you've collected data on six companies, three of which had low profits (1 million USD) in the past six months and three of which had high profits. Just like you suspected, highly profitable companies are more likely to hire consultants. Two out of the three high-profit companies hired them, while only one out of the three low-profit companies hired consultants (if the low sample bothers you, please pretend that each data point here actually represents 10,000 companies):

```
In [10]: df = pd.DataFrame(dict(
             profits_prev_6m=[1.0, 1.0, 1.0, 5.0, 5.0, 5.0],
             consultancy=[0, 0, 1, 0, 1, 1],
             profits_next_6m=[1, 1.1, 1.2, 5.5, 5.7, 5.7],
         ))

         df
```

	profits_prev_6m	consultancy	profits_next_6m
0	1.0	0	1.0
1	1.0	0	1.1
2	1.0	1	1.2
3	5.0	0	5.5
4	5.0	1	5.7
5	5.0	1	5.7

If you simply compare `profits_next_6m` of the companies that hired consultants with those that didn't, you'll get a difference of 1.66 MM in profits:

```
In [11]: (df.query("consultancy==1")["profits_next_6m"].mean()
          - df.query("consultancy==0")["profits_next_6m"].mean())
```

```
Out[11]: 1.666666666666667
```

But you know better. This is not the causal effect of consultancy on a company's performance, since the companies that performed better in the past are overrepresented in the group that hired consultants. To get an unbiased estimate of the effect of consultants, you need to look at companies with similar past performance. As you can see, this yields more modest results:

```
In [12]: avg_df = (df
                   .groupby(["consultancy", "profits_prev_6m"])
                   ["profits_next_6m"]
                   .mean())

         avg_df.loc[1] - avg_df.loc[0]
```

```
Out[12]: profits_prev_6m
         1.0    0.15
         5.0    0.20
         Name: profits_next_6m, dtype: float64
```

If you take the weighted average of these effects, where the weights are the size of each group, you end up with an unbiased estimate of the ATE. Here, since the two groups are of equal size, this is just a simple average, giving you an ATE of 175,000. Hence, if you are a manager deciding whether to hire consultants and you are presented with the preceding data, you can conclude that the impact of consultants on future profits is about 175k USD. Of course, in order to do that, you have to invoke the CIA. That is, you have to assume that past performance is the only common cause of hiring consultants and future performance.

You just went through a whole example of encoding your beliefs about a causal mechanism into a graph and using that graph to find out which variables you needed to condition on in order to estimate the ATE, even without randomizing the treatment. Then, you saw what that looked like with some data, where you estimated the ATE, following the adjustment formula and assuming conditional independence. The tools used here are fairly general and will inform you of many causal problems to come. Still, I don't think we are done yet. Some graphical structures—and the bias they entail—are much more common than others. It is worth going through them so you can start to get a feeling for the difficulties that lie ahead in your causal inference journey.

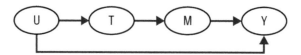
Confounding Bias

The first significant cause of bias is confounding. It's the bias we've been discussing so far. Now, we are just putting a name to it. *Confounding happens when there is an open backdoor path through which association flows noncausally, usually because the treatment and the outcome share a common cause.* For example, let's say that you work in HR and you want to know if your new management training program is increasing employers' engagement. However, since the training is optional, you believe only managers that are already doing great attend the program and those who need it the most, don't. When you measure engagement of the teams under the managers that took the training, it is much higher than that of the teams under the managers who didn't attend the training. But it's hard to know how much of this is causal. Since there is a common cause between treatment and outcome, they would move together regardless of a causal effect.

To identify that causal effect, you need to close all backdoor paths between the treatment and the outcome. If you do so, the only effect that will be left is the direct effect $T \rightarrow Y$. In our example, you could somehow control for the manager's quality prior to taking the training. In that situation, the difference in the outcome will be only due to the training, since manager quality prior to the training would be held constant between treatment and control. Simply put, *to adjust for confounding bias, you need to adjust for the common causes of the treatment and the outcome:*

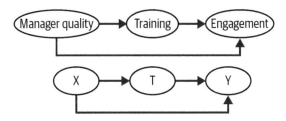

Unfortunately, it is not always possible to adjust for all common causes. Sometimes, there are unknown causes or known causes that you can't measure. The case of manager quality is one of them. Despite all the effort, we still haven't yet figured out how to measure management quality. If you can't observe manager quality, then you can't condition on it and the effect of training on engagement is not identifiable.

Surrogate Confounding

In some situations, you can't close all the backdoor paths due to unmeasured confounders. In the following example, once again, manager quality causes managers to opt in for the training and team's engagement. So there is confounding in the relationship between the treatment (training) and the outcome (team's engagement). But in this case, you can't condition on the confounder, because it is unmeasurable. In this case, the causal effect of the treatment on the outcome is not identifiable due to confounder bias. However, you have other measured variables that can act as proxies for the confounder manager's quality. Those variables are not in the backdoor path, but controlling for them will help reduce the bias (even though it won't eliminate it). Those variables are sometimes referred to as surrogate confounders.

In this example, you can't measure manager quality, but you can measure some of its causes, like the manager's tenure or level of education; and some of its effects, like the team's attrition or performance. Controlling for those surrogate variables is not sufficient to eliminate bias, but it sure helps:

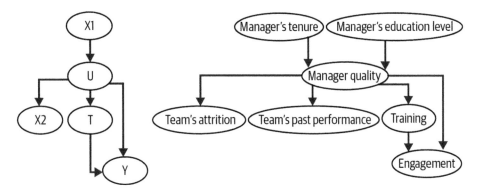

Randomization Revisited

In many important and very relevant research questions, confounders are a major issue, since you can never be sure that you've controlled for all of them. But if you are planning to use causal inference mostly in the industry, I have good news for you. In the industry, you are mostly interested in learning the causal effects of things that your company can control—like prices, customer service, and marketing budget—so that you can optimize them. In those situations, it is fairly easy to know what the confounders are, because the business usually knows what information it used to allocate the treatment. Not only that, even when it doesn't, it's almost always an option to intervene on the treatment variable. This is precisely the point of A/B tests. When you randomize the treatment, you can go from a graph with unobservable confounders to one where the only cause of the treatment is randomness:

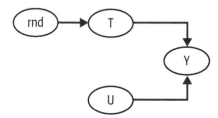

Consequently, besides trying to see what variables you need to condition on in order to identify the effect, you should also be asking yourself what are the possible interventions you could make that would change the graph into one where the causal quantity of interest is identifiable.

Not all is lost when you have unobserved confounders. In Part IV, I'll cover methods that can leverage time structure in the data to deal with unobserved confounders. Part V will cover the use of instrumental variables for the same purpose.

Sensitivity Analysis and Partial Identification

When you can't measure all common causes, instead of simply giving up, it is often much more fruitful to shift the discussion from "Am I measuring all confounders?" to "How strong should the unmeasured confounders be to change my analysis significantly?" This is the main idea behind sensitivity analysis. For a comprehensible review on this topic, I suggest you check out the paper "Making Sense of Sensitivity: Extending Omitted Variable Bias," by Cinelli and Hazlett.

Additionally, even when the causal quantity you care about can't be point identified, you can still use observable data to place bounds around it. This process is called *partial identification* and it is an active area of research.

Selection Bias

If you think confounding bias was already a sneaky little stone in your causal inference shoe, just wait until you hear about selection bias. While confounding bias happens when you don't control for common causes to the treatment and outcome, selection bias is more related to conditioning on common effects and mediators.

Bias Terminology

There isn't a consensus in the literature on the names of biases. For instance, economists tend to refer to all sorts of biases as selection bias. In contrast, some scientists like to further segment what I'm calling selection bias into collider bias and mediator bias. I'll use the same terminology as in the book *Causal Inference: What If*, by Miguel A. Hernán and James M. Robins (Chapman & Hall/CRC).

Conditioning on a Collider

Consider the case where you work for a software company and want to estimate the impact of a new feature you've just implemented. To avoid any sort of confounding bias, you do a randomized rollout of the feature: 10% of the customers are randomly chosen to get the new feature, while the rest don't. You want to know if this feature made your customer happier and more satisfied. Since satisfaction isn't directly measurable, you use Net Promoter Score (NPS) as a proxy for it. To measure NPS, you send a survey to the customers in the rollout (treated) and in the control groups, asking them if they would recommend your product. When the results arrive, you see that the customers who had the new feature and responded to the NPS survey had higher NPS scores than the ones that didn't have the new feature and also responded to the NPS survey. Can you say that this difference is entirely due to the causal effect of the new feature on NPS? To answer this question, you should start with the graph that represents this situation:

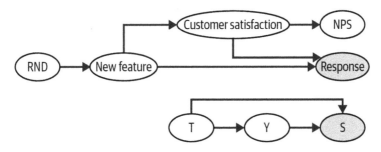

To cut to the chase, sadly, the answer is no. The issue here is that you can only measure NPS for those who responded to the NPS survey. You are estimating the difference between treated and control while also conditioning on customers who responded to the NPS survey. Even though randomization allows you to identify the ATE as the difference in outcome between treated and control, once you condition on the common effect, you also introduce selection bias. To see this, you can re-create this graph and delete the causal path from the new feature to customer satisfaction, which also closes the direct path to NPS. Then, you can check if NPS is still connected to the new features, once you condition on the response. You can see that it is, meaning that association flows between the two variables via a noncausal path, which is precisely what bias means:

```
In [13]: nps_model = nx.DiGraph([
             ("RND", "New Feature"),
         #     ("New Feature", "Customer Satisfaction"),
             ("Customer Satisfaction", "NPS"),
             ("Customer Satisfaction", "Response"),
             ("New Feature", "Response"),
         ])


         not(nx.d_separated(nps_model, {"NPS"}, {"New Feature"}, {"Response"}))

Out[13]: True
```

See Also

Causal identification under selection bias is very sneaky. This approach of deleting the causal path and checking if the treatment and outcome are still connected won't always work with selection bias. Unfortunately, at the time of this writing, I'm not aware of any Python libraries that deal with selection-biased graphs. But you can check DAGitty (*http://www.dagitty.net*), which works on your browser and has algorithms for identification under selection bias.

To develop your intuition about this bias, let's get your godlike powers back and pretend you can see into the world of counterfactual outcomes. That is, you can see both the NPS customers would have under the control, NPS_0, and under the treatment, NPS_1, for all customers, even those who didn't answer the survey. Let's also simulate data in such a way that we know the true effect. Here, the new feature increases NPS by 0.4 (which is a high number for any business standards, but bear with me for the sake of the example). Let's also say that both the new feature and customer satisfaction increases the chance of responding to the NPS survey, just like we've shown in the previous graph. With the power to measure counterfactuals, this is what you would see if you aggregated the data by the treated and control groups:

new_feature	responded	nps_0	nps_1	nps
0	0.183715	−0.005047	0.395015	−0.005047
1	0.639342	−0.005239	0.401082	0.401082

First, notice that 63% of those with the new feature responded to the NPS survey, while only 18% of those in the control responded to it. Next, if you look at both treated and control rows, you'll see an increase of 0.4 by going from NPS_0 to NPS_1. This simply means that the effect of the new feature is 0.4 for both groups. Finally, notice that the difference in NPS between treated (new_feature=1) and control (new_feature=0) is about 0.4. Again, if you could see the NPS of those who did not respond to the NPS survey, you could just compare treated and control groups to get the true ATE.

Of course, in reality, you can't see the columns NPS_0 and NPS_1. You also also can't see the NPS column like this, because you only have NPS for those who responded to the survey (18% of the control rows and 63% of the treated rows):

new_feature	responded	nps_0	nps_1	nps
0	0.183715	NaN	NaN	NaN
1	0.639342	NaN	NaN	NaN

If you further break down the analysis by respondents, you get to see the NPS of those where *Response* = 1. But notice how the difference between treated and control in that group is no longer 0.4, but only about half of that (0.22). How can that be? This is all due to selection bias:

responded	new_feature	nps_0	nps_1	nps
0	0	NaN	NaN	NaN
	1	NaN	NaN	NaN
1	0	NaN	NaN	0.314073
	1	NaN	NaN	0.536106

Adding back the unobservable quantities, you can see what is going on (focus on the respondents group here):

responded	new_feature	nps_0	nps_1	nps
0	0	−0.076869	0.320616	−0.076869
	1	−0.234852	0.161725	0.161725
1	0	0.314073	0.725585	0.314073
	1	0.124287	0.536106	0.536106

Initially, treated and control groups were comparable, in terms of their baseline satisfaction Y_0. But once you condition on those who responded the survey, the treatment group has lower baseline satisfaction $E[Y_0|T = 0, R = 1] > E[Y_0|T = 1, R = 1]$. This means that a simple difference in averages between treated and control does not identify the ATE, once you condition on those who responded:

$$E[Y|T = 1, R = 1] - E[Y|T = 1, R = 1] = \underbrace{E[Y_1 - Y_0|R = 1]}_{ATE}$$

$$+ \underbrace{E[Y_0|T = 0, R = 1] - E[Y_0|T = 1, R = 1]}_{SelectionBias}$$

That bias term won't be zero if the outcome, customer satisfaction, affects the response rate. Since satisfied customers are more likely to answer the NPS survey, identification is impossible in this situation. If the treatment increases satisfaction, then the control group will contain more customers whose baseline satisfaction is higher than the treatment group. That's because the treated group will have those who were satisfied (high baseline satisfaction) plus those who had low baseline satisfaction, but due to the treatment, became more satisfied and answered the survey.

See Also

Selection bias is a much more complex topic than I can give it justice in this chapter. For instance, you can have selection bias simply by conditioning on an effect of the outcome, even if that effect isn't shared with the treatment. This situation is called a *virtual collider*. To learn more about it and much more, I strongly recommend you check out the paper "A Crash Course in Good and Bad Controls," by Carlos Cinelli et al. It goes through everything covered in this chapter and more. The paper is also written in clear language, making it easy to read.

Adjusting for Selection Bias

Unfortunately, correcting selection bias is not at all trivial. In the example we've been discussing, even with a randomized control trial, the ATE is not identifiable, simply because you can't close the noncausal flow of association between the new feature and customer satisfaction, once you condition on those who responded to the survey. To make some progress, you need to make further assumptions, and here is where the graphical model starts to shine. It allows you to be very explicit and transparent about those assumptions.

For instance, you need to assume that the outcome doesn't cause selection. In our example, this would mean that customer satisfaction doesn't cause customers to be more or less likely to answer the survey. Instead, you would have some other *observable* variable (or variables) that cause both selection and the outcome. For example, it could be that the only thing that causes customers to respond to the survey is the time they spend in the app and the new feature. In this case, the noncausal association between treatment and control flows through time in the app:

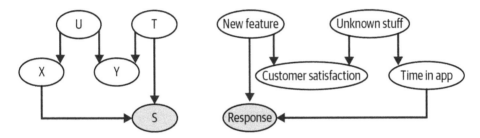

Only expert knowledge will be able to tell how strong of an assumption that is. But if it is correct, the effect of the new feature on satisfaction becomes identifiable once you control for time in the app.

Once again, you are applying the adjustment formula here. You are simply segmenting the data into groups defined by X so that treated and control groups become comparable within those segments. Then, you can just compute the weighted average of the in-group comparison between treated and control, using the size of each group as the weights. Only now, you are doing all of this while also conditioning on the selection variable:

$$ATE = \sum_x \{(E[Y|T = 1, R = 1, X] - E[Y|T = 0, R = 1, X])P(X|R = 1)\}$$

Generally speaking, to adjust for selection bias, you have to adjust for whatever causes selection and you also have to assume that neither the outcome nor the treatment causes selection directly or shares a hidden common cause with selection. For instance, in the following graph, you have selection bias since conditioning on S opens a noncausal association path between T and Y:

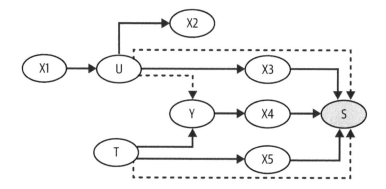

You can close two of these paths by adjusting for measurable variables that explain selection, $X3$, $X4$, and $X5$. However, there are two paths you cannot close (shown in dashed lines): $Y \to S \leftarrow T$ and $T \to S \leftarrow U \to Y$. That's because the treatment causes selection directly and the outcome shares a hidden common cause with selection. You can mitigate the bias from this last path by further conditioning on $X2$ and $X1$, as they account for some variation in U, but that will not eliminate the bias completely.

This graph reflects a more plausible situation you will encounter when it comes to selection bias, like the response bias we've just used as an example. In these situations, the best you can do is to condition on variables that explain the selection. This will reduce the bias, but it won't eliminate it because, as you saw, 1) there are things that cause selection that you don't know or can't measure, and 2) the outcome or the treatment might cause selection directly.

PRACTICAL EXAMPLE

The Hidden Bias in Survival Analysis

Survival analysis appears in many business applications that involve duration or time to an event. For instance, a bank is very interested in understanding how the size of a loan (loan amount) increases the chance of a customer defaulting on that loan. Consider a 3-year loan. The customer can default in the first, second, or third year, or they could not default at all. The goal of the bank is to know how loan amount impacts $P(Default | \text{yr} = 1)$, $P(Default | \text{yr} = 2)$, and $P(Default | \text{yr} = 3)$. Here, for simplicity's sake, consider that the bank has randomized the loan amount. Notice how only customers who survived (did not default) in year 1 are observed in year 2 and only customers who survived years 1 and 2 are observed in year 3. This selection makes it so that only the effect of loan size in the first year is identifiable.

Intuitively, even if the loan amount was randomized, it only stays that way in the first year. After that, if the loan amount increases the chance of default, customers with lower risk of defaulting will be overrepresented in the region with high loan amounts. Their risk will have to be low enough to offset the increase caused by a bigger loan amount; otherwise, they would have defaulted at year 1. If the bias is too extreme, it can even look like bigger loans cause risk to decrease in a year after year 1, which doesn't make any sense.

A simple solution for this selection bias problem is to focus on cumulative outcome (survival), $Y|time > t$, rather than yearly outcomes (hazard rates), $Y|time = t$. For example, even though you can't identify the effect of loan amount on default at year 2, $P(Default|yr = 2)$, you can easily identify the effect on default up to year 2, $P(Default|yr \leq 2)$:

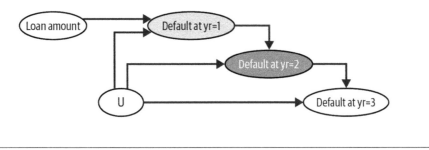

I also don't want to give you the false idea that just controlling for everything that causes selection is a good idea. In the following graph, conditioning on X opens a noncausal path, $Y \rightarrow X \leftarrow T$:

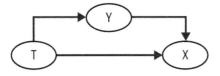

Conditioning on a Mediator

While the selection bias discussed so far is caused by unavoidable selection into a population (you were forced to condition on the respondent population), you can also cause selection bias inadvertently. For instance, let's suppose you are working in HR and you want to find out if there is gender discrimination; that is, if equally qualified men and women are paid differently. To do that analysis, you might consider controlling for seniority level; after all, you want to compare employees who are equally qualified, and seniority seems like a good proxy for that. In other words, you think that if men and women in the same position have different salaries, you will have evidence of a gender pay gap in your company.

The issue with this analysis is that the causal diagram probably looks something like this:

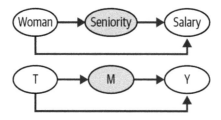

The seniority level is a *mediator* in the path between the treatment (woman) and salary. Intuitively, the difference in salary between women and men has a direct cause (the direct path, *woman → salary*) and an indirect cause, which flows through the seniority (the indirect path *woman → seniority → salary*). What this graph tells you is that one way women can suffer from discrimination is by being less likely to be promoted to higher seniorities. The difference in salary between men and women is partly the difference in salary at the same seniority level, but also the difference in seniority. Simply put, the path *woman → seniority → salary* is also a causal path between the treatment and the outcome, and you shouldn't close it in your analysis. If you compare salaries between men and women while controlling for seniority, you will only identify the direct discrimination, *woman → salary*.

It is also worth mentioning that conditioning on descendants of the mediator node also induces bias. This sort of selection doesn't completely shut the causal path, but it partially blocks it:

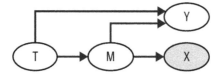

Key Ideas

In this chapter, you focused mostly on the identification part of causal inference. The goal was to learn how to use graphical models to be transparent about the assumptions you are making and to see what kind of association—causal or not—those assumptions entail. To do that, you had to learn how association flows in a graph. This cheat sheet is a good summary of those structures, so I recommend you keep it close by:

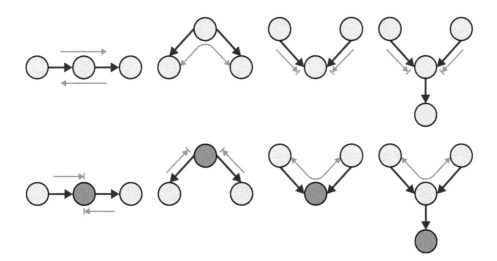

Then, you saw that identification amounts to isolating the causal flow of association from the noncausal ones in a graph. You could close noncausal paths of association by adjusting (conditioning) on some variables or even intervening on a graph, like in the case where you do a randomized experiment. Bayesian network software, like networkx, is particularly useful here, as it aids you when checking if two nodes are connected in a graph. For instance, to check for confounder bias, you can simply remove the causal path in a graph and check if the treatment and outcome nodes are still connected, even with that path removed. If they are, you have a backdoor path that needs to be closed.

Finally, you went through two very common structures of bias in causal problems. Confounding bias happens when the treatment and the outcome share a common cause. This common cause forms a fork structure, which creates a noncausal association flow between the treatment and the outcome:

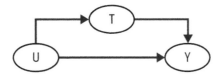

To fix confounding bias, you need to try to adjust for the common causes, directly or by the means of proxy variables. This motivated the idea of the adjustment formula:

$$ATE = \sum_{x}\{(E[Y\,|\,T = 1, X = x] - E[Y\,|\,T = 0, X = x])P(X = x)\},$$

and the conditional independence assumption, which states that, if treatment is as good as randomly assigned within groups of variables X, then you can identify causal quantities by conditioning on X.

Alternatively, if you can intervene on the treatment node, confounding becomes a lot easier to deal with. For instance, if you design a random experiment, you'll create a new graph where the arrows pointing to the treatment are all deleted, which effectively annihilates confounding bias.

You also learned about selection bias, which appears when you condition on a common effect (or descendant of a common effect) between the treatment and the outcome or when you condition on a mediator node (or a descendant of a mediator node). Selection bias is incredibly dangerous because it does not go away with experimentation. To make it even worse, it can be quite counterintuitive and hard to spot:

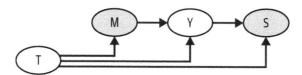

Again, it is worth mentioning that understanding a causal graph is like learning a new language. You'll learn most of it by seeing it again and again and by trying to use it.

PART II

Adjusting for Bias

CHAPTER 4

The Unreasonable Effectiveness of Linear Regression

In this chapter you'll add the first major debiasing technique in your causal inference arsenal: linear regression or ordinary least squares (OLS) and orthogonalization. You'll see how linear regression can adjust for confounders when estimating the relationship between a treatment and an outcome. But, more than that, I hope to equip you with the powerful concept of treatment orthogonalization. This idea, born in linear regression, will come in handy later on when you start to use machine learning models for causal inference.

All You Need Is Linear Regression

Before you skip to the next chapter because "oh, regression is so easy! It's the first model I learned as a data scientist" and yada yada, let me assure you that no, you actually don't know linear regression. In fact, regression is one of the most fascinating, powerful, and dangerous models in causal inference. Sure, it's more than one hundred years old. But, to this day, it frequently catches even the best causal inference researchers off guard.

OLS Research

Don't believe me? Just take a look at some recently published papers on the topic and you'll see. A good place to start is the article "Difference-in-Differences with Variation in Treatment Timing," by Andrew Goodman-Bacon, or the paper "Interpreting OLS Estimands When Treatment Effects Are Heterogeneous" by Tymon Słoczyński, or even the paper "Contamination Bias in Linear Regressions" by Goldsmith-Pinkham et al.

I assure you: not only is regression the workhorse for causal inference, but it will be the one you'll use the most. Regression is also a major building block for more advanced techniques, like most of the panel data methods (difference-in-differences and two-way fixed effects), machine learning methods (Double/Debiased Machine Learning), and alternative identification techniques (instrumental variables or discontinuity design).

Why We Need Models

Now that I hopefully convinced you to stay, we can get down to business. To motivate the use of regression, let's consider a pretty challenging problem in banking and the lending industry in general: understanding the impact of loan amount or credit card limits on default rate. Naturally, increasing someone's credit card limit will increase (or at least not decrease) the odds of them defaulting on the credit card bill. But, if you look at any banking data, you will see a negative correlation between credit lines and default rate. Obviously, this doesn't mean that higher lines cause customers to default less. Rather, it simply reflects the treatment assignment mechanism: banks and lending companies offer more credit to customers who have a lower chance of defaulting, as perceived by their underwriting models. The negative correlation you see is the effect of confounding bias:

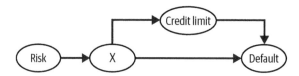

Of course the bank doesn't know the inherent risk of default, but it can use proxy variables X—like income or credit scores—to estimate it. In the previous chapters, you saw how you could adjust for variables to make the treatment look as good as randomly assigned. Specifically, you saw how the adjustment formula:

$$ATE = E_x\{E[Y|T = 1, X = x] - E[Y|T = 0, X = x]\},$$

which, together with the conditional independence assumption, $(Y_0, Y_1) \perp T|X$, allows you to identify the causal effect.

However, if you were to literally apply the adjustment formula, things can get out of hand pretty quickly. First, you would need to partition your data into segments defined by the feature X. This would be fine if you had very few discrete features. But what if there are many of them, with some being continuous? For example, let's say you know the bank used 10 variables, each with 3 groups, to underwrite customers and assign credit lines. That doesn't seem a lot, right? Well, it will already amount to

59,049, or 3^{10}, cells. Estimating the ATE in each of those cells and averaging the result is only possible if you have massive amounts of data. This is the *curse of dimensionality*, a problem very familiar to most data scientists. In the context of causal inference, one implication of this curse is that a naive application of the adjustment formula will suffer from data sparsity if you have lots of covariates.

Causal Inference Versus Machine Learning Lingo

The literature on machine learning, which is what most data scientists are familiar with, uses different terms from the literature on causal inference, which usually comes from econometrics or epidemiology. So, in the event that you need to translate from one to the other, here are some of the main equivalences you will encounter:

Feature
    Covariates or independent variables

Weights
    Parameters or coefficients

Target
    Outcome or dependent variable

One way out of this dimensionality problem is to assume that the *potential outcome can be modeled by something like linear regression*, which can interpolate and extrapolate the many individual X defined cells. You can think about linear regression in this context as a dimensionality reduction algorithm. It projects all the X variables into the outcome dimension and makes the comparison between treatment and control on that projection. It's quite elegant. But I'm getting ahead of myself. To really (and I mean truly, with every fiber of your heart) understand regression, you have to start small: regression in the context of an A/B test.

Regression in A/B Tests

Pretend you work for an online streaming company, perfecting its recommender system. Your team just finished a new version of this system, with cutting-edge technology and the latest ideas from the machine learning community. While that's all very impressive, what your manager really cares about is if this new system will increase the watch time of the streaming service. To test that, you decide to do an A/B test. First, you sample a representative but small fraction of your customer base. Then, you deploy the new recommender to a random 1/3 of that sample, while the rest continue to have the old version of the recommender. After a month, you collect the results in terms of average watch time per day:

```
In [1]: import pandas as pd
        import numpy as np

        data = pd.read_csv("./data/rec_ab_test.csv")
        data.head()
```

	recommender	age	tenure	watch_time
0	challenger	15	1	2.39
1	challenger	27	1	2.32
2	benchmark	17	0	2.74
3	benchmark	34	1	1.92
4	benchmark	14	1	2.47

Since the version of recommender was randomized, a simple comparison of average watch time between versions would already give you the ATE. But then you had to go through all the hassle of computing standard errors to get confidence intervals in order to check for statistical significance. So, what if I told you that you can interpret the results of an A/B test with regression, which will give you, for free, all the inference statistics you need? The idea behind regression is that you'll estimate the following equation or model:

$$WatchTime_i = \beta_0 + \beta_1 challenger_i + e_i$$

Where *challenger* is 1 for customers in the group that got the new version of the recommender and zero otherwise. If you estimate this model, the impact of the challenger version will be captured by the estimate of β_1, $\widehat{\beta_1}$.

To run that regression model in Python, you can use `statsmodels`' formula API. It allows you to express linear models succinctly, using R-style formulas. For example, you can represent the preceding model with the formula `'watch_time ~ C(recommender)'`. To estimate the model, just call the method `.fit()` and to read the results, call `.summary()` on a previously fitted model:

```
In [2]: import statsmodels.formula.api as smf

        result = smf.ols('watch_time ~ C(recommender)', data=data).fit()

        result.summary().tables[1]
```

	coef	std err	t	P>|t|	[0.025	0.975]
Intercept	2.0491	0.058	35.367	0.000	1.935	2.163
C(recommender)[T.challenger]	0.1427	0.095	1.501	0.134	−0.044	0.330

In that R-style formula, the outcome variable comes first, followed by a ~. Then, you add the explanatory variables. In this case, you'll just use the recommender variable, which is categorical with two categories (one for the challenger and one for the old version). You can wrap that variable in C(...) to explicitly state that the column is categorical.

Patsy

The formula syntactic sugar is an incredibly convenient way to do feature engineering. You can learn more about it in the patsy library (*https://oreil.ly/YuQG_*).

Next, look at the results. First, you have the intercept. This is the estimate for the β_0 parameter in your model. It tells you the expected value of the outcome when the other variables in the model are zero. Since the only other variable here is the challenger indicator, you can interpret the intercept as the expected watch time for those who received the old version of the recommender system. Here, it means that customers spend, on average, 2.04 hours per day watching your streaming content, when with the old version of the recommender system. Finally, looking at the parameter estimate associated with the challenger recommender, $\widehat{\beta_1}$, you can see the increase in watch time due to this new version. If $\widehat{\beta_0}$ is the estimate for the watch time under the old recommender, $\widehat{\beta_0} + \widehat{\beta_1}$ tells you the expected watch time for those who got the challenger version. In other words, $\widehat{\beta_1}$ is an estimate for the ATE. Due to randomization, you can assign causal meaning to that estimate: you can say that the new recommender system increased watch time by 0.14 hours per day, on average. However, that result is not statistically significant.

Forget the nonsignificant result for a moment, because what you just did was quite amazing. Not only did you estimate the ATE, but also got, for free, confidence intervals and p-values out of it! More than that, you can see for yourself that regression is doing exactly what it supposed to do—estimating $E[Y|T]$ for each treatment:

```
In [3]: (data
        .groupby("recommender")
        ["watch_time"]
        .mean())

Out[3]: recommender
        benchmark     2.049064
        challenger    2.191750
        Name: watch_time, dtype: float64
```

Just like I've said, the intercept is mathematically equivalent to the average watch time for those in the control—the old version of the recommender.

These numbers are identical because, in this case, regression is mathematically equivalent to simply doing a comparison between averages. This also means that $\widehat{\beta_1}$ is the average difference between the two groups: $2.191 - 2.049 = 0.1427$. OK, so you managed to, quite literally, reproduce group averages with regressions. But so what? It's not like you couldn't do this earlier, so what is the real gain here?

Adjusting with Regression

To appreciate the power of regression, let me take you back to the initial example: estimating the effect of credit lines on default. Bank data usually looks something like this, with a bunch of columns of customer features that might indicate credit worthiness, like monthly wage, lots of credit scores provided by credit bureaus, tenure at current company and so on. Then, there is the credit line given to that customer (the treatment in this case) and the column that tells you if a customer defaulted or not—the outcome variable:

```
In [4]: risk_data = pd.read_csv("./data/risk_data.csv")

        risk_data.head()
```

	wage	educ	exper	married	credit_score1	credit_score2	credit_limit	default
0	950.0	11	16	1	500.0	518.0	3200.0	0
1	780.0	11	7	1	414.0	429.0	1700.0	0
2	1230.0	14	9	1	586.0	571.0	4200.0	0
3	1040.0	15	8	1	379.0	411.0	1500.0	0
4	1000.0	16	1	1	379.0	518.0	1800.0	0

Simulated Data

Once again, I'm building from real-world data and changing it to fit the needs of this chapter. This time, I'm using the wage1 data, curated by professor Jeffrey M. Wooldridge and available in the "wooldridge" R package.

Here, the treatment, credit_limit, has way too many categories. In this situation, it is better to treat it as a continuous variable, rather than a categorical one. Instead of representing the ATE as the difference between multiple levels of the treatment, you can represent it as the derivative of the expected outcome with respect to the treatment:

$$ATE = \frac{\partial}{\partial t}E[y|t]$$

Don't worry if this sounds fancy. It simply means the amount you expect the outcome to change given a unit increase in the treatment. In this example, it represents how much you expect the default rate to change given a 1 USD increase in credit lines.

One way to estimate such a quantity is to run a regression. Specifically, you can estimate the model:

$$Default_i = \beta_0 + \beta_1 limit_i + e_i,$$

and the estimate $\hat{\beta}_1$ can be interpreted as the amount you expect risk to change given a 1 USD increase in limit. This parameter has a causal interpretation if the limit was randomized. But as you know very well that is not the case, as banks tend to give higher lines to customers who are less risky. In fact, if you run the preceding model, you'll get a negative estimate for β_1:

```
In [5]: model = smf.ols('default ~ credit_limit', data=risk_data).fit()
        model.summary().tables[1]
```

	coef	std err	t	P>|t|	[0.025	0.975]
Intercept	0.2192	0.004	59.715	0.000	0.212	0.226
credit_limit	−2.402e−05	1.16e−06	−20.689	0.000	−2.63e−05	−2.17e−05

That is not at all surprising, given the fact that the relationship between risk and credit limit is negative, due to confounding. If you plot the fitted regression line alongside the average default by credit limit, you can clearly see the negative trend:

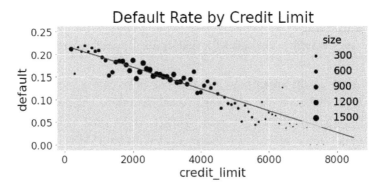

To adjust for this bias, you could, in theory, segment your data by all the confounders, run a regression of default on credit lines inside each segment, extract the slope parameter, and average the results. However, due to the curse of dimensionality, even if you try to do that for a moderate number of confounders—both credit scores—you will see that there are cells with only one sample, making it impossible for you to run your regression. Not to mention the many cells that are simply empty:

```
In [6]: risk_data.groupby(["credit_score1", "credit_score2"]).size().head()


Out[6]: credit_score1  credit_score2
        34.0           339.0            1
                       500.0            1
        52.0           518.0            1
        69.0           214.0            1
                       357.0            1
        dtype: int64
```

Thankfully, once more, regression comes to your aid here. Instead of manually adjusting for the confounders, you can simply add them to the model you'll estimate with OLS:

$$Default_i = \beta_0 + \beta_1 limit_i + \theta \mathbf{X}_i + e_i,$$

Here, $\mathbf{X}$ is a vector of confounder variables and θ is the vector of parameters associated with those confounders. There is nothing special about θ parameters. They behave exactly like β_1. I'm representing them differently because they are just there to help you get an unbiased estimate for β_1. That is, you don't really care about their causal interpretation (they are technically called *nuisance parameters*).

In the credit example, you could add the credit scores and wage confounders to the model. It would look like this:

$$Default_i = \beta_0 + \beta_1 limit_i + \theta_1 wage_i + \theta_2 creditScore1_i + \theta_3 creditScore2_i + e_i,$$

I'll get into more details about how including variables in the model will adjust for confounders, but there is a very easy way to see it right now. The preceding model is a model for $E[y|t, X]$. Recall that you want $\frac{\partial}{\partial t} E[y|t, X]$. So what happens if you differentiate the model with respect to the treatment—credit limit? Well, you simply get β_1! In a sense, β_1 can be seen as the partial derivative of the expected value of default with respect to credit limit. Or, more intuitively, it can be viewed as how much you should expect default to change, given a small increase in credit limit, *while holding fixed all other variables in the model*. This interpretation already tells you a bit of how regression adjusts for confounders: it holds them fixed while estimating the relationship between the treatment and the outcome.

To see this in action, you can estimate the preceding model. Just add some confounders and, like some kind of magic, the relationship between credit lines and default becomes positive!

```
In [7]: formula = 'default ~ credit_limit + wage+credit_score1+credit_score2'
        model = smf.ols(formula, data=risk_data).fit()
        model.summary().tables[1]
```

	coef	std err	t	P>|t|	[0.025	0.975]
Intercept	0.4037	0.009	46.939	0.000	0.387	0.421
credit_limit	3.063e−06	1.54e−06	1.987	0.047	4.16e−08	6.08e−06
wage	−8.822e−05	6.07e−06	−14.541	0.000	−0.000	−7.63e−05
credit_score1	−4.175e−05	1.83e−05	−2.278	0.023	−7.77e−05	−5.82e−06
credit_score2	−0.0003	1.52e−05	−20.055	0.000	−0.000	−0.000

Don't let the small estimate of β_1 fool you. Recall that limit is in the scales of 1,000s while default is either 0 or 1. So it is no surprise that increasing lines by 1 USD will increase expected default by a very small number. Still, that number is statistically significant and tells you that risk increases as you increase credit limit, which is much more in line with your intuition on how the world works.

Hold that thought because you are about to explore it more formally. It's finally time to learn one of the greatest causal inference tools of all: the *Frisch-Waugh-Lovell* (FWL) theorem. It's an incredible way to get rid of bias, which is unfortunately seldom known by data scientists. FWL is a prerequisite to understand more advanced debiasing methods, but the reason I find it most useful is that *it can be used as a debiasing pre-processing step*. To stick to the same banking example, imagine that many data scientists and analysts in this bank are trying to understand how credit limit impacts (causes) lots of different business metrics, not just risk. However, only you have the context about how the credit limit was assigned, which means you are the only expert who knows what sort of biases plague the credit limit treatment. With FWL, you can use that knowledge to debias the credit limit data in a way that it can be used by everyone else, regardless of what outcome variable they are interested in. *The Frisch-Waugh-Lovell theorem allows you to separate the debiasing step from the impact estimation step*. But in order to learn it, you must first quickly review a bit of regression theory.

Regression Theory

I don't intend to dive too deep into how linear regression is constructed and estimated. However, a little bit of theory will go a long way in explaining its power in causal inference. First of all, regression solves the best linear prediction problem. Let β^* be a vector of parameters:

$$\beta^* = \underset{\beta}{argmin} \ E\left[(Y_i - X_i'\beta)^2\right]$$

Linear regression finds the parameters that minimize the mean squared error (MSE). If you differentiate it and set it to zero, you will find that the linear solution to this problem is given by:

$$\beta^* = E[X'X]^{-1}E[X'Y]$$

You can estimate this beta using the sample equivalent:

$$\hat{\beta} = (X'X)^{-1}X'Y$$

But don't take my word for it. If you are one of those who understand code better than formulas, try for yourself. In the following code, I'm using the algebraic solution to OLS to estimate the parameters of the model you just saw (I'm adding the intercept as the final variables, so the first parameter estimate will be $\widehat{\beta_1}$):

```
In [8]: X_cols = ["credit_limit", "wage", "credit_score1", "credit_score2"]
        X = risk_data[X_cols].assign(intercep=1)
        y = risk_data["default"]

        def regress(y, X):
            return np.linalg.inv(X.T.dot(X)).dot(X.T.dot(y))

        beta = regress(y, X)
        beta

Out[8]: array([ 3.062e-06, -8.821e-05, -4.174e-05, -3.039e-04, 4.0364-01])
```

If you look back a bit, you will see that these are the exact same numbers you got earlier, when estimating the model with the ols function from statsmodels.

Assign

I tend to use the method `.assign()` from pandas quite a lot. If you are not familiar with it, it just returns a new data frame with the newly created columns passed to the method:

```
new_df = df.assign(new_col_1 = 1,
                   new_col_2 = df["old_col"] + 1)

new_df[["old_col", "new_col_1", "new_col_2"]].head()
   old_col  new_col_1  new_col_2
0        4          1          5
1        9          1         10
2        8          1          9
3        0          1          1
4        6          1          7
```

Single Variable Linear Regression

The $\hat{\beta}$ formula from the previous section is pretty general. However, it pays off to study the case where you only have one regressor. In causal inference, you often want to estimate the causal impact of a variable T on an outcome y. So, you use regression with this single variable to estimate this effect.

With a single regressor variable T, the parameter associated to it will be given by:

$$\hat{\tau} = \frac{Cov(Y_i, T_i)}{Var(T_i)} = \frac{E[(T_i - \bar{T})(Y_i - \bar{Y})]}{E[(T_i - \bar{T})^2]}$$

If T is randomly assigned, β_1 is the ATE. Importantly, with this simple formula, you can see what regression is doing. It's finding out how the treatment and outcome move together (as expressed by the covariance in the numerator) and scaling this by units of the treatment, which is achieved by dividing by the variance of the treatment.

You can also tie this to the general formula. Covariance is intimately related to dot products, so you can pretty much say that $X'X$ takes the role of the denominator in the covariance/variance formula, while $X'y$ takes the role of the numerator.

Multivariate Linear Regression

Turns out there is another way to see multivariate linear regression, beyond the general formula you saw earlier. This other way sheds some light into what regression is doing.

If you have more than one regressor, you can extend the one variable regression formula to accommodate that. Let's say those other variables are just auxiliary and that you are truly interested in estimating the parameter τ associated to T:

$$y_i = \beta_0 + \tau T_i + \beta_1 X_{1i} + \ldots + \beta_k X_{ki} + u_i$$

τ can be estimated with the following formula:

$$\hat{\tau} = \frac{Cov\left(Y_i, \widetilde{T_i}\right)}{Var\left(\widetilde{T_i}\right)}$$

where $\widetilde{T_i}$ is the residual from a regression of T_i on all of the other covariates $X_{1i} + \ldots + X_{ki}$.

Now, let's appreciate how cool this is. It means that the coefficient of a multivariate regression is the bivariate coefficient of the same regressor *after accounting for the effect of other variables in the model*. In causal inference terms, τ is the bivariate coefficient of T after having used all other variables to predict it.

This has a nice intuition behind it. If you can predict T using other variables, it means it's not random. However, you can make T look as good as random once you control for the all the confounder variables X. To do so, you can use linear regression to predict it from the confounder and then take the residuals of that regression $\widetilde{T}$. By definition, $\widetilde{T}$ cannot be predicted by the other variables X that you've already used to predict T. Quite elegantly, $\widetilde{T}$ is a version of the treatment that is not associated (uncorrelated) with any other variable in X.

I know this is a mouthful, but it is just amazing. In fact, it is already the work of the FWL theorem that I promised to teach you. So don't worry if you didn't quite get this multivariate regression part, as you are about to review it in a much more intuitive and visual way.

Frisch-Waugh-Lovell Theorem and Orthogonalization

FWL-style orthogonalization is the *first major debiasing technique you have at your disposal*. It's a simple yet powerful way to make nonexperimental data look as if the treatment has been randomized. FWL is mostly about linear regression; FWL-style orthogonalization has been expanded to work in more general contexts, as you'll see in Part III. The Frisch-Waugh-Lovell theorem states that a multivariate linear regression model can be estimated all at once or in three separate steps. For example, you can regress `default` on `credit_limit`, `wage`, `credit_score1`, `credit_score2`, just like you already did:

```
In [9]: formula = 'default ~ credit_limit + wage+credit_score1+credit_score2'
        model = smf.ols(formula, data=risk_data).fit()
        model.summary().tables[1]
```

	coef	std err	t	P>|t|	[0.025	0.975]
Intercept	0.4037	0.009	46.939	0.000	0.387	0.421
credit_limit	3.063e−06	1.54e−06	1.987	0.047	4.16e−08	6.08e−06
wage	−8.822e−05	6.07e−06	−14.541	0.000	−0.000	−7.63e−05
credit_score1	−4.175e−05	1.83e−05	−2.278	0.023	--7.77e−05	-5.82e−06
credit_score2	−0.0003	1.52e−05	−20.055	0.000	−0.000	−0.000

But, according to FWL, you can also break down this estimation into:

1. A debiasing step, where you regress the treatment T on confounders X and obtain the treatment residuals $\tilde{T} = T - \hat{T}$

2. A denoising step, where you regress the outcome Y on the confounder variables X and obtain the outcome residuals $\tilde{Y} = Y - \hat{Y}$

3. An outcome model where you regress the outcome residual $\tilde{Y}$ on the treatment residual $\tilde{T}$ to obtain an estimate for the causal effect of T on Y

Not surprisingly, this is just a restatement of the formula you just saw in "Multivariate Linear Regression" on page 105. The FWL theorem states an equivalence in estimation procedures with regression models. It also says that you can isolate the debiasing component of linear regression, which is the first step outlined in the preceding list.

To get a better intuition on what is going on, let's break it down step by step.

Debiasing Step

Recall that, initially, due to confounding bias, your data looked something like this, with default trending downward with credit line:

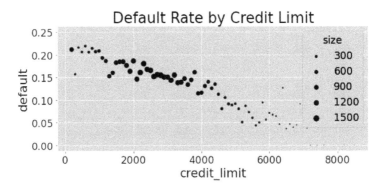

According to the FWL theorem, you can debias this data by fitting a regression model to predict the treatment—the credit limit—from the confounders. Then, you can take the residual from this model: $\widetilde{line}_i = line_i - \widehat{line}_i$. This residual can be viewed as a version of the treatment that is uncorrelated with the variables used in the debiasing model. That's because, by definition, the residual is orthogonal to the variables that generated the predictions.

This process will make $\widetilde{line}$ centered around zero. Optionally, you can add back the average treatment, $\overline{line}$:

$$\widetilde{line}_i = line_i - \widehat{line}_i + \overline{line}$$

This is not necessary for debiasing, but it puts $\widetilde{line}$ in the same range as the original *line*, which is better for visualization purposes:

```
In [10]: debiasing_model = smf.ols(
             'credit_limit ~ wage + credit_score1  + credit_score2',
             data=risk_data
         ).fit()

         risk_data_deb = risk_data.assign(
             # for visualization, avg(T) is added to the residuals
             credit_limit_res=(debiasing_model.resid
                             + risk_data["credit_limit"].mean())
         )
```

If you now run a simple linear regression, where you regress the outcome, *risk*, on the debiased or residualized version of the treatment, $\widetilde{line}$, you'll already get the effect of credit limit on risk while controlling for the confounders used in the debiasing model. The parameter estimate you get for β_1 here is exactly the same as the one you got earlier by running the complete model, where you've included both treatment and confounders:

```
In [11]: model_w_deb_data = smf.ols('default ~ credit_limit_res',
                                    data=risk_data_deb).fit()

         model_w_deb_data.summary().tables[1]
```

	coef	std err	t	P>|t|	[0.025	0.975]
Intercept	0.1421	0.005	30.001	0.000	0.133	0.151
credit_limit_res	3.063e-06	1.56e-06	1.957	0.050	-4.29e-09	6.13e-06

There is a difference, though. Look at the p-value. It is a bit higher than what you got earlier. That's because you are not applying the denoising step, which is responsible for reducing variance. Still, with only the debiasing step, you can already get the unbiased estimate of the causal impact of credit limit on risk, given that all the confounders were included in the debiasing model.

You can also visualize what is going on by plotting the debiased version of credit limit against default rate. You'll see that the relationship is no longer downward sloping, as when the data was biased:

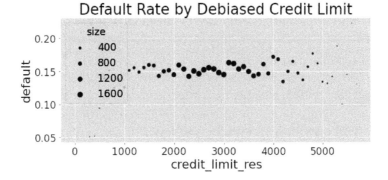

Denoising Step

While the debiasing step is crucial to estimate the correct causal effect, the denoising step is also nice to have, although not as important. It won't change the value of your treatment effect estimate, but it will reduce its variance. In this step, you'll regress the outcome on the covariates that are not the treatment. Then, you'll get the residual for the outcome $\overline{default_i} = default_i - \widehat{default_i}$.

Once again, for better visualization, you can add the average default rate to the denoised default variable for better visualization purposes:

$$\overline{default_i} = default_i - \widehat{default_i} + \overline{default}$$

```
In [12]: denoising_model = smf.ols(
             'default ~ wage + credit_score1  + credit_score2',
             data=risk_data_deb
         ).fit()

         risk_data_denoise = risk_data_deb.assign(
             default_res=denoising_model.resid + risk_data_deb["default"].mean()
         )
```

Standard Error of the Regression Estimator

Since we are talking about noise, I think it is a good time to see how to compute the regression standard error. The SE of the regression parameter estimate is given by the following formula:

$$SE(\hat{\beta}) = \frac{\sigma(\hat{\epsilon})}{\sigma(\tilde{T})\sqrt{n - DF}},$$

where $\hat{\epsilon}$ is the residual from the regression model and DF is the model's degree of freedom (number of parameters estimated by the model). If you prefer to see this in code, here it is:

```
In [13]: model_se = smf.ols(
             'default ~ wage + credit_score1  + credit_score2',
             data=risk_data
         ).fit()

         print("SE regression:", model_se.bse["wage"])


         model_wage_aux = smf.ols(
             'wage ~ credit_score1 + credit_score2',
             data=risk_data
         ).fit()

         # subtract the degrees of freedom - 4 model parameters - from N.
         se_formula = (np.std(model_se.resid)
                       /(np.std(model_wage_aux.resid)*np.sqrt(len(risk_data)-4)))
```

```
    print("SE formula:    ", se_formula)
```

```
Out[13]: SE regression: 5.364242347548197e-06
         SE formula:    5.364242347548201e-06
```

This formula is nice because it gives you further intuition about regression in general and the denoising step in particular. First, the numerator tells you that the better you can predict the outcome, the smaller the residuals will be and, hence, the lower the variance of the estimate. This is very much what the denoising step is all about. It also tells you that if the treatment explains the outcome a lot, its parameter estimate will also have a smaller standard error.

Interestingly, the error is also inversely proportional to the variance of the (residualized) treatment. This is also intuitive. If the treatment varies a lot, it will be easier to measure its impact. You'll learn more about this in "Noise Inducing Control" on page 136.

Experiments with Continuous Treatments

The standard error formula can also be useful if you plan to design an experiment where you care to measure the effect as the parameter estimate from a regression. This is a good idea if the treatment you want to randomize is continuous. In this case, the standard error formula can be approximated by:

$$SE \approx \frac{\sigma(y)}{\sigma(T)\sqrt{n-2}}$$

This approximation is conservative in the case of a single variable regression model, since $\sigma(y) \geq \sigma(\hat{e})$, because the treatment might explain a bit of the outcome. Then, you can take this standard error and plug in the sample size calculation formula from Chapter 2. Importantly, designing this test has the additional complexity of choosing a sampling distribution from T, which can also affect the standard error via $\sigma(T)$.

Final Outcome Model

With both residuals, $\tilde{Y}$ and $\tilde{T}$, you can run the final step outlined by the FWL theorem—just regress $\tilde{Y}$ on $\tilde{T}$:

```
In [14]: model_w_orthogonal = smf.ols('default_res ~ credit_limit_res',
                                  data=risk_data_denoise).fit()

         model_w_orthogonal.summary().tables[1]
```

	coef	std err	t	P>|t|	[0.025	0.975]
Intercept	0.1421	0.005	30.458	0.000	0.133	0.151
credit_limit_res	3.063e−06	1.54e−06	1.987	0.047	4.17e−08	6.08e−06

The parameter estimate for the treatment is exactly the same as the one you got in both the debiasing step and when running the regression model with credit limit plus all the other covariates. Additionally, the standard error and p-value are now also just like when you first ran the model, with all the variables included. This is the effect of the denoising step.

Of course, you can also plot the relationship between the debiased treatment with the denoised outcome, alongside the predictions from the final model to see what is going on:

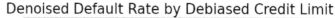
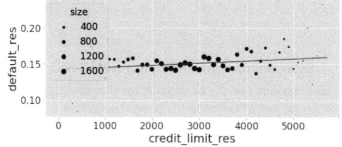

FWL Summary

I don't know if you can already tell, but I really like illustrative figures. Even if they don't reflect any real data, they can be quite useful to visualize what is going on behind some fairly technical concept. It wouldn't be different with FWL. So to summarize, consider that you want to estimate the relationship between a treatment T and an outcome Y but you have some confounder X. You plot the treatment on the x-axis, the outcome on the y-axis, and the confounder as the color dimension. You initially see a negative slope between treatment and outcome, but you have strong reasons (some domain knowledge) to believe that the relationship should be positive, so you decide to debias the data.

To do that, you first estimate $E[T|X]$ using linear regression. Then, you construct a debiased version of the treatment: $T - E[T|X]$ (see Figure 4-1). With this debiased treatment, you can already see the positive relationship you were hoping to find. But you still have a lot of noise.

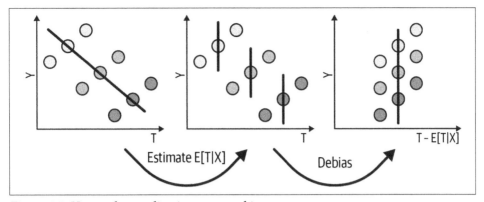

Figure 4-1. How orthogonalization removes bias

To deal with the noise, you estimate $E[Y|X]$, also using a regression model. Then, you construct a denoised version of the outcome: $Y - E[T|X]$ (see Figure 4-2). You can view this denoised outcome as the outcome after you've accounted for all the variance in it that was explained by X. If X explains a lot of the variance in Y, the denoised outcome will be less noisy, making it easier to see the relationship you really care about: that between T and Y.

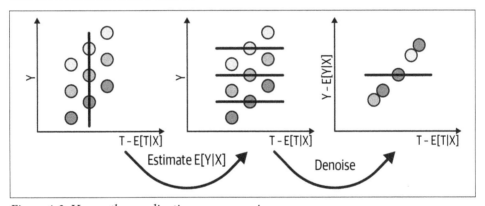

Figure 4-2. How orthogonalization removes noise

Finally, after both debiasing and denoising, you can clearly see a positive relationship between T and Y. All there is left to do is fit a final model to this data:

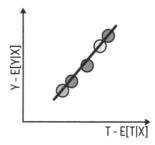

This final regression will have the exact same slope as the one where you regress Y on T and X at the same time.

Debiasing and the Intercept

One word of caution, though. In causal inference, you are mostly concerned with the slope of this regression line, since the slope is a linear approximation to the effect of the continuous treatment, $\frac{\partial}{\partial t}E[y|t]$. But, if you also care about the intercept—for instance, if you are trying to do counterfactual predictions—you should know that debiasing and denoising makes the intercept equal to zero.

Regression as an Outcome Model

Throughout this section I emphasized how regression works mostly by orthogonalizing the treatment. However, you can also see regression as a potential outcome imputation technique. Suppose that the treatment is binary. If regression of Y on X in the control population ($T = 0$) yields good approximation to $E[Y_0|X]$, then you can use that model to impute Y_0 and estimate the ATT:

$$ATT = \frac{1}{N_1}\sum \mathbb{1}(T_i = 1)(Y_i - \hat{\mu}_0(X_i)),$$

where N_1 is the number of treated units.

Indicator Function

Throughout this book, I'll use $\mathbb{1}(.)$ to represent the indicator function. This function returns 1 when the argument inside it evaluates to true and zero otherwise.

A similar argument can be made to show that if regression on the treated units can model $E[Y_1|X]$, you can use it to estimate the average effect on the untreated. If you put these two arguments side by side, you can estimate the ATE as follows:

$$ATE = \frac{1}{N}\sum\left(\hat{\mu}_1(X_i) - \hat{\mu}_0(X_i)\right)$$

This estimator will impute both potential outcomes for all units. It is equivalent to regressing Y on both X and T and reading the parameter estimate on T.

Alternatively, you can impute just the potential outcomes that are missing:

$$ATE = \frac{1}{N}\sum\left(\mathbb{1}(T_i = 1)[Y_i - \hat{\mu}_0(X_i)] + \mathbb{1}(T_i = 0)[\hat{\mu}_1(X_i) - Y_i]\right)$$

When T is continuous, this is a bit harder to conceptualize, but you can understand regression as imputing the whole treatment response function, which involves imputing the potential outcomes $Y(t)$ as if it was a line.

The fact that regression works if it can either correctly estimate $E[T|X]$ for orthogonalization or correctly estimate the potential outcomes $E[Y_t|X]$ grants it doubly robust properties, something you'll explore further in Chapter 5. Seeing regression through this lens will also be important when you learn about difference-in-differences in Part IV.

PRACTICAL EXAMPLE

Public or Private Schools?

In the book *Mastering Metrics* (Princeton University Press), Angrist and Pischke show how regression can be used to adjust for the bias when estimating the impact of going to private schools on one's income. Graduates of private school often make more money than those of public school, but it's hard to say how much of this relationship is causal. For instance, your parents' income might confound the relationship, as kids of richer families are both more likely to go to private schools and to earn more. Similarly, since private schools are very selective, it could be that they take in only the students who would already be better off anyway.

So much so that a naive regression of income on a private school dummy is almost sure to return a positive effect. In other words, estimating the following model would give you a positive and significant $\widehat{\beta_1}$:

$$income_i = \delta_0 + \beta_1 private + e_i$$

What Angrist and Pischke show, however, is that if you adjust for SAT score and parents' income, the measured impact decreases. That is, if you augment the model with these two variables, your $\widehat{\beta}_1$ will be smaller, compared to the one you would get with the short model:

$$income_i = \delta_0 + \beta_1 private + \delta_1 SAT_i + \delta_2 ParentInc_i + e_i$$

Still, after running a regression with parent income, the effect of private schools remained positive and significant, at least in the dataset used by the authors. However, one final set of controls managed to make the relationship insignificant. The authors included the average SAT of the school the students applied to (regardless of them being accepted). This can be interpreted as a proxy for ambition:

$$income_i = \delta_0 + \beta_1 private + \delta_1 SAT_i + \delta_2 ParentInc_i$$
$$+ \delta_3 AvgSATSchool_i + e_i$$

Once they added the ambition proxy controls, the estimated $\widehat{\beta}_1$ became insignificant. Interestingly, keeping only those controls and dropping the SAT and parents' income controls still resulted in a nonsignificant estimate. This indicates that, given your ambition level, it doesn't matter if you go to a public or private school, at least in terms of your earnings:

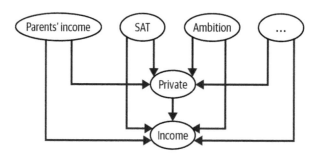

Positivity and Extrapolation

Since regression models the potential outcome as a parametric function, it allows for extrapolation outside the region where you have data on all treatment levels. This can be a blessing or a curse. It all depends on whether the extrapolation is reasonable. For example, consider that you have to estimate a treatment effect in a dataset with low overlap. Call it Dataset 1. Dataset 1 has no control units for high values of a covariate x and no treated units for low values of that same covariate. If you use regression to estimate the treatment effect on this data, it will impute Y_0 and Y_1 as shown by the lines in the first plot:

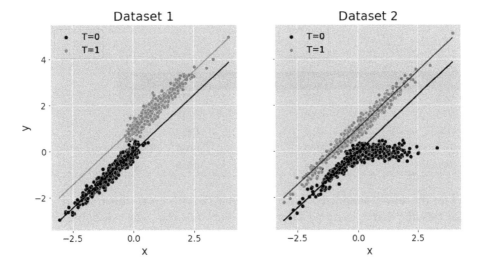

This is fine, so long as the same relationship between Y_0 and x you've fitted in the control for low levels of x is also valid for high values of x and that the Y_1 you've fitted on the treated also extrapolates well to low levels of x. Generally, if the trends in the outcome where you do have overlap look similar across the covariate space, a small level of extrapolation becomes less of an issue.

However, too much extrapolation is always dangerous. Let's suppose you've estimated the effect on Dataset 1, but then you collect more data, now randomizing the treatment. On this new data, call it Dataset 2, you see that the effect gets larger and larger for positive values of x. Consequently, if you evaluate your previous fit on this new data, you'll realize that you grossly underestimated the true effect of the treatment. This goes to show that you can never really know what will happen to the treatment effect in a region where you don't have positivity. You might choose to trust your extrapolations for those regions, but that is not without risk.

Nonlinearities in Linear Regression

Up until this point, the treatment response curve seemed pretty linear. It looked like an increase in credit line caused a constant increase in risk, regardless of the credit line level. Going from a line of 1,000 to 2,000 seemed to increase risk about the same as going from a line of 2,000 to 3,000. However, you are likely to encounter situations where this won't be the case.

As an example, consider the same data as before, but now your task is to estimate the causal effect of credit limit on credit card spend:

```
In [15]: spend_data = pd.read_csv("./data/spend_data.csv")

         spend_data.head()
```

	wage	educ	exper	married	credit_score1	credit_score2	credit_limit	spend
0	950.0	11	16	1	500.0	518.0	3200.0	3848
1	780.0	11	7	1	414.0	429.0	1700.0	3144
2	1230.0	14	9	1	586.0	571.0	4200.0	4486
3	1040.0	15	8	1	379.0	411.0	1500.0	3327
4	1000.0	16	1	1	379.0	518.0	1800.0	3508

And for the sake of simplicity, let's consider that the only confounder you have here is wage (assume that is the only information the bank uses when deciding the credit limit). The causal graph of this process looks something like this:

As a result, you have to condition on wage to identify the effect of credit lines on spending. If you want to use orthogonalization to estimate this effect, you can say that you need to debias credit lines by regressing it on wage and getting the residuals. Nothing new so far. But there is a catch. If you plot spend by credit lines for multiple wage levels, you can clearly see that the relationship is not linear:

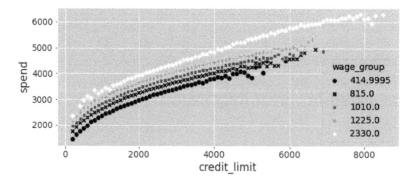

Rather, the treatment response curve seems to have some sort of concavity to it: the higher the credit limit, the lower the slope of this curve. Or, in causal inference language, since slopes and causal effects are intimately related, you can also say that the effect of lines on spend diminishes as you increase lines: going from a line of 1,000 to 2,000 increases spend more than going from 2,000 to 3,000.

Linearizing the Treatment

To deal with that, you first need to transform the treatment into something that does have a linear relationship with the outcome. For instance, you know that the relationship seems concave, so you can try to apply some concave function to lines. Some good candidates to try out are the log function, the square root function, or any function that takes credit lines to the power of a fraction.

In this case, let's try the square root:

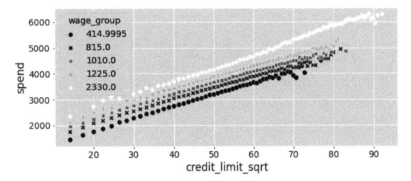

Now we are getting somewhere! The square root of the credit line seems to have a linear relationship with spend. It's definitely not perfect. If you look very closely, you can still see some curvature. But it might just do for now.

I'm sad to say that this process is fairly manual. You have to try a bunch of stuff and see what linearizes the treatment better. Once you find something that you are happy with, you can apply it when running a linear regression model. In this example, it means that you will be estimating the model:

$$spend_i = \beta_0 + \beta_1\sqrt{line}_i + e_i$$

and your causal parameter is β_1.

This model can be estimated with `statsmodels`, by using the NumPy square root function directly in the formula:

```
In [16]: model_spend = smf.ols(
             'spend ~ np.sqrt(credit_limit)',data=spend_data
         ).fit()
```

```
model_spend.summary().tables[1]
```

	coef	std err	t	P>|t|	[0.025	0.975]
Intercept	493.0044	6.501	75.832	0.000	480.262	505.747
np.sqrt(credit_limit)	63.2525	0.122	519.268	0.000	63.014	63.491

But you are not done yet. Recall that wage is confounding the relationship between credit lines and spend. You can see this by plotting the predictions from the preceding model against the original data. Notice how its slope is probably upward biased. That's because more wage causes both spend and credit lines to increase:

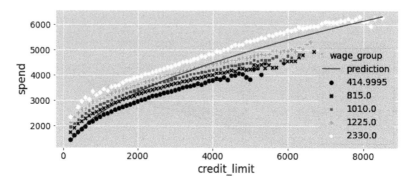

If you include wage in the model:

$$spend_i = \beta_0 + \beta_1\sqrt{line_i} + \beta_2 wage_i + e_i$$

and estimate β_1 again, you get an unbiased estimate of the effect of lines on spend (assuming wage is the only confounder, of course). This estimate is smaller than the one you got earlier. That is because including wage in the model fixed the upward bias:

```
In [17]: model_spend = smf.ols('spend ~ np.sqrt(credit_limit)+wage',
                                data=spend_data).fit()

         model_spend.summary().tables[1]
```

	coef	std err	t	P>|t|	[0.025	0.975]
Intercept	383.5002	2.746	139.662	0.000	378.118	388.882
np.sqrt(credit_limit)	43.8504	0.065	672.633	0.000	43.723	43.978
wage	1.0459	0.002	481.875	0.000	1.042	1.050

Nonlinear FWL and Debiasing

As to how the FWL theorem works with nonlinear data, it is exactly like before, but now you have to apply the nonlinearity first. That is, you can decompose the process of estimating a nonlinear model with linear regression as follows:

1. Find a function F that linearizes the relationship between T and Y.

2. A debiasing step, where you regress the treatment $F(T)$ on confounder variables X and obtain the treatment residuals $\widetilde{F(T)} = F(T) - \widehat{F(T)}$.

3. A denoising step, where you regress the outcome Y on the confounder variables X and obtain the outcome residuals $\tilde{Y} = Y - \hat{Y}$.

4. An outcome model where you regress the outcome residual $\tilde{Y}$ on the treatment residual $\widetilde{F(T)}$ to obtain an estimate for the causal effect of $F(T)$ on Y.

In the example, F is the square root, so here is how you can apply the FWL theorem considering the nonlinearity. (I'm also adding $\overline{F(lines)}$ and $\overline{spend}$ to the treatment and outcome residuals, respectively. This is optional, but it makes for better visualization):

```
In [18]: debias_spend_model = smf.ols(f'np.sqrt(credit_limit) ~ wage',
                                       data=spend_data).fit()
         denoise_spend_model = smf.ols(f'spend ~ wage', data=spend_data).fit()


         credit_limit_sqrt_deb = (debias_spend_model.resid
                       + np.sqrt(spend_data["credit_limit"]).mean())
         spend_den = denoise_spend_model.resid + spend_data["spend"].mean()


         spend_data_deb = (spend_data
                       .assign(credit_limit_sqrt_deb = credit_limit_sqrt_deb,
                               spend_den = spend_den))

         final_model = smf.ols(f'spend_den ~ credit_limit_sqrt_deb',
                               data=spend_data_deb).fit()

         final_model.summary().tables[1]
```

	coef	std err	t	P>|t|	[0.025	0.975]
Intercept	1493.6990	3.435	434.818	0.000	1486.966	1500.432
credit_limit_sqrt_deb	43.8504	0.065	672.640	0.000	43.723	43.978

Not surprisingly, the estimate you get here for β_1 is the exact same as the one you got earlier, by running the full model including both the wage confounder and the treatment. Also, if you plot the prediction from this model against the original data, you can see that it is not upward biased like before. Instead, it goes right through the middle of the wage groups:

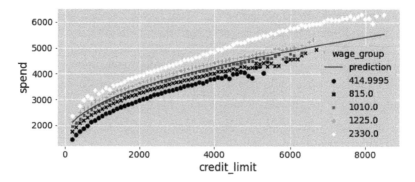

Regression for Dummies

Regression and orthogonalization are great and all, but ultimately you have to make an independence assumption. You have to assume that treatment looks as good as randomly assigned, when some covariates are accounted for. This can be quite a stretch. It's very hard to know if all confounders have been included in the model. For this reason, it makes a lot of sense for you to push for randomized experiments as much as you can. For instance, in the banking example, it would be great if the credit limit was randomized, as that would make it pretty straightforward to estimate its effect on default rate and customer spend. The thing is that this experiment would be incredibly expensive. You would be giving random credit lines to very risky customers, who would probably default and cause a huge loss.

Conditionally Random Experiments

The way around this conundrum is not the ideal randomized controlled trial, but it is the next best thing: *stratified or conditionally random experiments*. Instead of crafting an experiment where lines are completely random and drawn from the same probability distribution, you instead create multiple local experiments, where you draw samples from different distributions, depending on customer covariates. For instance, you know that the variable `credit_score1` is a proxy for customer risk. So you can use it to create groups of customers that are more or less risky, dividing them into buckets of similar `credit_score1`. Then, for the high-risk bucket—with low `credit_score1`—you randomize credit lines by sampling from a distribution with a lower average; for low-risk customers—with high `credit_score1`—you randomize credit lines by sampling from a distribution with a higher average:

```
In [19]: risk_data_rnd = pd.read_csv("./data/risk_data_rnd.csv")
         risk_data_rnd.head()
```

	wage	educ	exper	married	credit_score1	credit_score2	credit_score1_buckets	credit_limit	default
0	890.0	11	16	1	490.0	500.0	400	5400.0	0
1	670.0	11	7	1	196.0	481.0	200	3800.0	0
2	1220.0	14	9	1	392.0	611.0	400	5800.0	0
3	1210.0	15	8	1	627.0	519.0	600	6500.0	0
4	900.0	16	1	1	275.0	519.0	200	2100.0	0

Plotting the histogram of credit limit by `credit_score1_buckets`, you can see that lines were sampled from different distributions. The buckets with higher score—low-risk customers—have a histogram skewed to the left, with higher lines. The groups with risker customers—low score—have lines drawn from a distribution that is skewed to the right, with lower lines. This sort of experiment explores credit lines that are not too far from what is probably the optimal line, which lowers the cost of the test to a more manageable amount:

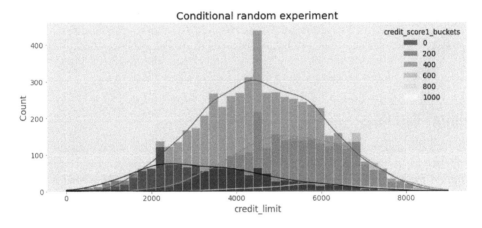

Beta Sampling

In this experiment, credit limit was sampled from Beta distributions. The Beta distribution can be understood as generalization of the uniform distribution, which makes it particularly handy when you want your sample to be confined to a specific range.

This doesn't mean that conditionally random experiments are better than completely random experiments. They sure are cheaper, but they add a tone of extra complexity. For this reason, if you opt for a conditionally random experiment, for whatever reason, try to keep it as close to a completely random experiment as possible. This means that:

- The lower the number of groups, the easier it will be to deal with the conditionally random test. In this example you only have 5 groups, since you divided `credit_score1` in buckets of 200 and the score goes from 0 to 1,000. Combining different groups with different treatment distribution increases the complexity, so sticking to fewer groups is a good idea.
- The bigger the overlap in the treatment distributions across groups, the easier your life will be. This has to do with the positivity assumption. In this example, if the high-risk group had zero probability of receiving high lines, you would have to rely on dangerous extrapolations to know what would happen if they were to receive those high lines.

If you crank these two rules of thumb to their maximum, you get back a completely random experiment, which means both of them carry a trade-off: the lower the number of groups and the higher the overlap, the easier it will be to read the experiment, but it will also be more expensive, and vice versa.

 Stratified experiments can also be used as a tool to minimize variance and to ensure balance between treatment and control on the stratified variables. But in those applications, the treatment distribution is designed to be the same across all groups or strata.

Dummy Variables

The neat thing about conditionally random experiments is that the conditional independence assumption is much more plausible, since you know lines were randomly assigned given a categorical variable of your choice. The downside is that a simple regression of the outcome on the treated will yield a biased estimate. For example, here is what happens when you estimate the model, without the confounder included:

$$default_i = \beta_0 + \beta_1 lines_i + e_i$$

```
In [20]: model = smf.ols("default ~ credit_limit", data=risk_data_rnd).fit()
         model.summary().tables[1]
```

	coef	std err	t	P>|t|	[0.025	0.975]
Intercept	0.1369	0.009	15.081	0.000	0.119	0.155
credit_limit	−9.344e−06	1.85e−06	−5.048	0.000	−1.3e−05	−5.72e−06

As you can see, the causal parameter estimate, $\widehat{\beta_1}$, is negative, which makes no sense here. Higher credit lines probably do not decrease a customer's risk. What happened is that, in this data, due to the way the experiment was designed, lower-risk customers —those with high `credit_score1`—got, on average, higher lines.

To adjust for that, you need to include in the model the group within which the treatment is randomly assigned. In this case, you need to control for `credit_score1_buck ets`. Even though this group is represented as a number, it is actually a categorical variable: it represents a group. So, the way to control for the group itself is to create *dummy variables*. A dummy is a binary column for a group. It is 1 if the customer belongs to that group and 0 otherwise. As a customer can only be from one group, at most one dummy column will be 1, with all the others being zero. If you come from a machine learning background, you might know this as one-hot encoding. They are exactly the same thing.

In pandas, you can use the `pd.get_dummies` function to create dummies. Here, I'm passing the column that represents the groups, `credit_score1_buckets`, and saying that I want to create dummy columns with the suffix `sb` (for score bucket). Also, I'm dropping the first dummy, that of the bucket 0 to 200. That's because one of the dummy columns is redundant. If I know that all the other columns are zero, the one that I dropped must be 1:

```
In [21]: risk_data_dummies = (
             risk_data_rnd
                 .join(pd.get_dummies(risk_data_rnd["credit_score1_buckets"],
                                      prefix="sb",
                                      drop_first=True))
         )
```

	wage	educ	exper	married	...	sb_400	sb_600	sb_800	sb_1000
0	890.0	11	16	1	...	1	0	0	0
1	670.0	11	7	1	...	0	0	0	0
2	1220.0	14	9	1	...	1	0	0	0
3	1210.0	15	8	1	...	0	1	0	0
4	900.0	16	1	1	...	0	0	0	0

Once you have the dummy columns, you can add them to your model and estimate β_1 again:

$$default_i = \beta_0 + \beta_1 lines_i + \theta \mathbf{G}_i + e_i$$

Now, you'll get a much more reasonable estimate, which is at least positive, indicating that more credit lines increase risk of default.

```
In [22]: model = smf.ols(
             "default ~ credit_limit + sb_200+sb_400+sb_600+sb_800+sb_1000",
             data=risk_data_dummies
         ).fit()

         model.summary().tables[1]
```

	coef	std err	t	P>|t|	[0.025	0.975]
Intercept	0.2253	0.056	4.000	0.000	0.115	0.336
credit_limit	4.652e−06	2.02e−06	2.305	0.021	6.97e−07	8.61e−06
sb_200	−0.0559	0.057	−0.981	0.327	−0.168	0.056
sb_400	−0.1442	0.057	−2.538	0.011	−0.256	−0.033
sb_600	−0.2148	0.057	−3.756	0.000	−0.327	−0.103
sb_800	−0.2489	0.060	−4.181	0.000	−0.366	−0.132
sb_1000	−0.2541	0.094	−2.715	0.007	−0.438	−0.071

I'm only showing you how to create dummies by hand so you know what happens under the hood. This will be very useful if you have to implement that sort of regression in some other framework that is not in Python. In Python, if you are using stats models, the C() function in the formula can do all of that for you:

```
In [23]: model = smf.ols("default ~ credit_limit + C(credit_score1_buckets)",
                         data=risk_data_rnd).fit()

         model.summary().tables[1]
```

	coef	std err	t	P>|t|	[0.025	0.975]
Intercept	0.2253	0.056	4.000	0.000	0.115	0.336
C(credit_score1_buckets)[T.200]	−0.0559	0.057	−0.981	0.327	−0.168	0.056
C(credit_score1_buckets)[T.400]	−0.1442	0.057	−2.538	0.011	−0.256	−0.033
C(credit_score1_buckets)[T.600]	−0.2148	0.057	−3.756	0.000	−0.327	−0.103
C(credit_score1_buckets)[T.800]	−0.2489	0.060	−4.181	0.000	−0.366	−0.132
C(credit_score1_buckets)[T.1000]	−0.2541	0.094	−2.715	0.007	−0.438	−0.071
credit_limit	4.652e−06	2.02e−06	2.305	0.021	6.97e−07	8.61e−06

Finally, here you only have one slope parameter. Adding dummies to control for confounding gives one intercept per group, but the same slope for all groups. We'll discuss this shortly, but this slope will be a variance weighted average of the regression in each group. If you plot the model's predictions for each group, you can clearly see that you have one line per group, but all of them have the same slope:

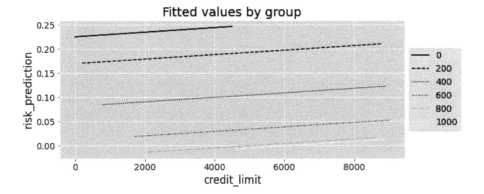

Fitted values by group

Saturated Regression Model

Remember how I started the chapter highlighting the similarities between regression and a conditional average? I showed you how running a regression with a binary treatment is exactly the same as comparing the average between treated and control group. Now, since dummies are binary columns, the parallel also applies here. If you take your conditionally random experiment data and give it to someone that is not as versed in regression as you are, their first instinct will probably be to simply segment the data by `credit_score1_buckets` and estimate the effect in each group separately:

```
In [24]: def regress(df, t, y):
             return smf.ols(f"{y}~{t}", data=df).fit().params[t]

         effect_by_group = (risk_data_rnd
                            .groupby("credit_score1_buckets")
                            .apply(regress, y="default", t="credit_limit"))
         effect_by_group

Out[24]: credit_score1_buckets
         0       -0.000071
         200      0.000007
         400      0.000005
         600      0.000003
         800      0.000002
         1000     0.000000
         dtype: float64
```

This would give an effect by group, which means you also have to decide how to average them out. A natural choice would be a weighted average, where the weights are the size of each group:

```
In [25]: group_size = risk_data_rnd.groupby("credit_score1_buckets").size()
         ate = (effect_by_group * group_size).sum() / group_size.sum()
```

```
ate
```

```
Out[25]: 4.490445628748722e-06
```

Of course, you can do the exact same thing with regression, by running what is called a *saturated model*. You can interact the dummies with the treatment to get an effect for each dummy defined group. In this case, because the first dummy is removed, the parameter associated with `credit_limit` actually represents the effect in the omitted dummy group, sb_100. It is the exact same number as the one estimated above for the credit_score1_bucketsearlier group 0 to 200: –0.000071:

```
In [26]: model = smf.ols("default ~ credit_limit * C(credit_score1_buckets)",
                          data=risk_data_rnd).fit()
         model.summary().tables[1]
```

	coef	std err	t	P>|t|	[0.025	0.975]
Intercept	0.3137	0.077	4.086	0.000	0.163	0.464
C(credit_score1_buckets)[T.200]	−0.1521	0.079	−1.926	0.054	−0.307	0.003
C(credit_score1_buckets)[T.400]	−0.2339	0.078	−3.005	0.003	−0.386	−0.081
C(credit_score1_buckets)[T.600]	−0.2957	0.080	−3.690	0.000	−0.453	−0.139
C(credit_score1_buckets)[T.800]	−0.3227	0.111	−2.919	0.004	−0.539	−0.106
C(credit_score1_buckets)[T.1000]	−0.3137	0.428	−0.733	0.464	−1.153	0.525
credit_limit	−7.072e−05	4.45e−05	−1.588	0.112	−0.000	1.66e−05
credit_limit:C(credit_score1_buckets)[T.200]	7.769e−05	4.48e−05	1.734	0.083	−1.01e−05	0.000
credit_limit:C(credit_score1_buckets)[T.400]	7.565e−05	4.46e−05	1.696	0.090	−1.18e−05	0.000
credit_limit:C(credit_score1_buckets)[T.600]	7.398e−05	4.47e−05	1.655	0.098	−1.37e−05	0.000
credit_limit:C(credit_score1_buckets)[T.800]	7.286e−05	4.65e−05	1.567	0.117	−1.83e−05	0.000
credit_limit:C(credit_score1_buckets)[T.1000]	7.072e−05	8.05e−05	0.878	0.380	−8.71e−05	0.000

The interaction parameters are interpreted in relation to the effect in the first (omitted) group. So, if you sum the parameter associated with `credit_limit` with other interaction terms, you can see the effects for each group estimated with regression. They are exactly the same as estimating one effect per group:

```
In [27]: (model.params[model.params.index.str.contains("credit_limit:")]
          + model.params["credit_limit"]).round(9)
```

```
Out[27]: credit_limit:C(credit_score1_buckets)[T.200]    0.000007
         credit_limit:C(credit_score1_buckets)[T.400]    0.000005
         credit_limit:C(credit_score1_buckets)[T.600]    0.000003
         credit_limit:C(credit_score1_buckets)[T.800]    0.000002
         credit_limit:C(credit_score1_buckets)[T.1000]   0.000000
         dtype: float64
```

Plotting this model's prediction by group will also show that, now, it is as if you are fitting a separate regression for each group. Each line will have not only a different intercept, but also a different slope. Besides, the saturated model has more parameters (degrees of freedom), which also means more variance, all else equal. If you look at the following plot, you'll see a line with negative slope, which doesn't make sense in this context. However, that slope is not statistically significant. It is probably just noise due to a small sample in that group:

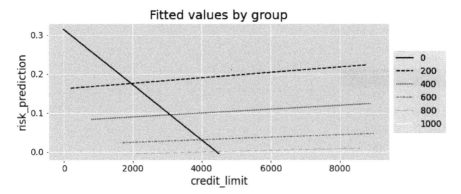

Regression as Variance Weighted Average

But if both the saturated regression and calculating the effect by group give you the exact same thing, there is a very important question you might be asking yourself. When you run the model `default ~ credit_limit + C(credit_score1_buckets)`, without the interaction term, you get a single effect: only one slope parameter. Importantly, if you look back, that effect estimate is different from the one you got by estimating an effect per group and averaging the results using the group size as weights. So, somehow, regression is combining the effects from different groups. And the way it does it is not a sample size weighted average. So what is it then?

Again, the best way to answer this question is by using some very illustrative simulated data. Here, let's simulate data from two different groups. Group 1 has a size of 1,000 and an average treatment effect of 1. Group 2 has a size of 500 and an average treatment effect of 2. Additionally, the standard deviation of the treatment in group 1 is 1 and 2 in group 2:

```
In [28]: np.random.seed(123)

         # std(t)=1
         t1 = np.random.normal(0, 1, size=1000)
         df1 = pd.DataFrame(dict(
             t=t1,
             y=1*t1, # ATE of 1
             g=1,
```

```
    ))

    # std(t)=2
    t2 = np.random.normal(0, 2, size=500)
    df2 = pd.DataFrame(dict(
        t=t2,
        y=2*t2, # ATE of 2
        g=2,
    ))

    df = pd.concat([df1, df2])
    df.head()
```

	t	y	g
0	−1.085631	−1.085631	1
1	0.997345	0.997345	1
2	0.282978	0.282978	1
3	−1.506295	−1.506295	1
4	−0.578600	−0.578600	1

If you estimate the effects for each group separately and average the results with the group size as weights, you'd get an ATE of around 1.33, $(1 * 1000 + 2 * 500)/1500$:

```
In [29]: effect_by_group = df.groupby("g").apply(regress, y="y", t="t")
         ate = (effect_by_group *
                 df.groupby("g").size()).sum() / df.groupby("g").size().sum()
         ate
```

```
Out[29]: 1.333333333333333
```

But if you run a regression of y on t while controlling for the group, you get a very different result. Now, the combined effect is closer to the effect of group 2, even though group 2 has half the sample of group 1:

```
In [30]: model = smf.ols("y ~ t + C(g)", data=df).fit()
         model.params
```

```
Out[30]: Intercept    0.024758
         C(g)[T.2]    0.019860
         t            1.625775
         dtype: float64
```

The reason for this is that regression doesn't combine the group effects by using the sample size as weights. Instead, it uses weights that are proportional to the variance of the treatment in each group. Regression prefers groups where the treatment varies a lot. This might seem odd at first, but if you think about it, it makes a lot of sense. If the treatment doesn't change much within a group, how can you be sure of its effect? If the treatment changes a lot, its impact on the outcome will be more evident.

To summarize, if you have multiple groups where the treatment is randomized inside each group, the conditionality principle states that the effect is a weighted average of the effect inside each group:

$$ATE = E\left\{ \left(\frac{\partial}{\partial t} E[Y_i \,|\, T = t, Group_i] \right) w(Group_i) \right\}$$

Depending on the method, you will have different weights. With regression, $w(Group_i) \propto \sigma^2(T)|Group$, but you can also choose to manually weight the group effects using the sample size as the weight: $w(Group_i) = N_{Group}$.

See Also

Knowing this difference is key to understanding what is going on behind the curtains with regression. The fact that regression weights the group effects by variance is something that even the best researchers need to be constantly reminded of. In 2020, the econometric field went through a renaissance regarding the diff-in-diff method (you'll see more about it in Part IV). At the center of the issue was regression not weighting effects by sample size. If you want to learn more about it, I recommend checking it out the paper "Difference-in-Differences with Variation in Treatment Timing," by Andrew Goodman-Bacon. Or just wait until we get to Part IV.

De-Meaning and Fixed Effects

You just saw how to include dummy variables in your model to account for different treatment assignments across groups. But it is with dummies where the FWL theorem really shines. If you have a ton of groups, adding one dummy for each is not only tedious, but also computationally expensive. You would be creating lots and lots of columns that are mostly zero. You can solve this easily by applying FWL and understanding how regression orthogonalizes the treatment when it comes to dummies.

You already know that the debiasing step in FWL involves predicting the treatment from the covariates, in this case, the dummies:

```
In [31]: model_deb = smf.ols("credit_limit ~ C(credit_score1_buckets)",
                             data=risk_data_rnd).fit()
         model_deb.summary().tables[1]
```

	coef	std err	t	P>|t|	[0.025	0.975]
Intercept	1173.0769	278.994	4.205	0.000	626.193	1719.961
C(credit_score1_buckets)[T.200]	2195.4337	281.554	7.798	0.000	1643.530	2747.337
C(credit_score1_buckets)[T.400]	3402.3796	279.642	12.167	0.000	2854.224	3950.535
C(credit_score1_buckets)[T.600]	4191.3235	280.345	14.951	0.000	3641.790	4740.857
C(credit_score1_buckets)[T.800]	4639.5105	291.400	15.921	0.000	4068.309	5210.712
C(credit_score1_buckets)[T.1000]	5006.9231	461.255	10.855	0.000	4102.771	5911.076

Since dummies work basically as group averages, you can see that, with this model, you are predicting exactly that: if `credit_score1_buckets=0`, you are predicting the average line for the group `credit_score1_buckets=0`; if `credit_score1_buckets=1`, you are predicting the average line for the group `credit_score1_buckets=1` (which is given by summing the intercept to the coefficient for that group 1173.0769 + 2195.4337 = 3368.510638) and so on and so forth. Those are exactly the group averages:

```
In [32]: risk_data_rnd.groupby("credit_score1_buckets")["credit_limit"].mean()


Out[32]: credit_score1_buckets
         0       1173.076923
         200     3368.510638
         400     4575.456498
         600     5364.400448
         800     5812.587413
         1000    6180.000000
         Name: credit_limit, dtype: float64
```

Which means that if you want to residualize the treatment, you can do that in a much simpler and effective way. First, calculate the average treatment for each group:

```
In [33]: risk_data_fe = risk_data_rnd.assign(
             credit_limit_avg = lambda d: (d
                                 .groupby("credit_score1_buckets")
                                 ["credit_limit"].transform("mean"))
         )
```

Then, to get the residuals, subtract that group average from the treatment. Since this approach subtracts the average treatment, it is sometimes referred to as de-meaning the treatment. If you want to do that inside the regression formula, you must wrap the mathematical operation around `I(...)`:

```
In [34]: model = smf.ols("default ~ I(credit_limit-credit_limit_avg)",
                         data=risk_data_fe).fit()
         model.summary().tables[1]
```

	coef	std err	t	P>|t|	[0.025	0.975]
Intercept	0.0935	0.003	32.121	0.000	0.088	0.099
I(credit_limit − credit_limit_avg)	4.652e−06	2.05e−06	2.273	0.023	6.4e−07	8.66e−06

The parameter estimate you got here is exactly the same as the one you got when adding dummies to your model. That's because, mathematically speaking, they are equivalent. This idea goes by the name of *fixed effects*, since you are controlling for anything that is fixed within a group. It comes from the literature of causal inference with temporal structures (panel data), which you'll explore more in Part IV.

Another idea from the same literature is to include the average treatment by group in the regression model (from Mundlak's, 1978). Regression will residualize the treatment from the additional variables included, so the effect here is about the same:

```
In [35]: model = smf.ols("default ~ credit_limit + credit_limit_avg",
                         data=risk_data_fe).fit()
         model.summary().tables[1]
```

	coef	std err	t	P>|t|	[0.025	0.975]
Intercept	0.4325	0.020	21.418	0.000	0.393	0.472
credit_limit	4.652e−06	2.02e−06	2.305	0.021	6.96e−07	8.61e−06
credit_limit_avg	-7.763e−05	4.75e−06	−16.334	0.000	−8.69e−05	−6.83e−05

PRACTICAL EXAMPLE

Marketing Mix Modeling

Measuring the impact of advertising on sales is very hard, since you usually can't randomize who gets to see your ads. One popular alternative to randomization in the advertising industry is the technique called marketing mix modeling (MMM). Despite the fancy name, MMMs are just regressions of sales on marketing strategies indicators and some confounders. For example, let's say you want to know the effect of your budget on TV, social media, and search advertising on your product's sales. You can run a regression model where each unit i is a day:

$$Sales_i = \delta_0 + \beta_1 TV_i + \beta_2 Social_i + \beta_3 Search_i$$
$$+ \delta_1 CompetitorSales_i + \delta_2 Month_i + \delta_3 Trend_i + e_i$$

To account for the fact that you might have increased your marketing budget on a good month, you can adjust for this confounder by including additional controls in your regression. For example, you can include your competitor's sales, a dummy for each month, and a trend variable.

Omitted Variable Bias: Confounding Through the Lens of Regression

I hope I made myself very clear in Chapter 3 when I said that common causes—confounders—will bias the estimated relationship between the treated and the outcome. That is why you need to account for them by, for example, including them in a regression model. However, regression has its own particular take on confounding bias. Sure, everything said up until now still holds. But regression allows you to be more precise about the confounding bias. For example, let's say you want to estimate the effect of credit lines on default and that wage is the only confounder:

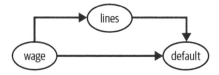

In this case, you know you should be estimating the model that includes the confounder:

$$default_i = \beta_0 + \beta_1 lines_i + \beta_2 > wage_i + e_i,$$

But if you instead estimate a shorter model, where the confounder is omitted:

$$default_i = \beta_0 + \beta_1 lines_i + e_i,$$

the resulting estimate becomes biased:

```
In [36]: short_model = smf.ols("default ~ credit_limit", data=risk_data).fit()
         short_model.params["credit_limit"]

Out[36]: -2.401961992596885e-05
```

As you can see, it looks like higher credit lines cause default to go down, which is nonsense. But you know that already. What you don't know is that you can be precise about the size of that bias. With regression, you can say that the bias due to an omitted variable is *equal to the effect in the model where it is included plus the effect of the omitted variable on the outcome times the regression of omitted on included.* Don't worry. I know this is a mouthful, so let's digest it little by little. First, it means that simple regression of Y on T will be the true causal parameter τ, plus a bias term:

$$\frac{Cov(T, Y)}{Var(T)} = \tau + \beta'_{omitted}\delta_{omitted}$$

This bias term is the coefficient of the omitted confounder on the outcome, $\beta_{omitted}$, times the coefficient of regressing the omitted variable on the treatment, $\delta_{omitted}$. To check that, you can obtain the biased parameter estimate you got earlier with the following code, which reproduces the omitted variable bias formula:

```
In [37]: long_model = smf.ols("default ~ credit_limit + wage",
                              data=risk_data).fit()

        omitted_model = smf.ols("wage ~ credit_limit", data=risk_data).fit()

        (long_model.params["credit_limit"]
          + long_model.params["wage"]*omitted_model.params["credit_limit"])


Out[37]: -2.4019619925968762e-05
```

Neutral Controls

By now, you probably have a good idea about how regression adjusts for confounder variables. If you want to know the effect of the treatment T on Y while adjusting for confounders X, all you have to do is include X in the model. Alternatively, to get the exact same result, you can predict T from X, get the residuals, and use that as a debiased version of the treatment. Regressing Y on those residuals will give you the relationship of T and Y while holding X fixed.

But what kind of variables should you include in X? Again, it's not because adding variables adjusts for them that you want to include everything in your regression model. As seen in the previous chapters, you don't want to include common effects (colliders) or mediators, as those would induce selection bias. But in the context of regression, there are more types of controls you should know about. Controls that, at first, seem like they are innocuous, but are actually quite harmful. These controls are named neutral because they don't influence the bias in your regression estimate. But they can have severe implications in terms of variance. As you'll see, there is a bias–variance trade-off when it comes to including certain variables in your regression. Consider, for instance, the following DAG:

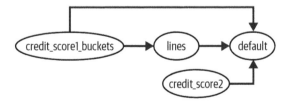

Should you include `credit_score2` in your model? If you don't include it, you'll get the same result you've been seeing all along. That result is unbiased, as you are adjusting for `credit_score1_buckets`. But, although you don't need to, look at what happens when you do include `credit_score2`. Compare the following results to the one you got earlier, which didn't include `credit_score2`. What changed?

```
In [38]: formula = "default~credit_limit+C(credit_score1_buckets)+credit_score2"
         model = smf.ols(formula, data=risk_data_rnd).fit()
         model.summary().tables[1]
```

	coef	std err	t	P>|t|	[0.025	0.975]
Intercept	0.5576	0.055	10.132	0.000	0.450	0.665
C(credit_score1_buckets)[T.200]	−0.0387	0.055	−0.710	0.478	−0.146	0.068
C(credit_score1_buckets)[T.400]	−0.1032	0.054	−1.898	0.058	−0.210	0.003
C(credit_score1_buckets)[T.600]	−0.1410	0.055	−2.574	0.010	−0.248	−0.034
C(credit_score1_buckets)[T.800]	−0.1161	0.057	−2.031	0.042	−0.228	−0.004
C(credit_score1_buckets)[T.1000]	−0.0430	0.090	−0.479	0.632	−0.219	0.133
credit_limit	4.928e−06	1.93e−06	2.551	0.011	1.14e−06	8.71e−06
credit_score2	−0.0007	2.34e−05	−30.225	0.000	−0.001	−0.001

First, the parameter estimate on `credit_limit` became a bit higher. But, more importantly, the standard error decreases. That's because `credit_score2` is a good predictor of the outcome Y and it will contribute to the denoising step of linear regression. In the final step of FWL, because `credit_score2` was included, the variance in $\tilde{Y}$ will be reduced, and regressing it on $\tilde{T}$ will yield more precise results.

This is a very interesting property of linear regression. It shows that it can be used not only to adjust for confounders, but also to reduce noise. For example, if you have data from a properly randomized A/B test, you don't need to worry about bias. But you can still use regression as a noise reduction tool. Just include variables that are highly predictive of the outcome (and that don't induce selection bias).

Noise Reduction Techniques

There are other noise reduction techniques out there. The most famous one is CUPED, which was developed by Microsoft researchers and is widely used in tech companies. CUPED is very similar to just doing the denoising part of the FWL theorem.

Noise Inducing Control

Just like controls can reduce noise, they can also increase it. For example, consider again the case of a conditionally random experiment. But this time, you are interested in the effect of credit limit on spend, rather than on risk. Just like in the previous example, credit limit was randomly assigned, given credit_score1. But this time, let's say that credit_score1 is not a confounder. It causes the treatment, but not the outcome. The causal graph for this data-generating process looks like this:

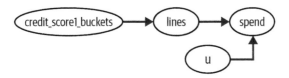

This means that you don't need to adjust for credit_score1 to get the causal effect of credit limit on spend. A single variable regression model would do. Here, I'm keeping the square root function to account for the concavity in the treatment response function:

```
In [39]: spend_data_rnd = pd.read_csv("data/spend_data_rnd.csv")

         model = smf.ols("spend ~ np.sqrt(credit_limit)",
                         data=spend_data_rnd).fit()

         model.summary().tables[1]
```

	coef	std err	t	P>|t|	[0.025	0.975]
Intercept	2153.2154	218.600	9.850	0.000	1723.723	2582.708
np.sqrt(credit_limit)	16.2915	2.988	5.452	0.000	10.420	22.163

But, what happens if you do include credit_score1_buckets?

```
In [40]: model = smf.ols("spend~np.sqrt(credit_limit)+C(credit_score1_buckets)",
                         data=spend_data_rnd).fit()

         model.summary().tables[1]
```

	coef	std err	t	P>|t|	[0.025	0.975]
Intercept	2367.4867	556.273	4.256	0.000	1274.528	3460.446
C(credit_score1_buckets)[T.200]	−144.7921	591.613	−0.245	0.807	−1307.185	1017.601
C(credit_score1_buckets)[T.400]	−118.3923	565.364	−0.209	0.834	−1229.211	992.427
C(credit_score1_buckets)[T.600]	−111.5738	570.471	−0.196	0.845	−1232.429	1009.281
C(credit_score1_buckets)[T.800]	−89.7366	574.645	−0.156	0.876	−1218.791	1039.318
C(credit_score1_buckets)[T.1000]	363.8990	608.014	0.599	0.550	−830.720	1558.518
np.sqrt(credit_limit)	14.5953	3.523	4.142	0.000	7.673	21.518

You can see that it increases the standard error, widening the confidence interval of the causal parameter. That is because, like you saw in "Regression as Variance Weighted Average" on page 129, OLS likes when the treatment has a high variance. But if you control for a covariate that explains the treatment, you are effectively reducing its variance.

Feature Selection: A Bias-Variance Trade-Off

In reality, it's really hard to have a situation where a covariate causes the treatment but not the outcome. Most likely, you will have a bunch of confounders that cause both T and Y, but to different degrees. In Figure 4-3, X_1 is a strong cause of T but a weak cause of Y, X_3 is a strong cause of Y but a weak cause of T, and X_2 is somewhere in the middle, as denoted by the thickness of each arrow.

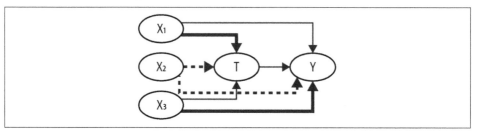

Figure 4-3. A confounder like X_1, which explains away the variance in the treatment more than it removes bias, might be causing more harm than good to your estimator

In these situations, you can quickly be caught between a rock and a hard place. On one hand, if you want to get rid of all the biases, you must include all the covariates; after all, they are confounders that need to be adjusted. On the other hand, adjusting for causes of the treatment will increase the variance of your estimator.

To see that, let's simulate data according to the causal graph in Figure 4-3. Here, the true ATE is 0.5. If you try to estimate this effect while controlling for all of the confounders, the standard error of your estimate will be too high to conclude anything:

```
In [41]: np.random.seed(123)

         n = 100
         (x1, x2, x3) = (np.random.normal(0, 1, n) for _ in range(3))
         t = np.random.normal(10*x1 + 5*x2 + x3)

         # ate = 0.05
         y = np.random.normal(0.05*t + x1 + 5*x2 + 10*x3, 5)
         df = pd.DataFrame(dict(y=y, t=t, x1=x1, x2=x2, x3=x3))

         smf.ols("y~t+x1+x2+x3", data=df).fit().summary().tables[1]
```

	coef	std err	t	P>|t|	[0.025	0.975]
Intercept	0.2707	0.527	0.514	0.608	−0.775	1.316
t	0.8664	0.607	1.427	0.157	−0.339	2.072
x1	−7.0628	6.038	−1.170	0.245	−19.049	4.923
x2	0.0143	3.128	0.005	0.996	−6.195	6.224
x3	9.6292	0.887	10.861	0.000	7.869	11.389

If you know that one of the confounders is a strong predictor of the treatment and a weak predictor of the outcome, you can choose to drop it from the model. In this example, that would be X_1. Now, be warned! This will bias your estimate. But maybe this is a price worth paying if it also decreases variance significantly:

```
In [42]: smf.ols("y~t+x2+x3", data=df).fit().summary().tables[1]
```

	coef	std err	t	P>|t|	[0.025	0.975]
Intercept	0.1889	0.523	0.361	0.719	−0.849	1.227
t	0.1585	0.046	3.410	0.001	0.066	0.251
x2	3.6095	0.582	6.197	0.000	2.453	4.766
x3	10.4549	0.537	19.453	0.000	9.388	11.522

The bottom line is that the more confounders you include (adjust for) in your model, the lower the bias in your causal estimate. However, if you include variables that are weak predictors of the outcome but strong predictors of the treatment, this bias reduction will come at a steep cost in terms of variance increase. Saying the same thing but differently, sometimes it is worth accepting a bit of bias in order to reduce variance. Also, you should be very aware that not all confounders are equal. Sure, all of them are common because of both T and Y. But if they explain the treatment too much and almost nothing about the outcome, you should really consider dropping it from your adjustment. This is valid for regression, but it will also be true for other adjustment strategies, like propensity score weighting (see Chapter 5).

Unfortunately, how weak the confounder should be in terms of explaining the treatment to justify removing it is still an open question in causal inference. Still, it is worth knowing that this bias-variance trade-off exists, as it will help you understand and explain what is going on with your linear regression.

Key Ideas

This chapter was about regression, but from a very different perspective than the one you usually see in machine learning books. Regression here is not a prediction tool. Notice how I didn't talk about R^2 even once! Rather, regression is used here as a way to primarily adjust for confounders and, sometimes, as a variance reduction technique.

The core of this chapter was orthogonalization as a means to make treatment look as good as randomly assigned if conditional independence holds. Formally, if $Y_t \perp T \mid X$, you can adjust for the confounding bias due to X by regressing T on X and obtaining the residuals. Those residuals can be seen as a debiased version of the treatment.

This approach was further developed using the Frisch-Waugh-Lovell theorem, which states that a multivariate regression can be decomposed into the following steps:

1. A debiasing step, where you regress the treatment T on confounders X and obtain the treatment residuals $\tilde{T} = T - \hat{T}$

2. A denoising step, where you regress the outcome Y on the confounder variables X and obtain the outcome residuals $\tilde{Y} = Y - \hat{Y}$

3. An outcome model where you regress the outcome residual $\tilde{Y}$ on the treatment residual $\tilde{T}$ to obtain an estimate for the causal effect of T on Y

Everything else in the chapter follows from this theorem—be it nonlinear treatment response functions, understanding how regression with categorical variables implements a weighted average, or the role of good and bad controls in regression.

CHAPTER 5

Propensity Score

In Chapter 4, you learned how to adjust for confounders using linear regression. In addition to that, you were introduced to the concept of debiasing through orthogonalization, which is one of the most useful bias-adjusting techniques available. However, there is another technique that you need to learn—propensity weighting. This technique involves modeling the treatment assignment mechanism and using the model's prediction to reweight the data, instead of building residuals like in orthogonalization. In this chapter, you will also learn how to combine the principles of Chapter 4 with propensity weighting to achieve what is known as double robustness.

The content of this chapter is better suited for when you have binary or discrete treatments. Still, I'll show an extension that allows you to use propensity weighting for continuous treatment.

The Impact of Management Training

A common phenomenon in tech companies is for talented individual contributors (ICs) to branch out to a management track. But because management often requires a very different skill set than the ones that made them talented ICs, this transition is often far from easy. It comes at a high personal cost, not only for the new managers, but for those they manage.

Hoping to make this transition less painful, a big multinational company decided to invest in manager training for its new managers. Also, to measure the effectiveness of the training, the company tried to randomly select managers into this program. The idea was to compare an engagement score for the employees whose managers got enrolled in the program with the engagement of those whose managers didn't. With proper randomization, this simple comparison would give the average treatment effect of the training.

Unfortunately, things are not that simple. Some managers didn't want to go to the training, so they simply didn't show up. Others managed to get the training even without being assigned to receive it. The result is that what was to be a randomized study ended up looking a lot like an observational one.

Noncompliance

People not getting the treatment they are intended to is called *noncompliance*. You will see more about this when we talk about instrumental variables in Chapter 11.

Now, as an analyst who has to read this data, you'll have to make treated and untreated comparable by adjusting for confounders. To do that, you are given data on the company managers along with some covariates that describe them:

```
In [1]: import pandas as pd
        import numpy as np

        df = pd.read_csv("data/management_training.csv")
        df.head()
```

	department_id	intervention	engagement_score	...	last_engagement_score	department_size
0	76	1	0.277359	...	0.614261	843
1	76	1	−0.449646	...	0.069636	843
2	76	1	0.769703	...	0.866918	843
3	76	1	−0.121763	...	0.029071	843
4	76	1	1.526147	...	0.589857	843

The treatment variable is `intervention` and your outcome of interest is `engagement_score`, which is the average standardized engagement score for that manager's employees. Beyond the treatment and the outcome, the covariates in this data are:

`department_id`
    A unique identifier for the department

`tenure`
    The number of years the manager has been with the company (as an employee, not necessarily as a manager)

`n_of_reports`
    The number of reports the manager has

`gender`
    Categorical variable for manager identified gender

role
> Job category inside the company

department_size
> The number of employees in that same department

department_score
> The average engagement score in that same department

last_engagement_score
> The average engagement score for that manager in the previous iteration of the engagement survey

You hope that, by controlling for some or all of these variables, you might manage to reduce or even eliminate the bias when estimating the causal relationship between management training and employee engagement.

 Simulated Data

This dataset was adapted from the one used in the study "Estimating Treatment Effects with Causal Forests: An Application," by Susan Athey and Stefan Wager.

Adjusting with Regression

Before moving on to propensity weighting, let's use regression to adjust for the confounders. In general, when learning something new, its always a good idea to have some benchmark that you trust to compare to. Here the idea is to check if the propensity weighting estimate is at least inline with the regression one. Now, let's get to it.

For starters, if you simply compare treated and control groups, this is what you'll get:

```
In [2]: import statsmodels.formula.api as smf

        smf.ols("engagement_score ~ intervention",
                data=df).fit().summary().tables[1]
```

	coef	std err	t	P>|t|	[0.025	0.975]
Intercept	−0.2347	0.014	−16.619	0.000	−0.262	−0.207
intervention	0.4346	0.019	22.616	0.000	0.397	0.472

But then again, this result is probably biased, since the treatment was not entirely random. To reduce this bias, you can adjust for the covariates you have in your data, estimating the following model:

$$engagement_i = \tau T_i + \theta X_i + e_i,$$

where X is all the confounders you have plus a constant column for the intercept. Additionally, gender and role are both categorical variables, so you have to wrap them in C() inside your OLS formula:

```
In [3]: model = smf.ols("""engagement_score ~ intervention
        + tenure + last_engagement_score + department_score
        + n_of_reports + C(gender) + C(role)""", data=df).fit()

        print("ATE:", model.params["intervention"])
        print("95% CI:", model.conf_int().loc["intervention", :].values.T)


Out[3]: ATE: 0.2677908576676856
        95% CI: [0.23357751 0.30200421]
```

Notice that the effect estimate here is considerably smaller than the one you got earlier. This is some indication of positive bias, which means that managers whose employees were already more engaged are more likely to have participated in the manager training program. OK, enough with the preamble. Let's see what propensity weighting is all about.

Propensity Score

Propensity weighting revolves around the concept of a propensity score, which itself comes from the realization that you don't need to directly control for confounders X to achieve conditional independence $(Y_1, Y_0) \perp T | X$. Instead, it is sufficient to control for a balancing score that estimates $E[T|X]$. This balancing score is often the conditional probability of the treatment, $P(T|X)$, also called the *propensity score, e(x)*.

The propensity score can be viewed as a dimensionality reduction technique. Instead of conditioning on X, which can be very high dimensional, you can simply condition on the propensity score in order to block the backdoor paths that flow through X: $(Y_1, Y_0) \perp T | P(x)$.

There is a formal proof (*https://oreil.ly/LkYaz*) for why this is. It's not complicated, but a bit beyond the scope of this book. Here, you can approach the matter in a more intuitive way. The propensity score is the conditional probability of receiving the treatment, right? So you can think of it as some sort of function that converts X into the treatment T. The propensity score makes this middle ground between the variable X and the treatment T. This is what it would look like in a causal graph:

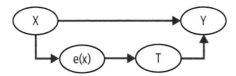

In this graph, if you know what $e(x)$ is, X alone gives you no further information about T. Which means that controlling for $e(x)$ works the same way as controlling for X directly.

Think of it in terms of the manager training program. Treated and nontreated are initially not comparable because the managers with more engaged direct reports are more likely to participate in the training. However, if you take two managers, one from the treated and one from the control group, but with the same probability of receiving the treatment, they are comparable. Think about it. If they have the exact same probability of receiving the treatment, the only reason one of them did it and the other didn't is by pure chance. Given the same propensity score, treatment is as good as random.

Propensity Score Estimation

In an ideal world, you would have the true propensity score $e(x)$. You might have this in the case of conditionally random experiment, where the assignment mechanism is nondeterministic, but known. However, in most cases, the mechanism that assigns the treatment is unknown and you'll need to replace the true propensity score by an estimation of $e(x)$.

Since you have a binary treatment, a good candidate for estimating $e(x)$ is using logistic regression. To fit a logistic regression with statsmodels, you can simply change the method ols to logit:

```
In [4]: ps_model = smf.logit("""intervention ~
        tenure + last_engagement_score + department_score
        + C(n_of_reports) + C(gender) + C(role)""", data=df).fit(disp=0)
```

Save your estimated propensity score in a data frame; you'll use it a lot in the following sections, where I'll show you how to use it and what it is doing:

```
In [5]: data_ps = df.assign(
            propensity_score = ps_model.predict(df),
        )

        data_ps[["intervention", "engagement_score", "propensity_score"]].head()
```

	intervention	engagement_score	propensity_score
0	1	0.277359	0.596106
1	1	−0.449646	0.391138
2	1	0.769703	0.602578
3	1	−0.121763	0.580990
4	1	1.526147	0.619976

Propensity Score and ML

Alternatively, you can use machine learning models to estimate the propensity score. But they require you to be more careful. First, you must ensure that your ML model outputs a calibrated probability prediction. Second, you need to use out-of-fold predictions to avoid bias due to overfitting. You can use sklearn's calibration module for the first task and the cross_val_predict function, from the model selection module, for the latter.

Propensity Score and Orthogonalization

If you recall from the previous chapter, according to the FLW theorem, linear regression also does something very similar to estimating a propensity score. In the debiasing step, it estimates $E[T|X]$. So, very much like the propensity score estimation, OLS is also modeling the treatment assignment mechanism. This means you can also use propensity score $\hat{e}(X)$ inside a linear regression in order to adjust for the confounders X:

```
In [6]: model = smf.ols("engagement_score ~ intervention + propensity_score",
                        data=data_ps).fit()
        model.params["intervention"]


Out[6]: 0.26331267490277066
```

The estimated ATE you get with this approach is remarkably similar to the one you got earlier, fitting a linear model with the treatment and confounder X. This is not at all surprising, as both approaches are simply orthogonalizing the treatment. The only difference is that OLS uses linear regression to model T, while this propensity score estimate was obtained from a logistic regression.

Propensity Score Matching

Another popular approach to control for the propensity score is the matching estimator. This method searches for pairs of units with similar observable characteristics and compares the outcomes of those who received the treatment to those who did not. If you have a background in data science, you can think of matching as a simple

K-Nearest-Neighbors (KNN) algorithm, where K=1. To start, you fit a KNN model on the treated units, using the propensity score as the only feature, and use it to impute Y_1 for the control group. Next, you fit a KNN model on the untreated units and use it to impute Y_0 for the treated units. In both cases, the imputed value is simply the outcome of the matched unit, where the match is based on the propensity score:

```
In [7]: from sklearn.neighbors import KNeighborsRegressor

        T = "intervention"
        X = "propensity_score"
        Y = "engagement_score"

        treated = data_ps.query(f"{T}==1")
        untreated = data_ps.query(f"{T}==0")

        mt0 = KNeighborsRegressor(n_neighbors=1).fit(untreated[[X]],
                                                      untreated[Y])

        mt1 = KNeighborsRegressor(n_neighbors=1).fit(treated[[X]], treated[Y])

        predicted = pd.concat([
            # find matches for the treated looking at the untreated knn model
            treated.assign(match=mt0.predict(treated[[X]])),

            # find matches for the untreated looking at the treated knn model
            untreated.assign(match=mt1.predict(untreated[[X]]))
        ])

        predicted.head()
```

	department_id	intervention	engagement_score	...	department_size	propensity_score	match
0	76	1	0.277359	...	843	0.596106	0.557680
1	76	1	−0.449646	...	843	0.391138	−0.952622
2	76	1	0.769703	...	843	0.602578	−0.618381
3	76	1	−0.121763	...	843	0.580990	−1.404962
4	76	1	1.526147	...	843	0.619976	0.000354

Once you have a match for each unit, you can estimate the ATE:

$$\widehat{ATE} = \frac{1}{N}\sum\left\{\left(Y_i - Y_{jm}(i)\right)T_i + \left(Y_{jm}(i) - Y_i\right)(1 - T_i)\right\},$$

where $Y_{jm}(i)$ is the match of unit i from the treatment group different from i's:

```
In [8]: np.mean((predicted[Y] - predicted["match"])*predicted[T]
              + (predicted["match"] - predicted[Y])*(1-predicted[T]))
```

```
Out[8]: 0.28777443474045966
```

Bias of the Matching Estimator

You don't need to use matching only with the propensity score. Instead, you could directly match on the raw features X used to construct the propensity score estimate $\hat{P}(T|X)$. However, the matching estimator is biased, and that bias increases with the dimension of X. With a high dimensionality, the data becomes sparse, and the matching becomes poorer. Say $\mu_0(X)$ and $\mu_1(X)$ are the expected outcome function in the control and treated group, respectively. The bias is the discrepancy between the expected outcome and the match's outcome: $\mu_0(X_i) - \mu_0(X_{jm})$ for the treated units and $\mu_1(X_{jm}) - \mu_1(X_i)$ for the control units, where X_{jm} are the covariates for the match.

This means that, if you want to use matching, but avoid its bias, you have to apply a bias correction term:

$$\widehat{ATE} = \frac{1}{N}\Sigma\left\{\left(Y_i - Y_{jm}(i) - \left(\hat{\mu}_0(X_i) - \hat{\mu}_0(X_{jm})\right)\right)T_i \right.$$
$$\left. + \left(Y_{jm}(i) - Y_i - \left(\hat{\mu}_1(X_{jm}) - \hat{\mu}_1(X_i)\right)\right)(1 - T_i)\right\},$$

where $\widehat{\mu_1}$ and $\widehat{\mu_0}$ can be estimated with something like linear regression.

To be completely honest, I'm not a huge fan of this estimator, first, because it is biased, second, because it is difficult to derive its variance, and third, because my experience in data science has led me to be suspicious of KNN, mostly because it is very inefficient with high dimensional X. This last problem is not an issue if you only match on the propensity score, but the first two problems remain. I'm teaching this method here mostly because it is very famous and you might see it here and there.

See Also

The paper "Why Propensity Scores Should Not Be Used for Matching," by King and Nielsen, provides a more technical discussion on the issue with propensity score matching.

Inverse Propensity Weighting

There is another widely used approach for utilizing propensity scores that I find preferable—inverse propensity weighting (IPW). By reweighting the data based on the inverse probability of treatment, this method can make the treatment appear to have been randomly assigned in the reweighted data. To do this, we reweight the sample by $1/P(T = t|X)$ in order to create a pseudo-population that approximates what would have happened if everyone had received the treatment t:

$$E[Y_t] = E\left[\frac{\mathbb{1}(T = t)Y}{P(T = t|X)}\right]$$

Once again, the proof for this is not complicated, but beside the point here. So let's stick with intuition. Suppose you want to know the expectation of Y_1, that is, of what would be the average engagement had all managers taken the training. To get that, you take all those who are treated and scale them by the inverse probability of getting the treatment. This puts a high weight on those with very low probability of treatment, but that nonetheless got it. You are essentially up-weighting rare treatment examples.

This makes sense, right? If a treated individual has a low probability of treatment, that individual looks a lot like the untreated. This must be interesting! This treated unit that looks like the untreated will probably be very informative of what would happen to the untreated, had they been treated, $Y_1|T = 0$. That is why you give a high weight to that unit. Same thing for the control. If a control unit looks a lot like the treated group, it is probably a good estimate for $Y_0|T = 1$, so you give it more weight.

Here is what this process looks like with the management training data, with weights depicted as the size of each dot:

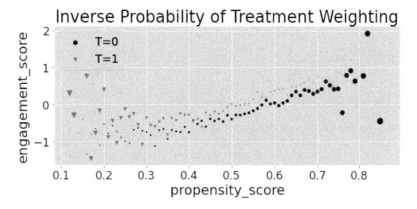

Notice how those managers who got the training, $T = 1$, have a high weight when $\hat{e}(X)$ is low. You are giving high importance to the treated that look like the untreated. Conversely, the untreated have a high weight when $\hat{e}(X)$ is high, or when $\hat{P}(T = 0 \mid X)$ is low. Here you are giving high importance to the untreated that look like the treated.

If you can use the propensity score to recover the average potential outcome, it also means you can use it to recover the ATE:

$$ATE = E\left[\frac{\mathbb{1}(T = 1)Y}{P(T = 1 \mid X)}\right] - E\left[\frac{\mathbb{1}(T = 0)Y}{P(T = 0 \mid X)}\right]$$

Both expectations can be estimated from data with very simple code:

```
In [9]: weight_t = 1/data_ps.query("intervention==1")["propensity_score"]
        weight_nt = 1/(1-data_ps.query("intervention==0")["propensity_score"])
        t1 = data_ps.query("intervention==1")["engagement_score"]
        t0 = data_ps.query("intervention==0")["engagement_score"]

        y1 = sum(t1*weight_t)/len(data_ps)
        y0 = sum(t0*weight_nt)/len(data_ps)

        print("E[Y1]:", y1)
        print("E[Y0]:", y0)
        print("ATE", y1 - y0)

Out[9]: E[Y1]: 0.11656317232946772
        E[Y0]: -0.1494155364781444
        ATE 0.2659787088076121
```

Using this approach, the ATE is once again smaller than the one you got naively, not adjusting for X. Moreover, this result looks pretty similar to the one you got by using OLS, which is a good check to make sure you didn't do anything wrong. It is also worth noticing that the ATE expression can be simplified to the following:

$$ATE = E\left[Y\frac{T - e(x)}{e(x)(1 - e(x))}\right]$$

Sure enough, it produces the exact same result as before:

```
In [10]: np.mean(data_ps["engagement_score"]
                 * (data_ps["intervention"] - data_ps["propensity_score"])
                 / (data_ps["propensity_score"]*(1-data_ps["propensity_score"])))

Out[10]: 0.26597870880761226
```

Regression and IPW

The preceding formula is very neat because it also gives you some insight into how IPW compares to regression. With regression, you are recovering the treatment effect with

$$\tau_{ols} = \frac{E[Y(T - E[T|X])]}{E[Var(T|X)]} .$$

With that in mind, recall that the variance of a Bernoulli variable with probability p is simply $p(1 - p)$. Hence, the IPW is recovering the treatment effect with

$$\tau_{ipw} = E\left[\frac{Y(T - E[T|X])}{Var(T|X)}\right].$$

Notice the similarity? To make it more transparent, since $1/E[Var(X|T)]$ is a constant, you can move it inside the expectation and rewrite the regression estimator as follows:

$$\tau_{ols} = E\left[\frac{Y(T - E[T|X])}{E[Var(T|X)]}\right] = E\left[\frac{Y(T - E[T|X])}{Var(T|X)} \star W\right]$$

with $W = Var(T|X)/E[Var(T|X)]$.

Now, the thing inside the expectation in the IPW estimator identifies the effect (CATE) in the groups defined by X. So, the difference between IPW and OLS is the first weights each sample by 1, while regression weights the group effects by the conditional treatment variance. This is in line with what you learned in the previous chapter, about regression upweighting effects where the treatment varies a lot. So, even though regression and IPW look different, they are doing almost same thing, up to the weighting point.

Variance of IPW

Unfortunately, computing the standard error for IPW is not as straightforward as with linear regression. The most straightforward way to obtain a confidence interval around your IPW estimate is by using the bootstrap method. With this method, you will repeatedly resample the data with replacement to obtain multiple IPW estimators. You can then calculate the 2.5th and 97.5th percentiles of these estimates to obtain a 95% confidence interval.

To code that, let's first wrap your IPW estimation into a reusable function. Notice how I'm replacing `statsmodels` with `sklearn`. The `logit` function in `statsmodels` is slower than the logistic regression model from sklearn, so this change will save you some time. Also, since you probably don't want to lose the convenience of formulas you get from statsmodels, I'm using patsy's dmatrix function. This function engineers a feature matrix based on an R-style formula, like the ones you've been using so far:

```
In [11]: from sklearn.linear_model import LogisticRegression
         from patsy import dmatrix

         # define function that computes the IPW estimator
         def est_ate_with_ps(df, ps_formula, T, Y):

             X = dmatrix(ps_formula, df)
             ps_model = LogisticRegression(penalty="none",
                                           max_iter=1000).fit(X, df[T])
             ps = ps_model.predict_proba(X)[:, 1]

             # compute the ATE
             return np.mean((df[T]-ps) / (ps*(1-ps)) * df[Y])
```

Probability Prediction

By default, sklearn's classifiers output 0 or 1 predictions following the logic $\hat{P}(Y|X) > 0.5$. Since you want your model to output a probability, you'll have to use the predict_proba method. This method outputs a two column matrix, where the first column is $\hat{P}(Y = 0|X)$ and the second column, $\hat{P}(Y = 1|X)$. You only want the second one, which in this case is $\hat{P}(T = 1|X)$. Hence, the indexing [:, 1].

Here is how you would use this function:

```
In [12]: formula = """tenure + last_engagement_score + department_score
         + C(n_of_reports) + C(gender) + C(role)"""
         T = "intervention"
         Y = "engagement_score"

         est_ate_with_ps(df, formula, T, Y)
```

```
Out[12]: 0.2659755621752663
```

Now that you have the code to compute ATE inside a neat function, you can apply it inside a bootstrap procedure. To speed things up, I'm also going to run the resampling in parallel. All you have to do is call the data frame method .sample(frac=1, replace=True) to get a bootstrap sample. Then, pass this sample to the function you created earlier. To make the bootstrap code more generic, one of its arguments is an estimator function, `est_fn`, which takes a data frame and returns a single number as an estimate. I'm using four jobs, but feel free to set this to the number of cores in your computer.

Run this estimator multiple times, one in each bootstrap sample, and you'll end up with an array of estimates. Finally, to get the 95% CI, just take the 2.5 and 97.5 percentiles of that array:

```
In [13]: from joblib import Parallel, delayed # for parallel processing

         def bootstrap(data, est_fn, rounds=200, seed=123, pcts=[2.5, 97.5]):
             np.random.seed(seed)

             stats = Parallel(n_jobs=4)(
                 delayed(est_fn)(data.sample(frac=1, replace=True))
                 for _ in range(rounds)
             )

             return np.percentile(stats, pcts)
```

I tend to lean toward functional programming in my code, which might not be familiar to everyone. For this reason, I'll add notes explaining some of the functional patterns that I'm using, starting with the `partial` function.

Partial

partial takes in a function and some of its arguments and returns another function just like the input one, but with the arguments that you passed already applied:

```
def addNumber(x, number):
    return x + number

add2 = partial(addNumber, number=2)
add4 = partial(addNumber, number=4)

add2(3)
>>> 5

add4(3)
>>> 7
```

I'll use `partial` to take the `est_ate_with_ps` function and partially apply the formula, the treatment, and the outcome arguments. This will give me a function that has a data frame as its only input and that outputs the ATE estimate. I can then pass this function as the `est_fn` argument to the bootstrap function I created earlier:

```
In [14]: from toolz import partial
```

```
    print(f"ATE: {est_ate_with_ps(df, formula, T, Y)}")

    est_fn = partial(est_ate_with_ps, ps_formula=formula, T=T, Y=Y)
    print(f"95% C.I.: ", bootstrap(df, est_fn))


Out[14]: ATE: 0.2659755621752663
         95% C.I.:  [0.22654315 0.30072595]
```

This 95% is about as wide as the one you got earlier, with linear regression. It's important to realize that the variance in the propensity score estimator will be large if you have big weights. Big weights means that some units have a big impact in the final estimate. A few units having a big impact in the final estimate is precisely what causes the variance.

You'll have big weights if you have few control units in the region with high propensity score or a few treated units in the region with low propensity score. This will cause you to have few units to estimate the counterfactuals $Y_0|T = 1$ and $Y_1|T = 0$, which might give you a very noisy result.

PRACTICAL EXAMPLE

Causal Contextual Bandits

Contextual bandits is a flavor of reinforcement learning where the goal is to learn an optional decision-making policy. It merges a sampling component, which balances gathering data in unexplored regions with allocating the best treatment, and an estimation component, which tries to figure out the best treatment with the available data.

The estimation component can be easily framed as a causal inference problem, where you wish to learn the best treatment assignment mechanism, where *best* is defined in terms of the expected value of a desired outcome Y you wish to optimize. Since the algorithm goal is to allocate the treatment in an optimal manner, the data it gathers is confounded (not random). This is why a causal approach to contextual bandits can yield significant improvements.

If the decision-making process is probabilistic, you can store the probability of assigning each treatment, which is exactly the propensity score $e(x)$. Then, you can use this propensity score to reweight the past data, where the treatment has already been selected and the outcome is already observed. This reweighted data should be unconfounded and hence much easier to learn what is the optimal treatment.

Stabilized Propensity Weights

Weighting the treated samples by $1/P(T = 1|X)$ creates a pseudo-population the same size as the original one, but as though everyone was treated. This means that the sum of the weights is about the same as the original sample size. Likewise, weighting the control by $1/P(T = 0|X)$ creates a pseudo-population that behaves as though everyone had the control.

If you come from a machine learning background, you might recognize IPW as an application of importance sampling. With importance sampling, you have data from an origin distribution $q(x)$ but want to sample from a target distribution $p(x)$. To do that, you can reweight the data from $q(x)$ by $p(x)/q(x)$. Bringing this to an IPW context, weighting the treated by $1/P(T = 1|X)$ essentially means you are taking data that came from $P(T = 1|X)$—which is biased if X also causes Y—and reconstructing $P(T = 1) = 1$, where the treatment probability does not depend on X, since it is just 1. This also explains why the resulting re-weighted sample behaves as if everyone in the original sample was treated.

Another way to see that is to notice how the sum of the weights for both the treatment and the untreated are pretty close to the original sample size:

```
In [15]: print("Original Sample Size", data_ps.shape[0])
         print("Treated Pseudo-Population Sample Size", sum(weight_t))
         print("Untreated Pseudo-Population Sample Size", sum(weight_nt))
```

```
Out[15]: Original Sample Size 10391
         Treated Pseudo-Population Sample Size 10435.089079197916
         Untreated Pseudo-Population Sample Size 10354.298899788304
```

This is fine, as long as you don't have weights that are too large. But if a treatment is very unlikely, $P(T|X)$ can be tiny, which might cause you some computational issues. A simple solution is to stabilize the weights using the marginal probability of treatment, $P(T = t)$:

$$w = \frac{P(T = t)}{P(T = t|X)}$$

With these weights, a treatment with low probability won't have massive weights because the small denominator will be balanced by the also small numerator. This won't change the results you got earlier, but it is more computationally stable.

Moreover, the stabilized weights reconstruct a pseudo-population where the effective size (sum of the weights) of both treated and control matches that of the original treated and control groups, respectively. Again, making a parallel with importance sampling, with stabilized weights, you are coming from a distribution where the treatment depends on X, $P(T = t|X)$, but reconstructing the marginal $P(T = t)$:

```
In [16]: p_of_t = data_ps["intervention"].mean()

         t1 = data_ps.query("intervention==1")
         t0 = data_ps.query("intervention==0")

         weight_t_stable = p_of_t/t1["propensity_score"]
         weight_nt_stable = (1-p_of_t)/(1-t0["propensity_score"])

         print("Treat size:", len(t1))
         print("W treat", sum(weight_t_stable))

         print("Control size:", len(t0))
         print("W treat", sum(weight_nt_stable))

Out[16]: Treat size: 5611
         W treat 5634.807508745978
         Control size: 4780
         W treat 4763.116999421415
```

Again, this stabilization keeps the same balancing properties of the original propensity score. You can verify that it yields the exact same ATE estimate as you had before:

```
In [17]: nt = len(t1)
         nc = len(t0)

         y1 = sum(t1["engagement_score"]*weight_t_stable)/nt
         y0 = sum(t0["engagement_score"]*weight_nt_stable)/nc

         print("ATE: ", y1 - y0)

Out[17]: ATE:  0.26597870880761176
```

Pseudo-Populations

I've mentioned pseudo-populations already, but understanding them better will help you appreciate how IPW removes bias. Let's first think about what bias means from the perspective of $P(T|X)$. If the treatment was randomly assigned with probability, say, 10%, you know that the treatment would not depend on X, or that $P(T|X) = P(T) = 10\%$. So, if the treatment is independent from X, you would not have confounding bias flowing through X and no adjustment would be needed. If you do have this sort of bias, then some units have a higher chance of getting the treatment. For example, it could be that very passionate managers, who already have a very engaged team, are more likely to take the training (have higher $e(T)$) than the managers whose teams are not so engaged.

If you plot the distribution of $\hat{e}(x)$ by treatment status, since managers don't have the same chance of taking the training (treatment is not random), treated individuals will have higher $\hat{e}(x)$. You can see that in the plot on the left in the following figure, where the treated distribution for $\hat{e}(x)$ is a bit shifted to the right:

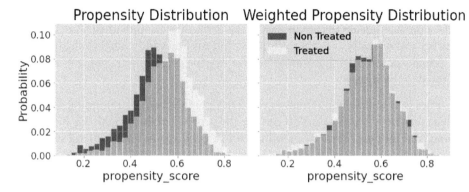

Contrast this with the plot on the right. Here, in the low $\hat{e}(X)$ region, treated are up-weighted and control, down-weighted. Similarly, when $\hat{e}(X)$ is high, treated units are down-weighted and control, up-weighted. These movements make the two distributions overlap. The fact that they do means that, on the weighted data, treated and control have the same chance of getting both the treatment or the control. In other words, treatment assignment looks as good as random (assuming no unobserved confounders, of course).

This also sheds some light on what IPW is doing. By taking the treated's outcome, $Y|T = 1$, and up-weighting those where $\hat{e}(X)$ is low and down-weighting those where $\hat{e}(X)$, you are trying to figure out what $Y_1|T = 0$ would look like. A similar argument can be made to show how you are also trying to learn $Y_0|T = 1$ by reweighting the control sample by $1/(1 - P(T = 1))$.

Selection Bias

The example used here is meant to show how propensity score weighting can be used to adjust for common causes, making the treatment similar to the control and vice versa. That is, you saw how to use propensity score weighting as a way to account and control for confounding bias. However, IPW can also be used to adjust for selection issues. In fact, the IPW estimator was initially used in this context, as presented by Horvitz and Thompson in 1952. For this reason, you might see the IPW estimator as the Horvitz-Thompson estimator.

To give an example, suppose you want to know the satisfaction of your customers with your app. So you send out a survey asking them to rate your product on a 1-to-5 scale. Naturally, some customers don't respond. But the issue with this is that it can bias your analysis. If the nonrespondents are mostly unsatisfied customers, the result you'll get back from the survey will be an artificially inflated rate.

To adjust for that you can estimate the probability of responding, R, given customer's covariates (like age, income, app usage, etc.), $P(R = 1|X)$. Then, you can reweight those who responded by $1/\hat{P}(R = 1)$. This will up-weight the respondents that look like the nonrespondents (have low $\hat{P}(R = 1)$). With this, an individual who answered the survey will not only account for himself, but for other individuals like him, creating a pseudo-population that should behave like the original one, but as if everyone responded to the survey.

Sometimes (but hopefully not many), you'll have to face both confounding and selection bias together. In this case, you can use the product of the weights for both selection and confounding. Since this product can be quite small, I recommend stabilizing the confounding bias weights with the marginal probability $P(T = t)$:

$$W = \frac{\hat{P}(T = t)}{\hat{P}(R = 1|X)\hat{P}(T = t|X)}$$

Bias-Variance Trade-Off

As the naive data scientist that I was, when I learned about propensity scores I thought "Oh boy! This is huge! I can transform a causal inference problem into a prediction problem. If I can just predict $e(x)$, I'm golden!" Unfortunately, it is not that simple. In my defense, that is an easy mistake to make. At first glance, it does seem that the better your estimate of the treatment assignment mechanism, the better your causal estimates will be. But that is simply not the case.

Remember when you learned about noise-inducing controls, in Chapter 4? The same logic applies here. If you have a covariate X_k that is a very good predictor of T, this variable will give you a very accurate model of $e(x)$. But if that same variable does not cause Y, it is not a confounder and it will only increase the variance of your IPW estimate. To see this, think about what would happen if you have a very good model of T. This model would output a very high $\hat{e}(x)$ for all treated units (as it correctly predicts that they are treated) and a very low $\hat{e}(x)$ for all the control units (as it correctly predicts that they are untreated). This would leave you no treated units with low $\hat{e}(x)$ to estimate $Y_1|T = 0$ and no control units with high $\hat{e}(x)$ to estimate $Y_0|T = 1$.

In contrast, think about what would happen if the treatment was randomized. In this case, the predictive power of $\hat{e}(x)$ should be zero! In the managers training example, under randomization, managers with higher $\hat{e}(x)$ would not be more likely to participate in the training than those with lower $\hat{e}(x)$. Still, even with no predictive power, this is the best situation you'll get in terms of estimating the treatment effect.

As you can see, there is also a bias-variance trade-off when it comes to IPW. In general, the more precise the propensity score model, the lower the bias. However, a very precise model for $e(x)$ will generate a very imprecise effect estimate. This means you have to make your model precise enough to control for the bias, but not too much, or you'll run into variance issues.

Trimming

One way to lower the variance of the IPW estimator is to trim the propensity score to be always above a certain number—say, 1%—to avoid weights that are too big—say, above 100. Equivalently, you can directly clip the weights to never be too large. The IPW with clipped weights is no longer unbiased, but it might have lower mean square error if the variance reduction is expressive.

Positivity

The bias–variance trade-off can also be viewed in the light of two causal inference assumptions: conditional independence (unconfoundedness) and positivity. The more precise you make your model for $e(x)$, say, by adding more variables to it, the more you go in the direction of making the CIA hold. However, you also make positivity less plausible for the reasons you already saw: you'll concentrate the treatment in a low $\hat{e}(x)$ region, far away from the controls and vice versa.

The IPW reconstruction is only possible if you have samples to reweight. If there are no treated samples in the region with low propensity score (high chance of being the control), there is no amount of reweight you can do to reconstruct Y_1 in that region. This is what positivity violations look like in terms of IPW. Also, even if positivity is not entirely violated, but some units have very small or large propensity scores, IPW will suffer from high variance.

To see this on a more intuitive level, consider the following simulated data. Here, the true ATE is 1. However, x confounds the relationship between T and Y. The higher the X, the smaller the Y, but the higher the chance of receiving the treatment. Hence, a naive comparison in the average outcome between treated and control will be downward biased and can even be negative:

```
In [18]: np.random.seed(1)

         n = 1000
         x = np.random.normal(0, 1, n)
         t = np.random.normal(x, 0.5, n) > 0

         y0 = -x
         y1 = y0 + t  # ate of 1

         y = np.random.normal((1-t)*y0 + t*y1, 0.2)
```

```
df_no_pos = pd.DataFrame(dict(x=x,t=t.astype(int),y=y))

df_no_pos.head()
```

	x	t	y
0	1.624345	1	−0.526442
1	−0.611756	0	0.659516
2	−0.528172	0	0.438549
3	−1.072969	0	0.950810
4	0.865408	1	−0.271397

If you estimate the propensity score in this data, some units (with high x) have a propensity score very close to 1, meaning it is almost impossible for them to get the control. In a similar manner, some units have almost zero chance of getting the treatment (those with low x). You can see this in the following image's middle plot. Notice the lack of overlap between the treated and untreated propensity score distribution. This is very troublesome, as it means that a huge chunk of the control distribution is condensed where $e(x)$ is close to zero, but you have no treated unit to reconstruct that region. As a consequence, you end up lacking a good estimate for $Y_1|T = 0$ for a good portion of the data:

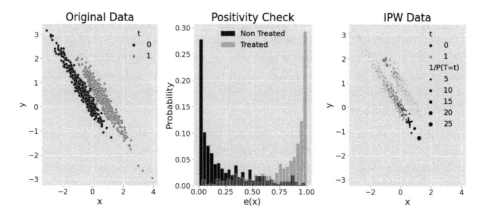

Additionally, as you can see in the third plot, the control units to the right (high $e(x)$) have massive weights. A similar thing can be said about the treated units to the left (small $e(x)$). As you know by now, these huge weights will generally increase the variance of the IPW estimator.

Combine these two problems—high variance and positivity violation—and you'll see how the IPW estimator fails to recover the ATE of 1 in this data:

```
In [19]: est_fn = partial(est_ate_with_ps, ps_formula="x", T="t", Y="y")
         print("ATE:", est_fn(df_no_pos))
         print(f"95% C.I.: ", bootstrap(df_no_pos, est_fn))


Out[19]: ATE: 0.6478011810615735
         95% C.I.: [0.41710504 0.88840195]
```

It's important to note that this isn't simply a problem of high variance. Sure, the 95% CI of this estimator is large, but it is more than that. Specifically, the upper end of the confidence interval still appears to be significantly lower than the true ATE of 1.

Lack of positivity is a problem not only for the IPW estimator. However, IPW can be more transparent about positivity issues. For instance, if you plot the distribution of the propensity score (the plot in the middle of the preceding image) for the treatment variants, you can visually check if you have decent levels of positivity.

In fact, let's contrast the IPW estimator with linear regression. You know that regression will not be very transparent about positivity violations. Instead, it will extrapolate to the regions where you have no data whatsoever. In some very lucky situations, this might even work. For instance, in this very simple simulated data, regression manages to recover the ATE of 1, but only because it correctly extrapolates both Y_0 and Y_1 to the treated and control region where there is no actual data:

```
In [20]: smf.ols("y ~ x + t", data=df_no_pos).fit().params["t"]


Out[20]: 1.0165855487679483
```

In a sense, regression can replace the positivity assumption for a parametric assumption on $E[Y|T, X]$, which is essentially an assumption about smoothness in the potential outcomes. If the linear model has a good fit to the conditional expectation, it will manage to recover the ATE even in regions where positivity doesn't hold. In contrast, IPW makes no assumptions on the shape of the potential outcome. As a result, it fails when extrapolation is needed.

Design- Versus Model-Based Identification

You've just learned how to use propensity score weighting to estimate the treatment effect. Along with regression, this already gives two—and the most important—methods to debias nonexperimental data. But which one should you use and when? Regression or IPW?

Implicit in this choice is the discussion of *model-based versus design-based* identification. Model-based identification involves making assumptions in the form of a model of the potential outcomes conditioned on the treatment and additional covariates.

From this perspective, the goal is to impute the missing potential outcomes required for estimation. In contrast, design-based identification is all about making assumptions about the treatment assignment mechanism. In Chapter 4, you saw how regression fits both kinds of strategy: from the perspective of orthogonalization, it is design-based; from the perspective of an estimator for the potential outcome model, it is model-based. In this chapter, you learned about IPW, which is purely design-based, and in later chapters, you'll learn about Synthetic Control, which is purely model-based.

So, in order to choose between a design- or model-based identification, you need to ask yourself which type of assumption you are more comfortable with. Do you have a good understanding of how the treatment was assigned? Or do you have a better chance in correctly specifying a potential outcome model?

Doubly Robust Estimation

The good news is that, when in doubt, you can just choose both! Doubly robust (DR) estimation is a way of combining both model- and design-based identification, hoping that at least one of them is correct. Here, let's see how to combine propensity score and linear regression in a way that only one of them needs to be rightly specified. Let me show you a popular DR estimator and tell you why it is awesome.

Quite generally, a doubly robust estimator for the counterfactual Y_t can be written as follows:

$$\hat{\mu}_t^{DR}(\hat{m}, \hat{e}) = \frac{1}{N}\sum \hat{m}(X) + \frac{1}{N}\sum\left[\frac{T}{\hat{e}(x)}(Y - \hat{m}(X))\right]$$

where $\hat{m}(X)$ is a model for $E[Y_t|X]$ (linear regression, for example) and $\hat{e}(X)$ is a propensity score model for $P(T|X)$. Now, the reason why this is amazing—and why it is called doubly robust—is that it only requires one of the models, $\hat{m}(X)$ or $\hat{e}(X)$, to be correctly specified.

For example, suppose that the propensity score model was wrong, but the outcome model $\hat{m}(X)$ was correct. In this case, the second term would converge to zero, since $E[Y = \hat{m}(X)] = 0$. You would be left with the first term, which is just the outcome model, which is correct.

Next, let's consider a scenario where the outcome model is incorrect, but the propensity score model is accurate. To explore this possibility, you can perform some algebraic manipulation on the preceding formula and rewrite it as follows:

$$\hat{\mu}_t^{DR}(\hat{m}, \hat{e}) = \frac{1}{N}\sum \frac{TY}{\hat{e}(X)} + \frac{1}{N}\sum\left[\frac{T - \hat{e}(X)}{\hat{e}(X)}\hat{m}(X)\right]$$

I hope this makes it more clear. If the propensity model is correct, $T - \hat{e}(X)$ would converge to zero. That would leave you only the first term, which is the IPW estimator. And since the propensity model is correct, this estimator would be too. That's the beauty of this doubly robust estimator: it converges to whichever model is correct.

The preceding estimator would estimate the average counterfactual outcome Y_t. If you want to estimate the average treatment effect, all you have to do is put two of those estimators together, one for $E[Y_0]$ and one for $E[Y_1]$, and take the difference:

$$ATE = \hat{\mu}_1^{DR}(\hat{m}, \hat{e}) - \hat{\mu}_0^{DR}(\hat{m}, \hat{e})$$

Having understood the theory behind DR, it's time to code it up. The models $\hat{e}$ and $\hat{m}$ don't have to be a logistic and linear regression, respectively, but I think those are very good candidates for a starter. Once again, I'll begin by using the R-style formula from patsy's dmatrix to engineer my covariate matrix X. Next, I'm using logistic regression to fit the propensity model and get $\hat{e}(X)$. Then comes the output model part. I'm fitting one linear regression per treatment variant, giving me two of them—one for the treated and one for the control. Each model is fitted on the subset of the data of its treatment variant, but makes predictions for the entire dataset. For example, the control model fits only in the data where $T = 0$, but it predicts everything. This prediction is an estimate for Y_0.

Finally, I'm combining the two models to form the DR estimator for both $E[Y_0]$ and $E[Y_1]$. This is simply the translation of the formula you just saw into code:

```
In [21]: from sklearn.linear_model import LinearRegression

         def doubly_robust(df, formula, T, Y):
             X = dmatrix(formula, df)

             ps_model = LogisticRegression(penalty="none",
                                           max_iter=1000).fit(X, df[T])
             ps = ps_model.predict_proba(X)[:, 1]

             m0 = LinearRegression().fit(X[df[T]==0, :], df.query(f"{T}==0")[Y])
             m1 = LinearRegression().fit(X[df[T]==1, :], df.query(f"{T}==1")[Y])

             m0_hat = m0.predict(X)
             m1_hat = m1.predict(X)

             return (
                 np.mean(df[T]*(df[Y] - m1_hat)/ps + m1_hat) -
                 np.mean((1-df[T])*(df[Y] - m0_hat)/(1-ps) + m0_hat)
             )
```

Let's see how it performs in the manager training data. You can also pass it to your bootstrap function to construct a confidence interval for the DR ATE estimate:

```
In [22]: formula = """tenure + last_engagement_score + department_score
         + C(n_of_reports) + C(gender) + C(role)"""
         T = "intervention"
         Y = "engagement_score"

         print("DR ATE:", doubly_robust(df, formula, T, Y))

         est_fn = partial(doubly_robust, formula=formula, T=T, Y=Y)
         print("95% CI", bootstrap(df, est_fn))


Out[22]: DR ATE: 0.27115831057931455
         95% CI [0.23012681 0.30524944]
```

As you can see, the result is pretty in line with both the IPW and the regression estimator you saw earlier. This is good news, as it means the DR estimator is not doing anything crazy. But honestly, it is kind of boring and it doesn't exactly show the power of DR. So, to better understand why DR is so interesting, let's craft two new examples. They will be fairly simple, but very illustrative.

Treatment Is Easy to Model

The first example is one where the treatment assignment is fairly easy to model, but the outcome model is a bit more complicated. Specifically, the treatment follows a Bernoulli distribution with probability given by the following propensity score:

$$e(x) = \frac{1}{1 + e^{-(1 + 1.5x)}}$$

In case you didn't recognize, this is exactly the kind of form the logistic regression assumes, so it should be pretty easy to estimate it. Moreover, since $P(T|X)$ is easy to model, the IPW score should have no problem finding the true ATE here, which is close to 2. In contrast, since the outcome Y is a bit trickier, a regression model might run into some trouble:

```
In [23]: np.random.seed(123)

         n = 10000
         x = np.random.beta(1,1, n).round(2)*2
         e = 1/(1+np.exp(-(1+1.5*x)))
         t = np.random.binomial(1, e)

         y1 = 1
         y0 = 1 - 1*x**3
         y = t*(y1) + (1-t)*y0 + np.random.normal(0, 1, n)
```

```
df_easy_t = pd.DataFrame(dict(y=y, x=x, t=t))

print("True ATE:", np.mean(y1-y0))
```

Out[23]: True ATE: 2.0056243152

The following two plots show what this data looks like. It is interesting to notice the effect heterogeneity in the data, which is easy to see in the second plot. Notice how the effect is 0 for low values of x and it increases nonlinearly as x increases. This sort of heterogeneity is oftentimes hard for regression to get it right:

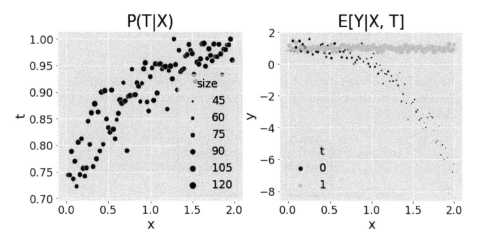

Now, let's see how regression does in this data. Here I'm once again fitting $\widehat{m}_1$ and $\widehat{m}_0$ separately and estimating the ATE as the average of the different predictions in the entire dataset, $N^{-1}\sum\left(\widehat{m}_1(x) - \widehat{m}_0(X)\right)$:

```
In [24]: m0 = smf.ols("y~x", data=df_easy_t.query("t==0")).fit()
         m1 = smf.ols("y~x", data=df_easy_t.query("t==1")).fit()
         regr_ate = (m1.predict(df_easy_t) - m0.predict(df_easy_t)).mean()

         print("Regression ATE:", regr_ate)
```

Out[24]: Regression ATE: 1.786678396833022

As expected, the regression model fails to recover the true ATE of 2. If you plot the predicted values against the original data you can see why. Regression fails to capture the curvature in the control group:

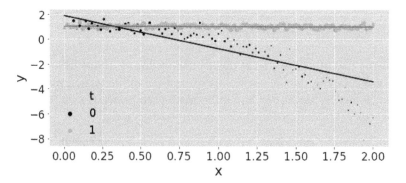

To be clear, this doesn't mean it is not possible to correctly estimate the ATE with regression. If you knew about the true curvature of the data, you could pretty much model it correctly:

```
In [25]: m = smf.ols("y~t*(x + np.power(x, 3))", data=df_easy_t).fit()
         regr_ate = (m.predict(df_easy_t.assign(t=1))
                     - m.predict(df_easy_t.assign(t=0))).mean()

         print("Regression ATE:", regr_ate)


Out[25]: Regression ATE: 1.9970999747190072
```

But, of course, in reality, you don't really know how the data was generated. So, more likely than not, regression would have failed you here. In contrast, let's see how IPW does. Again, since it is pretty easy to model the treatment assignment, you should expect IPW to perform quite well on this data:

```
In [26]: est_fn = partial(est_ate_with_ps, ps_formula="x", T="t", Y="y")
         print("Propensity Score ATE:", est_fn(df_easy_t))
         print("95% CI", bootstrap(df_easy_t, est_fn))


Out[26]: Propensity Score ATE: 2.002350388474011
         95% CI [1.80802227 2.22565667]
```

Notice how IPW pretty much nails the correct ATE.

Finally, the moment you've been waiting for, let's see the DR estimate in action. Remember, DR requires one of the models—$P(T|X)$ or $E[Y_t|X]$—to be correct, but not necessarily both. In this data, the model for $P(T|X)$ will be correct, but the model for $E[Y_t|X]$ will be wrong:

```
In [27]: est_fn = partial(doubly_robust, formula="x", T="t", Y="y")
         print("DR ATE:", est_fn(df_easy_t))
         print("95% CI", bootstrap(df_easy_t, est_fn))


Out[27]: DR ATE: 2.001617934263116
         95% CI [1.87088771 2.145382]
```

As expected, the DR performs quite well here, also recovering the true ATE. But there is more. Notice how the 95% CI is smaller than that of pure IPW estimate, meaning the DR estimator is more precise here. This simple example shows how DR can perform well when $P(T|X)$ is easy to model even if it gets $E[Y_t|X]$ wrong. But what about the other way around?

Outcome Is Easy to Model

In this next simple yet illustrative example, the complexity is in $P(T|X)$ rather than $E[Y_t|X]$. Notice the nonlinearity in $P(T|X)$, while the outcome function is simply linear. Here, the true ATE is −1:

```
In [28]: np.random.seed(123)

         n = 10000
         x = np.random.beta(1,1, n).round(2)*2
         e = 1/(1+np.exp(-(2*x - x**3)))
         t = np.random.binomial(1, e)

         y1 = x
         y0 = y1 + 1 # ate of -1
         y = t*(y1) + (1-t)*y0 + np.random.normal(0, 1, n)

         df_easy_y = pd.DataFrame(dict(y=y, x=x, t=t))

         print("True ATE:", np.mean(y1-y0))


Out[28]: True ATE: -1.0
```

The same kind of plot from before can be used to show the complex functional form for $P(T|X)$ and the simplicity of $E[Y_t|X]$:

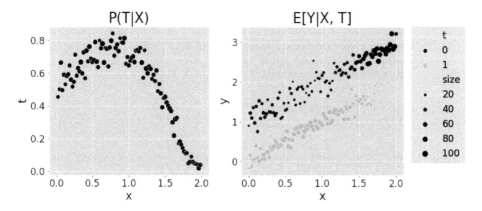

With this data, since the propensity score is relatively complex to model, IPW does not manage to recover the true ATE:

```
In [29]: est_fn = partial(est_ate_with_ps, ps_formula="x", T="t", Y="y")
         print("Propensity Score ATE:", est_fn(df_easy_y))
         print("95% CI", bootstrap(df_easy_y, est_fn))


Out[29]: Propensity Score ATE: -1.1042900278680896
         95% CI [-1.14326893 -1.06576358]
```

But regression manages to get it precisely right:

```
In [30]: m0 = smf.ols("y~x", data=df_easy_y.query("t==0")).fit()
         m1 = smf.ols("y~x", data=df_easy_y.query("t==1")).fit()
         regr_ate = (m1.predict(df_easy_y) - m0.predict(df_easy_y)).mean()

         print("Regression ATE:", regr_ate)


Out[30]: Regression ATE: -1.0008783612504342
```

Once again, because DR only needs one of the models to be correctly specified, it also manages to recover the true ATE here:

```
In [31]: est_fn = partial(doubly_robust, formula="x", T="t", Y="y")
         print("DR ATE:", est_fn(df_easy_y))
         print("95% CI", bootstrap(df_easy_y, est_fn))


Out[31]: DR ATE: -1.0028459347805823
         95% CI [-1.04156952 -0.96353366]
```

I hope these two examples made it more clear why doubly robust estimation can be very interesting. The bottom line is that it gives you two shots at being correct. In some cases, it's hard to model $P(T|X)$, but easy to model $E[Y_t|X]$. In others, the reverse might be true. Regardless, as long as you can model one of them correctly, you can combine a model for $P(T|X)$ and a model for $E[Y_t|X]$ in a way that only one of them needs to be correct. This is the true power of the doubly robust estimator.

See Also

The DR estimator covered here is only one of the many out there. Just to give some examples, you could take the DR estimator covered in this chapter but fit the regression model with weights set to $\hat{e}(x)$. Or, you could add $\hat{e}(x)$ to the regression model. Interestingly, linear regression alone is a DR estimator that models the treatment as $e(x) = \beta X$. It is not a very good DR estimator, since βX is not bounded between 0 and 1, as a probability model should be, but it is nonetheless a DR estimator. To learn more about other DR estimators, check out the excellent discussion in "Comment: Performance of Double-Robust Estimators When 'Inverse Probability' Weights Are Highly Variable," 2008, by Robins et al.

Generalized Propensity Score for Continuous Treatment

Until now, this chapter has only shown how to use propensity scores for discrete treatment. There is a pretty good reason for that. Continuous treatments are way more complicated to deal with. So much so that I would say that causal inference as a science doesn't have a very good answer on how to deal with them.

In Chapter 4, you managed to get away with continuous treatment by assuming a functional form for the treatment response. Something like $y = a + bt$ (linear form) or $y = a + b\sqrt{t}$ (square root form), which you could then estimate with OLS. But when it comes to propensity weighting, there is no such thing as a parametric response function. The potential outcomes are estimated nonparametrically, by reweighting and taking averages. When T is continuous, there exist infinitely many potential outcomes Y_t. Furthermore, since the probability of a continuous variable is always zero, it is not feasible to estimate $P(T = t|X)$ in this scenario.

The simplest way out of these issues is to discretize the continuous treatment into a coarser version that can then be treated as discrete. But there is another way out, which is to use the generalized propensity score. If you make some changes to the traditional propensity score, you'll be able to accommodate any type of treatment. To see how this would work, consider the following example.

A bank wants to know how a loan's interest rates affect the duration (in months) that the customer chooses to pay back that loan. Intuitively speaking, the effect of interest on the duration should be negative, since people like to pay back high-rate loans as fast as possible to avoid paying too much on interest.

To answer this question, the bank could randomize the interest rate, but this would be costly, both in money and in time. Instead, it wants to use the data it already has. The bank knows that interest rates were assigned by two machine learning models: ml_1 and ml_2. Additionally, since the bank's data scientists were very smart, they added a random Gaussian noise to the interest rate decision-making process. This ensures that the policy is nondeterministic and that the positivity assumption is not violated. The observational (nonrandomized) interest data, along with information on the confounders ml_1 and ml_2 and the outcome duration is stored in the df_cont_t data frame:

```
In [32]: df_cont_t = pd.read_csv("./data/interest_rate.csv")

         df_cont_t.head()
```

	ml_1	ml_2	interest	duration
0	0.392938	0.326285	7.1	12.0
1	−0.427721	0.679573	5.6	17.0
2	−0.546297	0.647309	11.1	12.0
3	0.102630	−0.264776	7.2	18.0
4	0.438938	−0.648818	9.5	19.0

Your task is to unbias the relationship between interest rate and duration, adjusting for ml_1 and ml_2. Notice that, if you estimate the treatment effect naively, not adjusting for anything, you'll find a positive treatment effect. As discussed already, this makes no business sense, so this result is probably biased:

```
In [33]: m_naive = smf.ols("duration ~ interest", data=df_cont_t).fit()
         m_naive.summary().tables[1]
```

	coef	std err	t	P>|t|	[0.025	0.975]
Intercept	14.5033	0.226	64.283	0.000	14.061	14.946
interest	0.3393	0.029	11.697	0.000	0.282	0.396

To adjust for ml_1 and ml_2, you could just include them in your model, but let's see how to manage the same thing with reweighting. The first challenge that needs to be addressed is the fact that continuous variables have a probability of zero everywhere, i.e., $P(T = t) = 0$. This occurs because the probability is represented by the area under the density, and the area of a single point is always zero. One possible solution is to work with the conditional density function $f(T|X)$ instead of the conditional probability $P(T = t|X)$. However, this approach presents another issue, which is specifying the distribution of the treatment.

Here, for simplicity's sake, let's assume it is drawn from a normal distribution $T \sim N(\mu_i, \sigma^2)$. This is a fairly reasonable simplification, especially since the normal distribution can be used to approximate other distributions. Moreover, let's assume constant variance σ^2, instead of one that changes for each individual.

Recall that the density of the normal distribution is given by the following function:

$$f(t_i) = \frac{exp\left(-\frac{1}{2}\left(\frac{t_i - \mu_i}{\sigma}\right)^2\right)}{\sigma\sqrt{2\pi}}$$

Now you need to estimate the parameters of this conditional Gaussian, that is, the mean and standard deviation. The simplest way to do that is using OLS to fit the treatment variable:

```
In [34]: model_t = smf.ols("interest~ml_1+ml_2", data=df_cont_t).fit()
```

Then, the fitted values will be used as μ_i and the standard deviation of the residual will be σ. With this, you have an estimate for the conditional density. Next, you'll need to evaluate that conditional density at the given treatment, which is why I'm passing T to the x argument in the density function in the following code:

```
In [35]: def conditional_density(x, mean, std):
             denom = std*np.sqrt(2*np.pi)
             num = np.exp(-((1/2)*((x-mean)/std)**2))
             return (num/denom).ravel()


         gps = conditional_density(df_cont_t["interest"],
                                   model_t.fittedvalues,
                                   np.std(model_t.resid))

         gps

Out[35]: array([0.1989118, 0.14524168, 0.03338421, ..., 0.07339096, 0.19365006,
                0.15732008])
```

Alternatively, you can (and probably should) import the normal distribution from scipy and use that instead:

```
In [36]: from scipy.stats import norm


         gps = norm(loc=model_t.fittedvalues,
```

```
            scale=np.std(model_t.resid)).pdf(df_cont_t["interest"])
gps
```

Out[36]: array([0.1989118, 0.14524168, 0.03338421, ..., 0.07339096, 0.19365006,
         0.15732008])

Beyond the Normal

If the treatment follows another distribution other than the normal, you can use generalized linear models (glm) to fit it. For example, if T was assigned according to a Poisson distribution, you could build the GPS weights with something like the following code:

```
import statsmodels.api as sm
from scipy.stats import poisson

mt = smf.glm("t~x1+x2",
             data=df, family=sm.families.Poisson()).fit()

gps = poisson(mu=m_pois.fittedvalues).pmf(df["t"])

w = 1/gps
```

Using the inverse of the GPS as weights in a regression model can adjust for the bias. You can see that now you'll find a negative effect of interest on duration, which makes more business sense:

```
In [37]: final_model = smf.wls("duration~interest",
                    data=df_cont_t, weights=1/gps).fit()

         final_model.params["interest"]
```

Out[37]: -0.6673977919925854

There is still one more improvement that can be made, which will provide a more intuitive understanding of GPS. Using this score to construct weights will assign greater importance to points with unlikely treatments. Specifically, you will assign high weights to units with high residuals in the treatment model that you have fitted. Additionally, due to the exponential nature of the normal density, the weights will increase exponentially with the size of the residual.

To illustrate this point, suppose you fit the interest rate using only ml_1, instead of both ml_1 and ml_2. This simplification enables presenting everything in a single plot. The resulting weights are displayed in the next figure. The first plot shows the original data, color-coded by the confounder ml_1. Customers with low scores on `ml_1` typically select longer durations to repay their loan. Furthermore, customers with low `ml_1` scores are assigned higher interest rates. Consequently, an upward bias exists in the relationship between interest rate and duration.

The second plot shows the fitted values of the treatment model and the weights constructed by the GPS, obtained from that model. They are larger the farther you go from the fitted line. This makes sense, as the GPS gives more weight to unlikely treatments. But look how big the weights can get. Some are bigger than 1,000!

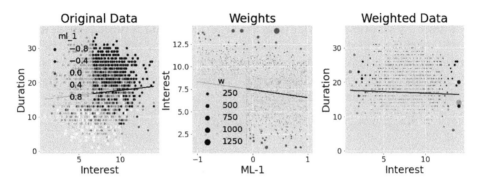

The last plot shows the same weights, but in the relationship between interest and duration. Since both low interest rates at low values of `ml_1` and high interest at high values of `ml_1` are unlikely, inverse GPS weight gives high importance to those points. This manages to reverse the positive (and biased) relationship between interest and duration. But this estimator will have huge variance, as it is practically just using a few data points—those with very high weights. Moreover, because this data was simulated, I know for a fact that the true ATE is –0.8, but the preceding estimate is only –0.66.

To improve upon it, you can stabilize the weights by the marginal density $f(t)$. Unlike with discrete treatment, where weight stabilization was just nice to have, with the GPS, I would say it is a must. To estimate $f(t)$, you can simply use the average treatment value. Then, evaluate the resulting density at the given treatments.

Notice how this produces weights that sum to (almost) the original sample size. Thinking about this in the light of importance sampling, these weights take you from $f(t|x)$ to $f(t)$, a density where the treatment does not depend on x:

```
In [38]: stabilizer = norm(
             loc=df_cont_t["interest"].mean(),
             scale=np.std(df_cont_t["interest"] - df_cont_t["interest"].mean())
         ).pdf(df_cont_t["interest"])

         gipw = stabilizer/gps

         print("Original Sample Size:", len(df_cont_t))
```

```
                print("Effective Stable Weights Sample Size:", sum(gipw))

Out[38]: Original Sample Size: 10000
         Effective Stable Weights Sample Size: 9988.19595174861
```

Again, to understand what is going on, suppose you fit $f(t|x)$ using only ml_1. Once again, inverse propensity weighting gives high importance to points that are far from the fitted values of the treatment model, as they fall in a low-density region of $f(t|x)$. But additionally, the stabilization also gives low importance to points that are far away from $f(t)$, that is, points far from the mean. The result is twofold. First, the stabilized weights are much smaller, which gives you lower variance. Second, it becomes clearer that you are now giving more importance to points with both low values of ml_1 and low interest rate (and vice versa). You can see this by the change in the color pattern between the first and third plots:

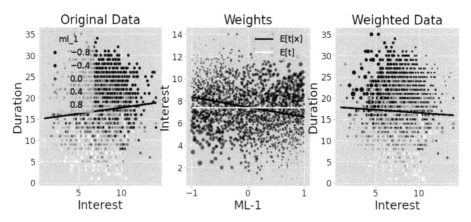

Also, these stabilized weights give you an estimate that is much closer to the true ATE of –0.8:

```
In [39]: final_model = smf.wls("duration ~ interest",
                               data=df_cont_t, weights=gipw).fit()

         final_model.params["interest"]

Out[39]: -0.7787046278134069
```

As you can see, even though weight stabilization didn't have an impact in the case where T was discrete, it is very relevant for continuous treatments. It gets you closer to the true value of the parameter you are trying to estimate and it also significantly reduces the variance. Since it is a bit repetitive, I'm omitting the code to compute the 95% CI of the estimates, but it is pretty much what you did before: just wrap the whole thing in a function and bootstrap it. But just so you can see it for yourself, here are the 95% CI with and without stabilization:

```
95% CI, non-stable:  [-0.81074164 -0.52605933]
95% CI, stable:  [-0.85834311 -0.71001914]
```

Notice how both contain the true value of –0.8, but the one with stabilization is much narrower.

Continuous Treatment Literature

There are other ways to estimate the treatment effect with models that predict the treatment. One idea (by Hirano and Imbens) is to include the GPS as a covariate in a regression function. Another option (by Imai and van Dyk) is fit T, segment the data based on the predictions $\hat{T}$, regress the treatment on the outcome on each segment defined by $\hat{T}$, and combine the results using a weighted average, where the weights are the size of each group.

For a more comprehensive survey of the available options, I recommend checking out Douglas Galagate's PhD thesis, "Causal Inference with a Continuous Treatment and Outcome."

There is also a Python package named `causal-curve` (*https://oreil.ly/8CteT*) that provides a scikit-learn–like API for modeling continuous treatment with GPS, if you don't want to code all of this by hand.

Key Ideas

Along with regression—and orthogonalization in general—inverse propensity weighting is the second workhorse for bias adjustment in your causal inference toolbox. Both techniques require you to model the treatment. This should serve as a reminder of how important it is to think about the treatment assignment mechanism in any causal inference problem. However, each technique makes use of that treatment model in a very unique way. Orthogonalization residualized the treatment, projecting it to a new space where it becomes linearly independent (orthogonal) to the covariates X that were used to model the treatment. IPW keeps the same treatment dimension, but reweights the data by the inverse of the treatment propensity:

$$w = \frac{P(T)}{P(T \mid X)}$$

This makes it look like the treatment was drawn from a distribution $P(T)$, which does not depend on the covariates X that were used to create the propensity model.

Figure 5-1 shows a simple comparison between the two approaches. In this data, treatment effect is positive, but confounded by x, which is depicted in the color schema of the data points. The first plot contains the original data along a regression line of y on y. The negative slope is due to the bias that comes from x. The next two plots show how orthogonalization and IPW debias this data using very distinct ideas. Both manage to recover a positive causal effect of t on y, as shown by their respective regression lines.

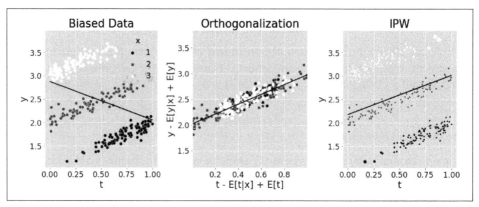

Figure 5-1. How orthogonalization and IPW remove bias

If both procedures manage to debias the data, a natural question that arises is which one should you choose. This is a bit personal, but here is my take on it. I really like IPW for when the treatment is discrete, especially if you pair it with outcome modeling in a doubly robust approach. However, when the treatment is continuous, I tend to gravitate toward regression modeling of the kind you saw in Chapter 4. With continuous treatment, you'll have very few data points around any specific treatment. As a result, a method like IPW, which doesn't pose a parametric assumption on the treatment response function, becomes less appealing. For me, it is more productive to assume some smoothness in the treatment response function, allowing you to pool information from neighboring points around a particular treatment to infer its response.

Sure, I think it is very much worth understanding approaches like the Generalized Propensity Score, as it gives you further intuition into IPW in general. That is why I've included it in this chapter. Also, as the continuous treatment literature advances, I want you to be able to keep up with it, if you wish to. But, day-to-day, when T is continuous, I think you'll be better off with outcome models like linear regression.

PART III

Effect Heterogeneity and Personalization

CHAPTER 6

Effect Heterogeneity

This chapter introduces what is perhaps the most interesting development of causal inference applied to the industry: effect heterogeneity. Up until this point, you understood the general impact of a treatment. Now, you'll focus on finding how it can affect people differently. The idea that the treatment effect is not constant is simple, yet incredibly powerful. Knowing which units respond better to a certain treatment is key in deciding who gets it. Effect heterogeneity offers a causal inference approach to the cherished idea of personalization.

You'll start by understanding effect heterogeneity on a theoretical level, what the challenges are in estimating effect heterogeneity, and how you can expand what you already learned to work around those challenges. Next, you'll see that estimating heterogeneous effects is closely related to predictive problems, which are already very familiar to data scientists. Consequently, you'll see how the idea of cross-validation and model selection still applies in treatment heterogeneity models. However, validating your effect estimate is much more challenging than evaluating a simple predictive model, which is why you'll see some novel ideas on how to do it.

The chapter closes with some guidelines and examples on how to use effect heterogeneity to guide decision making. Although not exhaustive, I hope those examples will inform you on how to use these ideas on your own business problems.

From ATE to CATE

So far, every time you've estimated the causal impact of a treatment, it was mostly the average treatment effect:

$$\tau = E[Y_1 - Y_0]$$

or the continuous treatment equivalent:

$$\tau = E[y'(t)]$$

where $y'(t)$ is the derivative of the treatment response function. That is, you've learned techniques to uncover the general effectiveness of a treatment. ATE estimation is the bedrock of causal inference. It's a super useful tool for the decision-making problem that is referred to as program evaluation: when you want to know if you should roll out a treatment to the entire population or not.

Now, it's time to learn how to inform another type of decision: *which unit* should you treat? For that, you'll need to allow the decision to change from one unit to another. For example, it might be beneficial to give a discount coupon to one customer but not to another, since one customer might be more sensitive to discounts. Or, it might make sense to prioritize a vaccine to one group over another, as those would benefit more from such treatment. In this type of situation, personalization is key.

One way to achieve this personalization is by taking effect heterogeneity into account, which involves estimating the conditional average treatment effect (CATE). By considering the unique characteristics of each unit, you can determine the most effective treatment for that particular case:

$$E[Y_1 - Y_0 | X] \text{ or } E[y'(t) | X]$$

The conditioning on X means that you now allow the treatment effect to be different depending on the characteristics, as defined by the covariates X of each unit. Again, here, you believe that not all entities respond equally well to the treatment and you want to leverage that heterogeneity. You want to treat only the right units (in the binary case) or figure out the optimal treatment dosage for each unit (in the continuous case).

For instance, if you are a bank that has to decide the loan each customer is eligible for, you can be sure that it's not a good idea to give loads of money to everyone, although it might be reasonable for some. You will have to be smart with your treatment (loan amount). Perhaps, depending on the customer credit score, you can figure out what the proper loan amount is. Of course, you don't need to be a big institution to leverage personalization. There's no shortage of examples where it applies. What days of the year should you do sales? How much should you charge for a product? How much exercise is too much exercise for each person?

Why Prediction Is Not the Answer

Think of it this way. You have a bunch of customers and a treatment (price, discount, loan…) and you want to personalize the treatment—for example, give different discounts to different customers. And say you can organize your customers in the following treatment by outcome plot:

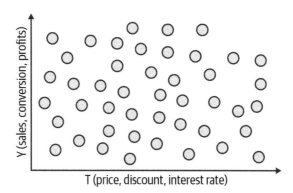

You can think about the personalization task as problem of customer segmentation. You want to create groups of customers based on how they respond to your treatment. For example, say you want to find customers who respond well to discounts and customers who respond poorly to them. Well, the customer's response to a treatment is given by the conditional treatment effect $\frac{\delta Y}{\delta T}$. So, if you could somehow estimate that for each customer, you would be able to group those who respond great to the treatment (high treatment effect) and those who don't respond very well to it. If you did that, you would split the customer space somewhat like the following image:

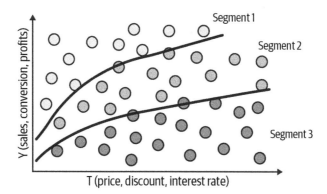

That would be wonderful because now you would be able to estimate different treatment effects on each group. Again, since the effect is just the slope of the treatment response function, if you can produce groups where that slope differs, entities on those partitions will have different responsiveness to the treatment:

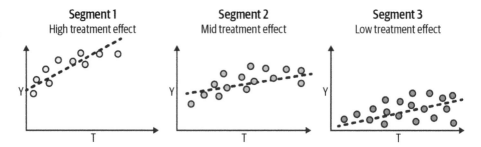

Now, contrast this with what you would get with a traditional machine learning approach. You would probably try to predict Y, rather than the derivative $\frac{\delta Y}{\delta T}$ for each unit. This would essentially partition the space on the y-axis, assuming that your predictive model can approximate the target well. However, this wouldn't necessarily lead to groups with different treatment effects. Which is why simply predicting the outcome is not always useful for decision making:

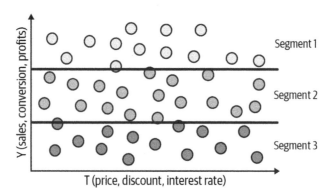

OK, you might say, I get that I have to estimate the effect, instead of just predict the outcome, but it's kind of tricky. How can I predict the slope $\frac{\delta Sales}{\delta Discount}$ if I can't see it?

That's a good point. Unlike the raw outcome Y, slopes (or rate of changes) are essentially nonobservable on a unit level. For you to see the individual slopes, you would have to observe each unit under different treatment levels and calculate how the outcome changes for each of those treatments:

$$\frac{\delta Y_i}{\delta T_i} \approx \frac{Y(T_i) - Y(T_i + \epsilon)}{T_i - (T_i + \epsilon)}$$

This is the fundamental problem of causal inference all over again. You can't ever see the same unit under different treatment conditions. So, what can you do?

CATE and ITE

Keep in mind that the CATE is different from the individual treatment effect (ITE). For instance, suppose you have two groups, $x = 1$ and $x = 2$, each with 4 units, and you want to know the effect of a new drug on an illness that usually kills 50% of those with it. For group $x = 1$, the medicine is detrimental to one patient, killing it, but it saves another. For the group $x = 2$, the effect of the drug is null, and 1 of them dies (remember that the illness kills 50%). In both groups, the CATE is 0.5, but the ITE of no single unit is 0.5.

CATE with Regression

I think you probably saw it coming: as with most things in applied causal inference, the answer tends to start with linear regression. But before going that route, let's make things a bit more tangible. Pretend that you work for a chain of restaurants that operate across the country. A key component of this business is understanding *when* it should give discounts to its customers. For this reason, the company ran a nationwide experiment that lasted three years, where it randomized discounts in six different restaurants in the chain. The data is stored in the following data frame:

```
In [1]: data = pd.read_csv("./data/daily_restaurant_sales.csv")

        data.head()
```

	rest_id	day	month	weekday	...	is_nov	competitors_price	discounts	sales
0	0	2016-01-01	1	4	...	False	2.88	0	79.0
1	0	2016-01-02	1	5	...	False	2.64	0	57.0
2	0	2016-01-03	1	6	...	False	2.08	5	294.0
3	0	2016-01-04	1	0	...	False	3.37	15	676.5
4	0	2016-01-05	1	1	...	False	3.79	0	66.0

Your goal here is to understand when it is the best time to give discounts. In this data, you have one row per restaurant and day combination. This is a bit different from most of the examples used in this book, where the unit was customers. Now, the unit is a day–restaurant combination. Even so, you can still apply the same reasoning from before, only instead of treating customers, you'll "treat" (give a discount) days instead of customers. You could also have a different price at each restaurant at each day, but let's simplify the problem to keeping prices consistent across restaurants.

You can frame this business problem as a CATE estimation problem. If you can create a model that outputs the sales sensitivity to discount for each day and covariate, that is:

$$\frac{\partial}{\partial t} E[Sales(t)|X],$$

then, you can use that model to decide when to give a discount and how much discount to give.

CATE Identification

Throughout this chapter, you won't have to worry too much about identification, since the treatment is randomized in the evaluation set. However, the whole idea of estimating the CATE is based on making $E[Sales(t)|X] = E[Sales|T = t, X]$.

Now that you have something more tangible to work with, let's see how regression can help you. Recall that you were left in a complicated situation. You need to predict $\frac{\delta Y_i}{\delta T_i}$, which is sadly not observable. So it's not like you could simply use an ML algorithm and plug that as its target. But maybe you don't need to observe $\frac{\delta Y_i}{\delta T_i}$ in order to predict it.

For instance, let's say you fit the following linear model to your data:

$$y_i = \beta_0 + \beta_1 t_i + \beta_2 X_i + e_i$$

If you differentiate it on the treatment, you will end up with the following:

$$\frac{\delta y_i}{\delta t_i} = \beta_1$$

which is the ATE, in the case of a randomized treatment.

Since you can estimate the preceding model to get $\widehat{\beta_1}$, you might even go ahead to say that *you can predict slopes even though you can't observe them*. In the example, it is a rather simple prediction. You are predicting the constant value $\widehat{\beta_1}$ for everyone. That's something, but not quite what you want. That's the ATE, not the CATE. This doesn't help you in your task of figuring out when to give discounts, simply because every unit (day and restaurant combination) gets the same slope prediction.

To improve upon it, you can do the following simple change:

$$y_i = \beta_0 + \beta_1 t_i + \beta_2 X_i + \beta_3 t_i X_i + e_i$$

which would, in turn, give you the following slope prediction:

$$\frac{\widehat{\delta y_i}}{\delta t_i} = \widehat{\beta_1} + \widehat{\beta_3} X_i$$

where β_3 is a vector coefficient for the features in X. Now you are getting somewhere! Each entity defined by a different X_i will have a different slope prediction. In other words, the slope prediction will change as X changes. Intuitively speaking, including the interaction between the treatment and the covariates allows the model to learn how the effect changes by those same covariates. This is how regression can give you a way of estimating the CATE, even though you can't predict it directly.

Enough of theory for now. Let's see how to code this up. First, you need to define the covariates. In this example, the covariates are basically date-specific features, like the month, the day of the week, and if it is a holiday. I'm also including the average competitor's price, as this will probably affect how customers respond to discounts in each restaurant.

Once you have the covariates, you need to interact them with the treatment. The * operator does exactly that. It creates an additive term for the left and right side plus an interaction term. For example, a*b will include the terms a, b and a * b in your regression. In your example, this would result in the following:

$$sales_i = \beta_0 + \beta_1 discount_i + \beta_2 X_i * discount_i + \beta_3 X_i + e_i$$

```
In [2]: import statsmodels.formula.api as smf

        X = ["C(month)", "C(weekday)", "is_holiday", "competitors_price"]
        regr_cate = smf.ols(f"sales ~ discounts*({'+'.join(X)})",
                            data=data).fit()
```

* and : Operators

If you only want the multiplicative term, you can use the : operator inside the formula.

Once you've estimated the model, the predicted slope can be extracted from the parameter estimates:

$$\frac{\overline{\delta sales_i}}{\delta discounts_i} = \widehat{\beta_1} + \widehat{\beta_3}X_i$$

where β_1 is the discount coefficient and β_3 is the vector for the interaction coefficients. You could just extract those parameters from the fitted model, but an easier way to get the slope predictions is to use the definition of the derivative:

$$\frac{\delta y}{\delta t} = \frac{y(t + \epsilon) - y(t)}{(t + \epsilon) - t}$$

with ϵ going to zero. You can approximate this definition by replacing ϵ with 1:

$$\frac{\delta y}{\delta t} \approx \hat{y}(t + 1) - \hat{y}(t)$$

where $\hat{y}$ is given by your model's predictions. Since this is a linear model, the approximation is exact.

In other words, you'll make two predictions with your models: one passing the original data and another passing the original data but with the treatment incremented by one unit. The difference between those predictions is your CATE prediction. Here is what this looks like with some code:

```
In [3]: ols_cate_pred = (
            regr_cate.predict(data.assign(discounts=data["discounts"]+1))
            -regr_cate.predict(data)
        )
```

OK, you have your CATE model and its predictions. But there is still a lurking question: how good is it? In other words, how can you evaluate this model? As you can probably tell, comparing actuals and predicted values won't do here, since the actual treatment effect is not observed at a unit level.

PRACTICAL EXAMPLE

Price Discrimination

In the microeconomic literature, the example used in this chapter is what's called *price discrimination*. Despite the bad-sounding name, it simply means that firms can discriminate consumers into those who are willing to pay more and charge them more.

A very well known example of price discrimination is when an airline company changes the airfare depending on how far in advance the ticket is bought: customers who need to book a flight for next week can expect to pay much more than those booking one for next year. This is called *intertemporal price discrimination*, since the company manages to distinguish the price sensitivity of customers based on time. It is a very similar situation to the restaurant example you saw in this chapter.

A more infamous example would be when a wine company sells the same exact wine in two different bottles, one marketed as premium at a much steeper price and one market as average, sold at a more modest value. Yet a third way of price discriminating is when you have half-price entry tickets for students. In this case, the company knows that students make less money on average, meaning they have less to spend.

Evaluating CATE Predictions

If you come from a traditional data science background, you can probably see that this sort of CATE prediction looks a lot like regular machine learning prediction, but with a sneaky target that is not observed at a unit level. This means that a lot of the model evaluation techniques used in traditional machine learning—like cross-validation—still apply here, while others will need some adaptation.

So, to keep with tradition, let's split the data into a train and a test set. Since you have a time dimension, let's use that. The train will contain data from 2016 and 2017 and the test, from 2018 onward:

```
In [4]: train = data.query("day<'2018-01-01'")
        test = data.query("day>='2018-01-01'")
```

Now, let's refit the regression model for CATE from before, but using only the training data for estimation and making predictions on the test set:

```
In [5]: X = ["C(month)", "C(weekday)", "is_holiday", "competitors_price"]
        regr_model = smf.ols(f"sales ~ discounts*({'+'.join(X)})",
                             data=train).fit()

        cate_pred = (
            regr_model.predict(test.assign(discounts=test["discounts"]+1))
            -regr_model.predict(test)
        )
```

To make things interesting, let's benchmark this regression model with a purely predictive machine learning model. This ML model simply tries to predict the outcome Y:

```
In [6]: from sklearn.ensemble import GradientBoostingRegressor

        X = ["month", "weekday", "is_holiday", "competitors_price", "discounts"]
        y = "sales"

        np.random.seed(1)
        ml_model = GradientBoostingRegressor(n_estimators=50).fit(train[X],
                                                                  train[y])

        ml_pred = ml_model.predict(test[X])
```

Finally, let's also include a very bad model in our comparisons. This model simply outputs random numbers between –1 and 1. It is obviously nonsense, but an interesting benchmark to keep an eye on. Ultimately, you want to know if allocating the treatment by a CATE model will be better than simply at random, which is what this last model does.

For convenience, I'm storing everything in a new data frame, `test_pred`:

```
In [7]: np.random.seed(123)

        test_pred = test.assign(
            ml_pred=ml_pred,
            cate_pred=cate_pred,
            rand_m_pred=np.random.uniform(-1, 1, len(test)),
        )
```

	rest_id	day	sales	ml_pred	cate_pred	rand_m_pred
731	0	2018-01-01	251.5	236.312960	41.355802	0.392938
732	0	2018-01-02	541.0	470.218050	44.743887	−0.427721
733	0	2018-01-03	431.0	429.180652	39.783798	−0.546297
734	0	2018-01-04	760.0	769.159322	40.770278	0.102630
735	0	2018-01-05	78.0	83.426070	40.666949	0.438938

Once you have your models, it's time to figure out how to evaluate and compare them. Namely, you'll have to deal with the fact that the ground truth is non-observable. As you'll soon see, the trick is to realize that even though you can't measure the treatment effect for a single individual, you can estimate it for very small groups. Hence, if you wish to come up with a way to evaluate your model in terms of CATE, you'll have to rely on group-level metrics.

Effect by Model Quantile

The idea of making CATE models came from the necessity of finding which units are more sensitive to the treatment with the goal of allocating the treatment more efficiently. It came from a desire for personalization. If that is the goal, it would be very useful if you could somehow order units from more sensitive to less sensitive. And since you have the predicted CATE, you can order units by that prediction and hope it also orders them by the real CATE. Sadly, you can't evaluate that ordering on a unit level. But, what if you don't need to? What if, instead, you evaluate groups defined by the ordering?

First, recall that if the treatment is randomly assigned, you don't have to worry about confounding bias here. Estimating the effect for a group of units is easy. All you need is to compare the outcome between the treated and untreated. Or, more generally, run a simple regression of Y on T inside that group:

$$y_i = \beta_0 + \beta_1 t_i + e_i | X = x$$

From the theory on simple linear regression, you know that:

$$\widehat{\beta_1} = \frac{\Sigma(t_i - \bar{t})y_i}{\Sigma(t_i - \bar{t})^2}$$

where $\bar{t}$ is the group sample average for the treatment and $\bar{y}$ is the group sample average for the outcome.

Curry

The curry decorator is a way to create functions that can be partially applied:

```
@curry
def addN(x, N):
    return x+N

ad5 = addN(N=5)
ad13 = addN(N=13)

print(ad5(5))
>>> 10

print(ad13(5))
>>> 18
```

To code the slope parameter estimate of a single variable regression, you can use curry. It's very useful when you need to create functions that accept a data frame as its only argument:

```
In [8]: from toolz import curry

        @curry
        def effect(data, y, t):
                return (np.sum((data[t] - data[t].mean())*data[y]) /
                        np.sum((data[t] - data[t].mean())**2))
```

Applying this function to the entire test set yields the ATE:

```
In [9]: effect(test, "sales", "discounts")


Out[9]: 32.16196368039615
```

But that is not what you want. Instead, you want to know if the models you've just fitted can create partitions in the data that separate units into those that are more sensitive to the treatment from those that are less sensitive. For that, you can segment the data by quantiles of your model's prediction and estimate the effect for each quantile. If the estimated effect in each quantile is ordered, you know that the model is also good at ordering the true CATE.

Response Curve Shape

Here the effect is defined as estimated slope of regressing Y on T. If you think this is not a good effect metric, you could use others. For instance, if you think the response function is concave, you could define the effect as the slope of regressing Y on $log(T)$ or $\sqrt{T}$. If you have a binary outcome, it might make sense to use the parameter estimate of a logistic regression, instead of the one from a linear regression. The key thing here is to see that, if T is continuous, you have to summarize the entire treatment response function into a single effect number.

Let's code a function to calculate the effect by quantile. It first uses pd.qcut to segment the data by q quantiles (10, by default). I'm wrapping it in pd.IntervalIndex to extract the midpoint of each group returned by pd.qcut. The rounding is just so the results look prettier.

Then, I'm creating a column in the data with these groups, partitioning the data by them and estimating the effect in each partition. For this last step, I'm using the .apply(...) method from pandas. This method takes a function that has a data frame as an input and outputs a number: f(DataFrame) -> float. Here is where the effect function you created earlier comes into play. You can call it passing just the outcome and treatment arguments. This will return a partially applied `effect` function that has the data frame as the only missing argument. It is the type of function `.apply(...)` expects.

The result of using this function in the `test_pred` data frame is a column where the indexes are the quantiles of your model's prediction and the values, the treatment effect in that quantile:

```
In [10]: def effect_by_quantile(df, pred, y, t, q=10):

             # makes quantile partitions
             groups = np.round(pd.IntervalIndex(pd.qcut(df[pred], q=q)).mid, 2)

             return (df
                     .assign(**{f"{pred}_quantile": groups})
                     .groupby(f"{pred}_quantile")
                     # estimate the effect on each quantile
                     .apply(effect(y=y, t=t)))


         effect_by_quantile(test_pred, "cate_pred", y="sales", t="discounts")

Out[10]: cate_pred_quantile
         17.50     20.494153
         23.93     24.782101
         26.85     27.494156
         28.95     28.833993
         30.81     29.604257
         32.68     32.216500
         34.65     35.889459
         36.75     36.846889
         39.40     39.125449
         47.36     44.272549
         dtype: float64
```

Notice how the estimated effect in the first quantile is lower than the estimated effect in the second quantile, which is lower than the estimated effect in the third quantile, and so on. This is evidence that your CATE prediction is indeed ordering the effect: days with lower predictive value also have low sensitivity to discount and vice versa. Also, the midpoint prediction in each quantile (the index in the preceding column) is very close to the estimated effect for the same quantile. This means that your CATE model not only orders the true CATE quite well, but it also manages to predict it correctly. In other words, you have a calibrated model for the CATE.

Next, so you have other models to compare against, you can apply the same function, but passing the predictive ML model and the random model. The following plot shows the effect by quantile for the three models defined earlier:

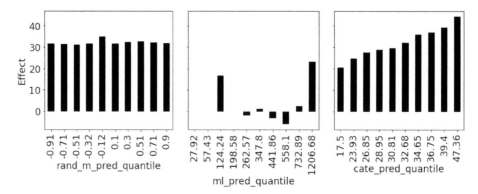

First, look at the random model (rand_m_pred). It has roughly the same estimated effect in each of its partitions. You can already see just by looking at the plot that it won't help you with personalization since it can't distinguish between days with high and low discount sensitivity. The effect in all of its partitions is just the ATE. Next, consider the ML predictive model, ml_pred. That model is a bit more interesting. It looks like groups with high sales predictions and low sales predictions are both more sensitive to discounts. It doesn't exactly produce an ordering score, though, but you could use it for personalization, maybe giving more discounts when sales predictions are either very high or very low, as those indicate high treatment sensitivity.

Finally, look at the CATE model you got from regression, cate_pred. The group with low CATE prediction has indeed lower CATE than the groups with high CATE predictions. It looks like this model can distinguish high from low effects pretty well. You can tell by the staircase shape of its effect by a quantile plot. In general, the steeper the staircase shape, the better the model in terms of ordering CATE.

In this example, it is pretty clear which model is better in terms of ordering sensitivity to discount. But if you have two decent models, the comparison might not be that clear cut. Also, visual validations are nice, but not ideal if you want to do model selection (like hyperparameter tuning or feature selection). Ideally, you should be able to summarize the quality of your model in a single number. We'll get there, but to do so, you first need to learn about the cumulative effect curve.

Cumulative Effect

If you understood the effect by quantile plot, this next one will be pretty easy. Once again, the idea is to use your model to define groups and estimate effects inside those groups. However, instead of estimating the effect by group, you will accumulate one group on top of the other.

First, you need to sort your data by a score—usually a CATE model, but it can be anything really. Then, you'll estimate the effect on the top 1%, according to that ordering. Next, you'll add the following 1% and calculate the effect on the top 2%, and then on the top 3% and so on and so forth. The result will be a curve of effect by cumulative sample. Here is a simple code to do that:

```
In [11]: def cumulative_effect_curve(dataset, prediction, y, t,
                                      ascending=False, steps=100):
             size = len(dataset)
             ordered_df = (dataset
                          .sort_values(prediction, ascending=ascending)
                          .reset_index(drop=True))

             steps = np.linspace(size/steps, size, steps).round(0)

             return np.array([effect(ordered_df.query(f"index<={row}"), t=t, y=y)
                             for row in steps])

         cumulative_effect_curve(test_pred, "cate_pred", "sales", "discounts")

Out[11]: array([49.65116279, 49.37712454, 46.20360341, ...,
                32.46981935, 32.33428884, 32.16196368])
```

If the score you used to sort the data is also good for ordering the true CATE, the resulting curve will start very high and gradually decrease to the ATE. In contrast, a bad model will either quickly converge to the ATE or simply fluctuate around it all the time. To better understand this, here is the cumulative effect curve for the three models you've created:

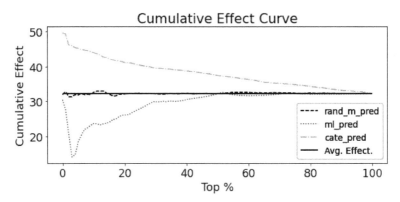

First, notice how the regression CATE model starts very high and gradually converges to the ATE. For instance, if you sort your data by this model, the ATE in the top 20% will be around 42, the ATE of the top 50% would be something like 37, and the ATE of the top 100% will simply be the global effect of the treatment (ATE). In contrast, a model that simply outputs random numbers will just gravitate around the ATE and a model that reverse orders the effect will start below the ATE.

Order Asymmetry

It's important to mention that this ordering is not symmetric. That is, taking a score and reversing it won't simply flip the curve around the ATE line.

The cumulative effect curve is somewhat nicer than the effect by the quantile curve because it allows a summarization into a single number. For instance, you could compute the area between the curve and the ATE and use that to compare different models. The bigger the area, the better the model. But there is still a downside. If you do this, the beginning of the curve will have the biggest area. But that is exactly where the uncertainty is the largest, due to the smaller sample size. Fortunately, there is a very easy fix: the cumulative gain curve.

Cumulative Gain

If you take the exact same logic from the cumulative effect curve, but multiply each point by the cumulative sample, N_{cum}/N, you get the cumulative gain curve. Now, even though the beginning of the curve will have the highest effect (for a good model, that is), it will get downscaled by the small relative size.

Taking a look at the code, what changes is that I'm now multiplying the effect by (row/size) at each iteration. Additionally, I can choose to normalize this curve by the ATE, which is why I'm also subtracting a normalizer from the effect at each iteration:

```
In [12]: def cumulative_gain_curve(df, prediction, y, t,
                                    ascending=False, normalize=False, steps=100):

            effect_fn = effect(t=t, y=y)
            normalizer = effect_fn(df) if normalize else 0

            size = len(df)
            ordered_df = (df
                          .sort_values(prediction, ascending=ascending)
                          .reset_index(drop=True))

            steps = np.linspace(size/steps, size, steps).round(0)
            effects = [(effect_fn(ordered_df.query(f"index<={row}"))
                        -normalizer)*(row/size)
                       for row in steps]
```

```
        return np.array([0] + effects)


    cumulative_gain_curve(test_pred, "cate_pred", "sales", "discounts")


Out[12]: array([ 0.       ,  0.50387597,  0.982917  , ...,  31.82346463,
         32.00615008, 32.16196368])
```

See Also

If you don't want to bother implementing all these functions, I've been working along with some colleagues on a Python library to handle that for you. You can simply import all the curves and their AUC from fklearn causal module (*https://oreil.ly/mgYoJ*):

```
from fklearn.causal.validation.auc import *
from fklearn.causal.validation.curves import *
```

Both the cumulative gain and normalized cumulative gain for the three models are shown in the following image. Here, the better model in terms of ordering CATE is the one that has the biggest area between the curve and the dashed line representing the ATE:

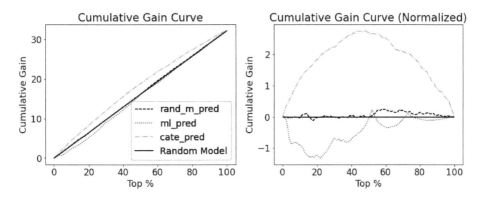

To summarize the model performance into a single number, you can just sum the values from the normalized cumulative gain curve. The model with the biggest value will be the best one in terms of ordering CATE. Here is the area under the curve (AUC) for the three models you've been evaluating so far. Notice that the area for the ML model is negative because it reverse-orders CATE:

```
AUC for rand_m_pred: 6.0745233598544495
AUC for ml_pred: -45.44063124684
AUC for cate_pred: 181.74573239200615
```

Again, the fact that you can condense your model's performance into a single number is amazing, as it allows for automated model selection. Still, as much as I like this last curve, there are some caveats you need to be aware of when using them.

First, in all the curves that you saw, it's important to keep in mind that each point in this curve is an estimate, not a ground truth value. It is the estimate of the regression slope on a particular—and sometimes very small—group. And since it is a regression estimate, it depends on the relationship between T and Y being correctly specified. Even with randomization, if the relationship between the treatment and the outcome is, let's say, a log function, estimating the effect as if it were a line will yield wrong results. If you know the shape of the treatment response function, you can adjust your effect function to be the slope of y~log(t) instead of y~t. But you need to know the correct shape in order to do that.

Second, these curves don't really care if you get the CATE right. All they care about is if the *ordering is correct*. For example, if you take any of your models and subtract –1,000 from their predictions, their cumulative gain curve will remain unchanged. Hence, even if you have a biased estimator for the CATE, this bias won't show up in these curves. Now, this might not be a problem, if all you care about is prioritizing the treatment. In this case, ordering is enough. But if you do care about precisely estimating the CATE, these curves might be misleading. If you come from a data science background, you can draw a parallel between the cumulative gain curve and the ROC curve. Similarly, a model with good ROC-AUC won't necessarily be calibrated.

Third, and perhaps most importantly, *all of the preceding methods require unconfounded data*. If you have any bias, the effects you'll estimate—in the subgroups or the ATE—will be wrong. If the treatment is not randomized, in theory, you can still use these evaluation techniques, provided you debiased the data before, by using something like orthogonalization of IPW. However, I'm a bit skeptical of this. Instead, I strongly recommend you invest in some experimental data, even if it is just a little, only for the purpose of evaluation. That way you can focus on effect heterogeneity without having to worry about confounding creeping in.

See Also

All the curves presented here are an attempt to generalize the curves traditionally used for uplift modeling, when the treatment is binary. If you want to review that literature, I recommend the papers "Causal Inference and Uplift Modeling a Review of the Literature," by Pierre Gutierrez and Jean-Yves Gérardy and "Empirical Analysis of Model Selection for Heterogeneous Causal Effect Estimation," by Divyat Mahajan et al.

Evaluation of causal models is an area of research that is still developing. As such, it still has many blindspots. For instance, the curves presented so far only tell you how good a model is in terms of ordering the CATE. I haven't found a good solution to checking if your model correctly predicts CATE. One thing that I like to do is to use the effect by quantile plot alongside the cumulative gain curve, since the first one gives me some idea on how calibrated the model is while the second gives me an idea how well it orders the CATE. As for the normalized cumulative gain, it is just a zoom-in that makes visualization easier.

But I'll admit that this is not ideal. If you are looking for a summary metric like the R^2 or the MSE—both commonly used in predictive models—I'm sad to say I haven't found any good parallel to those in the causal modeling world. Here is what I did find, though—target transformation.

Target Transformation

It turns out that even though you can't observe the true treatment effect $\tau(x_i)$, you can create a target variable that approximates it in expectation:

$$Y_i^* = \frac{\left(Y_i - \hat{\mu}_y(X_i)\right)\left(T_i - \hat{\mu}_t(X_i)\right)}{\left(T_i - \hat{\mu}_t(X_i)\right)^2} = \frac{Y_i - \hat{\mu}_y(X_i)}{T_i - \hat{\mu}_t(X_i)}$$

where μ_y is a model for the outcome and μ_t is a model for the treatment. This target is interesting because $E[Y_i^*] = \tau_i$. Notice how it looks a lot like the formula for the regression coefficient, with the numerator being the covariance between Y and T and the denominator, the variance of T. However, instead of using expectations to define those, it is computed on a unit level.

Since this target approximates the true treatment effect, you can use it to compute deviance metrics, like the mean squared error (MSE). If your model for CATE is good in terms of predicting the individual level effect τ_i, then the MSE of its prediction with respect to this target should be small.

There is a catch, though. This target will be incredibly noisy when close to the treatment average, where the denominator will tend toward zero. To fix that, you can apply weights that assign low importance to points where $T_i - \hat{\mu}_t(X_i)$ is small. For instance, you can weight the units by $\left(T_i - \hat{\mu}_t(X_i)\right)^2$.

Foreshadowing the R-Loss

There is a good theoretical reason for using those weights. You'll learn more about it when we talk about nonparametric Double/Debiased Machine Learning in Chapter 7. For now, you'll have to take my word for it.

To code this target, you can simply divide the residuals of an outcome and a treatment model:

```
In [13]: X = ["C(month)", "C(weekday)", "is_holiday", "competitors_price"]

         y_res = smf.ols(f"sales ~ {'+'.join(X)}", data=test).fit().resid
         t_res = smf.ols(f"discounts ~ {'+'.join(X)}", data=test).fit().resid

         tau_hat = y_res/t_res
```

Next, you can use it to compute the MSE of all your models. Notice how I'm also using weights like discussed previously:

```
In [14]: from sklearn.metrics import mean_squared_error

         for m in ["rand_m_pred", "ml_pred", "cate_pred"]:
             wmse = mean_squared_error(tau_hat, test_pred[m],
                                       sample_weight=t_res**2)
             print(f"MSE for {m}:", wmse)

Out[14]: MSE for rand_m_pred: 1115.803515760459
         MSE for ml_pred: 576256.7425385397
         MSE for cate_pred: 42.90447405550281
```

According to this weighted MSE, once again, the regression model used to estimate the CATE performs better than the other two. Also, there is something interesting here. The ML model performs worse than the random model. This is not surprising, as the ML model is trying to predict Y not τ_i.

See Also

Like I said before, the literature on evaluating causal models is still in its infancy. It's quite an exciting problem, where new methods are being proposed all the time. For example, in the paper "Intelligent Credit Limit Management in Consumer Loans Based on Causal Inference," the scientists from Ant Financial Services Group propose partitioning the units into groups that have similar covariates (they use over 6,000 groups!), pretending that outcome is the treatment effect plus some Gaussian random noise $\hat{y}_i = \hat{\tau}(x_i) + e_i$, computing outcome MSE in each group $N^{-1}\Sigma(y_i - \hat{y}_i)$ and averaging the results using the sample size in each group.

Predicting Y will only be good in terms of ordering or predicting τ_i when the effect is correlated with the outcome. This won't generally be the case, but there are some situations in which it might happen. Some of those are fairly common in business, so it is worth taking a look at them.

When Prediction Models Are Good for Effect Ordering

Like I said before, for a model that predicts Y to also be good at ordering the CATE, it must be the case that Y and the CATE $\tau(x_i)$ are also correlated. For instance, in the context of finding days where customers are more responsive to discounts in a restaurant, if the days when sales are high coincide with the days when people are more sensitive to discounts, then a model that predicts Y will also be good at ordering the effect of T on Y. More generally, this can happen when the treatment response function is nonlinear.

Marginal Decreasing Returns

When the treatment response function is concave, additional units of the treatment will have less and less effect. This is a very common phenomenon in business, as things tend to have a saturation point. For example, the number of sales can only go so high, even if you set a discount to 100%, as there are factors that limit the amount you can produce. Or, the effect of your marketing budget will eventually flatten out, since there are only so many customers you can advertise to.

A marginally decreasing treatment response function looks something like this:

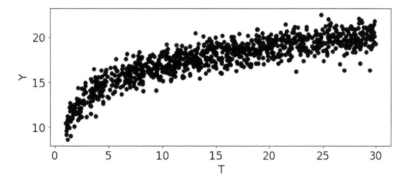

It is easy to see why, in this case, a model that is good at predicting the outcome Y can also be good at ordering the CATE: the higher the outcome, the lower the effect. Hence, if you take the model that predicts Y and sort your units by the inverse of these predictions, you'll probably manage to get a decent CATE ordering.

Binary Outcomes

Another common situation where a model that predicts Y can be good for ordering the CATE is when the outcome is binary. In this case, $E[Y|T]$ has an S shape, flattening out at 0 and 1:

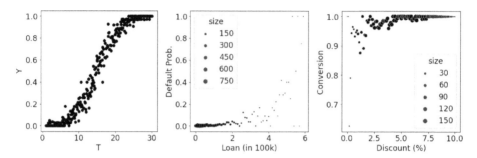

In most business applications, the data will be concentrated at one or the other end of this S-shaped function. For example, in banking, only a small fraction of customers will default on their loans, which means you would be mostly to the left side of this curve, where it looks exponential. As a result, if you have a model that predicts customer default, there is a good chance that customers with higher predictions will also be more sensitive to the treatment. Intuitively speaking, those are customers close to the tipping point between not defaulting and defaulting. For them, a small change in the treatment can make all the difference.

In contrast, let's say you work at an online shopping business where most of the customers that enter your site do buy something (convert). In this case, you are more to the right of the S-shaped curve. Hence, if you have a model that predicts conversion, there is a good chance that the same model can also order the effect of something like discounts. The higher the chances of conversion, the lower the effect size. That's because at the right side, the S curve looks a bit like the marginally diminishing returns case you saw before.

In general, when the outcome is binary, the closer you are to the middle—that is, to $E[Y|X] = 50\%$—the higher the effect will be.

PRACTICAL EXAMPLE

Prioritizing Vaccines

You saw how binary outcome induces a nonlinearity in the treatment response function, which allows you to use the predictive value of the outcome to allocate the treatment. A very interesting application of this principle was seen in the COVID-19 pandemic. In 2021, the world managed to deliver its first batch of approved COVID-19 vaccines to the general public. Back then, a crucial question was who

---

should receive the vaccine first. This is, not surprisingly, a heterogeneous treatment effect problem. Policymakers would like to vaccinate those who would benefit the most first. In this situation, the treatment effect is avoiding death or hospitalization. So, whose death or hospitalization decreased the most when given a shot? In most countries, they were the elderly and those with prior health conditions (comorbidities). Now, these are the people that are more likely to die when getting COVID-19. Also COVID-19 mortality rate is thankfully much lower than 50%, which puts you to the left of logistic function. In this region, by the same context we made for default rates, it would make sense to treat those with a high baseline probability of death when getting COVID-19, which are precisely the groups mentioned earlier. Is this a coincidence? Maybe. Keep in mind that I'm not a health expert, so I might be very wrong here. But the logic makes a lot of sense to me.

When the treatment response function is nonlinear, like in the binary outcome or in the case where the outcome is marginally decreasing, a predictive model might yield a good ordering of the CATE. Still, this doesn't mean that it will be the best model nor that it can't be outperformed by a model that aims at directly predicting the CATE. Moreover, even though such a model might order the treatment effect, it does not predict that treatment effect. This is only OK if all you care about is sorting units by their sensitivity to the treatment. But in case your decision making depends on correctly estimating the CATE, additional effect by group estimation will be required.

See Also

Sometimes outcome prediction can outperform CATE prediction because CATE tends to be very noisy. Fernández-Loría and Provost discuss this further in their paper, "Causal Classification: Treatment Effect Estimation vs. Outcome Prediction."

Speaking of that, I think it is worth spelling out how you could use the CATE for decision making. You probably already have a good idea how to do that, but maybe I have some piece of advice you haven't thought about.

CATE for Decision Making

When the treatment is binary, the decision-making process is pretty straightforward. You essentially care about who responds positively to the treatment. If you have an unlimited supply of treatments, then all you have to do is treat everyone whose CATE is positive. If you don't have a model that predicts the CATE, but you do have one that orders it—as in the case of the predictive models discussed in the previous section—you can use the effect by model quantile plot. Just partition your data by quantiles of your model, estimate the treatment effect in each quantile, and treat everyone up to the point where the effect is still positive.

If you don't have an unlimited supply of the treatment, then you need to add a second rule. Not only will you treat only those with positive effect, but also those with the highest CATE. For example, if you only have 1,000 units of the treatment, you probably want to treat the top 1,000 units, according to some CATE ordering model, provided that they all have positive effect.

If the treatment is continuous or ordered, things get a bit more complicated. You now have to decide not only who to treat, but also how much to treat. This is very business specific. Each problem will have its own treatment response function to optimize. This means I can't give you very detailed guidelines on how to do it, but I can walk you through a typical example.

Consider once again the problem of deciding how much discount to give each day on a chain of restaurants. Since deciding how much discount to give is just another way of deciding what price to charge ($Price = Price_{base} * (1 - Discount)$), let's reframe that problem as a price optimization one. In all business problems there is a cost (even if not monetary) and a revenues function. Let's say that the revenue of the restaurant is given by the following equations:

$$Demand_i = 50 - \tau(X_i)Price_i$$

$$Revenue_i = Demand_iPrice_i$$

Revenue on a day i is just the price times the number of meals (demand) the restaurant serves. However, the number of meals people are willing to buy on a particular day is inversely proportional to the price charged on that day. That is, it has a component $-\tau(X_i)Price_i$, where $\tau(X_i)$ is how sensitive customers are to price increases on that day (notice that this depends on the date-specific features, X_i). In other words, that sensitivity is the conditional average treatment effect of price on demand.

If you plot the demand curve for different values of τ, you will see that τ is nothing more than the slope of the demand curve. If you take the demand curve and multiply it by the revenues curve, you would get a quadratic shape. In this curve, the day in which customers are less sensitive to price ($\tau = 1$) peak at a latter price value:

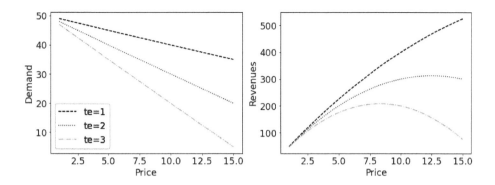

Next, suppose that you spend 3 dollars in order to produce your meal. This means that the cost is simply the quantity you produce, q, times 3:

$$Costs(q_i) = 3q_i$$

Keep in mind that the cost equation doesn't depend on the treatment effect directly, but if you recall that the quantity produced is just the quantity of customer orders—that is, the demand—then, the higher the price, the lower the cost, as customers will demand fewer meals.

Finally, once you have both revenues and costs, you can combine them to get the amount of profit as a function price:

$$Profit_i = Demand_i * Price_i - Cost(Demand_i)$$

If you plot the profits by price for different values of τ_i, you'll see that each yields a different optimal price. The lower τ_i, the less sensitive customers are to price increase, which allows the restaurant to increase prices in order to make more profits:

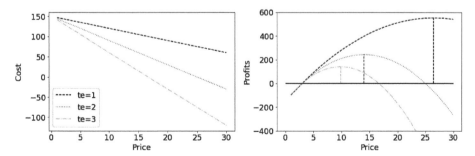

Economists will quickly realize that this is the famous problem of the firm. Setting the marginal cost equal to the marginal revenue and isolating price gives a numerical solution to the profit maximizing price:

$$(P(50 - \tau(X)P))' = (3(50 - \tau(X)P))'$$

$$P* = \frac{3\tau(X) + 50}{2\tau(X)}$$

Notice that, in this case, the only unknown is the effect of price on demand, $\tau(X)$. So, if you can estimate it using a model that predicts CATE, you can convert that CATE prediction to the optimal price.

Again, this is highly dependent on the form of the revenue and cost curve, which in turn depends a lot on your business. But, in general, almost any treatment you care to optimize has an upside—revenues, in this example—and a downside—costs, in this example. To use CATE for deciding the level of a continuous treatment you have to understand how it impacts both of those sides.

Corner Solution

In some rare situations, the treatment level that optimizes a business is none at all or the maximum allowed level. For instance, let's say that your local government sets a price cap on the product you are selling. That cap is below the price that would maximize your profits. In this case, the optimal price would simply be the maximum allowed by the government. This situation is rare, however. In most cases, corner solutions arise when hidden prices are not taken into account. For example, if you are trying to optimize cross-sell emails, you can argue that the cost of sending an email is negligible, so you should just go ahead and send it to everyone. But I would argue back saying that you are not taking into account the costs in terms of customer attention: if you spam your customers, eventually they will get tired of you and unsubscribe to your emails, which will cost you future sales that would come through the email channel. These hidden costs are much harder to take into account, but it doesn't mean that they aren't there. In fact, finding good proxies for those costs tend to be an invaluable data science task.

Key Ideas

This chapter introduces the idea of treatment heterogeneity. The key insight is that each unit i can have a different treatment effect τ_i. If you knew this effect, you could use it to better allocate the treatment among units. Sadly, due to the fundamental problem of causal inference, this effect is unobservable. Still, if you assume that it depends on observable features of the units, $\tau(x_i)$, then you can make some progress; namely, you can go from estimating the average treatment effect to estimating the conditional average treatment effect (CATE):

$$CATE = \frac{\partial}{\partial t} E[Y(t) | X]$$

So, even though the treatment effect is not observed at a unit level, you can still estimate group effects. A simple way of doing that is with linear regression, by including an interaction term between the treatment and the covariates:

$$y_i = \beta_0 + \tau_0 T_i + \tau X_i T_i + \beta X_i + e_i$$

Estimating this model would give you the following CATE estimate:

$$\widehat{CATE} = \tau_0 + \tau X_i$$

Next, you saw some ideas on how to pair cross-validation with CATE evaluation techniques in order to evaluate your CATE estimates. Since the CATE is not defined for a single unit, you had to rely on group-specific metrics, like the effect by quantile curve or the cumulative gain curve. If that is not enough, you could also define a target that approximates the individual-level treatment effect and use that to calculate deviance metrics, like the MSE.

Finally, it's worth emphasizing that everything discussed in this chapter hinges on the fact that the CATE, a causal quantity, can be identified from the conditional expectation, a statistical quantity recoverable from data:

$$\frac{\partial}{\partial t} E[Y(t) | X] = \frac{\partial}{\partial t} E[Y | X, T = t].$$

Without that, the idea of CATE as a group effect you can estimate no longer holds, which is why randomized data is so important for CATE estimation problems, even if just for evaluating your treatment heterogeneity models.

CHAPTER 7

Metalearners

Just to recap, in Part III you're focusing on treatment effect heterogeneity, that is, identifying how units respond differently to the treatment. In this framework, you want to estimate:

$$\tau_i(x) = E\big[Y_i(1) - Y_i(0)\big|X\big] = E\big[\tau_i\big|X\big]$$

or, $E\big[\delta Y_i(t)\big|X\big]$ in the continuous case. In other words, you want to know how sensitive the units are to the treatment. This is super useful in the case where you can't treat everyone and need to do some prioritization of the treatment; for example, when you want to give discounts but have a limited budget. Or when the treatment effect is positive for some units but negative for others.

Previously, you saw how you could use regression with interaction terms to get conditional average treatment effect (CATE) estimates. Now, it's time to throw some machine learning algorithms into the mix.

Metalearners are an effortless way to leverage off-the-shelf predictive machine learning algorithms for approximating treatment effects. They can be used to estimate the ATE, but, in general, they are mostly used for CATE estimation, since they can deal pretty well with high-dimensional data. Metalearners serve to recycle predictive models for causal inference. All predictive models, such as linear regression, boosted decision trees, neural networks, or Gaussian processes, can be repurposed for causal inference using the approaches described in this chapter. Therefore, the success of the metalearner is highly contingent on the machine learning technique it uses under the hood. Oftentimes you'll just have to try out many different things and see what works best.

Metalearners for Discrete Treatments

Suppose you work for the marketing team at an online retailer. Your goal is to figure out which customers are receptive to a marketing email. You know this email has the potential of making customers spend more, but you also know that some customers don't really like to receive marketing emails. To solve this problem, you intend to estimate the conditional average treatment effect of the email on customers' future purchase volume. That way, your team can use this estimate to decide who to send it to.

As with most business applications, you have a bunch of historical data where you've sent marketing emails to customers. You can use that abundant data to fit your CATE model. On top of that, you also have a few data points from an experiment where the marketing email was randomized. You plan on using this precious data only for evaluating your model, as you have so little of it:

```
In [1]: import pandas as pd
        import numpy as np

        data_biased = pd.read_csv("./data/email_obs_data.csv")
        data_rnd = pd.read_csv("./data/email_rnd_data.csv")

        print(len(data_biased), len(data_rnd))
        data_rnd.head()

Out[1]: 300000 10000
```

	mkt_email	next_mnth_pv	age	tenure	...	jewel	books	music_books_movies	health
0	0	244.26	61.0	1.0	...	1	0	0	2
1	0	29.67	36.0	1.0	...	1	0	2	2
2	0	11.73	64.0	0.0	...	0	1	0	1
3	0	41.41	74.0	0.0	...	0	4	1	0
4	0	447.89	59.0	0.0	...	1	1	2	1

Both random and observational data have the exact same columns. The treatment variable is mkt_email and the outcome you care about is the purchase volume 1 month after receiving the email—next_mnth_pv. In addition to these columns, the data also contains a bunch of covariates such as customer's age, time since first purchase on your website (tenure), and also a bunch of data on how much they bought in each category. These covariates will dictate the treatment heterogeneity you plan on fitting.

To streamline the development of your CATE models, you can create variables to store the treatment, outcome, and covariates, as well as the training and testing set.

Once you have all of that, constructing pretty much all the metalearners will be straightforward:

```
In [2]: y = "next_mnth_pv"
        T = "mkt_email"
        X = list(data_rnd.drop(columns=[y, T]).columns)

        train, test = data_biased, data_rnd
```

Now that you have everything set, let's see our first metalearner.

Causal Inference Libraries

All of the following metalearners are implemented in most causal inference packages. However, since they are very simple to code, I'll not rely on external libraries, but instead teach you how to build them from the ground up. Also, at the time of this writing, all the causal inference packages are in their early stage, making it hard to predict which one will attain dominance in the industry. This doesn't mean you shouldn't check them out for yourself, of course. Two that I particularly like are Microsoft's econml and Uber's causalml.

T-Learner

If you have a categorical treatment, the first learner you should try is the T-learner. It is pretty straightforward and I'm guessing it is something you thought about already. It fits one outcome model $\mu_t(x)$ for every treatment in order to estimate the potential outcome Y_t. In the binary case, there are only two models that you need to estimate (hence the name T):

$$\mu_0(x) = E[Y \mid T = 0, X]$$

$$\mu_1(x) = E[Y \mid T = 1, X]$$

Once you have those models, you can make counterfactual predictions for each treatment and get the CATE as follows:

$$\hat{\tau}(x)_i = \hat{\mu}_1(X_i) - \hat{\mu}_0(X_i)$$

Figure 7-1 shows a diagram of this learner.

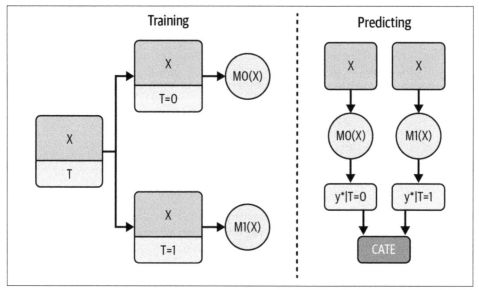

Figure 7-1. A T-learner trains an ML model on T = 1 and another at T = 0; at predic-tion time, it uses both models to estimate the difference between treatment and control

To code it, I'll use boosted regression trees for the outcome models. Specifically, I'll use `LGBMRegressor`, which is a very popular regression model. I'm also using the default parameters, but feel free to optimize this if you wish too:

```
In [3]: from lightgbm import LGBMRegressor

        np.random.seed(123)

        m0 = LGBMRegressor()
        m1 = LGBMRegressor()

        m0.fit(train.query(f"{T}==0")[X], train.query(f"{T}==0")[y])
        m1.fit(train.query(f"{T}==1")[X], train.query(f"{T}==1")[y]);
```

Now that I have the two models, making CATE predictions on the test set is pretty easy:

```
In [4]: t_learner_cate_test = test.assign(
            cate=m1.predict(test[X]) - m0.predict(test[X])
        )
```

To evaluate this model, I'm using the relative cumulative gain curve and the area under that curve, both concepts that you learned in Chapter 6. Recall that this evalua-tion method only cares if you sort customers correctly, from the one with the highest treatment effect to the one with the lowest:

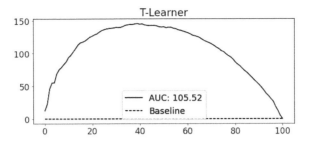

The T-learner works just fine in this dataset. It looks like it can produce a pretty good ordering of customers by CATE, as you can see by the curved cumulative gain curve.

In general, the T-learner tends to be a reasonable first choice, mainly owing to its simplicity. But it has a potential issue that might manifest depending on the situation: it is prone to regularization bias.

Consider a situation where you have lots of data for the untreated and very little data for the treated. This is pretty common in many applications where the treatment is expensive. Now suppose you have some nonlinearity in the outcome Y, but the *treatment effect is constant*. This is depicted on the first plot in the following image:

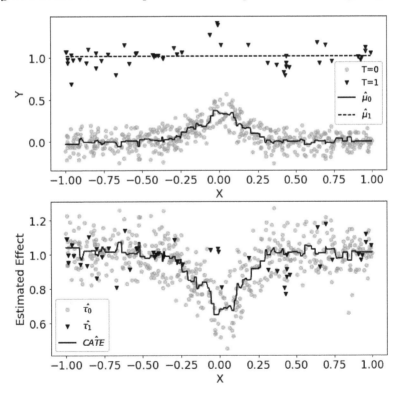

If the data looks like this, with very few treated observations compared to untreated ones, there's a good chance the $\hat{\mu}_1$ model will end up being simple to avoid overfitting. In contrast, $\hat{\mu}_0$ will be more complicated, but that's OK because the abundance of data prevents overfitting. Importantly, this can happen even if you use the same hyperparameters for both models. For instance, to generate the preceding figures, I used an LGBM Regressor with `min_child_samples=25` and everything else set to the default. A lot of ML algorithms self-regularize when dealing with fewer data points, as is the case of `min_child_samples`. It forces the tree in the LGBM to have at least 25 samples in each leaf node, causing the tree to be smaller if the sample size is also small.

Self-regularization makes a lot of sense from a machine learning standpoint. If you have little data, you should use simpler models. So much so that both models in the preceding image have pretty decent predictive performance, as they are each optimized for the sample size they have. However, if you use these models to compute the CATE $\hat{\tau} = \mu_1(X) - \mu_0(X)$, the nonlinearity of $\mu_0(X)$ minus the linearity of $\mu_1(X)$ will result in a nonlinear CATE (dashed line minus the solid line), which is wrong, since the CATE is constant and equal to 1 in this case. You can see this happening in the second plot in the preceding image.

What happens here is that the model for the untreated can pick up the nonlinearity, but the model for the treated cannot, because it is regularized to deal with a small sample size. Of course, you could use less regularization on that model, but then it runs into the risk of overfitting. Seems like you are caught between a rock and a hard place here. How can you deal with this? Here is where the X-learner comes in.

See Also

The issue outlined here is further explored in the paper "Metalearners for Estimating Heterogeneous Treatment Effects using Machine Learning," by Kunzel et al.

X-Learner

The X-learner is significantly more complex to explain than the previous learner, but its implementation is quite simple, so don't worry if you don't understand it at first. The X-learner has two stages and a propensity score model. The first one is identical to the T-learner. First, you split the samples into treated and untreated and fit a model for each group:

$$\hat{\mu}_0(X) \approx E[Y \mid T = 0, X]$$

$$\hat{\mu}_1(X) \approx E[Y \mid T = 1, X]$$

Now, things start to take a turn. For the second stage, you'll first need to impute the missing potential outcomes, using the models you've fitted earlier:

$$\hat{\tau}(X, T = 0) = \hat{\mu}_1(X, T = 0) - Y_{T = 0}$$

$$\hat{\tau}(X, T = 1) = Y_{T = 1} - \hat{\mu}_0(X, T = 1)$$

Then, you'll fit two more models to predict those estimated effects. The idea is that this second stage of models will approximate the CATE on the control and treated populations:

$$\hat{\mu}(X)_{\tau 0} \approx E[\tau(X) | T = 0]$$

$$\hat{\mu}(X)_{\tau 1} \approx E[\tau(X) | T = 1]$$

In the illustrative data from before, the $\hat{\tau}(X, T = 0)$ and $\hat{\tau}(X, T = 1)$ are the data points in the second plot. In the following image, I'm reproducing that same data, alongside the predictive models models, $\hat{\mu}(X)_{\tau 0}$ and $\hat{\mu}(X)_{\tau 1}$. Notice that even though you have more control data, $\hat{\tau}(X, T = 0)$ *is wrong*. That is because it was constructed using $\widehat{\mu_1}$, which was fitted in a very small sample. Consequently, because $\hat{\tau}(X, T = 0)$ is wrong, $\hat{\mu}(X)_{\tau 0}$ will also be misleading. In contrast, $\hat{\mu}(X)_{\tau 1}$ will probably be correct, since $\hat{\tau}(X, T = 1)$ is also correct, as it was generated using the $\widehat{\mu_0}$ model:

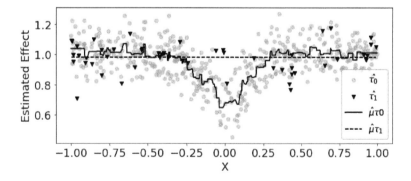

In summary, you have one model that is wrong because you've imputed the treatment effects incorrectly and another model that is correct because you've correctly imputed those values. Now, you need a way to combine the two in a way that gives more weight to the correct model. For that, you can use a propensity score model. With it, you can combine the two second stage models as follows:

$$\widehat{\tau(x)} = \hat{\mu}(X)_{\tau 0}\hat{e}(x) + \hat{\mu}(X)_{\tau 1}(1 - \hat{e}(x))$$

In this example, since there are very few treated units, $\hat{e}(x)$ is very small, which gives a very small weight to the wrong CATE model, $\hat{\mu}(X)_{\tau 0}$. In contrast, $1 - \hat{e}(x)$ is close to 1, so you will give more weight to the correct CATE model $\hat{\mu}(X)_{\tau 1}$. More generally, this weighted average using the propensity score will favor the treatment effect estimates that were obtained from the $\widehat{\mu_t}$ model that was trained using more data.

The following image shows the estimated CATE given by the X-learner, as well as the weights assigned to each data point. Notice how it practically discards the wrong data:

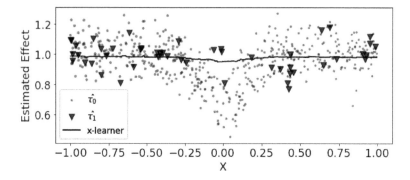

As you can see, compared to the T-learner, the X-learner does a much better job in correcting the wrong CATE estimated at the nonlinearity. In general the X-learner performs better when a treatment group is much larger than the other.

I know this might be a lot to digest, but hopefully it will be clearer when you look at the code. Figure 7-2 summarizes this learner.

Another thing you can try is the *domain adaptation learner*. It is the X-learner, but using the propensity score model to estimate $\hat{\mu}_t(X)$ with weights set to $1/\hat{P}(T = t)$.

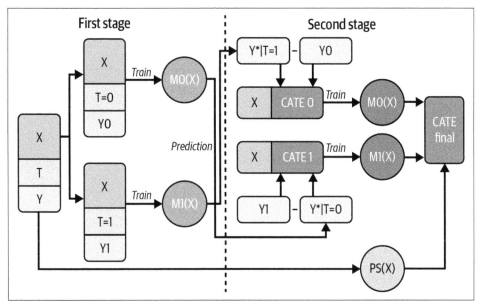

Figure 7-2. An X-learner trains two stages of ML models plus a propensity score model; at prediction time, it uses only the models from the second stage and the propensity score model

Let's see how to code all of this. Here, you have the first stage, which is exactly the same as the T-learner. If you plan on using the propensity score for domain adaptation, you need to reweight the training sample by $1/P(T = t)$, so now is also the time to fit that propensity score:

```
In [5]: from sklearn.linear_model import LogisticRegression
        from lightgbm import LGBMRegressor

        # propensity score model
        ps_model = LogisticRegression(penalty='none')
        ps_model.fit(train[X], train[T])


        # first stage models
        train_t0 = train.query(f"{T}==0")
        train_t1 = train.query(f"{T}==1")

        m0 = LGBMRegressor()
        m1 = LGBMRegressor()

        np.random.seed(123)

        m0.fit(train_t0[X], train_t0[y],
               sample_weight=1/ps_model.predict_proba(train_t0[X])[:, 0])
```

```
m1.fit(train_t1[X], train_t1[y],
        sample_weight=1/ps_model.predict_proba(train_t1[X])[:, 1]);
```

Next, you need to predict the treatment effect and fit the second stage models on those predicted effects:

```
In [6]: # second stage
        tau_hat_0 = m1.predict(train_t0[X]) - train_t0[y]
        tau_hat_1 = train_t1[y] - m0.predict(train_t1[X])

        m_tau_0 = LGBMRegressor()
        m_tau_1 = LGBMRegressor()

        np.random.seed(123)

        m_tau_0.fit(train_t0[X], tau_hat_0)
        m_tau_1.fit(train_t1[X], tau_hat_1);
```

Finally, once you have all of that, you can combine the predictions from the second-stage models using the propensity score model to obtain the CATE. All of which can be estimated on the test set:

```
In [7]: # estimate the CATE
        ps_test = ps_model.predict_proba(test[X])[:, 1]

        x_cate_test = test.assign(
            cate=(ps_test*m_tau_0.predict(test[X]) +
                (1-ps_test)*m_tau_1.predict(test[X])
                )
        )
```

Let's see how the X-learner does in terms of the cumulative gain. In this data set, the treatment and control are almost the same size, so don't expect a huge difference. The issue the X-learner tries to correct probably does not manifest here:

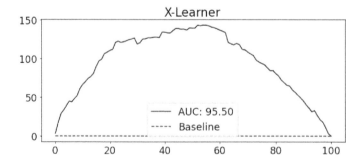

As expected, the X-learner performance is not very different from what you got with the T-learner. In fact, it slightly underperforms it, in terms of the area under the curve. Keep in mind that the quality of these learners is situation-dependent. Like I said earlier, in this specific data, both the treatment and control have a decent enough sample size so as to not run into the type of problem that the X-learner tries to solve. This might explain the similar performance between the two models.

Metalearners for Continuous Treatments

As always, when the treatment is continuous, things can get a bit complicated. It is no different with the metalearners. As a running example, let's use the data from the previous chapter. Recall that it has three years' worth of data from a chain of restaurants. The chain randomized discounts on six of its restaurants and it now wants to know which are the best days to give more discounts. To answer this question, you need to understand on which days customers are more sensitive to discounts (more sensitive to prices). If the restaurant chain can learn this, they will be better equipped to decide when to give more or fewer discounts.

As you can see, this is a problem where you need to estimate the CATE. If you manage to do so, the company can use your CATE predictions to decide on a discount policy—the higher the predicted CATE, the more customers are sensitive to discounts, so the higher the discounts should be:

```
In [8]: data_cont = pd.read_csv("./data/discount_data.csv")
        data_cont.head()
```

	rest_id	day	month	weekday	...	is_nov	competitors_price	discounts	sales
0	0	2016-01-01	1	4	...	False	2.88	0	79.0
1	0	2016-01-02	1	5	...	False	2.64	0	57.0
2	0	2016-01-03	1	6	...	False	2.08	5	294.0
3	0	2016-01-04	1	0	...	False	3.37	15	676.5
4	0	2016-01-05	1	1	...	False	3.79	0	66.0

In this data, discounts is the treatment and sales is the outcome. You also have some engineered date features, like the month, the day of the week, if it is a holiday and so on. Since the goal here is CATE prediction, it is probably best to split your dataset into a training and a test set. Here, you can take advantage of the time dimension and use it to create those sets:

```
In [9]: train = data_cont.query("day<'2018-01-01'")
        test = data_cont.query("day>='2018-01-01'")
```

Now that you are familiar with the data, let's see which of the metalearners can deal with this continuous treatment.

S-Learner

The first learner you should try is the S-learner. This is the simplest learner there is. You'll use a single (hence the S) machine learning model $\hat{\mu}_s$ to estimate:

$$\mu(x) = E[Y \mid T, X]$$

To do so, you will include the treatment as a feature in the model that tries to predict the outcome Y. That's pretty much it:

```
In [10]: X = ["month", "weekday", "is_holiday", "competitors_price"]
         T = "discounts"
         y = "sales"

         np.random.seed(123)
         s_learner = LGBMRegressor()
         s_learner.fit(train[X+[T]], train[y]);
```

But this model does not output a treatment effect directly. Rather, it outputs counterfactual predictions. That is, it can make predictions under different treatment regimes. If the treatment were binary, this model would still work and the difference in predictions between the test and control will be the CATE estimate:

$$\hat{\tau}(x)_i = M_s(X_i, T = 1) - M_s(X_i, T = 0)$$

Figure 7-3 contains a diagram that explain what it would look like.

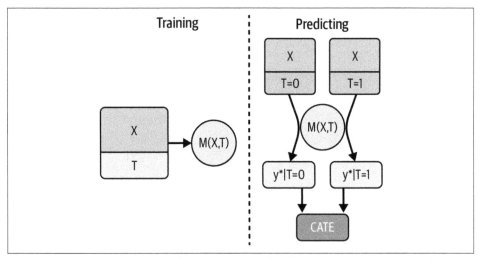

Figure 7-3. An S-learner is simply an ML model that has the treatment as one of its features

In the continuous case, you have to do a bit of extra work. First, you need to define a grid of treatments. In the example, the discounts go from zero to about 40%, so you can try a [0, 10, 20, 30, 40] grid. Next, you need to expand the data you want to make predictions on so that each line gets one copy for each treatment value in the grid. The easiest way I can find to do that is to cross-join a data frame with the grid values into the data where I want to make predictions—the test set. In pandas, you can do a cross-join by using a constant key. This will replicate each line in the original data, changing only the treatment value. Finally, you can use your fitted S-learner to make counterfactual predictions in this expanded data. Here is a simple piece of code to do all of that:

```
In [11]: t_grid = pd.DataFrame(dict(key=1,
                                     discounts=np.array([0, 10, 20, 30, 40])))

         test_cf = (test
                    .drop(columns=["discounts"])
                    .assign(key=1)
                    .merge(t_grid)
                    # make predictions after expansion
                    .assign(sales_hat = lambda d: s_learner.predict(d[X+[T]])))

         test_cf.head(8)
```

	rest_id	day	month	weekday	...	sales	key	discounts	sales_hat
0	0	2018-01-01	1	0	...	251.5	1	0	67.957972
1	0	2018-01-01	1	0	...	251.5	1	10	444.245941
2	0	2018-01-01	1	0	...	251.5	1	20	793.045769
3	0	2018-01-01	1	0	...	251.5	1	30	1279.640793
4	0	2018-01-01	1	0	...	251.5	1	40	1512.630767
5	0	2018-01-02	1	1	...	541.0	1	0	65.672080
6	0	2018-01-02	1	1	...	541.0	1	10	495.669220
7	0	2018-01-02	1	1	...	541.0	1	20	1015.401471

In the previous step, you've essentially estimated a coarse version of the treatment response function $Y(t)$ for each unit. You can even plot this curve for a handful of units (days, in our case) to see what they look like. In the following plot, you can see that the estimated response function for 2018-12-25—that is, Christmas—is steeper than the one for a day like 2018-06-18. This means that your model learned that customers are more sensitive to discounts on Christmas, compared to that particular day in June:

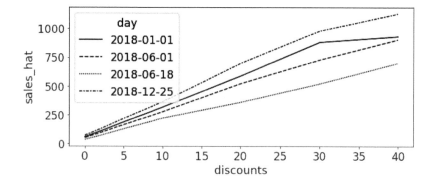

Whether those counterfactual predictions are correct is a whole other issue. To evaluate this model, you first need to realize that you still don't have a CATE prediction. This means that the evaluation methods you learned in Chapter 6 can't be used here. In order to get a CATE prediction, you have to somehow summarize the unit level curves into a single number that represents the treatment effect. Surprisingly—or not that much—linear regression is a good way of doing that. Simply put, you can run a regression for each unit and extract the slope parameter on the treatment as your CATE estimate.

Since all you care about is the slope parameter, you can do this much more efficiently, using the formula for the slope of the single variable linear regression:

$$\hat{\beta} = Cov(t, y)/Var(t)$$

Let's see the code to do that. First, I'm defining a function that summarizes each individual curve into a slope parameter. Then, I'm grouping the expanded test data by the restaurant ID and day and applying the slope function to each of those units. This gives me a pandas series, with indexes `rest_id` and day. I'm naming this series `cate`. Finally, I'm joining the series into the original test set (not the expanded one) to get a CATE prediction for each day and restaurant in the testing set:

```
In [12]: from toolz import curry

         @curry
         def linear_effect(df, y, t):
             return np.cov(df[y], df[t])[0, 1]/df[t].var()


         cate = (test_cf
                 .groupby(["rest_id", "day"])
                 .apply(linear_effect(t="discounts", y="sales_hat"))
                 .rename("cate"))

         test_s_learner_pred = test.set_index(["rest_id", "day"]).join(cate)

         test_s_learner_pred.head()
```

rest_id	day	month	weekday	weekend	...	competitors_price	discounts	sales	cate
0	2018-01-01	1	0	False	...	4.92	5	251.5	37.247404
	2018-01-02	1	1	False	...	3.06	10	541.0	40.269854
	2018-01-03	1	2	False	...	4.61	10	431.0	37.412988
	2018-01-04	1	3	False	...	4.84	20	760.0	38.436815
	2018-01-05	1	4	False	...	6.29	0	78.0	31.428603

Now that you have a CATE prediction, you can use the methods you learned from the previous chapter to validate your model. Here, let's stick with the cumulative gain:

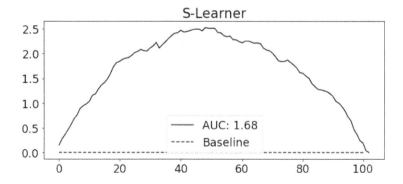

As you can see from the cumulative gain, the S-learner, although simple, can perform OK on this dataset. Again, keep in mind that this performance is highly particular to this dataset. This is a particularly easy dataset, as you have lots of random data, which you can use even to train your learner. In practice, I find that the S-learner is a good first bet for any causal problem, mostly due to its simplicity. It also tends to perform OK, even if it doesn't have random data to train. Moreover, the S-learner supports both binary and continuous treatment, making it an excellent default choice.

The major disadvantage of the S-learner is that it tends to bias the treatment effect toward zero. Since the S-learner employs what is usually a regularized machine learning model, that regularization can restrict the estimated treatment effect.

The following plot replicates a result from the paper, "Double/Debiased/Neyman Machine Learning of Treatment Effects," by Chernozhukov et al. To make this plot, I simulated data with 20 covariates and a binary treatment with a true ATE of 1. I then tried to estimate that ATE using an S-learner. I repeated this simulation and estimation steps 500 times and plotted the distribution of the estimated ATE alongside the true ATE:

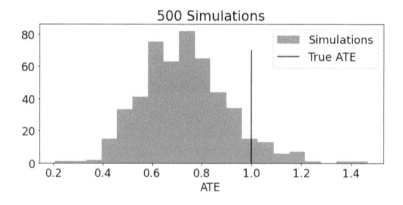

You can see that the distribution of estimated ATEs is concentrated to the left of the true ATE, being biased toward zero. In other words, the true causal effect is frequently bigger than the estimated one.

Even worse, if the treatment is very weak relative to the impact other covariates play in explaining the outcome, the S-learner can discard the treatment variable completely. Notice that this is highly related to the chosen ML model you employ. The greater the regularization, the greater the problem. A way around this, proposed in the same paper by Chernozhukov et al., is Double/Debiased Machine Learning, or the R-learner.

Double/Debiased Machine Learning

Double/Debiased ML or the R-learner can be seen as a buffed version of the Frisch-Waugh-Lovell theorem. The idea is very simple—use ML models when constructing the outcome and treatment residuals:

$$Y_i - \hat{\mu}_y(X_i) = \tau \cdot \left(T_i - \hat{\mu}_t(X_i)\right) + \epsilon_i$$

where $\hat{\mu}_y(X_i)$ is estimating $E[Y|X]$ and $\hat{\mu}_t(X_i)$ is estimating $E[T|X]$.

Since the ML models can be super flexible, they are better suited to capture interactions and nonlinearities when estimating the Y and T residuals while still maintaining an FWL-style orthogonalization. This means you don't have to make any parametric assumption about the relationship between the covariates X and the outcome Y nor between the covariates and the treatment in order to get the correct treatment effect. Provided you don't have unobserved confounders, you can recover the ATE with the following orthogonalization procedure:

1. Estimate the outcome Y with features X using a flexible ML regression model μ_y.

2. Estimate the treatment T with features X using a flexible ML regression model μ_t.

3. Obtain the residuals $\tilde{Y} = Y - \mu_y(X)$ and $\tilde{T} = T - \mu_t(X)$.

4. Regress the residuals of the outcome on the residuals of the treatment $\tilde{Y} = \alpha + \tau\tilde{T}$, where τ is the causal parameter ATE, which you can estimate, for example, with OLS.

The power you gain with ML is flexibility. ML is so powerful that it can capture complicated functional forms in the nuisance relationships. But that flexibility is also troublesome, because it means you now have to take into account the possibility of overfitting. The paper by Chernozhukov et al. has a much more in-depth and rigorous explanation about how overfitting can be troublesome and I definitely recommend you check it out. But here, I'll go on with a more intuition-based explanation.

To see the issue, suppose that your μ_y model is overfitting. The result is that the residual $\tilde{Y}$ will be smaller than it should be. It also means that μ_y is capturing more than only the relationship between X and Y. Part of that something more is the relationship between T and Y, and if μ_y is capturing some of that, the residual regression will be biased toward zero. In other words, μ_y is capturing the causal relationship and not leaving it to the final residual regression.

Now, to see the problem in overfitting μ_t, notice that it will explain more of the variance in T than it should. As a result, the treatment residual will have less variance than it should. If there is less variance in the treatment, the variance of the final estimator will be high. It is as if the treatment is the same for almost everyone, or if the positivity assumption was violated. If everyone has almost the same treatment level, it becomes very difficult to estimate what would happen under different treatment.

Those are the problems you have when using ML models. But how can you work around them? The answer lies in cross predictions and out-of-fold residuals. Instead of getting the residuals in the same data used to fit the model, you'll partition your data into K folds, estimating the model in K–1 of those folds and getting the residuals in the fold that was left out. Repeat the same procedure K times to get the residuals for the entire dataset. With this approach, even if the model does overfit, it won't drive the residuals to zero artificially.

This looks complicated in theory but it is actually very easy to code. You can use the cross_val_predict function from sklearn to get out-of-fold predictions from any machine learning model. Here is how you can get those residuals with just a few lines of code:

```
In [13]: from sklearn.model_selection import cross_val_predict

         X = ["month", "weekday", "is_holiday", "competitors_price"]
         T = "discounts"
         y = "sales"

         debias_m = LGBMRegressor()
         denoise_m = LGBMRegressor()

         t_res =  train[T] - cross_val_predict(debias_m,train[X],train[T],cv=5)
         y_res =  train[y] - cross_val_predict(denoise_m,train[X],train[y],cv=5)
```

If you only cared about the ATE, you could simply regress the residual of the outcome on the residual of the treatment (just don't trust those standard errors, as they don't account for the variance in estimating the residuals):

```
In [14]: import statsmodels.api as sm

         sm.OLS(y_res, t_res).fit().summary().tables[1]
```

	coef	std err	t	P>|t|	[0.025	0.975]
discounts	31.4615	0.151	208.990	0.000	31.166	31.757

But in this chapter, we are focusing on CATE. So how exactly do you get that with Double-ML?

Double-ML for CATE estimation

To get CATE predictions from your Double-ML model, you'll need a few adaptations. Essentially, you need to allow the causal parameter τ to change depending on the unit's covariates:

$$Y_i = \hat{\mu}_y(X_i) + \tau(X_i)(T_i - \hat{\mu}_t(X)) + \hat{\epsilon}_i$$

where $\hat{\mu}_y$ and $\hat{\mu}_t$ are models that, respectively, predict the outcome and treatment from the features X. If you rearrange the terms, you can isolate the error:

$$\hat{\epsilon}_i = \left(Y_i - \hat{\mu}_y(X_i)\right) - \tau(X_i)(T_i - \hat{\mu}_t(X))$$

This is nothing short of awesome, because now you can call this a *causal loss function*. Which means that, if you minimize the square of this loss, you'll be estimating the expected value of $\tau(X_i)$, which is the CATE you wanted:

$$\hat{L}_n(\tau(x)) = \frac{1}{n}\sum_{i=1}^{n}\left(\left(Y_i - \widehat{M}_y(X_i)\right) - \tau(X_i)\left(T_i - \widehat{M}_t(X)\right)\right)^2$$

This loss is also called the *R-Loss*, since it's what the R-learner minimizes. OK, but how do you minimize this loss function? There are multiple ways, actually, but here you'll see the simplest one. First, to declutter the technical notation, let's rewrite the loss function using the residualized version of treatment and outcome:

$$\hat{L}_n(\tau(x)) = \frac{1}{n}\sum_{i=1}^{n}\left(\tilde{Y}_i - \tau(X_i)\tilde{T}_i\right)^2$$

Finally, you can do some algebraic parkour to take $\tilde{T}_i$ out of the parentheses and isolate $\tau(X_i)$ in the square part of the loss function:

$$\hat{L}_n(\tau(x)) = \frac{1}{n}\sum_{i=1}^{n}\tilde{T}_i^2\left(\frac{\tilde{Y}_i}{\tilde{T}_i} - \tau(X_i)\right)^2$$

Minimizing the preceding loss is equivalent to minimizing what is inside the parentheses, but weighting each term by $\tilde{T}_i^2$. Any predictive ML model can do that.

But wait a minute! You saw this already! This is the transformed target you used to compute the mean square error in Chapter 6! Indeed it is. Then, I asked you to trust my word for it, but now I offer you the reason why it works. Again, coding this up is very simple:

```
In [15]: y_star = y_res/t_res
         w = t_res**2

         cate_model = LGBMRegressor().fit(train[X], y_star, sample_weight=w)

         test_r_learner_pred = test.assign(cate = cate_model.predict(test[X]))
```

What I really like about this learner is that it directly outputs CATE estimates. There is no need for all those extra steps you had to take with the S-learner. Also, as you can see in the following plot, it does a pretty decent job in terms of ordering the CATE, as measured by the cumulative gain:

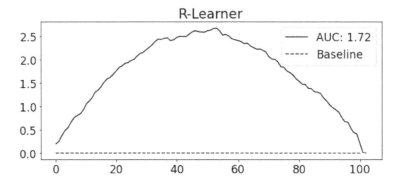

In this example, Double/Debiased-ML has a pretty similar performance to the S-learner. That is probably because the treatment is strong enough so that the ML model in S-learner assigns high importance to it. Also, the treatment is randomized, which means that the μ_t model in Double-ML is not doing anything really. So, in order to get a better understanding of the true power of Double-ML, let's go through a more illustrative example.

Visual intuition for Double-ML

Consider the following simulated data. In it, you have two covariates: x_c is a confounder and x_h is not. Also, x_h drives effect heterogeneity. There are only three values for x_h: 1, 2, and 3. The CATE for each of them is 2, 3, and 4, respectively, since the treatment effect is given by $t + tx_h$. Also, since x_h is uniformly distributed, the ATE is just a simple average of the CATEs—that is, 3. Finally, notice how the confounder x_c affects both treatment and outcome nonlinearly:

```
In [16]: np.random.seed(123)
         n = 5000

         x_h = np.random.randint(1, 4, n)
         x_c = np.random.uniform(-1, 1, n)
```

```
t = np.random.normal(10 + 1*x_c + 3*x_c**2 + x_c**3, 0.3)
y = np.random.normal(t + x_h*t - 5*x_c - x_c**2 - x_c**3, 0.3)

df_sim = pd.DataFrame(dict(x_h=x_h, x_c=x_c, t=t, y=y))
```

Here is a plot for this data. Each blob of points is a group defined by x_h. The color coding represents the value of the confounder x_c. Notice the nonlinear shape in it:

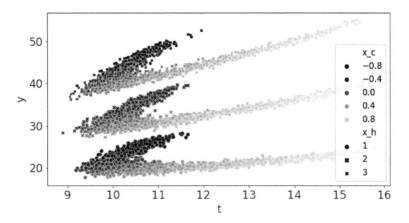

Now, let's see how Double-ML processes this data. First, let's get the residuals $\tilde{T}$ and $\tilde{Y}$. Since you don't have a lot of data here, constrain your ML models to have trees with max_depth=3. I'm including only x_c in the debiasing model, since that is the only confounder. The denoise model has both covariates, as both cause the outcome and including them will reduce noise:

```
In [17]: debias_m = LGBMRegressor(max_depth=3)
         denoise_m = LGBMRegressor(max_depth=3)

         t_res = cross_val_predict(debias_m, df_sim[["x_c"]], df_sim["t"],
                           cv=10)

         y_res = cross_val_predict(denoise_m, df_sim[["x_c", "x_h"]],df_sim["y"],
                           cv=10)

         df_res = df_sim.assign(
             t_res =  df_sim["t"] - t_res,
             y_res =  df_sim["y"] - y_res
         )
```

Once you have those residuals, the confounding bias due to x_c should be gone. Even though it is nonlinear, our ML model should be able to capture that nonlinearity and get rid of all the bias. So much so that if you run a simple regression of $\tilde{Y}$ on $\tilde{T}$, it should give you the correct ATE:

```
In [18]: import statsmodels.formula.api as smf

         smf.ols("y_res~t_res", data=df_res).fit().params["t_res"]

Out[18]: 3.045230146006292
```

Next, let's turn our attention to CATE estimation. The left plot in the following figure shows the relationship between the residuals and color codes each point by the confounder x_c. Notice that there are no patterns in the color of this plot. This shows that all confounding due to x_c was removed. The data looks as if the treatment was randomly assigned.

The next plot color codes the same relationship by the x_h, the feature that drives treatment heterogeneity. The darkest points ($x_h = 1$) seem to be less sensitive to the treatment, as shown by the lower slope. In contrast, the lighter ones ($x_h = 3$) seem to be more sensitive to the treatment. Looking at this plot, can you think of a way to extract those sensitivities?

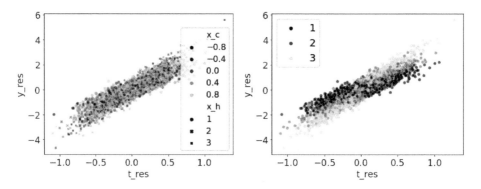

To answer this question, notice that both residuals are centered around zero. This means that the lines that dictate the slope of all the groups defined by x_h should cross zero. Now, recall that the slope of a line can be estimated from two points as $\Delta y/\Delta t$. But, since the intercept of this line should be zero, this simplifies to y/t. Hence, you can see the Y^* target from Double-ML as the slope of the line that goes through the point and has zero as its intercept.

But there is a catch. Both $\tilde{T}$ and $\tilde{Y}$ have a mean close to zero. You know what happens when you divide by a number close to zero? That's right, it can be very unstable, giving you tremendous amounts of noise. Here is where the weights $\tilde{T}^2$ come into play. By giving more importance to points with high values of $\tilde{T}$, you are essentially focusing on the region where the variance is low. To see that this works, you can compute the average of Y^*, weighted by $\tilde{T}^2$, for each value of x_h. This will get you pretty close to the true CATE of 2, 3, and 4, for $x_h = 1, 2, 3$, respectively:

```
In [19]: df_star = df_res.assign(
             y_star = df_res["y_res"]/df_res["t_res"],
             weight = df_res["t_res"]**2,
         )

         for x in range(1, 4):
             cate = np.average(df_star.query(f"x_h=={x}")["y_star"],
                            weights=df_star.query(f"x_h=={x}")["weight"])

             print(f"CATE x_h={x}", cate)


Out[19]: CATE x_h=1 2.019759619990067
         CATE x_h=2 2.974967932350952
         CATE x_h=3 3.9962382855476957
```

You can also see what I'm talking about in the plot of $\tilde{Y}^*$ by $\tilde{T}$. Here, I'm again color coding by x_h, but now I'm adding weights equal to $\tilde{T}^2$. I've also included the average estimated CATE for each group as a horizontal line:

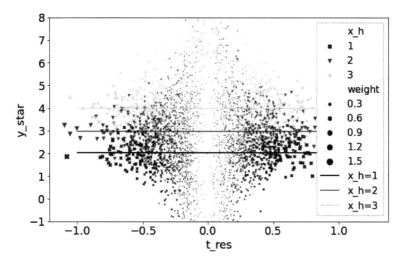

I like this plot because it clearly shows the role of the weights. The variance of $\tilde{Y}^*$ increases a lot as you approach the center of the plot. You can't see it because I've limited the range of the y-axis, but you actually have points that go all the way to both −2,000 and 2,000! Fortunately, those are all close to $\tilde{T} = 0$, so they have very small weights. And now you know on a more intuitive level what is going on with Double-ML.

Tree-Based Learners and Neural Net Learners

This chapter doesn't intend to be an exhaustive list of all the meta-learners there currently are. I've only included the ones that I personally find most useful. However, beyond the four learners presented here, there are some others that are worth mentioning.

First, Susan Athey and Stefan Wager did a lot of pioneering work on effect heterogeneity using modified decision trees. You can find tree-based CATE learners in causal inference libraries such as `econml` and `causalml`. I did not include them in this chapter because, at the time of this writing, I've never managed to use them successfully. Mostly because the implementations currently available are in pure Python, which makes them quite slow to fit on large datasets. I do expect that sometime soon a faster implementation will arise, making tree-based learners an interesting option to try out. If you want to learn more about tree-based learners, I suggest the documentation of the causal inference packages that implement them. There is also a fantastic online series of videos from Stanford Business School, by Athey and Wager, called *Machine Learning & Causal Inference: A Short Course*.

Second, there are neural network–based algorithms you can try. However, I think those are still in their infancy and the amount of complexity they bring is not worth the potential gain. At least not yet. Still, if you want to venture yourself in this literature, I recommend you check the papers "Nonparametric Estimation of Heterogeneous Treatment Effects: From Theory to Learning Algorithms", by Curth and Schaar, and "Learning Representations for Counterfactual Inference," by Shalit et al.

Key Ideas

This chapter expands on the idea of learning group-level treatment effects $\tau(x_i)$. Instead of just interacting the treatment variable with the covariates X in a regression model, you learned how to repurpose generic machine learning models for conditional average treatment effect (CATE) estimation: the so-called metalearners. Specifically, you learned about four meta-learners, two that work only with categorical treatments and two that work with any type of treatment.

First, the T-learner fits a machine learning model to predict the Y for each treatment T. Then, the resulting outcome models $\widehat{\mu}_t$ can be used to estimate the treatment effect. For instance, in the case of a binary treatment:

$$\widehat{\tau}(X_i) = \widehat{\mu_1}(X_i) - \widehat{\mu_0}(X_i)$$

the T-learner works fine if you have lots of observations for all treatment levels. Otherwise, the model estimated in a small dataset can suffer from regularization bias. The next learner you saw, the X-learner, tried to address this issue by using a propensity score model to lower the importance of any $\widehat{\mu}_t$ trained on a small sample.

To handle continuous treatment, you learned about the S-learner, which simply estimates $E[Y|T, X]$. That is, it predicts the outcome with the treatment included as a feature. This model can be used to make counterfactual predictions of Y_t, given a grid of treatment values. This results in a unit-specific coarse treatment response function, which later needs to be summarized into a single slope parameter.

Last, but not least, you learned about Double-ML. The idea was to use generic ML models and out-of-fold prediction to get treatment and outcome residuals, $T - E[T|X]$ and $T - E[Y|X]$, respectively. This can be understood as a buffed version of FWL orthogonalization. Once you have those residuals—call them $\tilde{T}$ and $\tilde{Y}$—you could construct a target that approximates $\tau(x_i)$:

$$Y^* = \tilde{Y}/\tilde{T}$$

Using any ML model to predict that target while also using weights $\tilde{T}^2$ resulted in a ML model that could output CATE predictions directly.

Finally, it's worth remembering that all these methods rely on the unconfoundedness assumptions. It doesn't matter how cool-sounding the algorithm you are trying to use for CATE estimation is; for them to be able to remove bias, you need to have in your data all the relevant confounders. Specifically, unconfoundedness allows you to interpret rates of change on the conditional expectation as if it was the slope of the treatment response function:

$$\frac{\partial}{\partial t}E[Y(t)|X] = \frac{\partial}{\partial t}E[Y|T = t, X]$$

PART IV

Panel Data

CHAPTER 8

Difference-in-Differences

After discussing treatment effect heterogeneity, it's time to switch gears a bit, back into average treatment effects. Over the next few chapters, you'll learn how to leverage *panel data for causal inference.*

A panel is a data structure that has repeated observations across time. The fact that you observe the same unit in multiple time periods allows you to see, for the same unit, what happens before and after a treatment takes place. This makes panel data a promising alternative to identifying the causal effects when randomization is not possible. When you have observational (nonrandomized) data and the likely presence of unobserved confounders, panel data methods are as good as it gets in terms of properly identifying the treatment effect.

In this chapter, you'll see why panel data is so interesting for causal inference. Then, you'll learn the most famous causal inference estimator for panel data: difference-in-differences—and many variations of it. To keep things interesting, you'll do all of this in the context of figuring out the effect of an offline marketing campaign.

Data Regimes

In contrast to *panel data* or longitudinal design, *cross-sectional* data is characterized by each unit appearing only once. A third category, which falls between the two, is known as *repeated cross-sectional data*. This type of data involves multiple time entries, but the units in each entry are not necessarily the same. Up until this point, you have worked with data that includes repeated observations of the same unit over time (for example, when trying to determine the effect of discounts on restaurant sales), but for the sake of simplicity, we treated that data as cross-sectional. This is sometimes referred to as *pooled cross-section*.

Panel Data

To motivate the use of panel data, I'll mostly talk about causal inference applications to marketing. Marketing is particularly interesting for its notorious difficulty in running randomized experiments. In marketing, you often can't control who receives the treatment, that is, who sees your advertisements. When a new user comes to your site or downloads your app, you have no good way of knowing if that user came because they saw one of your campaigns or due to some other reason. Even if you know that the customer clicked one of your marketing links, it's hard to tell if they wouldn't have gotten your product regardless. For example, if the customer clicked your sponsored Google link, they might just as well have scrolled down a bit and clicked the unpaid link, if they were really looking for your product.

The problem is even bigger with offline marketing. How can you know if placing some billboards in a city brings value in excess of its costs? Because of that, a common practice in marketing is to run geo-experiments: you can deploy a marketing campaign to some geographical region but not others and compare them. In this design, panel data methods are particularly interesting: you can collect data on an entire geography (unit) across multiple periods of time.

Like I've said, panel data is when you have multiple units i over multiple periods of time t. In some marketplace websites, units might be the person and t the days or months. But the unit doesn't need to be a single customer. For example, in the context of an offline marketing campaign, i could be cities where you can place a billboard for your product.

So you can follow along with something more tangible, the following data frame, `mkt_data`, has marketing data in a panel format. Each line is a (day, city) combination:

```
In [1]: import pandas as pd
        import numpy as np

        mkt_data = (pd.read_csv("./data/short_offline_mkt_south.csv")
                    .astype({"date":"datetime64[ns]"}))

        mkt_data.head()
```

	date	city	region	treated	tau	downloads	post
0	2021-05-01	5	S	0	0.0	51.0	0
1	2021-05-02	5	S	0	0.0	51.0	0
2	2021-05-03	5	S	0	0.0	51.0	0
3	2021-05-04	5	S	0	0.0	50.0	0
4	2021-05-05	5	S	0	0.0	49.0	0

This data frame is sorted by date and city. The outcome variable you care about is number of downloads. Since t will be used to represent time, to avoid confusion, from now on, I'll use D to denote the treatment. Also, in the panel data literature, the treatment is often referred to as an intervention. I'll use both terms interchangeably. In this example, the marketing team launched an offline campaign on the cities with $D_i = 1$. As for the time dimension, let's establish that T will be the number of periods, with T_{pre} being the periods before the intervention. You can think about the time vector as $t = \{1, 2, \ldots, T_{pre}, T_{pre} + 1, \ldots, T\}$. Periods after the treatment, $T_{pre}, \ldots, T$, are conveniently called post intervention. To simplify the notation, I'll often use a *Post* dummy, which is 1 when $t > T_{pre}$ and 0 otherwise.

The intervention only happens to treated units, $D = 1$, at the post-intervention period, $t > T_{pre}$. The combination of treatment and post intervention will be denoted by $W = D * \mathbb{1}(t > T_{pre})$ or $W = D * Post$. Here is an example of what this looks like in the marketing data:

```
In [2]: (mkt_data
         .assign(w = lambda d: d["treated"]*d["post"])
         .groupby(["w"])
         .agg({"date":[min, max]}))
```

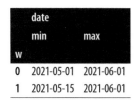

As you can see, the pre-intervention period is from 2021-05-01 to 2021-05-15 and the post-intervention period, from 2021-05-15 to 2021-06-01.

This dataset also has a τ variable to denote the treatment effect. Since this data is simulated, I know exactly what that effect is. I've included it in this dataset just for you to check if the methods you'll learn about are doing a good job in identifying the causal effect. But don't get used to it. In real life, you won't have this luxury.

Now that you understand the data better and have learned a new bit of technical notation, you can restate your goal more precisely. You want to understand the effect of the offline marketing campaign on the cities that got treated, after the treatment takes place:

$$ATT = E\left[Y_{it}(1) - Y_{it}(0) \mid D = 1, t > T_{pre}\right]$$

This is the ATT since you are only focusing on understanding the impact the campaign had on the cities with $D = 1$, after the campaign was launched $t > T_{pre}$. Since $Y_{it}(1)$ is observable, you can achieve this goal by imputing the missing potential outcome $E[Y(0)|D = 1, Post = 1]$.

Figure 8-1 shows why panel data becomes particularly interesting when you represent the observed outcomes in a unit-by-time matrix. This matrix highlights the fact that $Y(1)$ is only observable for treated units during the post-treatment period, while for all other cells, you can observe $Y(0)$. Despite this, these cells can still be useful for estimating the missing potential outcome $E[Y(0)|D = 1, t > T_{pre}]$. You can leverage the correlation between units by using the outcome of the control units in the post-intervention period, and you can also leverage correlation across time by using the treated units' outcome in the pre-treatment period.

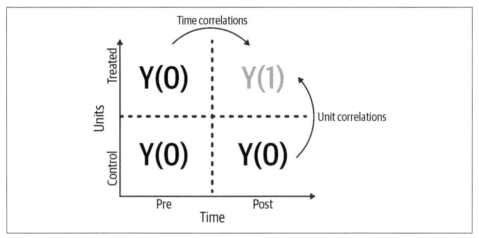

Figure 8-1. By observing the same units across multiple time periods, panel data allows you to leverage the correlation between units and across time to impute the missing potential outcome $T(1)$

Figure 8-1 also shows why you should focus on ATT in most applications with panel data: it's much easier to impute $Y(0)$ for the treated units. If instead you wanted the ATC (average effect on the control), you would have to impute $Y(1)$. However, you would only have one cell where that potential outcome is observable.

Now that you had your brief introduction to panel data, it's time to explore some of the machinery that leverages it to identify and estimate the treatment effect.

Canonical Difference-in-Differences

The basic idea behind difference-in-differences is to impute the missing potential outcome $E[Y(0)|D = 1, Post = 1]$ by using the baseline from the treated units, but applying the evolution of the outcome (growth) from the control units:

$$E[Y(0)|D = 1, Post = 1] = E[Y|D = 1, Post = 0]$$
$$+ (E[Y|D = 0, Post = 1] - E[Y|D = 0, Post = 0])$$

where you can estimate $E[Y(0)|D = 1, Post = 1]$ by replacing the righthand side expectations with sample averages. The reason this is called the difference-in-differences (DID) estimator is because, if you substitute the preceding expression for $E[Y(0)|D = 1, Post = 1]$ in the ATT, you get, quite literally, the difference in differences:

$$ATT = (E[Y|D = 1, Post = 1] - E[Y|D = 1, Post = 0])$$
$$- (E[Y|D = 0, Post = 1] - E[Y|D = 0, Post = 0])$$

Don't let all those expectations scare you. In its canonical form, you can get the DID estimate quite easily. First, you divide the time periods in your data into pre- and post-intervention. Then, you divide the units in a treated and control group. Finally, you can simply compute the averages of all the four cells: pre-treatment and control, pre-treatment and treated, post-treatment and control, and post-treatment and treated:

```
In [3]: did_data = (mkt_data
                    .groupby(["treated", "post"])
                    .agg({"downloads":"mean", "date": "min"}))

        did_data
```

treated	post	downloads	date
0	0	50.335034	2021-05-01
	1	50.556878	2021-05-15
1	0	50.944444	2021-05-01
	1	51.858025	2021-05-15

Those are all the numbers you need to get the DID estimate. For the treatment baseline, $E[Y|D = 1, Post = 0]$, you can index into the treatment with did_data.loc[1] and then into the pre-treatment period with a follow up .loc[0]. To get the evolution in the outcome for the control, $E[Y|D = 0, Post = 1] - E[Y|D = 0, Post = 0]$, you can index into the control with did_data.loc[0], compute the difference with .diff(), and index into the last row with a follow-up .loc[1]. Adding the control trend into the treated baseline gives you an estimate for the counterfactual $E[Y(0)|D=1, Post=1]$. To get the ATT, you can subtract that from the average outcome of the treated in the post-intervention period:

```
In [4]: y0_est = (did_data.loc[1].loc[0, "downloads"] # treated baseline
                  # control evolution
                  + did_data.loc[0].diff().loc[1, "downloads"])

        att = did_data.loc[1].loc[1, "downloads"] - y0_est
        att
```

```
Out[4]: 0.6917359536407233
```

If you compare this number with the true ATT (filtering the treated units and the post-treatment period), you can see that the DID estimate is quite close to what it tries to estimate:

```
In [5]: mkt_data.query("post==1").query("treated==1")["tau"].mean()
```

```
Out[5]: 0.7660316402518457
```

PRACTICAL EXAMPLE

Minimum Wages and Employment

In the '90s, David Card and Alan Krueger used a 2 × 2 DID to challenge the conventional economic theory that states that a rise in minimum wage leads to a decrease in employment. They looked at data from fast-food restaurants in New Jersey and Pennsylvania, before and after an increase in New Jersey's minimum wage. The study found no evidence of reduced employment due to the minimum wage increase. This paper was incredibly influential and got revisited many times and that result proved to be very robust. Eventually, due to its influence and for helping to popularize DID, Card was awarded the Nobel Prize in 2021.

Diff-in-Diff with Outcome Growth

Another very interesting take on DID is to realize it is differentiating the data in the time dimension. Let's define the difference in the outcome across time for unit i as $\Delta y_i = E\left[y_i \mid t > T_{pre}\right] - E\left[y_i \mid t \le T_{pre}\right]$. Now, let's convert your original data, which was by time and unit, into a data frame with Δy_i, where the time dimension has been differentiated out:

```
In [6]: pre = mkt_data.query("post==0").groupby("city")["downloads"].mean()
        post = mkt_data.query("post==1").groupby("city")["downloads"].mean()

        delta_y = ((post - pre)
                   .rename("delta_y")
                   .to_frame()
                   # add the treatment dummy
                   .join(mkt_data.groupby("city")["treated"].max()))

        delta_y.tail()
```

city	delta_y	treated
192	0.555556	0
193	0.166667	0
195	0.420635	0
196	0.119048	0
197	1.595238	1

Next, you can use potential outcome notation to define the ATT in terms of Δy:

$$ATT = E[\Delta y_1 - \Delta y_0],$$

which DID tries to identify by replacing Δy_0 with the average of the control units:

$$ATT = E[\Delta y | D = 1] - E[\Delta y | D = 0]$$

If you replace those expectations with sample averages, you'll see that you get back the same DID estimate you got before:

```
In [7]: (delta_y.query("treated==1")["delta_y"].mean()
         - delta_y.query("treated==0")["delta_y"].mean())
```

```
Out[7]: 0.6917359536407155
```

This is an interesting take on DID because it makes very clear what it is assuming, that is, $E[\Delta y_0] = E[\Delta y | D = 0]$, but we'll talk more about this later.

Since this has all been very technical and full of math, I wanted to give you a more visual understanding of DID by plotting the observed outcomes of the treated and control group over time, alongside the estimated counterfactual outcome for the treated unit. In the following image, the DID estimate for $E[Y(0)|D = 1]$ is shown as a dashed line. It was obtained by applying the trajectory from the control into the treatment baseline. The estimated ATT would then be the difference between the estimated counterfactual outcome $Y(0)$ and the observed outcome $Y(1)$, both in the post-treatment period (difference between the dot and the cross):

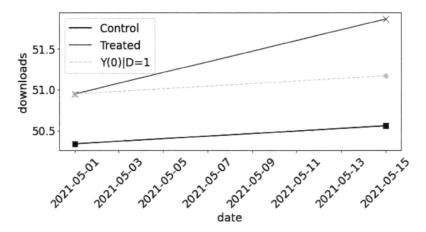

Diff-in-Diff with OLS

Even though you can implement DID by hand, computing averages or taking deltas, this wouldn't be a respectable causal inference chapter if it didn't include a fair amount of linear regression. Not surprisingly, you can get the exact same DID estimator with a saturated regression model. First, let's group your daily data by city and period—post- and pre-treatment. Then, for each city and period combination, you can get the average number of daily downloads. I'm also getting the start date for each period and the treatment status for each city. The start date isn't used in the estimator, but it's good for understanding when the treatment takes place:

```
In [8]: did_data = (mkt_data
                    .groupby(["city", "post"])
                    .agg({"downloads":"mean", "date": "min", "treated": "max"})
                    .reset_index())

        did_data.head()
```

	city	post	downloads	date	treated
0	5	0	50.642857	2021-05-01	0
1	5	1	50.166667	2021-05-15	0
2	15	0	49.142857	2021-05-01	0
3	15	1	49.166667	2021-05-15	0
4	20	0	48.785714	2021-05-01	0

With this city by period dataset, you can estimate the following linear model:

$$Y_{it} = \beta_0 + \beta_1 D_i + \beta_2 Post_t + \beta_3 D_i Post_t + e_{it}$$

and the parameter estimate $\widehat{\beta_3}$ will be the DID estimate. To see why that is, notice that β_0 is the baseline of the control. In this case, β_0 is the level of downloads in control cities, prior to 2021-05-15. If you turn on the treated city dummy, you get $\beta_0 + \beta_1$. So $\beta_0 + \beta_1$ is the baseline of treated cities, also before the intervention. β_1 is simply the difference in baseline between treated and control cities. If you turn the treatment dummy off and turn the post-treatment dummy on, you get $\beta_0 + \beta_2$, which is the level of the control cities after the intervention. β_2 is then the trend of the control. It's how much the control grows from the pre- to the post-intervention period.

As a recap, β_1 is the increment you get by going from the control to the treated, β_2 is the increment you get by going from the pre- to the post-treatment period. Finally, if you turn both treated and post dummies on, you get $\beta_0 + \beta_1 + \beta_2 + \beta_3$. This is the level of the treated cities after the intervention, which means that β_3 is the increment in the outcome that you get by going from treated to control cities and from pre- to post-intervention period. In other words, it is the difference-in-differences estimator:

```
In [9]: import statsmodels.formula.api as smf

        smf.ols(
            'downloads ~ treated*post', data=did_data
        ).fit().params["treated:post"]

Out[9]: 0.691735953640
```

Diff-in-Diff with Fixed Effects

Yet another way to understand DID is with time- and unit-fixed effect model (two-way fixed effects or TWFE). In this model, you have treatment effect τ, unit- and time-fixed effects, α_i and γ_t, respectively:

$$Y_{it} = \tau W_{it} + \alpha_i + \gamma_t + e_{it}.$$

In order to declutter, I'm using $W_{it} = D_i Post_t$ here.

If you estimate this model, the parameter estimate associated with W will match the DID estimate you got earlier and recover the ATT. To do so, recall from Chapter 4 that you can estimate fixed effects by using dummies or by de-meaning the data. Here, for the sake of simplicity, let's just use the dummies approach. That is, let's include city and period dummies with C(city) and C(post). Also, you need to create *W* by multiplying the treated and the post dummies. Just remember that the * operator creates the interaction between two terms and the terms by themselves. Since you only want the interaction, you need the : operator:

```
In [10]: m = smf.ols('downloads ~ treated:post + C(city) + C(post)',
                     data=did_data).fit()

         m.params["treated:post"]

Out[10]: 0.691735953640
```

Once again, you get the exact same parameter estimate.

Multiple Time Periods

The canonical DID setting requires you to have only four data cells: pre- and post-intervention, treated and control groups. But it doesn't require that the pre and post time periods be aggregated into a single block. Canonical DID only requires that you have what is called a block design: a group of units that are never treated and a group of units that are eventually treated *at the same time period*. That is, you can't have the treatment rolling out to units at different moments (you'll learn about that shortly). The marketing example you are working with has exactly this format, which means you don't have to aggregate it by a pre- and a post-treatment period. You can just use it as is.

You can visualize this block design in the following figure, which plots the treatment assignment for each city over time. It also shows the evolution of the outcome across time so that you can get a better feeling of what DID is looking at. Namely, it is trying to see if the difference between treated and control groups increases after the intervention takes place:

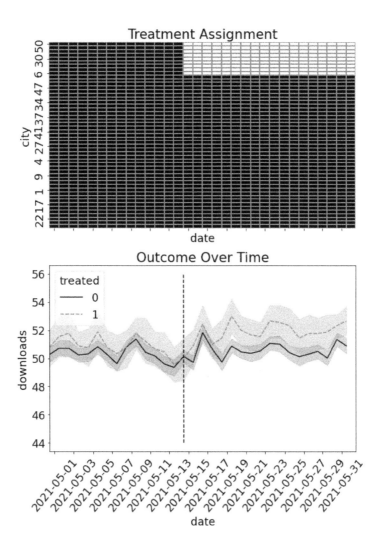

To get the DID estimate with this disaggregated data, you can use the exact same formulas as before. That is, you can either regress the outcome on a treated and post dummies and the interaction between them:

```
In [11]: m = smf.ols('downloads ~ treated*post', data=mkt_data).fit()

         m.params["treated:post"]


Out[11]: 0.6917359536407226
```

or you can use the fixed effect specification:

```
In [12]: m = smf.ols('downloads ~ treated:post + C(city) + C(date)',
                      data=mkt_data).fit()

         m.params["treated:post"]


Out[12]: 0.691735953640
```

I've just shown a bunch of ways to get the exact same DID estimate. By doing so, I hope you can pool insights from all of them, increasing your chances of understanding what is going on. But if you look carefully, I've deliberately hidden the confidence intervals from the regressions you just ran. That's because the confidence intervals from those regressions are probably wrong.

Inference

I said probably wrong because, in all honesty, doing inference with panel data is incredibly tricky. There has been a lot of recent research on the topic, which is of course nice, but it also highlights that it is something we as a field are still learning how to do. The issue here is that you have $N \cdot T$ data points, but they are not independent and identically distributed, since the same unit appears multiple times. In fact, the treatment is assigned to the unit, not to the time period, so you can argue that your sample size is actually just N, not $N \cdot T$, even though this last one is what your regression will consider when computing standard errors.

To correct the overly optimistic standard errors from your regression, you can cluster the standard errors by the unit (cities, in our example):

```
In [13]: m = smf.ols(
             'downloads ~ treated:post + C(city) + C(date)', data=mkt_data
         ).fit(cov_type='cluster', cov_kwds={'groups': mkt_data['city']})

         print("ATT:", m.params["treated:post"])
         m.conf_int().loc["treated:post"]


Out[13]: ATT: 0.6917359536407017


Out[13]: 0    0.296101
         1    1.087370
         Name: treated:post, dtype: float64
```

Clustering the errors will give you wider confidence intervals than no clustering at all:

```
In [14]: m = smf.ols('downloads ~ treated:post + C(city) + C(date)',
                      data=mkt_data).fit()
```

```
        print("ATT:", m.params["treated:post"])
        m.conf_int().loc["treated:post"]

Out[14]: ATT: 0.6917359536407017


Out[14]: 0    0.478014
         1    0.905457
         Name: treated:post, dtype: float64
```

Additionally, look what happens when you replace the daily data frame, mkt_data, from the one that you've aggregated by unit and pre- and post-treatment periods:

```
In [15]: m = smf.ols(
             'downloads ~ treated:post + C(city) + C(date)', data=did_data
         ).fit(cov_type='cluster', cov_kwds={'groups': did_data['city']})

         print("ATT:", m.params["treated:post"])
         m.conf_int().loc["treated:post"]

Out[15]: ATT: 0.6917359536407091


Out[15]: 0    0.138188
         1    1.245284
         Name: treated:post, dtype: float64
```

The confidence interval gets even wider! This just shows that, even though the sample size should come from the units and not from the time periods, having more time periods per unit clusters can decrease the variance.

As you'll see later in this chapter, some noncanonical flavors of DID won't have a standard way to compute confidence intervals. In those situations, you can choose to bootstrap the entire estimation procedure. You just need to be a bit careful here. Since you have repeated units, the model's error for the same unit will be correlated. Hence, you need to sample (with replacement) the entire unit. This procedure is called *block bootstrap*. To implement it, you first need to write a function that samples units with replacement:

```
In [16]: def block_sample(df, unit_col):

             units = df[unit_col].unique()
             sample = np.random.choice(units, size=len(units), replace=True)

             return (df
                     .set_index(unit_col)
                     .loc[sample]
                     .reset_index(level=[unit_col]))
```

Once you have this function, you can adapt the bootstrap code from Chapter 5 to implement the block bootstrap:

```
In [17]: from joblib import Parallel, delayed

         def block_bootstrap(data, est_fn, unit_col,
                             rounds=200, seed=123, pcts=[2.5, 97.5]):
             np.random.seed(seed)

             stats = Parallel(n_jobs=4)(
                 delayed(est_fn)(block_sample(data, unit_col=unit_col))
                 for _ in range(rounds))

             return np.percentile(stats, pcts)
```

Finally, just to check if everything is working as expected, you can use this function to calculate the 95% CI for the DID estimator applied to the marketing data. The resulting CI is pretty similar to the one you got earlier, with standard errors clustered by units. This is a good indicator that your block bootstrap function is working:

```
In [18]: def est_fn(df):
             m = smf.ols('downloads ~ treated:post + C(city) + C(date)',
                     data=df).fit()
             return m.params["treated:post"]

         block_bootstrap(mkt_data, est_fn, "city")

Out[18]: array([0.23162214, 1.14002646])
```

Before ending this section, I want to warn you that, although very convenient, there are some issues with block bootstrap. For instance, if the number of treated units is small, you might end up with a sample with no treated units. Again, inference with panel data is a complex topic that I feel we don't have a clear answer to yet.

See Also

If you want to learn more about it, you can check out the paper "When Should You Adjust Standard Errors for Clustering" (2022-09) from Abadie, Athey, Imbens, and Wooldridge, four fantastic researchers in the causal inference field. I also recommend you check some alternative ways to do inference, like the one outlined in the paper "An Exact and Robust Conformal Inference Method for Counterfactual and Synthetic Controls," by Victor Chernozhukov et al.

Identification Assumptions

As you probably know by now, causal inference is a constant interaction between statistical tools and assumptions. In this chapter, I chose to begin with the statistical tool, showing how DID could leverage unit and time relationships to estimate the treatment effect. That gave you a concrete example to hold on to. Now, it's time to dig a little deeper into what kind of assumptions you were making when using DID, sometimes even without realizing it.

Parallel Trends

Previously in this book, when working with cross-sectional data, a key identification assumption was that the treatment was independent of the potential outcomes, conditioned on observed covariates. DID makes a similar, but weaker assumption: *parallel trends*.

If you think about it, the DID estimator is quite intuitive when it comes to leveraging time and unit correlations. If all you had was units (no time dimension), you would have to use the control to estimate $Y(0)$ for the treated group. On the other hand, if you had a time dimension, but no control group (all units were treated at some point in time), you would have to use past $Y(0)$ from the treated units in a sort of before and after comparison. Both approaches require pretty strong assumptions. You either have to assume that the outcome of the control can identify $E[Y(0)|D = 1, Post = 1]$, which is only plausible if treated and control are comparable (like in a RCT), or if the outcome of the treated unit is a flat line across time, in which case you could use the past outcome of the treated units to identify $E[Y(0)|D = 1, Post = 1]$. In contrast, difference-in-differences makes a weaker assumption: that *the trajectory of outcomes across time would be the same, on average, for treatment and control groups, in the absence of the treatment*. It assumes that the trends in $Y(0)$ are parallel:

$$E\left[Y(0)_{it\,=\,1} - Y(0)_{it\,=\,0}\middle| D = 1\right] = E\left[Y(0)_{it\,=\,1} - Y(0)_{it\,=\,0}\middle| D = 0\right]$$

This assumption is untestable because it contains a term that is nonobservable: $E[Y(0)_{it\,=\,1}|D = 1]$. Still, for the sake of understanding it, let's pretend for a moment you could observe the $Y(0)$ potential outcome for all time periods. In the following plots, I'm representing them as dashed lines. Here you can see the potential outcome $Y(0)$ for four periods, for both treatment and control. Additionally, each plot has four points representing the observed data for the treated and control groups and the DID estimated trajectory of the treated under the control, represented as a dotted line. The difference between this dotted line and the post-treatment outcome for the treated group is the DID estimate for the ATT.

The true ATT, however, is the difference between the post-treatment outcome for the treated group, but with respect to the dashed gray line, which represents the unobserved $Y(0)$ for the treated group:

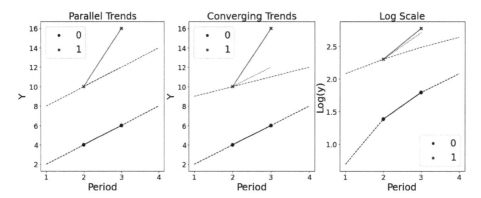

In the first plot, the estimated and actual $Y(0)|D = 1$ coincide. In this case, the parallel trend assumption is satisfied and the DID estimator recovers the true ATT. In the second plot, the trends converge. The estimated trend is steeper than the actual trend for $Y(0)|D = 1$. As a result, the DID estimate would be downward biased: the difference between $E[Y(1)|D = 1, Post = 1]$ and the estimated trend is smaller than the difference between $E[Y(1)|D = 1, Post = 1]$ and the actual, but unobservable, $E[Y(0)|D = 1, Post = 1]$.

Finally, the last plot shows how the *parallel trends assumption is not scale invariant*. This plot simply takes the data from the first plot and applies the log transformation to the outcome. This transformation takes a trend that was parallel and makes it convergent. I'm showing this to warn you to be very careful with DID. For instance, if you have level data, but want to measure the effect as a percent change, converting the outcome to a percentage can mess up your trends.

See Also

In the paper "When Is Parallel Trends Sensitive to Functional Form?" Jonathan Roth and Pedro Sant'Anna derive a more strict version of parallel trends that is invariant to monotonic transformation of the outcome and discuss in which situation that assumption is plausible.

An alternative way to think about the parallel trends assumption is in relation to the conditional independence assumption (CIA). While the CIA states that the level of $Y(0)$ is the same, on average, in the treated and control groups, parallel trends states that the *growth of $Y(0)$ is the same between treated and control groups*. This can be expressed in terms of the ΔYs you saw earlier:

$$(\Delta y_0, \Delta y_1) \perp T$$

Here lies the power of panel data: even if the treatment is not randomly assigned, so long as the treated and control groups have the same counterfactual growth, the ATT can be identified.

Just like with the independence assumption, you can relax the parallel trend assumption to be conditioned on covariates. That is, given a set of pre-treatment covariates X, the trend in $Y(0)$ is the same between treated and control group. You'll see later in this chapter how to incorporate covariates in DID.

No Anticipation Assumption and SUTVA

If the parallel trend assumption can be seen as a panel data version of the independence assumption, the no anticipation assumption is more related to the stable unit of treatment value assumption (SUTVA). Recall that SUTVA violations happen when the effect spills over from treatment into the control units (or vice versa)? Well, here it is the same thing, but across time periods: you don't want the effect to spill over to periods when the treatment hasn't yet taken place.

If you think there is no way this can happen, consider you are trying to estimate the effect of Black Friday on sales of cell phones. If you try this, you'll see that many businesses anticipate the Black Friday discount, knowing that the period prior to Black Friday is one where customers are already shopping for products. This will likely cause you to see a spike in sales before the treatment (Black Friday) even takes place.

The fact that you have to worry about time spillover doesn't mean you don't have to worry about unit spillover. Good old SUTVA is still a big issue in panel data analysis, especially when the unit is a geographic region. That's because people are constantly moving across the geographic borders, which makes the treatment likely to spill out of the treated units.

Spatial Spillover

Much like with everything in the panel data literature, dealing with spatial spillover is something the causal inference community is still learning about. A very good paper on this subject is "Difference-in-Differences Estimation with Spatial Spillovers," by Kyle Butts. The paper is not hard to read and the proposed solution is easy to implement. The basic idea is to expand the two-way fixed effect formulation of DID with a dummy, S which is 1 if a control unit is deemed close enough to a treated unit:

$$Y_{it} = \tau_{it} W_{it} + \eta_0 S_i (1 - W_{it}) + \eta_1 S_i W_{it} + \alpha_i + \gamma_t + e_{it}$$

Strict Exogeneity

The strict exogeneity assumption is a pretty technical assumption that is usually stated in terms of the fixed effect model's residuals:

$$Y_{it} = \alpha_i + X_{it}\beta + \epsilon_{it}$$

Strict exogeneity states that:

$$E\big[\epsilon_{it} \mid X_{it}, \alpha_i\big] = 0$$

This assumption is stronger and implies parallel trends. It is also fairly obscure, so I think it is best if we talk about it in terms of what it implies:

1. No time varying confounders

2. No feedback

3. No carryover effect

You can also make this assumption more palpable by showing it in a DAG:

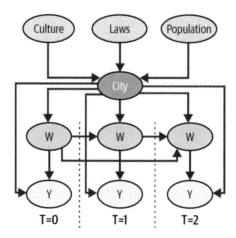

Now, let's walk through what it really means.

No Time Varying Confounders

Let me start with some good news. Do you remember how I mentioned that panel data can utilize time and unit correlations? It's worth noting that having repeated observations over time can help you *identify the causal effect even when unobserved confounders are present*. This is true as long as those confounders are constant over

---

time or across all units. To understand this better, let's revisit the marketing example. Each city has its unique culture, laws, and population, all of which can significantly influence both the treatment and outcome variables. Some of these variables, such as culture and laws, are challenging to quantify, making them unobserved confounders that you need to account for. However, how can you do that when you can't measure them?

The trick is to see that, by zooming in on a unit and tracking how it evolves over time, you are already controlling for anything that is fixed over time. That includes any time-fixed confounders, even those that are unmeasured. In the marketing example, if downloads increase over time in a particular city, you know it cannot be due to any change in the city culture (at least not in a short time frame), simply because that confounder is fixed over time. The bottom line is that even though you can't control for time-fixed confounders, since you can't measure it, you can still block the back-door path that goes through it, if you control for the unit itself.

If you are more of a math person, you can also see how the process of demeaning the data wipes out any time-fixed covariate. Recall that adding unit-fixed effects can be achieved by adding unit dummies, but also by computing the average of both outcome and treatment by unit and subtracting that from the original variables:

$$\ddot{Y}_{it} = Y_{it} - \bar{Y}_i$$

$$\ddot{W}_{it} = W_{it} - \bar{W}_i$$

Here, I'm using $W_{it} = D_i Post_t$ to denote the treatment, since D_i is time fixed. With demeaning, any unobserved U_i vanishes. Since U_i is constant across time, you have that $U_i = \bar{U}_i$, which makes $\ddot{U}_{it} = 0$ everywhere. In plain terms, unit-fixed effects wipe out any variable that is constant across time.

I'm focusing on unit-fixed effects, but a similar argument can be used to show how time-fixed effects can wipe out any variable that is fixed across units, but changes in time. In our example, those could be the country's exchange rate or inflation. Since those are nationwide variables, they are the same for all the cities.

Of course, if the unobserved confounder changes over time and unit, there is not much you can do here.

No Feedback

You might have noticed that the previous graph has another vital assumption in it. Specifically, there are no arrows extending from past outcomes, Y_{it-1}, toward current treatment, W_{it}. In other words, there is no feedback. This implies that the treatment cannot be decided based on the outcome trajectory. To illustrate, imagine the treatment was a vector indexed by time $W = (w_0, w_1, \ldots, w_T)$. In this scenario, the entire vector would have to be decided on one go. This is plausible in block designs like the one you saw before, where the treatment turns on at a particular time period and continues indefinitely. However, even then the no feedback assumption could be violated. For instance, suppose that the marketing team decided that they would do an offline marketing campaign whenever a city reached 1,000 downloads. This would violate the no feedback assumption.

Sequential Ignorability

If you want to be able to condition on past outcomes, you need to look into methods that work under sequential ignorability. Sadly, you can either control for past outcomes or time-fixed confounders, but not both. For more about this topic, I suggest you check out the paper "Causal Inference with Time-Series Cross-Sectional Data: A Reflection," by Yiqing Xu, or the book *Causal Inference* by M.A. Hernán and J.M. Robins.

No Carryover and No Lagged Dependent Variable

Beyond no feedback, you might observe that the graph also assumes *no carryover effect*, since there are no arrows from past treatment to current outcomes. Fortunately, this assumption can be relaxed if you expand the model, including lagged versions of the treatment. For example, if you believe that treatment at period $t - 1$ impacts the outcome at time t, you can use the following model:

$$Y_{it} = \tau_{it} W_{it} + \theta W_{it-1} + \alpha_i + \gamma_t + e_{it}.$$

Finally, the graph also assumes no lagged dependent variable, meaning that past outcome doesn't directly cause current outcome. Lucky for you, this assumption is not really necessary; adding arrows from past Ys to future Ys doesn't hinder identification.

See Also

Representing panel data in DAG is not something trivial, but there are two great papers that try to do so. They really helped me understand what strict exogeneity implied. First, the paper "When Should We Use Unit Fixed Effects Regression Models for Causal Inference with Longitudinal Data?" by Imai and Kim. Second, the paper "Causal Inference with Time-Series Cross-Sectional Data: A Reflection," by Yiqing Xu.

Effect Dynamics over Time

By now you probably have a pretty decent understanding about canonical DID, which means you can now try to diverge from it into its more apocryphal flavors. A slightly more complicated approach is when you want to incorporate effect dynamics over time. If you look back at the plot that shows outcome evolution, you can see that the difference between treated and control group doesn't increase right after the treatment takes place. Instead, it takes some time for the treatment to reach its full effect. In other words, the treatment effect is not instantaneous. This is a fairly common phenomenon not only in marketing, but with any sort of intervention on entire geographies. It also means that you might be underestimating the final treatment effect, because you are including periods where it hasn't fully matured yet.

One simple way around this problem is to estimate the ATT over time. If you are really clever, you can achieve this by creating dummies for each post-treatment period, but my favorite way of getting effects over time involves using a bit of brute force: iterating over all the time periods and running DID as if only that period was the post-treatment one.

In order to do that, let's create a function that takes a data frame and a date and runs DID as if that date was the post treatment period:

```
In [19]: def did_date(df, date):
             df_date = (df
                        .query("date==@date | post==0")
                        .query("date <= @date")
                        .assign(post = lambda d: (d["date"]==date).astype(int)))

             m = smf.ols(
                 'downloads ~ I(treated*post) + C(city) + C(date)', data=df_date
             ).fit(cov_type='cluster', cov_kwds={'groups': df_date['city']})

             att = m.params["I(treated * post)"]
             ci = m.conf_int().loc["I(treated * post)"]

             return pd.DataFrame({"att": att, "ci_low": ci[0], "ci_up": ci[1]},
                                 index=[date])
```

First, this function filters only the pre-treatment period and the passed date. Next, it filters the dates equal to or before the passed date. If the passed date is from the post-treatment period, this filter is innocuous. If the date is from the pre-treatment period, it tosses away the dates after it. This allows you to run DID even for the period before the treatment. Actually, to do that, you need the next line of code, where the function reassigns the post-treatment period to be the specified date. Now, if you pass a date from the pre-treatment, the function will pretend that it comes from the post-treatment period, in what is sort of a placebo test in the time dimension. Finally, the function estimates a DID model, extracting the ATT and the confidence interval around it. It then stores everything in a data frame with a single line.

This function works for a single date. To get the effect for all possible dates, you can iterate over them, getting the DID estimate each time. Just keep in mind that you need to skip the first date, as you need at least two time periods for DID to run. If you store all the results in a list, you can call pd.concat on that list to merge all the results into a single data frame:

```
In [20]: post_dates = sorted(mkt_data["date"].unique())[1:]

         atts = pd.concat([did_date(mkt_data, date)
                           for date in post_dates])

         atts.head()
```

	att	ci_low	ci_up
2021-05-02	0.325397	-0.491741	1.142534
2021-05-03	0.384921	-0.388389	1.158231
2021-05-04	-0.156085	-1.247491	0.935321
2021-05-05	-0.299603	-0.949935	0.350729
2021-05-06	0.347619	0.013115	0.682123

You can then plot the effect over time alongside its confidence interval. This plot shows that the effect doesn't climb after the treatment takes place. It also seems like the ATT is a bit higher if you discard the early periods, where it hasn't fully matured yet. I'm also plotting the true effect τ so you can see how this approach manages to recover it pretty well:

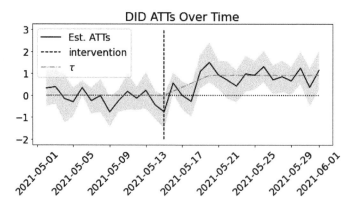

The pre-treatment part of this plot also deserves your attention. During this period, all estimated effects are indistinguishable from zero, which indicates that the effect does not occur prior to treatment. This provides strong evidence that the no-anticipation assumption may be valid in this case.

Diff-in-Diff with Covariates

Another variation of DID you need to learn is how to include pre-treatment covariates in your model. This is useful in case you suspect that parallel trend doesn't hold, but conditional parallel trend does:

$$E\big[Y(0)_{it=1} - Y(0)_{it=0}\big|D=1, X\big] = E\big[Y(0)_{it=1} - Y(0)_{it=0}\big|D=0, X\big]$$

Consider this situation: you have the same marketing data as before, but now, you have data on multiple regions of the country. If you plot the treatment and control outcome for each region, you'll see something interesting:

```
In [21]: mkt_data_all = (pd.read_csv("./data/short_offline_mkt_all_regions.csv")
                        .astype({"date":"datetime64[ns]"}))
```

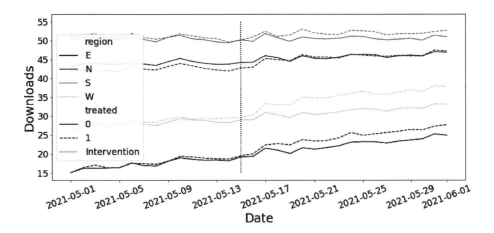

The pre-treatment trends seem to be parallel *within a region*, but not across regions. As a result, if you simply run the two-way fixed effect specification of DID here, you'll get a biased estimate for the ATT:

```
In [22]: print("True ATT: ", mkt_data_all.query("treated*post==1")["tau"].mean())

        m = smf.ols('downloads ~ treated:post + C(city) + C(date)',
                    data=mkt_data_all).fit()

        print("Estimated ATT:", m.params["treated:post"])
```

```
Out[22]: True ATT:  1.7208921056102682
         Estimated ATT: 2.068391984256296
```

Somehow, you need to account for the different trends in each region. You might think that simply adding the region as an extra covariate in the regression will solve the problem. But think again! Remember how using unit-fixed effects wipes out the effect of any time-fixed covariate? This is true not only for unobservable confounders, but also for the region covariate, which is constant across time. The end result is that naively adding it to the regression is innocuous. You'll get the same result as before:

```
In [23]: m = smf.ols('downloads ~ treated:post + C(city) + C(date) + C(region)',
                     data=mkt_data_all).fit()
         m.params["treated:post"]


Out[23]: 2.071153674125536
```

To properly include pre-treatment covariates in your DID model, you need to recall that DID works by estimating two important pieces: the treated baseline and the control trend. It then projects the control trend into the treated baseline. This means you have to estimate the control trend for each region separately. The overkill way of doing this is to simply run a separate difference-in-differences regression for each region. You could literally loop through the regions or interact the entire DID model with region dummies:

```
In [24]: m_saturated = smf.ols('downloads ~ (post*treated)*C(region)',
             data=mkt_data_all).fit()

atts = m_saturated.params[
         m_saturated.params.index.str.contains("post:treated")
         ]atts
Out[24]: post:treated              1.676808
         post:treated:C(region)[T.N]   -0.343667
         post:treated:C(region)[T.S]   -0.985072
         post:treated:C(region)[T.W]    1.369363
dtype: float64
```

Just keep in mind that the ATT estimates should be interpreted with respect to the baseline group, which in this case is the East region. So, the effect on the North region is 1.67–0.34, the effect on the South region is 1.67–0.98, and so on. Next, you can aggregate the different ATTs using a weighted average, where the number of cities in a region is the weight:

```
In [25]: reg_size = (mkt_data_all.groupby("region").size()
                     /len(mkt_data_all["date"].unique()))

         base = atts[0]
```

```
np.array([reg_size[0]*base]+
         [(att+base)*size
          for att, size in zip(atts[1:], reg_size[1:])]
        ).sum()/sum(reg_size)
```

```
Out[25]: 1.6940400451471818
```

Even though I said this is overkill, it is actually a pretty good idea. It is very easy to implement and hard to get it wrong. Still, it has some problems. For instance, if you have many covariates or a continuous covariate, this approach will be impractical. Which is why I think you should know that there is another way. Instead of interacting the region with both post and treated dummies, you can interact with the post dummy alone. This model will estimate the trend (pre- and post-outcome levels) for the treated in each region separately, but it will fit a single intercept shift to the treated and post period:

```
In [26]: m = smf.ols('downloads ~ post*(treated + C(region))',
                      data=mkt_data_all).fit()

         m.summary().tables[1]
```

	coef	std err	t	P>|t|	[0.025	0.975]
Intercept	17.3522	0.101	172.218	0.000	17.155	17.550
C(region)[T.N]	26.2770	0.137	191.739	0.000	26.008	26.546
C(region)[T.S]	33.0815	0.135	245.772	0.000	32.818	33.345
C(region)[T.W]	10.7118	0.135	79.581	0.000	10.448	10.976
post	4.9807	0.134	37.074	0.000	4.717	5.244
post:C(region)[T.N]	-3.3458	0.183	-18.310	0.000	-3.704	-2.988
post:C(region)[T.S]	-4.9334	0.179	-27.489	0.000	-5.285	-4.582
post:C(region)[T.W]	-1.5408	0.179	-8.585	0.000	-1.893	-1.189
treated	0.0503	0.117	0.429	0.668	-0.179	0.280
post:treated	1.6811	0.156	10.758	0.000	1.375	1.987

The parameter associated with `post:treated` can be interpreted as the ATT. It is not exactly the same ATT that you got before, but it is pretty close. The difference appears because—as you should know by now—regression averages the regions ATT by variance, while before, you averaged them by region size. This means that regression will overweight regions where the treatment is more evenly distributed (has higher variance).

This second approach is much faster to run, but the downside is that it requires careful thinking on how you go about doing the interactions. For this reason, I recommend you use it only if you really know what you are doing. Or, before you use it, try to build some simulated data where you know the true ATT and see if you can recover it with your model. And remember: there is no shame in just running a DID model for each region and averaging the results. In fact, it is a particularly clever idea.

Doubly Robust Diff-in-Diff

Another way of incorporating pre-treatment and time invariant covariates to allow for conditionally parallel trends is by making a doubly robust version of difference-in-differences (DRDID). To do this, you can take a lot of the ideas from Chapter 5, when you learned how to craft a doubly robust estimator. However, you'll need to make some adjustments. First, instead of having a raw outcome model, since DID works with Δy, you'll also need a model for the delta outcome over time. Second, since you only care about the ATT, you just need to reconstruct the treated population from the control units. All of this will make more sense as I show you the steps to build DRDID.

Propensity Score Model

The first step in DRDID is a propensity score model $\hat{e}(X)$ that uses the pre-treatment covariates to *estimate the probability that a unit comes from the treated group*. This model doesn't care about the time dimension, which means you only need one period worth of data to estimate it:

```
In [27]: unit_df = (mkt_data_all
                    # keep only the first date
                    .astype({"date": str})
                    .query(f"date=='{mkt_data_all['date'].astype(str).min()}'")
                    .drop(columns=["date"])) # just to avoid confusion

         ps_model = smf.logit("treated~C(region)", data=unit_df).fit(disp=0)
```

Delta Outcome Model

Next, you need the outcome model for Δy, which means that first you need to construct the delta outcome data. To do that you need to take the difference between the average outcome at the pre- and post-treatment periods. Once you do that, you'll again end up with one row for each unit, since the time dimension has been differentiated out:

```
In [28]: delta_y = (
             mkt_data_all.query("post==1").groupby("city")["downloads"].mean()
             - mkt_data_all.query("post==0").groupby("city")["downloads"].mean()
         )
```

Now that you have Δy, you can join it back into the unit dataset and fit the outcome model in it:

```
In [29]: df_delta_y = (unit_df
                       .set_index("city")
                       .join(delta_y.rename("delta_y")))

         outcome_model = smf.ols("delta_y ~ C(region)", data=df_delta_y).fit()
```

All Together Now

It's time to join all the pieces. Let's start by gathering all the data you need into a single data frame. For the final estimator, you'll need the actual Δy, the propensity score, and the delta outcome prediction. For that, you can start from the df_delta_y you used to build your outcome model and make predictions using both the propensity score model, $\hat{e}(x)$, and the outcome model, $\hat{m}(x)$. The result is, once more, a unit-level data frame:

```
In [30]: df_dr = (df_delta_y
                  .assign(y_hat = lambda d: outcome_model.predict(d))
                  .assign(ps = lambda d: ps_model.predict(d)))

         df_dr.head()
```

city	region	treated	tau	downloads	post	delta_y	y_hat	ps
1	W	0	0.0	27.0	0	3.087302	3.736539	0.176471
2	N	0	0.0	40.0	0	1.436508	1.992570	0.212766
3	W	0	0.0	30.0	0	2.761905	3.736539	0.176471
4	W	0	0.0	26.0	0	3.396825	3.736539	0.176471
5	S	0	0.0	51.0	0	-0.476190	0.343915	0.176471

With that, let's think about what a doubly robust DID would look like. As with all DID, the ATT estimate is the difference between the trend, had the units been treated, from the trend they would have under the control. Since those are counterfactual quantities, I'll represent them with Δy_1 and Δy_0, respectively. So, to summarize, the ATT would be given by:

$$\hat{\tau}_{DRDID} = \widehat{\Delta y_1}^{DR} - \widehat{\Delta y_0}^{DR}$$

It's not much, I'll admit, but it's a nice start. From there, you need to think how to estimate the Δy_Ds in a doubly robust manner.

Let's focus on Δy_1. To estimate the treated counterfactual you would weight $y - \widehat{m}(x)$ by the inverse of the propensity score, which would reconstruct y_1 for the entire population (see Chapter 5). Here, since you only care about the ATT, you don't need that; you already got the treatment population. Hence, the first term becomes:

$$\widehat{\Delta y_1}^{DR} = 1/N_{tr} \sum_{i \in tr} (\Delta y - \widehat{m}(X))$$

For the other term, you would use weights $1/(1 - \hat{e}(x))$ to reconstruct the general population under the control. But again, since you care about the ATT, you need to reconstruct the treatment population under the control. To do that, you can simply multiply the weights by the chance of being a treated unit, which, conveniently, is just the propensity score:

$$w_{co} = \hat{e}(X) \frac{1}{1 - \hat{e}(X)}$$

Having defined the weight, you can use it to obtain the estimate for Δy_0:

$$\widehat{\Delta y_0}^{DR} = \sum_{i \in co} w_{co}(\Delta y - \widehat{m}(X)) / \sum w_{co}$$

That is pretty much it. As (almost) always, it looks a lot simpler in code than in math:

```
In [31]: tr = df_dr.query("treated==1")
         co = df_dr.query("treated==0")

         dy1_treat = (tr["delta_y"] - tr["y_hat"]).mean()

         w_cont = co["ps"]/(1-co["ps"])
         dy0_treat = np.average(co["delta_y"] - co["y_hat"], weights=w_cont)

         print("ATT:", dy1_treat - dy0_treat)

Out[31]: ATT: 1.6773180394442853
```

It is remarkably close to the true ATT and to the ATT you got earlier when you added covariates to DID. The advantage here is that you get two shots at getting the estimation right. The DRDID will work if either (but not necessarily both) the propensity score model or the outcome model are correct. I won't do it here to avoid making this chapter too long, but I encourage you to try replacing either the ps columns or the y_hat column by a randomly generated column and recompute the preceding estimate. You'll see that the end result will still be close to the actual one.

See Also

This method was proposed in the paper "Doubly Robust Difference-in-Differences Estimators," by Sant'Anna and Zhao. The paper has a lot more content, including how to do inference on this estimator and how to achieve double robustness when you have repeated cross-sectional data (when units can change at each time period) as opposed to a panel data (when all units are the same).

Just like when you did doubly robust estimation with cross-sectional data, to get confidence intervals for DRDID, you would need to use the block bootstrap function you implemented earlier, wrapping the entire procedure—outcome model, propensity score model, and putting it all together—in a single estimation function.

Staggered Adoption

Up until this point, the type of data you've been looking at followed a block design, with only two periods: a pre- and post-treatment. Even though each period had multiple dates, at the end of the day, all that mattered was that you had a group of units that were all treated at the same point in time and a group of units that were never treated. This block design is the poster child to difference-in-differences analysis since it keeps things extremely simple, allowing you to estimate the baselines and trends nonparametrically—that is, by simply computing a bunch of sample averages and comparing them. But it can also be fairly limited. What if the treatment gets rolled out to the units at different points in time?

A much more common situation with panel data is the *staggered adoption design*, where you have multiple groups of units, which I'll call G, and each group gets treated at a different point in time (or never). Since the timing of the treatment is what defines a group, it's common to refer to them as a cohort: the group G that gets the treatment at time t is the cohort G_t.

Bringing this to the marketing data you've been looking at, you had two cohorts: a never treated cohort, or G_∞, and a group that got the treatment at 2021-05-15, or $G_{15/05}$. But that's only because I've hidden what happens after 2021-06-01. Now that you're ready for a more complex situation, look at the mkt_data_cohorts data frame, which also contains data on cities from all the regions, but now up until 2021-07-31:

```
In [32]: mkt_data_cohorts = (pd.read_csv("./data/offline_mkt_staggered.csv")
                             .astype({
                                 "date":"datetime64[ns]",
                                 "cohort":"datetime64[ns]"}))

         mkt_data_cohorts.head()
```

	date	city	region	cohort	treated	tau	downloads	post
0	2021-05-01	1	W	2021-06-20	1	0.0	27.0	0
1	2021-05-02	1	W	2021-06-20	1	0.0	28.0	0
2	2021-05-03	1	W	2021-06-20	1	0.0	28.0	0
3	2021-05-04	1	W	2021-06-20	1	0.0	26.0	0
4	2021-05-05	1	W	2021-06-20	1	0.0	28.0	0

It's hard to see all the data by just looking at the top rows, but Figure 8-2 shows the treatment status across time. There you can see what a staggered adoption design looks like.

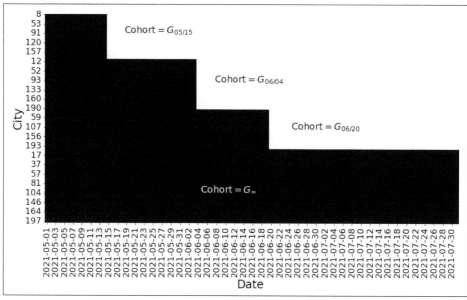

Figure 8-2. In a staggered adoption design, the treatment gets gradually rolled out to more and more units

Previously, you had data up until 2021-06-01, so it looked like you had a small treatment group and a huge never treated group. But once you expand your data, you can see that the offline marketing campaign got rolled out to other cities later on. Now, you have four different cohorts, three of which are treated and a never treated group (which has cohort 2100-01-01 in this dataset).

Just like with the block design, with staggered adoption you'll assume that once the treatment turns on, it stays that way forever. This is important to keep things tractable. In panel data analysis, the potential outcomes are defined by vectors representing the trajectory of outcome at each time period, $D = \left(Y_{d1}, Y_{d2}, \ldots, Y_{dT}\right)$, and the treatment effect is defined by contrasting two of those trajectories. This means there are about 2^T ways to define the treatment effect if you allow the treatment to turn on and off.

To take things one bite at a time, let's forget about covariates for now, focusing only on the West region. I'll show how to handle covariates later. For now, just focus on the staggered adoption component of the problem:

```
In [33]: mkt_data_cohorts_w = mkt_data_cohorts.query("region=='W'")
         mkt_data_cohorts_w.head()
```

	date	city	region	cohort	treated	tau	downloads	post
0	2021-05-01	1	W	2021-06-20	1	0.0	27.0	0
1	2021-05-02	1	W	2021-06-20	1	0.0	28.0	0
2	2021-05-03	1	W	2021-06-20	1	0.0	28.0	0
3	2021-05-04	1	W	2021-06-20	1	0.0	26.0	0
4	2021-05-05	1	W	2021-06-20	1	0.0	28.0	0

If you plot the average downloads over time for each cohort, you can see a clear picture. The outcome of $G = 05/15$ shows an increase right after the date 2021-15-05. The same is true for the cohorts $G = 06/04$ and $G = 06/20$. Meanwhile, the group that was never treated follows what appears to be a beautifully parallel trend to the treated groups prior to the treatment. Another thing to pay attention to is that the effect takes some time to mature, something you've seen before. This becomes even clearer if you plot the outcome after aligning the cohorts, which you can see in the second image:

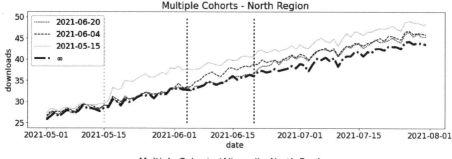

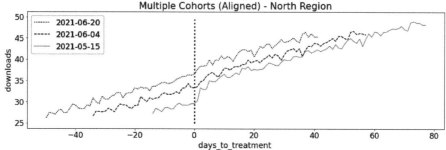

You might argue that the preceding data is extraordinarily well behaved, which makes it obvious it was simulated. You might even be tempted to conclude that diff-in-diff will have no problem recovering the true ATT. Well, let's try it out:

```
In [34]: twfe_model = smf.ols(
             "downloads ~ treated:post + C(date) + C(city)",
             data=mkt_data_cohorts_w
         ).fit()

         true_tau = mkt_data_cohorts_w.query("post==1&treated==1")["tau"].mean()

         print("True Effect: ", true_tau)
         print("Estimated ATT:", twfe_model.params["treated:post"])


Out[34]: True Effect:  2.2625252108176266
         Estimated ATT: 1.7599504780633743
```

As you can see, something is off. The effects seems downward biased! What is going on here?

This issue has been at the center of the very recent literature on panel data. Unfortunately, this chapter would be too long if I tried to give you a full explanation. What I can do is give you a glimpse and, if you are interested, point you to further resources. The root of this problem lies in the fact that, when you have staggered adoption, beyond the traditional DID assumptions you saw earlier, *you also need to assume that*

---

effects are homogeneous across time. As discussed earlier, this is not the case with this data. The effect takes some time to mature, meaning it is lower just after the treatment takes place and gradually climbs up afterward. This effect change over time causes bias in your ATT estimate.

Let's examine two groups of cities to understand why. The first group, which I'll call the *early treated* cohort, received treatment on 06/04. The second group, which I'll refer to as the *late treated* cohort, received treatment on 06/20. The two-way fixed effect model you just estimated actually uses a series of 2 × 2 diff-in-diff runs and combines them into a final estimate. In one of these runs, the model estimates the effect of treatment on the early treated cohort using the late treated group as a control. This is valid since the late treated cohort can be considered a not-yet-treated group. However, the model is also estimating the effect on the late treated cohort by using the early treated cohort as a control. This approach is acceptable, but only if the treatment effect is not variable across time. You can see why in the following image. The picture shows both comparisons as well as the estimated counterfactual, Y_0. It's worth noting that the role played by each cohort reverses from one plot to the next:

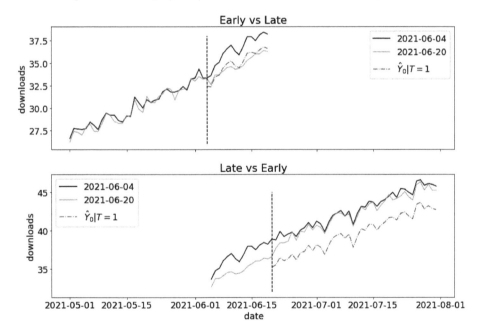

As you can see, the early versus late comparison seems fine. The issue is on the late versus early. The control group (cohort 06/04) is already treated, even though it serves as a control here. Moreover, since the effect is heterogeneous, gradually climbing up, the trend in the control (early treated) is steeper than it would be, had the cohort not yet been treated. This extra steepness from the gradually increasing effect causes an overestimate in the control trend, which in turns translates to a downward-biased ATT estimate. This is why using the already treated as a control will bias your results if the treatment effect is heterogeneous across time.

See Also

Like I said, there is a bunch of recent literature on this limitation of the two-way fixed effect model. If you want to learn more, I strongly recommend the paper "Difference-in-Differences with Variation in Treatment Timing," by Andrew Goodman-Bacon. His diagnosis of the problem is very neat and intuitive. Not to mention it comes with nice pictures to help with the general understanding of the paper.

Now that you know the problem, it's time to look at the solution. Since the issue lies on effect heterogeneity, the remedy will be to use a more flexible model, one that fully takes into account those heterogeneities.

PRACTICAL EXAMPLE

Higher Education and Growth in Developing Countries

In a more recent paper, "Higher Education Expansion, Labor Market, and Firm Productivity in Vietnam," Khoa Vu and Tu-Anh Vu-Thanh looked at the rapid increase at the number of universities in Vietnam to figure out the impact of higher education on wage. They took advantage that the higher education expansion was different for each province, which allowed them to identify the effect of universities using difference-in-differences.

> We collect a dataset on the timing and location of university openings and estimate that individuals' exposure to a university opening increases their chances of completing college by over 30%. It also raises their wage by 3.9% and household expenditure by 14%.

Heterogeneous Effect over Time

There is good news and bad news. First, the good news: you've identified the problem. Namely, you know that TWFE is biased when applied to staggered adoption data that has time-heterogeneous effects. In a more technical notation, your data generating process has different effect parameters:

$$Y_{it} = \tau_{it} W_{it} + \alpha_i + \gamma_t + e_{it},$$

but you were assuming that the effect was constant:

$$Y_{it} = \tau W_{it} + \alpha_i + \gamma_t + e_{it}.$$

If that is the problem, an easy fix would be to simply allow for a different effect for each time and unit. You could, in theory, achieve something like that with the following formula:

```
downloads ~ treated:post:C(date):C(city) + C(date) + C(city)
```

That's it right? Problem solved? Well, not quite. Now for the bad news: this model would have more parameters than there are data points. Since you are interacting date and unit, you would have one treatment effect parameter for each unit for each time period. But this is exactly the number of samples you have! OLS wouldn't even run here.

OK, so you need to reduce the number of treatment effect parameters of the model. To achieve that, can you think of a way of somehow grouping units? If you scratch your head a little, you can see a very natural way to group units: by cohort! You know that the effect in an entire cohort follows the same pattern over time. So, a natural improvement on that impractical model is to allow the effect to change by cohort, instead of by units:

$$Y_{it} = \tau_{gt} W_{it} + \alpha_i + \gamma_t + e_{it}.$$

That model has a more reasonable number of treatment effect parameters, since the number of cohorts is usually much smaller than the number of units. Now, you can finally run the model:

```
In [35]: formula = "downloads ~ treated:post:C(cohort):C(date) + C(city)+C(date)"

         twfe_model = smf.ols(formula, data=mkt_data_cohorts_w).fit()
```

This will give you multiple ATT estimates: one for each cohort and date. So, to see if you got it right, you can compute the estimated individual treatment effect implied by your model and average out the result. To do that, just compare the actual outcome at the post-treatment period from the treated units with what your models predict for $\hat{y}_0$:

```
In [36]: df_pred = (
             mkt_data_cohorts_w
             .query("post==1 & treated==1")
             .assign(y_hat_0=lambda d: twfe_model.predict(d.assign(treated=0)))
             .assign(effect_hat=lambda d: d["downloads"] - d["y_hat_0"])
         )

         print("Number of param.:", len(twfe_model.params))
         print("True Effect: ", df_pred["tau"].mean())
```

```
print("Pred. Effect: ", df_pred["effect_hat"].mean())
```

```
Out[36]: Number of param.: 510
         True Effect:  2.2625252108176266
         Pred. Effect:  2.259766144685074
```

Finally! This gives you a model with a bunch of parameters (510!), but it does manage to recover the true ATT. You can even extract those ATTs and plot them:

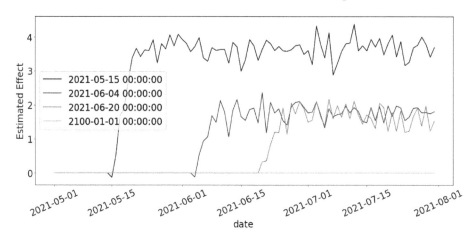

The nice thing about this plot is that it's in accordance with your intuition of how the effect should behave: it gradually climbs up and it stays constant after a while. Also, it shows you that the effect is zero for all the pre-treatment periods and, consequently, for the never treated cohort. This might give you some idea on how to reduce the number of parameters from this model. For instance, you could only consider effects from time periods that are greater than the cohort:

$$Y_{it} = \tau_{g,\, t \geq g} W_{it} + \alpha_i + \gamma_t + e_{it}.$$

This would involve a nontrivial amount of feature engineering, though, as you would have to group the dates prior to the treatment, but it's good to know it is possible.

See Also

This solution to the treatment effect heterogeneity problem was inspired by the papers "Estimating Dynamic Treatment Effects in Event Studies with Heterogeneous Treatment Effects," by Sun and Abraham, and the paper "Two-Way Fixed Effects, the Two-Way Mundlak Regression, and Difference-in-Differences Estimators," by Jeffrey Wooldridge.

Just like when you approached the problem of including covariates in the diff-in-diff model, there are two types of solutions for this TWFE bias. The one you just saw involves cleverly interacting dummies when running the two-way fixed effect model. Another approach involves breaking the problem into multiple 2 × 2 diff-in-diffs, solving each one individually and combining the results. One way to do this is by estimating one diff-in-diff model for each cohort, using the never treated group as a control:

```
In [37]: cohorts = sorted(mkt_data_cohorts_w["cohort"].unique())

         treated_G = cohorts[:-1]
         nvr_treated = cohorts[-1]

         def did_g_vs_nvr_treated(df: pd.DataFrame,
                                  cohort: str,
                                  nvr_treated: str,
                                  cohort_col: str = "cohort",
                                  date_col: str = "date",
                                  y_col: str = "downloads"):
             did_g = (
                 df
                 .loc[lambda d:(d[cohort_col] == cohort)|
                              (d[cohort_col] == nvr_treated)]
                 .assign(treated = lambda d: (d[cohort_col] == cohort)*1)
                 .assign(post = lambda d:(pd.to_datetime(d[date_col])>=cohort)*1)
             )

             att_g = smf.ols(f"{y_col} ~ treated*post",
                            data=did_g).fit().params["treated:post"]
             size = len(did_g.query("treated==1 & post==1"))
             return {"att_g": att_g, "size": size}


         atts = pd.DataFrame(
             [did_g_vs_nvr_treated(mkt_data_cohorts_w, cohort, nvr_treated)
              for cohort in treated_G]
         )

         atts
```

	att_g	size
0	3.455535	702
1	1.659068	1044
2	1.573687	420

Then, you can combine the result with a weighted average, where the weights are the sample size $(T*N)$ of each cohort. The resulting estimate is remarkably similar to what you estimated before:

```
In [38]: (atts["att_g"]*atts["size"]).sum()/atts["size"].sum()


Out[38]: 2.2247467740558697
```

Alternatively, instead of using the never treated as the control, you could use the not yet treated, which increases the sample size of the control. This is a bit more cumbersome, as you would have to run diff-in-diff multiple times for the same cohort.

See Also

This second solution to the effect heterogeneity problem was inspired by the paper "Difference-in-Differences with Multiple Time Periods," by Pedro H. C. Sant'Anna and Brantly Callaway. In the paper, they also cover how to use the not-yet treated as a control group and how to use doubly robust difference-in-differences.

Covariates

Having gotten the TWFE bias issue out the way, all there is left to do is see how to use the entire dataset, all time periods, with staggered adoption design, and all regions, which will require you to include covariates in your model.

Fortunately, there is nothing particularly new here. All you have to do is remember how you've added covariates to the diff-in-diff model earlier. In that case, you've interacted the covariates with the post treatment dummy. Here, analogous to the post-treatment dummy is the date column, which marks the passage of time. Hence, all you have to do is interact the covariates with that column:

```
In [39]: formula = """
         downloads ~ treated:post:C(cohort):C(date)
         + C(date):C(region) + C(city) + C(date)"""

         twfe_model = smf.ols(formula, data=mkt_data_cohorts).fit()
```

Once more, since this model will give you a bunch of parameter estimates, you can get the ATT by computing the individual effects and averaging them out:

```
In [40]: df_pred = (
             mkt_data_cohorts
             .query("post==1 & treated==1")
             .assign(y_hat_0=lambda d: twfe_model.predict(d.assign(treated=0)))
             .assign(effect_hat=lambda d: d["downloads"] - d["y_hat_0"])
         )
```

```
        print("Number of param.:", len(twfe_model.params))
        print("True Effect: ",  df_pred["tau"].mean())
        print("Pred. Effect: ", df_pred["effect_hat"].mean())


Out[40]: Number of param.: 935
         True Effect:  2.078397729895905
         Pred. Effect:  2.0426262863584568
```

If you choose to break down staggered adoption into multiple 2×2 blocks, you could also add covariates in each DID model individually, pretty much like you did earlier.

Key Ideas

Panel data methods is an exciting and rapidly evolving field in causal inference. A lot of the promises come from the fact that having an extra time dimension allows you to estimate counterfactuals for the treated not only from the control units, but also from the treated units' past.

In this chapter, you've explored multiple ways of applying difference-in-differences. DID relaxes the traditional unconfoundedness assumption, $Y_d \perp T | X$ to the conditional parallel assumption:

$$\Delta Y_d \perp T | X$$

This gives you some hope if you have unobservable confounders. With panel data, you can still identify the ATT, as long as those confounders are constant across time (for the same unit) or across units (for the same time period).

Despite its great powers, DID doesn't come without its complexities. If you move beyond the canonical DID formulation, you need to be very careful with your modeling. While 2×2 DID has the flexibility of a nonparametric model, the same cannot be said about the more general staggered adoption setting, which requires you to make additional functional form assumptions.

This chapter teaches you how to deal with many extensions beyond the simple 2×2 case, adding covariates, estimating the effect evolution over time, and allowing different treatment timing. However, keep in mind that all of this is very new, and I wouldn't be surprised if the field moves beyond what's in here in the near future. Still, this chapter should give you a pretty solid foundation to catch up quickly, should the necessity arise.

CHAPTER 9

Synthetic Control

In the previous chapter you learned about the advantages of panel data for causal identification. Namely, the fact that you could not only compare units with each other, but also with their former selves, allows you to estimate counterfactuals Y_0 with more plausible assumptions. You also learned about difference-in-differences (DID)—and many variations of it—one of the many causal inference tools that leverage panel data. By relying on similar (parallel) growth trajectories between treated and control, DID was able to identify the treatment effect even if the levels of Y_0 between treated and control were different. In this chapter, you'll learn another popular technique for panel datasets: synthetic control (SC).

While DID works great if you have a relatively large number of units N compared to time periods T, it falls short when the reverse is true. In contrast, synthetic control was designed to work with very few, even one, treatment unit. The idea behind it is quite simple: combine the control units in order to craft a synthetic control that would approximate the behavior of the treated units in the absence of treatment. By doing that, it avoids making a parallel trend assumption as the synthetic control, when well crafted, won't be just parallel, but perfectly overlapping with the counterfactual $E[Y_0|D = 1]$.

At the end of this chapter, you'll also learn how to combine both DID and SC. This combined estimator is not only very powerful, but, most importantly, it will give you a whole new perspective on difference-in-differences and synthetic control in particular, and panel data methods in general.

Online Marketing Dataset

As a use case for synthetic control, you'll be working with an online marketing dataset. Online marketing allows for better tracking than offline marketing, but it doesn't mean it comes without its challenges for causal inference. For instance, it is true that online marketing allows better attribution: you know if a customer reached your product through some paid marketing link. But that doesn't mean you know what would have happened to that customer if they didn't see your online ad. Perhaps customers only came because they saw the ad, in which case it is bringing in extra customers. But perhaps customers would have come either way and the fact that they did through the paid link was just because that link was at the top of the page.

Since attribution is not the same as incrementality, and since you can't randomize who gets to see your ads, treating entire geographies and doing some sort of panel data analysis, much like in the previous chapter, is also a good idea for online marketing. Hence, the data you have here is not much different from the data you saw in the previous chapter. Once again, you have the city as the unit and date as the time dimension, a treated column, which marks if the city is eventually treated, and a post-treatment column, which marks the post-intervention period. You also have some auxiliary columns, like the population in that city (recorded in 2013, so fixed in time) and the state:

```
In [1]: import pandas as pd
        import numpy as np

        df = (pd.read_csv("./data/online_mkt.csv")
              .astype({"date":"datetime64[ns]"}))

        df.head()
```

	app_download	population	city	state	date	post	treated
0	3066.0	12396372	sao_paulo	sao_paulo	2022-03-01	0	1
1	2701.0	12396372	sao_paulo	sao_paulo	2022-03-02	0	1
2	1927.0	12396372	sao_paulo	sao_paulo	2022-03-03	0	1
3	1451.0	12396372	sao_paulo	sao_paulo	2022-03-04	0	1
4	1248.0	12396372	sao_paulo	sao_paulo	2022-03-05	0	1

Here, the outcome variable is daily app downloads and the treatment is having the marketing campaign turned on for that city. The treatment is implemented on the treated cities at the same time, which means you have a simple block design. The catch here is that you have a much smaller number of treated units—only three cities:

```
In [2]: treated = list(df.query("treated==1")["city"].unique())
        treated

Out[2]: ['sao_paulo', 'porto_alegre', 'joao_pessoa']
```

If you paid attention to the population column in the data frame, you might have noticed that one of those cities, Sao Paulo, has a massive population of over 12MM. In fact, it is one of the biggest cities in the world! This also means that the number of app downloads in Sao Paulo will be a lot larger than in other cities, which poses some challenges. It is very hard to combine other cities to make a synthetic control that matches Sao Paulo's downloads. This issue is exacerbated here, but, in general, entire markets will have different sizes, making comparison across them difficult. Hence, a common approach is to *normalize the outcome by the market size*. This means dividing the number of app downloads by the city's population to create a normalized version of the outcome. This new outcome, app_download_pct, represents the number of daily downloads as a percentage of the market size:

```
In [3]: df_norm = df.assign(
            app_download_pct = 100*df["app_download"]/df["population"]
        )

        df_norm.head()
```

	app_download	population	city	state	date	post	treated	app_download_pct
0	3066.0	12396372	sao_paulo	sao_paulo	2022-03-01	0	1	0.024733
1	2701.0	12396372	sao_paulo	sao_paulo	2022-03-02	0	1	0.021789
2	1927.0	12396372	sao_paulo	sao_paulo	2022-03-03	0	1	0.015545
3	1451.0	12396372	sao_paulo	sao_paulo	2022-03-04	0	1	0.011705
4	1248.0	12396372	sao_paulo	sao_paulo	2022-03-05	0	1	0.010067

Moving forward with your exploratory analysis, you'll find out that an online marketing campaign was launched for those cities in 2022-05-01. The campaign also stayed on for the remainder of the analyzed time window:

```
In [4]: tr_period = df_norm.query("post==1")["date"].min()
        tr_period


Out[4]: Timestamp('2022-05-01 00:00:00')
```

This is a good time to review some of the panel notation you'll be using. Recall that, to avoid confusion, I'll use D to denote the treatment variable and t to denote time. T will be the number of periods, with T_{pre} being the number of periods before the intervention and T_{post}, the number of periods after the intervention. Hence, the treatment takes place when $D = 1$ and $t > T_{pre}$. To declutter, I'll sometimes use a post dummy to indicate $t > T_{pre}$. The combination of both treated and post-treatment will be represented by $W_{it} = D_i * Post_t$.

For you to get a sense of what this data looks like, the following plot shows the evolution of the average outcome of the three treated cities, and a sample of control cities, in the background, in light gray. The beginning of the post-treatment period is marked by a horizontal dashed line:

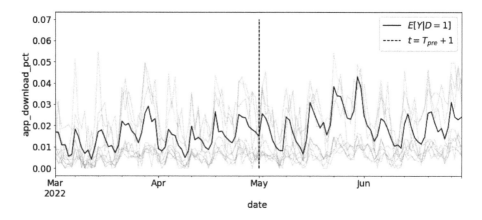

Looking at this plot, you can kind of see an increase in the treated units' outcome after the intervention, but it is not 100% clear. To be more precise, you would have to estimate the counterfactual and compare it to the observed outcome to get an estimate for average treatment effect on the treated (ATT):

$$ATT = E[Y|D = 1, Post = 1] - E\big[Y_0\big|D = 1, Post = 1\big]$$

Here is where synthetic control comes in. It is an incredibly *clever way to use (but not condition on) past outcomes in order to estimate* $E\big[Y_0\big|D = 1, Post = 1\big]$.

Matrix Representation

In the previous chapter, I showed you an image that represents panel data as a matrix, where one dimension is the time period and the other dimension denotes the units. Synthetic control makes explicit use of that matrix, so it is worth reviewing it. Let's say that the rows of the matrix are the time periods and the columns of the matrix are the cities (units). You can represent the treatment assignment with four blocks:

$$W = \begin{bmatrix} 0_{pre,\,co} & 0_{pre,\,tr} \\ 0_{post,\,co} & 1_{post,\,tr} \end{bmatrix}$$

The first block in your matrix (top left) corresponds to the control units prior to the treatment period; the second one (top right) corresponds to the treated units prior to the treatment period; the third block (bottom left) contains the control units after the treatment period; and the fourth block (bottom right) is the treated unit after the treatment period. The treatment indicator w_{ti} is zero everywhere except for the block with the treated units after the treatment period (bottom right).

This assignment matrix will lead to the following observed potential outcome matrix:

$$Y = \begin{bmatrix} Y(0)_{pre, co} & Y(0)_{pre, tr} \\ Y(0)_{post, co} & Y(1)_{post, tr} \end{bmatrix}$$

Again, notice how the post-treatment period is on the bottom and the treated units are to the right. Your goal is to estimate the $ATT = Y(1)_{post, tr} - Y(0)_{post, tr}$. For that, you need to somehow estimate the missing potential outcome $Y(0)_{post, tr}$, which is not observed. In words, you need to know what would have happened to the treated units at the post-treatment period had they not been treated. To achieve that, you would ideally leverage all the other three blocks at your disposal, $Y(0)_{pre, co}$, $Y(0)_{pre, tr}$, and $Y(0)_{post, co}$. Before I show you how synthetic control does that, let's create a function to represent the data in this matrix format.

The following code uses the `.pivot()` method to reshape the data frame so that you end up with one row per time period (date) and one column per city, while the outcome becomes the values of the matrix. Then, it partitions the matrix into treated and control units. It further partitions them into a pre- and post-intervention period:

```
In [5]: def reshape_sc_data(df: pd.DataFrame,
                            geo_col: str,
                            time_col: str,
                            y_col: str,
                            tr_geos: str,
                            tr_start: str):

            df_pivot = df.pivot(time_col, geo_col, y_col)

            y_co = df_pivot.drop(columns=tr_geos)
            y_tr = df_pivot[tr_geos]

            y_pre_co = y_co[df_pivot.index < tr_start]
            y_pre_tr = y_tr[df_pivot.index < tr_start]

            y_post_co = y_co[df_pivot.index >= tr_start]
            y_post_tr = y_tr[df_pivot.index >= tr_start]

            return y_pre_co, y_pre_tr, y_post_co, y_post_tr
```

You'll use this four-block matrix representation throughout the chapter. If you ever forget what you are working with, just come back to this function. To see how it works, passing df_norm to reshape_sc_data returns you the Ys in matrix format. Here are the first five rows of y_pre_tr:

```
In [6]: y_pre_co, y_pre_tr, y_post_co, y_post_tr = reshape_sc_data(
            df_norm,
            geo_col="city",
            time_col="date",
            y_col="app_download_pct",
            tr_geos=treated,
            tr_start=str(tr_period)
        )

        y_pre_tr.head()
```

city date	sao_paulo	porto_alegre	joao_pessoa
2022-03-01	0.024733	0.004288	0.022039
2022-03-02	0.021789	0.008107	0.020344
2022-03-03	0.015545	0.004891	0.012352
2022-03-04	0.011705	0.002948	0.018285
2022-03-05	0.010067	0.006767	0.000000

Synthetic Control as Horizontal Regression

The main idea behind synthetic control is quite simple. Using the pre-treatment period, you'll find a way to combine the control units to approximate the average outcome of the treated units. In mathematical terms, this can be framed as an optimization problem, where you'll look for unit weights w_i (not to be confused with $w_{it} = Post_t * D_i$) such that, when you multiply each weight by its unit's outcome, $w_i y_i$, you get something resembling the treated unit's outcome:

$$\hat{\omega}^{sc} = \underset{\omega}{\text{argmin}} \ \|\bar{y}_{pre,\,tr} - Y_{pre,\,co}\omega_{co}\|^2$$

Then, to estimate $E[Y(0)|D = 1, Post = 1]$ and get the ATT estimate, you can use the synthetic control $Y_{post,\,co}\omega_{co}$.

If this seems a bit cryptic, perhaps a good alternative explanation is one that compares synthetic control to a more familiar tool: linear regression. Recall that regression could also be represented by an optimization problem where the goal was to minimize the (squared) difference between the outcome and a linear combination of the covariates X:

$$\beta^* = \underset{\beta}{argmin} \; ||Y_i - X_i'\beta||^2$$

Outcome Modeling

Here, you can draw a parallel between synthetic control and potential outcome modeling, which you saw in Chapter 5, when reading about Doubly Robust Estimation. There, you also had to build a regression model that was estimated in the control group. Then, you used that model to impute the missing potential outcome, Y_0, for those that where treated. The idea is pretty much the same here.

As you can see, both objectives are identical! This means that synthetic control is nothing more than *a regression that uses the outcome of the control as features to try to predict the average outcome of the treated units*. The trick is that it does this by using only the pre-intervention period so that the regression estimates $E[Y_0|D = 1]$.

In fact, to prove my point, let's use OLS to build a synthetic control right now. All you have to do is to use y_pre_co as if it was the covariate matrix X and the column average of y_pre_tr as the outcome y. Once you fit this model, the weights can be extracted with .coef_:

```
In [7]: from sklearn.linear_model import LinearRegression

        model = LinearRegression(fit_intercept=False)
        model.fit(y_pre_co, y_pre_tr.mean(axis=1))

        # extract the weights
        weights_lr = model.coef_
        weights_lr.round(3)


Out[7]: array([-0.65 , -0.058, -0.239,  0.971,  0.03 , -0.204,  0.007,  0.095,
                0.102,  0.106,  0.074,  0.079,  0.032, -0.5  , -0.041, -0.154,
               -0.014,  0.132,  0.115,  0.094,  0.151, -0.058, -0.353,  0.049,
               -0.476, -0.11 ,  0.158, -0.002,  0.036, -0.129, -0.066,  0.024,
               -0.047,  0.089, -0.057,  0.429,  0.23 , -0.086,  0.098,  0.351,
               -0.128,  0.128, -0.205,  0.088,  0.147,  0.555,  0.229])
```

As you can see, you have one weight for each control city. Usually, regression is used when you have a bunch of units (large N), which allows you to use the units as the rows and the covariates as the columns. But synthetic control is designed to work when you have relatively few units, but a larger time horizon T_{pre}. In order to do that, SC quite literally flips the data on its head, using the units as if they were covariates. This is why synthetic control is also called horizontal regression (see Figure 9-1).

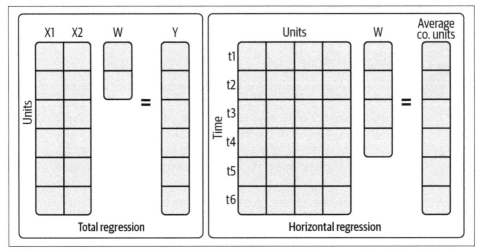

Figure 9-1. In traditional regression, units are the rows of the regression table; in horizontal regression, the rows are time periods and the units are the columns

Once you've estimated your regression parameters (or weights), you can use them to predict what $E[Y_0|D=1]$ would look like, not only on the pre-intervention period, but on the entire time horizon:

```
In [8]: # same as y0_tr_hat = model.predict(y_post_co)
        y0_tr_hat = y_post_co.dot(weights_lr)
```

Here, `y0_tr_hat` can be seen as a synthetic control: a combination of control units that come together to approximate the behavior of the treated units' average, had they not been treated.

Average of Synthetic Controls

Alternatively, instead of finding one synthetic control to replicate the average outcome of the treated units, you could also fit one synthetic control for each treatment unit individually and then average the synthetic controls:

```
model = LinearRegression(fit_intercept=False)
model.fit(y_pre_co, y_pre_tr)
y0_tr_hat = model.predict(y_co).mean(axis=1)
```

If you plot this synthetic control alongside the observed outcome, you'll get this:

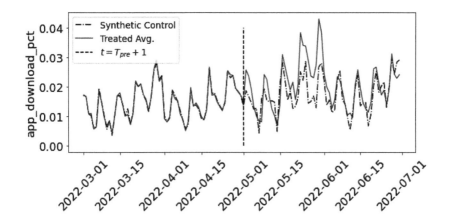

Notice how the predicted value (the synthetic control) is below the actual outcome of the treated units. It means that the observed outcome was higher than you've estimated it to be, had the treatment not taken place. This indicates a positive marketing effect from the online marketing campaign. You can compute that ATT estimate by contrasting the observed outcome with the synthetic control:

```
In [9]: att = y_post_tr.mean(axis=1) - y0_tr_hat
```

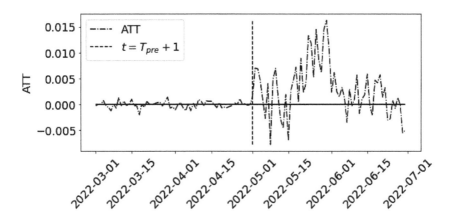

The plot presents a couple of intriguing aspects. Firstly, it suggests that the effect takes some time to reach its peak before gradually declining. The gradual increase is frequently observed in marketing since it usually requires time for individuals to take action after seeing an advertisement. Additionally, the effect wearing off can often be attributed to a novelty effect that gradually fades over time.

The second interesting thing is the size of the ATT in the pre-intervention period. In that time frame, the ATT can be interpreted simply as the residual (in sample error) from your OLS model. You might think that it being close to zero is a good thing; after all, you don't want to see an effect prior to the treatment (anticipation). But there is more to it. The fact that the pre-intervention error is incredibly low can also mean that the OLS model is probably overfitting. As a result, the out-of-sample prediction, which should estimate $E[Y_0|D=1, Post=1]$, might be off.

This is why simple regression is not commonly used as a method to build synthetic controls. Because of the relatively large number of columns (control cities), it tends to overfit, not generalizing to the post-intervention period. For this reason, the original synthetic control method is not a simple regression, but one that imposes some reasonable and intuitive constraints.

Canonical Synthetic Control

The canonical synthetic control formulation imposes two constraints on the regression model:

1. That the weights are all positive
2. That the weights add up to one

Mathematically, the optimization objective becomes:

$$\hat{w}^{sc} = \underset{w}{\operatorname{argmin}} \ ||\bar{\mathbf{y}}_{pre, tr} - \mathbf{Y}_{pre, co} w_{co}||^2$$
$$\text{s.t} \ \ \sum w_i = 1 \ \text{and} \ \ w_i > 0 \ \forall \ i$$

The idea behind the constraints is to force the synthetic control to be a convex combination of the treated units, *avoiding extrapolation*. This means that if the treated unit has an outcome greater (or lower) than all the control units, this canonical formulation won't be able to craft a synthetic control to recover $E[Y_0|D=1]$. You can view this as a limitation, but it is actually meant as a guardrail. It's a way of saying that the treatment units you are trying to reconstruct are very different from the ones in the control group and therefore you shouldn't even try.

To code the canonical version of SC, you can use convex optimization software, like cvxpy. cvxpy allows you to define an optimization objective with cp.Minimize. For SC, you want to minimize the squared error, so cp.Minimize(cp.sum_squares(y_co_pre@w - y_tr_pre)). It also allows you to pass optimization constraints. Here, you want all the ws to be nonnegative and np.sum(w)==1.

In the following code, I'm building the synthetic control model following scikit-learn's boilerplate. To do that, you can extend BaseEstimator and RegressorMixin and define a .fit and a .predict method. The rest of the code, like check_X_y, check_array, and check_is_fitted are just some standard checks you don't need to worry about:

```
In [10]: from sklearn.base import BaseEstimator, RegressorMixin
         from sklearn.utils.validation import (check_X_y, check_array,
                                               check_is_fitted)
         import cvxpy as cp

         class SyntheticControl(BaseEstimator, RegressorMixin):

             def __init__(self,):
                 pass

             def fit(self, y_pre_co, y_pre_tr):

                 y_pre_co, y_pre_tr = check_X_y(y_pre_co, y_pre_tr)

                 w = cp.Variable(y_pre_co.shape[1])

                 objective = cp.Minimize(cp.sum_squares(y_pre_co@w - y_pre_tr))
                 constraints = [cp.sum(w) == 1, w >= 0]

                 problem = cp.Problem(objective, constraints)

                 self.loss_ = problem.solve(verbose=False)
                 self.w_ = w.value

                 self.is_fitted_ = True
                 return self


             def predict(self, y_co):

                 check_is_fitted(self)
                 y_co = check_array(y_co)

                 return y_co @ self.w_
```

Having defined the SyntheticControl class, you can use it pretty much like you used LinearRegression before. Notice that I'm storing the final loss of the estimated model. This will come in handy if you want to incorporate covariates in your model, as you'll soon see. Also, after the model is fitted, you can access the weights with .w_:

```
In [11]: model = SyntheticControl()
         model.fit(y_pre_co, y_pre_tr.mean(axis=1))

         # extrac the weights
         model.w_.round(3)
```

```
Out[11]: array([-0.    , -0.    , -0.    , -0.    , -0.    , -0.    ,  0.076,  0.037,
                  0.083,  0.01 , -0.    , -0.    , -0.    , -0.    , -0.    , -0.    ,
                  0.061,  0.123,  0.008,  0.074, -0.    ,  0.    , -0.    , -0.    ,
                 -0.    , -0.    , -0.    , -0.    , -0.    ,  0.    , -0.    ,  0.092,
                 -0.    , -0.    ,  0.    ,  0.046,  0.089,  0.    ,  0.067,  0.061,
                  0.    , -0.    , -0.    ,  0.088,  0.    ,  0.086, -0.    ])
```

Notice another interesting thing: the convexity constraints you've imposed give a sparse solution to the optimization problem. Only a handful of cities are used to craft the final synthetic control. From this point onward, it's exactly the same thing as before. You can make predictions on the entire dataset to obtain the synthetic control estimate for $E[Y_0|D = 1]$ and use that to get the ATT estimate:

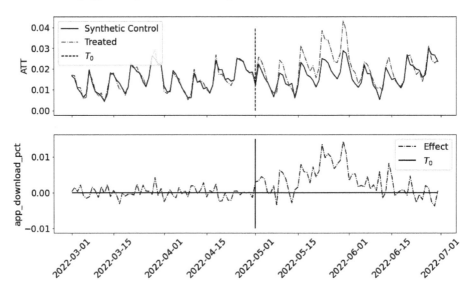

Compare this ATT plot with the one you got earlier, using unconstrained regression. Now, the training (pre-treatment) error is a bit larger, but the ATT is less noisy. This is regularization in action.

Regularized Regression

Once you realize that synthetic control is just horizontal regression, you can find other ways to regularize it. For instance, you can use lasso or ridge regression. Still, it makes a lot of sense to not allow negative weights, especially if the units are geographies, as the outcome tends to be positively correlated among those.

Synthetic Control Assumptions

Just like with difference-in-differences, you also have to assume no anticipation of the treatment and no spillovers when using synthetic control. The main difference between the two methods is the parametric assumption about the potential outcome model. In diff-in-diff, you had to assume that the trend in Y_0 for the treated units was parallel to the Y_0 trend from the control units. Synthetic control, on the other hand, allows a more flexible (but also more complicated) model for that potential outcome: a vector autoregressive model or a linear factor model. For the factor model:

$$Y_{0it} = \lambda_i' \mathbf{f}_t + e_{it},$$

if you set $\lambda_1 = 1$, $f_1 = \beta_t$ and $\lambda_1 = \alpha_i$, $f_1 = 1$, you can see that it becomes a generalization of the two-way-fixed-effects model $Y_{0it} = \alpha_i + \beta_t + e_{it}$.

In the paper "Using Synthetic Controls: Feasibility, Data Requirements, and Methodological Aspects," Alberto Abadie argues that if the potential outcome follows either the vector autoregressive or the linear factor model *and* the synthetic control matches the treated unit, then the synthetic control method produces an unbiased estimate to the ATT. In practice, that SC can only approximate the treated unit, so some bias is to be expected.

Synthetic Control with Covariants

Usually, synthetic control uses just the pre-treatment outcome from the control units as features to predict $\bar{Y}_{tr}$. That's because those tend to be the most predictive feature at your disposal. However, you might wish to include some additional covariates in the model, if you think they have a good predictive power. This is quite rare, though, so, if you are short of time, you can skip this section.

Let's say you somehow manage to get data on the daily number of downloads from your main competitor, which you've also normalized by the market size, comp_download_pct. You think this covariate is a good predictor of $\bar{Y}_{tr}$, so you want to include it in the synthetic control model:

```
In [12]: df_norm_cov = (pd.read_csv("./data/online_mkt_cov.csv")
                        .astype({"date":"datetime64[ns]"}))

         df_norm_cov.head()
```

	app_download	city	date	post	treated	app_download_pct	comp_download_pct
0	3066.0	sao_paulo	2022-03-01	0	1	0.024733	0.026280
1	2701.0	sao_paulo	2022-03-02	0	1	0.021789	0.023925
2	1927.0	sao_paulo	2022-03-03	0	1	0.015545	0.018930
3	1451.0	sao_paulo	2022-03-04	0	1	0.011705	0.015858
4	1248.0	sao_paulo	2022-03-05	0	1	0.010067	0.014548

In mathematical notation, you want to construct a synthetic control such that the weight w_i is not only multiplied by y_{co}, but also by this extra covariate, x_{co}, in order to approximate $\bar{Y}_{tr}$. The issue here is that x_{co} and y_{co} might be in completely different scales or one can be more predictive than the other, which is why you need to multiply each covariate, including y_{co}, by a scaling factor v, *before* solving the SC optimization problem. To take that into account, you can rewrite the objective in terms of covariates X, treating y_{co} as just another covariate:

$$\hat{w}^{sc} = \underset{\omega}{\operatorname{argmin}} \left\| \bar{y}_{pre,tr} - \sum v_k^* X_{k,pre,co} \omega_{co} \right\|^2$$

$$\text{s.t } \sum \omega_i = 1 \text{ and } \omega_i > 0 \ \forall \ i$$

However, this objective doesn't tell you how to find the optimal v. In order to do that, you'll have to wrap the entire synthetic control into yet another optimization objective. If it sounds complicated, don't worry. It is a lot easier to understand it in code. First, let's create the X matrix for both covariates, comp_download_pct and $Y_{pre,co}$, app_download_pct:

```
In [13]: from toolz import partial

         reshaper = partial(reshape_sc_data,
                            df=df_norm_cov,
                            geo_col="city",
                            time_col="date",
                            tr_geos=treated,
                            tr_start=str(tr_period))

         y_pre_co, y_pre_tr, y_post_co, y_post_tr = reshaper(
             y_col="app_download_pct"
         )

         x_pre_co, _, x_post_co, _ = reshaper(y_col="comp_download_pct")
```

Next, let's write a function which, when given a list of *vs*, one for each covariate, returns the synthetic control weights and the optimization loss. Remember that you can access the objective loss from a fitted SyntheticControl model with .loss_.

To check if this is working, you can pass [1, 0] as the *vs* and [y_pre_co, x_pre_co] as the covariate list. You should get back the original synthetic control, since the extra covariate has zero weight in this case:

```
In [14]: def find_w_given_vs(vs, x_co_list, y_tr_pre):
             X_times_v = sum([x*v for x, v in zip(x_co_list, vs)])

             model = SyntheticControl()
             model.fit(X_times_v, y_tr_pre)

             return {"loss": model.loss_, "w": model.w_}


         find_w_given_vs([1, 0],
                         [y_pre_co, x_pre_co],
                         y_pre_tr.mean(axis=1)).get("w").round(3)

Out[14]: array([-0.   , -0.   ,  0.   , -0.   , -0.   , -0.   ,  0.084,  0.039,
                  0.085,  0.003, -0.   , -0.   , -0.   , -0.   , -0.   ,  0.   ,
                  0.062,  0.121, -0.   ,  0.072, -0.   ,  0.   , -0.   ,  0.   ,
                 -0.   , -0.   ,  0.   , -0.   , -0.   ,  0.   , -0.   ,  0.095,
                  0.   , -0.   ,  0.   ,  0.022,  0.116, -0.   ,  0.068,  0.046,
                 -0.   , -0.   , -0.   ,  0.088,  0.   ,  0.098, -0.   ])
```

Finally, you can wrap `find_w_given_vs` in a function that just takes the array of *vs* and returns the optimization loss. Then, you can then pass this function to scipy `mini mize` function, which will iteratively look for the best *vs* and return them to you:

```
In [15]: from scipy.optimize import minimize

         def v_loss(vs):
             return find_w_given_vs(vs,
                                    [y_pre_co, x_pre_co],
                                    y_pre_tr.mean(axis=1)).get("loss")


         v_solution = minimize(v_loss, [0, 0], method='L-BFGS-B')
         v_solution.x

Out[15]: array([1.88034589, 0.00269853])
```

With the optimal *vs*, you can go back to `find_w_given_vs` to obtain the synthetic control weights that take the covariates into account. One thing to notice, though, is that the final solution is not much different from the one without covariants. This is not surprising, since the optimal v for the `comp_download_pct` covariate is a very small number and it is not on a much larger scale than `app_download_pct`:

```
In [16]: w_cov = find_w_given_vs(v_solution.x,
                             [y_pre_co, x_pre_co],
                             y_pre_tr.mean(axis=1)).get("w").round(3)

         w_cov
```

```
Out[16]: array([-0.   , -0.   , 0.   , -0.   , -0.   , -0.   , 0.078, 0.001,
                 0.033, 0.   , -0.   , 0.034, -0.   , -0.   , -0.   , 0.   ,
                 0.016, 0.047, 0.03 , 0.01 , -0.   , -0.   , 0.   , 0.055,
                 -0.   , 0.   , -0.   , 0.   , 0.   , 0.   , -0.   , 0.046,
                 0.078, 0.007, 0.   , 0.   , 0.138, 0.   , 0.022, 0.008,
                 -0.   , 0.201, 0.   , 0.035, 0.   , 0.161, -0.   ])
```

With these weights, you can make predictions for $Y(0)$ and obtain the final ATT estimate that considers covariates:

```
In [17]: y0_hat = sum([x*v for x, v
                      in zip([y_post_co, x_post_co], v_solution.x)]).dot(w_cov)

         att = y_post_tr.mean(axis=1) - y0_hat
```

The following plot shows the resulting ATT, alongside the ATT estimate from the canonical SC, without covariates. As you can see, both are pretty similar:

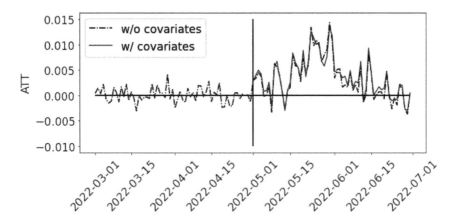

Although not hard, including covariates requires a fair amount of extra complexity. For this reason and due to the fact that $Y_{pre,co}$ tends to be enough to predict Y_{tr}, I usually don't bother with adding covariates. But maybe you can find very predictive features that would justify it.

Generic Horizontal Regression

A simpler way to add covariates is to just concatenate any additional time series you deem worthy as a column to $\mathbf{Y}_{pre,co}$. This would be equivalent to adding additional covariates in the horizontal regression:

$$\left[\mathbf{Y}_{pre,co} \middle| \mathbf{X}_{pre,co}\right]\omega$$

This wouldn't be a synthetic control in the strict sense of the words, since you are now estimating $E\left[Y(0)_{tr}\right]$ with the control units *and* those extra time series. As a result, you'll end up with weights not only for the units, but for each additional column that you've concatenated.

Debiasing Synthetic Control

Much like with powerful machine learning models, these prediction techniques are prone to overfitting, especially when the number of pre-treatment periods T_{pre} is small. Even the constraints imposed on the canonical synthetic control doesn't solve that completely. As a result, *SC is known to be biased*. To understand that, let's redefine the ATT as the average across time in the post-intervention periods:

$$ATT = \frac{1}{T1} \sum_{t=T0+1}^{T} \left(\bar{Y}_{1t} - \bar{Y}_{0t}\right),$$

where $T0$ and $T1$ are the size of the pre- and post-intervention periods, respectively, and $\bar{Y}_{dt}$ is the average potential outcome of the treated units. This simply averages the ATT for each individual post-intervention period into a single number, making it easier to work with it. Now, to check for bias in the SC method, you can compare that single number against its estimate. Figure 9-2 shows that bias.

I'm simulating a bunch of data following the synthetic control specification—with the treated unit being a weighted combination of some control units. Here, $N = 16$ and $T_{pre} = 15$, so there are more columns than rows in the horizontal regression. Also, the true ATT is zero. Still, the resulting distribution of ATT estimates you get with synthetic control is not centered at zero, showing how it is indeed biased.

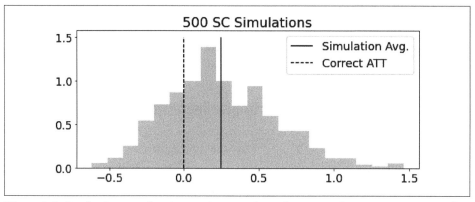

Figure 9-2. Synthetic control estimator is not unbiased, as it rarely manages to correctly specify the outcome model

Fortunately, you learned how to solve for overfitting bias in Chapter 7, when you saw Double/Debiased ML. The answer lies in *cross-fitting*. The idea is to partition the pre-intervention period into K blocks, each of size $min\{T_{pre}/K, T_{post}\}$ (the reason for this min function will become clear soon. For now, just trust me). Then, you'll treat each block as a hold-out set and fit a synthetic control model on $Y^{-k}_{pre, co}$ and $Y^{-k}_{pre, tr}$, where $-k$ means you'll drop the block from training. This step will give you weights $\widehat{\omega}^{-k}$. Next, you'll use those weights to make out-of-sample predictions using the held-out data $Y^{k}_{pre, co}$. The average difference between the predictions and the observed values in the hold-out data is an estimate for the bias:

$$\widehat{Bias}^k = avg\left(\mathbf{Y}^k_{pre, tr} - \mathbf{Y}^k_{pre, co}\widehat{\omega}^{-k}\right),$$

which means you can use it to adjust the ATT estimate:

$$\widehat{ATT}^k = \mathbf{Y}_{post, tr} - \mathbf{Y}_{post, co}\widehat{\omega}^{-k} - \widehat{Bias}^k$$

Notice that this will give you K different *ATTs*. You can average them out to get a final ATT estimate.

Now, let's put this into Python code. The trickiest part here is to define the blocks. So, to make it more clear, let's go over a simple example, shown in Figure 9-3.

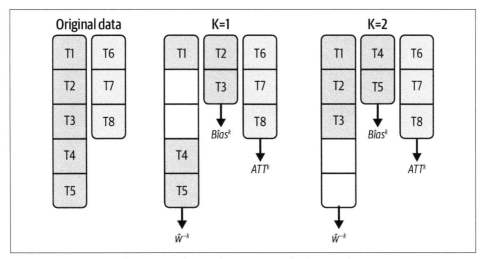

Figure 9-3. Cross-prediction can be used to estimate the bias and correct it

Suppose that you have five pre-intervention periods and three post-intervention periods and you want to build $K = 2$ blocks. The block size is 2.5, which is not an integer, so you have to floor it to two. This means you'll take two blocks of size two out of the pre-intervention period. 2×2 will give you four time periods, but you have five. So, I'm choosing to take the blocks from the end of the pre-intervention period, which will cause the first time period to never be removed. This is rather arbitrary, but doesn't have a huge impact on the whole procedure. You could also choose to trim the pre-intervention period to make it divisible by K.

Then, for each of the two blocks, you'll take it out of the training set, and estimate an SC model to obtain $\widehat{\omega}^{-k}$. With these weights, you'll move to the removed block and estimate the bias term. Finally, you'll use both weights and bias estimates to make an ATT estimate in the post-intervention period.

Even though it is a bit complicated to describe, it is fairly easy to get these blocks with NumPy. First, you'll index into the end of the pre-intervention period, `y_pre_tr.index[-K*block_size:]` to get an index with exactly K blocks. Then, you can use `np.split` to break those indexes into K blocks. This will return an array with K rows, each one containing the index that you want to remove in each iteration. Once you have those blocks, you can iterate over them, fitting an SC model, estimating the bias and the ATT in the post-intervention period. The result can be stored in a data frame for convenient display:

```
In [18]: def debiased_sc_atts(y_pre_co, y_pre_tr, y_post_co, y_post_tr, K=3):

            block_size = int(min(np.floor(len(y_pre_tr)/K), len(y_post_tr)))
            blocks = np.split(y_pre_tr.index[-K*block_size:], K)
```

```
def fold_effect(hold_out):
    model = SyntheticControl()
    model.fit(
        y_pre_co.drop(hold_out),
        y_pre_tr.drop(hold_out)
    )

    bias_hat = np.mean(y_pre_tr.loc[hold_out]
                        - model.predict(y_pre_co.loc[hold_out]))

    y0_hat = model.predict(y_post_co)
    return (y_post_tr - y0_hat) - bias_hat


return pd.DataFrame([fold_effect(block) for block in blocks]).T
```

To apply this function to the (already pivoted) marketing data, you just need to remember to average the treated units. The result is a data frame with all the ATT estimates. It has K columns and one row for each post-intervention period:

```
In [19]: deb_atts = debiased_sc_atts(y_pre_co,
                                      y_pre_tr.mean(axis=1),
                                      y_post_co,
                                      y_post_tr.mean(axis=1),
                                      K=3)


         deb_atts.head()
```

date	0	1	2
2022-05-01	0.003314	0.002475	0.003228
2022-05-02	0.003544	0.002844	0.003356
2022-05-03	0.004644	0.003698	0.004744
2022-05-04	0.004706	0.002866	0.003630
2022-05-05	0.000134	-0.000541	0.000243

To get a final ATT estimate for each post-intervention period you can average out the columns, deb_atts.mean(axis=1), or, if you want a single ATT for the entire period, just average everything: deb_atts.mean(axis=1).mean(). Plotting the debiased ATT alongside the canonical SC ATT you got earlier also shows that, for most parts, the debiasing increased the ATT estimate, although not by much:

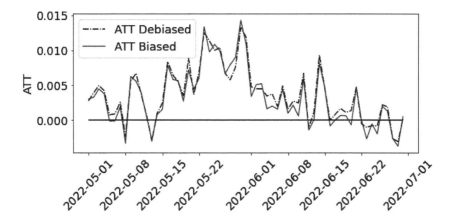

It's difficult to see a difference in your marketing data, but to show why debiasing is important, I can redo the simulations from before, but now using the debiasing procedure. Now, the distribution of ATTs from the simulation has mean zero, as it should be:

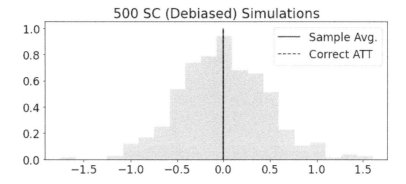

Inference

The debiasing procedure is useful on its own, but there is also a second reason why it is interesting, which is to place a confidence interval around the synthetic control ATT estimate. Doing inference with synthetic control has proven to be a daunting task, mostly because there are usually very few control units, or even just one. The block bootstrap you learned in Chapter 8 won't work here because a lot of the bootstrap samples will throw out all the treated units, making the ATT undefined.

Inference for the synthetic control method is an active area of research, which is rapidly changing. Over the last few years, many approaches have been proposed. Most of them rely on permuting the time dimension, as bootstrapping the units seems problematic. Here, I chose one of those methods that I find quite simple to implement and very computationally efficient. Especially if you already dealt with the debiasing part, because it uses it as a starting point. Just as a refresher, recall that debiasing gave you one ATT estimate for each of the K folds and for each post-intervention time period, which are represented as the columns of the following data frame:

```
In [20]: deb_atts.head()
```

date	0	1	2
2022-05-01	0.003314	0.002475	0.003228
2022-05-02	0.003544	0.002844	0.003356
2022-05-03	0.004644	0.003698	0.004744
2022-05-04	0.004706	0.002866	0.003630
2022-05-05	0.000134	-0.000541	0.000243

Now, let's say that you are interested in placing a confidence interval around the overall ATT estimate in the post-intervention period. To do so, the first thing you need is the $\widehat{ATT}$ itself. You can average out the rows of this data frame, which will give you a single ATT for each of the K folds. Then, you can take the average of that:

```
In [21]: atts_k = deb_atts.mean(axis=0).values
         att = np.mean(atts_k)

         print("atts_k:", atts_k)
         print("ATT:", att)


Out[21]: atts_k: [0.00414872 0.00260513 0.00318584]
         ATT: 0.003313226501636449
```

Now, for the inference part. The idea here is to construct a standard error estimate based on each of the ATT^k:

$$\hat{\sigma} = \sqrt{1 + \frac{BlockSize * K}{T_{post}}} * \sqrt{\frac{1}{K-1} \sum_{k=1}^{K} \left(ATT^k - ATT \right)}$$

$$\widehat{SE} = \hat{\sigma}/\sqrt{K}$$

When coding this, you just need to be careful to use the sample standard deviation, which means passing ddof=1 to np.std:

```
In [22]: K = len(atts_k)
         T0 = len(y_pre_co)
         T1 = len(y_post_co)
         block_size = min(np.floor(T0/K), T1)

         se_hat=np.sqrt(1+((K*block_size)/T1))*np.std(atts_k, ddof=1)/np.sqrt(K)

         print("SE:", se_hat)

Out[22]: SE: 0.0006339596260850461
```

With that standard error, you can construct a test statistic $\widehat{ATT}/\widehat{SE}$ which, under the null hypothesis $H0:ATT = 0$, has asymptotic t-distribution with $K - 1$ degrees of freedom. This means you can leverage it to construct a confidence interval using the t-distribution. For instance, here is how you can construct a 90% CI ($\alpha = 0.1$):

```
In [23]: from scipy.stats import t
         alpha = 0.1

         [att - t.ppf(1-alpha/2, K-1)*se_hat,
          att + t.ppf(1-alpha/2, K-1)*se_hat]

Out[23]: [0.0014620735349405393, 0.005164379468332358]
```

You might look at that K in the denominator of the standard error formula and be tempted to set it to a very large number. However, there is no free lunch here. Higher values of K result in smaller confidence intervals at the cost of lowering the coverage of those intervals. For high Ks, the $1 - \alpha$ CIs will contain the true ATT less than $1 - \alpha$ of the time, especially when the number of pre-treatment periods is small. In this case, a reasonable choice of K is 3. When T_0 is very large, compared to N, you can try larger values of K to decrease the length of the confidence interval.

Another important point is that this method does not apply to the treatment effect trajectory. That is, it can't be used for a per-period inference, as its theory requires both T0 and T1 to be relatively large.

See Also

This inference methods was proposed in the paper "A T-Test for Synthetic Controls," by Victor Chernozhukov et al. If you want to perform per-period inference, the same authors have a complementary paper that proposes conformal inference for synthetic controls: "An Exact and Robust Conformal Inference Method for Counterfactual and Synthetic Controls."

Synthetic Difference-in-Differences

To close this chapter, I wanted to give you yet another perspective on synthetic control, which is how it relates to difference-in-differences. By doing so, you'll also learn how to combine both methods into a single synthetic difference-in-differences (SDID) estimator. The idea here is quite simple. First, construct a synthetic control. Then, use it as the control unit in a DID setting. The end result is something much more interesting than the sum of its parts. First, the parallel assumption required for DID becomes much more plausible, since you are crafting a synthetic control for $E[Y(0)_{ti}|D=1]$. Second, because you are using DID, the synthetic control can focus on capturing just the trend of the treated unit, as it can have a different level of $Y(0)$. But first, before going into SDID, let's review some DID theory.

DID Refresher

In its canonical form, with one control block (never treated) and one treated block that gets treated all at the same time period, you could write DID with two-way fixed effects:

$$\hat{\tau}^{did} = \underset{\mu, \alpha, \beta, \tau}{argmin} \left\{ \sum_{n=1}^{N} \sum_{t=1}^{T} \left(Y_{it} - \mu + \alpha_i + \beta_t + \tau W_{it}\right)^2 \right\},$$

where τ is the ATT you care about, α_i are the unit-fixed effects, and β_t are the time-fixed effects. In this formulation, the unit effects capture the difference in intercepts for each unit while the time effects capture the general trend across both treated and control units. The main assumption behind the DID method is that the treated and untreated have the same Y_0 trend:

$$\Delta Y(d)_i \perp D$$

Synthetic Controls Revisited

Next, let's see how you can recast the synthetic control estimator into something that resembles the preceding DID formulation. Interestingly enough, you can write the SC estimator as solving the following optimization problems:

$$\hat{\tau}^{sc} = \underset{\beta, \tau}{argmin} \left\{ \sum_{n=1}^{N} \sum_{t=1}^{T} \left(Y_{it} - \beta_t - \tau W_{it}\right)^2 \hat{\omega}_i^{sc} \right\},$$

where the weights for the control units $\hat{\omega}_i^{sc}$ are obtained by optimizing the synthetic control objective you saw at the beginning of the chapter. Since the preceding formulation of the SC objective is defined for all units, not just the control, you also need to think about the treatment units' weight. Here, since you care about the ATT, they are simply N_{tr}/N (uniform weighting).

To verify that this new formulation is indeed equivalent to the one you learned earlier, let's compare the two. First, estimate SC as you've done so far and compute the ATT:

```
In [24]: sc_model = SyntheticControl()
         sc_model.fit(y_pre_co, y_pre_tr.mean(axis=1))

         (y_post_tr.mean(axis=1) - sc_model.predict(y_post_co)).mean()


Out[24]: 0.0033467270830624114
```

Next, let's add these synthetic control weights to the original marketing data frame, before the matrix reshaping. To do that, you can create a unit weights data frame that maps each control city to its weight:

```
In [25]: unit_w = pd.DataFrame(zip(y_pre_co.columns, sc_model.w_),
                               columns=["city", "unit_weight"])

         unit_w.head()
```

	city	unit_weight
0	ananindeua	-1.649964e-19
1	aparecida_de_goiania	-7.047642e-21
2	aracaju	4.150540e-19
3	belem	-3.238918e-19
4	belford_roxo	-5.756475e-19

Then, you can merge this unit weight data frame into the original marketing data frame using city as the key. This will leave the treatment unit with NaN weights. You can fill those up with the average of the treatment dummy, which is N_{tr}/N.

I'll also take this opportunity to create the W_{it} variable, by multiplying $D_i * Post_i$:

```
In [26]: df_with_w = (df_norm
                      .assign(tr_post = lambda d: d["post"]*d["treated"])
                      .merge(unit_w, on=["city"], how="left")
                      .fillna({"unit_weight": df_norm["treated"].mean()}))

         df_with_w.head()
```

	app_download	population	city	...	app_download_pct	tr_post	unit_weight
0	3066.0	12396372	sao_paulo	...	0.024733	0	0.06
1	2701.0	12396372	sao_paulo	...	0.021789	0	0.06
2	1927.0	12396372	sao_paulo	...	0.015545	0	0.06
3	1451.0	12396372	sao_paulo	...	0.011705	0	0.06
4	1248.0	12396372	sao_paulo	...	0.010067	0	0.06

Finally, you can run weighted OLS with time-fixed effects, following the alternative synthetic control formulation from earlier. Just be careful to remove the rows with very small weights, otherwise you might run into some errors while trying to run this regression:

```
In [27]: mod = smf.wls(
             "app_download_pct ~ tr_post + C(date)",
             data=df_with_w.query("unit_weight>=1e-10"),
             weights=df_with_w.query("unit_weight>=1e-10")["unit_weight"]
         )

         mod.fit().params["tr_post"]

Out[27]: 0.00334672708306243
```

Indeed, the ATT obtained here is exactly the same as the one you got earlier, which shows that both synthetic control formulations are equivalent. But more importantly, it's easier to compare the new SC formulation with the TWFE formulation of DID. First, it looks like SC has time-fixed effects, but not unit-fixed effects. Meanwhile DID has both time- and unit-fixed effects, but no unit weights. This suggests a merger between the two models that include elements from both SC and DID:

$$\hat{\tau}^{sdid} = \underset{\mu, \alpha, \beta, \tau}{argmin} \left\{ \sum_{n=1}^{N} \sum_{t=1}^{T} \left(Y_{it} - (\mu + \alpha_i + \beta_t + \tau D_{it}) \right)^2 \hat{\omega}_i \right\}$$

And while you are at it, why only weigh the units? Always remember the end goal here: to estimate $E[Y_0 | Post = 1, Tr = 1]$. The purpose of unit weights is to use the control units to approximate the treated units. But there is also a time dimension here, which means you could also use weights in the pre-treatment periods to better approximate the post-treatment period. This would give you the following SDID formulation:

$$\hat{\tau}^{sdid} = \underset{\mu, \alpha, \beta, \tau}{argmin} \left\{ \sum_{n=1}^{N} \sum_{t=1}^{T} \left(Y_{it} - (\mu + \alpha_i + \beta_t + \tau D_{it}) \right)^2 \hat{\omega}_i \hat{\lambda}_t \right\},$$

where $\hat{\lambda}_t$ are time weights.

Estimating Time Weights

Remember how, in order to get the unit weights, you've regressed the average outcome of the treated units on the outcome of the control units, both in the pretreatment period?

$$\hat{\omega}_i^{sc} = \underset{\omega}{\mathrm{argmin}} \ \|\bar{\mathbf{y}}_{pre, tr} - \mathbf{Y}_{pre, co}\omega_{co}\|^2$$

$$\mathrm{s.t} \ \sum \omega_i = 1 \ \mathrm{and} \ \omega_i > 0 \ \forall \ i$$

Well, to get time weights, you just need to transpose the $\mathbf{Y}_{pre, co}$ and regress it on the average outcome of the control on the *post-treatment* period:

$$\hat{\lambda}_t^{sc} = \underset{w}{\mathrm{argmin}} \ \|\bar{\mathbf{y}}'_{pre, co} - \mathbf{Y}'_{pre, co}\lambda_{pre}\|^2$$

$$\mathrm{s.t} \ \sum \lambda_i = 1 \ \mathrm{and} \ \lambda_i > 0 \ \forall \ i$$

But there is an additional catch here. Remember how SC doesn't allow for extrapolations? This would be a problem if you had some kind of trend in the outcome. If that was the case, the average post-treatment period would have a higher or lower outcome than all the pre-treatment periods and you would need to extrapolate in order to get a good fit. For this reason, the SDID formulation allows for an intercept shift λ_0 when finding the time weights:

$$\hat{\lambda}_t^{sc} = \underset{w}{\mathrm{argmin}} \ \|\bar{\mathbf{y}}'_{pre, co} - \left(\mathbf{Y}'_{pre, co}\lambda_{pre} + \lambda_0\right)\|^2$$

$$\mathrm{s.t} \ \sum \lambda_i = 1 \ \mathrm{and} \ \lambda_i > 0 \ \forall \ i$$

Fortunately, it is fairly easy to modify the SyntheticControl code to optionally fit the intercept, using a fit_intercept parameter. First, you'll create an intercept column that is always 1 if fit_intercept=True and zero otherwise. You can take advantage of the fact that multiplying True*1=1 in Python. Then, you'll prepend this column into y_pre_co and use that in the objective function. Also, when building the constraints, you don't want to include the intercept. In the end, you'll get rid of the intercept parameter, returning only the units' weights.

I won't show the entire code because it is fairly repetitive, but here is just the part that changes:

```
# add intercept
intercept = np.ones((y_pre_co.shape[0], 1))*self.fit_intercept
X = np.concatenate([intercept, y_pre_co], axis=1)
w = cp.Variable(X.shape[1])

objective = cp.Minimize(cp.sum_squares(X@w - y_pre_tr))
constraints = [cp.sum(w[1:]) == 1, w[1:] >= 0]

problem = cp.Problem(objective, constraints)

self.loss_ = problem.solve(verbose=False)
self.w_ = w.value[1:] # remove intercept
```

Once you deal with that, you can move on to estimate the time weights:

```
In [28]: time_sc = SyntheticControl(fit_intercept=True)

         time_sc.fit(
             y_pre_co.T,
             y_post_co.mean(axis=0)
         )

         time_w = pd.DataFrame(zip(y_pre_co.index, time_sc.w_),
                               columns=["date", "time_weight"])

         time_w.tail()
```

	date	time_weight
56	2022-04-26	-0.000011
57	2022-04-27	0.071965
58	2022-04-28	-0.000002
59	2022-04-29	0.078350
60	2022-04-30	0.000002

I also already stored the weights in a data frame, which you'll use later. You can also plot these weights to see how the pre-treatment time periods are being used to reconstruct the average outcome of the control in the post-treatment period:

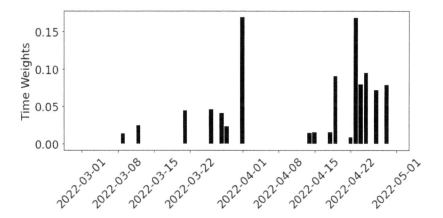

Synthetic Control and DID

OK. So you have weights for the pre-intervention period and weights for all the units. All there is left to do is join these pieces into a final estimator. You can start from the previously defined data frame df_with_w and join in the time weights data frame, using date as the key. Since time_w has weights only for the pre-intervention period, you need to fill in the post-intervention time weights with T_{post}/T (also uniformly weighting them). Finally, multiply both λ_t and ω_i and you are good to go:

```
In [29]: scdid_df = (
             df_with_w
             .merge(time_w, on=["date"], how="left")
             .fillna({"time_weight":df_norm["post"].mean()})
             .assign(weight = lambda d: (d["time_weight"]*d["unit_weight"]))
         )
```

You can now run DID using the scdid_df data and weighted regression. The parameter estimate associated with $W_{it} = D_i * Post_t$ is the ATT estimate you care about:

```
In [30]: did_model = smf.wls(
             "app_download_pct ~ treated*post",
             data=scdid_df.query("weight>1e-10"),
             weights=scdid_df.query("weight>1e-10")["weight"]).fit()

         did_model.params["treated:post"]


Out[30]: 0.004098194485564245
```

To grasp what SDID is doing, you can plot the diff-in-diff lines for the treated units and the counterfactual trend (dashed line) obtained by using the synthetic control's trend and projecting it into the treated's baseline. The difference between the two is the ATT estimate you just estimated. I'm also plotting the time weights on a second plot. You can see how SDID uses mostly time periods that are closer to the post-intervention period:

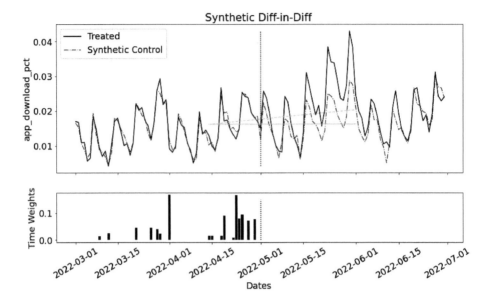

This SDID estimate is a bit higher, but not much different from the ATT of the canonical SC. So, why is SDID interesting? The SC component of the estimator makes the DID's parallel trend assumption more plausible. It's much easier to get parallel trends if you first craft a synthetic control to mimic the treated units. As a result, SDID tends to have lower bias, compared to both DID and SC. Second, SDID also tends to have lower variance than both methods. The original paper has simulation results to show this, in case you are interested.

The Original SDID

This SDID estimator is a simplification on top of the original SDID estimator, which was proposed in the paper "Synthetic Difference in Differences," by Dmitry Arkhangelsky et al. The paper proposes a slightly different optimization objective for the unit weights:

$$\hat{\omega}_i^{scdid} = \underset{\omega}{\text{argmin}} \; \|\bar{\mathbf{y}}_{pre, tr} - \left(\mathbf{Y}_{pre, co}\omega_{co} + \omega_0\right)\|_2^2 + \zeta^2 T_{pre}\|\omega_{co}\|_2^2$$

$$\text{s.t} \; \sum \omega_i = 1 \; \text{and} \; \omega_i > 0 \; \forall \; i$$

First, this objective also allows an intercept shift. The reason here is that the synthetic control doesn't need to exactly match the treated unit, only its trend, since you'll plug them in a DID model afterward. Second, they add an L2 penalty on the unit weights, which includes this new ζ term:

$$\zeta = \left(N_{tr} {}^{*} T_{post}\right)^{1/4} \sigma\left(Y_{it} - Y_{i(t-1)}\right)$$

There is a complicated theoretical reason for this ζ that I won't go into, but the main idea behind the additional L2 penalty is to make sure no single unit gets a disproportionately large weight. As a result, these weights tend to be more spread out across more units than that of the canonical synthetic control method.

The paper also proposed a new inference procedure, designed specifically for SDID. If that isn't enough reasons to check it out, I don't know what is.

Of course, there is no free lunch. By allowing intercept shifts, SDID removes the convexity guardrail from SC. Depending on the situation, you can view this as either good, since SDID allows more flexibility, or bad, since it also allows dangerous extrapolations.

Key Ideas

If there is one thing I want you to take out from this chapter is that you can have a model-based approach to estimating $E\left[Y(0)_t \mid D = 1, Post = 1\right]$: just fit a model to predict pre-treatment outcome of the treated on a bunch of equally pre-treatment time series and use that model to make predictions on the post-treatment period. Usually, those time series are the outcome of control units, and this approach amounts to a horizontal regression of the treated outcome on the control outcome, all in the pre-intervention period:

$$\hat{\omega}^{sc} = \underset{\omega}{\operatorname{argmin}} \ \lVert \bar{\mathbf{y}}_{pre,\,tr} - \mathbf{Y}_{pre,\,co}\omega_{co} \rVert_2^2$$

The result is a set of weights which, when multiplied by the control units, yields a synthetic control: a combination of control units that approximate the behavior of the treated units, at least in the pre-intervention period. If that approximation is good and generalizes into the post-intervention period, you can use it to estimate the ATT:

$$\widehat{ATT} = \mathbf{Y}_{post,\,tr} - \mathbf{Y}_{post,\,co}\hat{\omega}_{co}$$

That is the basic idea. You can build up from it. For example, in the canonical synthetic control setting, you would add the constraints $\sum \omega_i = 1$ and $\omega_i > 0 \ \forall \ i$ or use something like lasso regression. But the basic idea remains: use the pre-intervention period to regress the pre-treatment outcome on very predictive time series and extend those predictions to the post-intervention period.

See Also

Yiqing Xu has a bunch of papers on generalizing synthetic control, as well as software implementing those approaches. To name a few, the paper "Generalized Synthetic Control Method: Causal Inference with Interactive Fixed Effects Models" also mixes qualities from both DID and synthetic control, generalizing this last one to variable treatment periods (staggered adoption design). In "Bayesian Alternative to Synthetic Control for Comparative Case Studies," the authors also propose a Bayesian model to estimate counterfactuals.

PRACTICAL EXAMPLE

Causal Impact

Google's research team capitalized on the main idea behind synthetic controls to build the `causalimpact` library. They use Bayesian structural time-series models to estimate the counterfactual time series for $E[Y(0)|D = 1]$ by using other time series that are themselves not affected by the treatment. The fact that the method is Bayesian also allows them to give uncertainty metrics quite naturally.

Alternative Experimental Designs

CHAPTER 10

Geo and Switchback Experiments

In Part IV of this book, you learned how to use repeated observations over time to aid in the process of causal inference. Now, in this chapter, you will approach the same problem from a different angle. What if, instead of having to use panel data to identify a treatment effect, you had to design an experiment to gather that data? Part V of this book is dedicated to alternative experimental design when simple A/B testing won't work.

For example, let's consider the marketing problem from the previous chapter. Remember that inferring the impact of marketing is challenging because you cannot randomize people who are not yet your customers. Online marketing provides you with attribution tools, but attribution is not the same as incrementality. In this case, a promising alternative is to conduct a geo-experiment: treat entire markets, such as a city or a state, while leaving others as control. This approach would provide you with panel data to which you could apply the techniques learned in Part IV. However, in Part IV, you took the panel data as given and did not learn how to best select the treated and control markets in such an experiment. In this chapter, you will cover that gap. The first part of this chapter will teach you how to select geographical treatment units to get an effect estimate that approximates the effect you would have if the entire market (country, state) were treated.

The idea is to zoom out the unit of analysis from customers to cities or states. Of course, this comes at a price in terms of sample size since there are far more customers than there are cities. In some extreme cases, even randomizing cities may not be possible. For instance, if you are a small company operating locally, you may not have many markets in which to conduct an experiment. In the limit, you may have only a single unit of analysis. Fortunately, there is still a way out. Switchback experiments involve turning a treatment on and off multiple times. This approach can work even if you have only a single treatment unit. For example, if you are a small food delivery marketplace operating within a single city and you want to know what happens if you increase the delivery fee, you can increase and decrease prices multiple times and conduct a series of before-and-after analyses. The remainder of this chapter will expand on this idea and how to design a switchback experiment.

Geo-Experiments

To motivate the use of geo-experiments, let's take the same data and example from the previous chapter. Again, you have the city as the unit and date as the time dimension; a treated column, which marks if the city is eventually treated; and a post-treatment column, which marks the post-intervention period. You also have some auxiliary columns, like the population in that city (recorded in 2013, so fixed in time) and the state. Here, you'll work with the outcome: number of app downloads. And since the goal is to decide which city to treat, you'll discard the post-intervention period:

```
In [1]: import pandas as pd
        import numpy as np

        df = (pd.read_csv("./data/online_mkt.csv")
              .astype({"date":"datetime64[ns]"})
              .query("post==0"))

        df.head()
```

	app_download	population	city	state	date	post	treated
0	3066.0	12396372	sao_paulo	sao_paulo	2022-03-01	0	1
1	2701.0	12396372	sao_paulo	sao_paulo	2022-03-02	0	1
2	1927.0	12396372	sao_paulo	sao_paulo	2022-03-03	0	1
3	1451.0	12396372	sao_paulo	sao_paulo	2022-03-04	0	1
4	1248.0	12396372	sao_paulo	sao_paulo	2022-03-05	0	1

The objective is to select a group of cities that is representative of the total market. That way, if you treat that group, you'll get an idea of what would happen if the entire market (i.e., country) was treated. Before you do anything fancy, it's worth trying the simple things. If you have lots of geographical units (i.e., many cities), perhaps a simple A/B testing would work just fine. Simply choose at random a fraction of the cities to compose the treatment group. The only difference here is that you would be shifting the unit of analysis from people (potential customers) to entire cities.

Still, it's hard to know how many cities are enough. You could start with the sample size formula from Chapter 2 ($n = 16\sigma^2/\delta^2$). For instance, if you wish to detect an effect of 5%, it would tell you that you need about 40k cities to run that experiment:

```
In [2]: detectable_diff = df["app_download"].mean()*0.05
        sigma_2 = df.groupby("city")["app_download"].mean().var()
```

```
      np.ceil((sigma_2*16)/(detectable_diff)**2)
```

```
Out[2]: 36663.0
```

But that formula doesn't take into account that each city has a different variance of the outcome (cities with more people have lower variance) nor that you can leverage repeated observations of the same unit to increase the precision of your estimate. Even so, 40k cities seems a lot more than the 50 cities that you have in this data. So what can you do if you are short of units?

When considering different experimental options, it's essential to take into account how you will interpret the results. For example, if you plan on using the difference-in-differences method, you can identify pairs of cities that have similar trends in the outcome variable and randomize within each pair. One city would receive the treatment, while the other would serve as the control. However, it's worth noting that the diff-in-diff method estimates the average treatment effect on the treated (ATT). If you want to know the overall effect of the treatment, such as deploying the marketing campaign nationwide, the ATT estimate may not recover that. In this chapter, we will explore an idea that aims to maximize the external validity of the experiment by identifying a treatment group that is representative of the entire market.

Synthetic Control Design

Finding a group of units whose time series can best approximate the outcome of interest is exactly what you've been doing with synthetic controls. So, it's not surprising that you can repurpose the method to find a synthetic treatment unit that approximates the average behavior of all units. To do so, you'll only need the data in matrix form, where the rows are the time periods and the columns are the cities, $Y_{T,n}$:

```
In [3]: df_piv = (df
                  .pivot("date", "city", "app_download"))

        df_piv.head()
```

city date	ananindeua	aparecida_de_goiania	aracaju	...	teresina	uberlandia	vila_velha
2022-03-01	11.0	54.0	65.0	...	68.0	29.0	63.0
2022-03-02	5.0	20.0	42.0	...	17.0	29.0	11.0
2022-03-03	2.0	0.0	0.0	...	55.0	30.0	14.0
2022-03-04	0.0	0.0	11.0	...	49.0	35.0	0.0
2022-03-05	5.0	5.0	0.0	...	31.0	6.0	1.0

Now, let's think of what you want to achieve. First, let's keep in mind that each city contributes differently for the average. To get the global average you first need to know how much each city contributes to it. This can be represented by a city weight vector $\mathbf{f}$ where each entry i represents the size of city i as a share of the total market:

```
In [4]: f = (df.groupby("city")["population"].first()
             /df.groupby("city")["population"].first().sum())
```

Once $\mathbf{f}$ is defined, you can see that your objective is first to find a set of weights $\mathbf{w}$ such that:

$$\mathbf{Y}_{post}\mathbf{f} = \mathbf{Y}_{post}\mathbf{w}$$

Translating that to words, you want to find a combination of treatment cities that, when combined with weights $\mathbf{w}$, will give you the average outcome of the market. Leaving it like this, the obvious solution would be to set $\mathbf{f} = \mathbf{w}$, but that would mean treating every city, which would leave you without any control units to estimate the treatment effect, so you have to add a constraint that the number of nonzero elements in $\mathbf{w}$ must be smaller than N, the number of cities: $|\mathbf{w}|_0 < N$ ($|.|_0$ is the L0 norm, which is the number of nonzero elements). Moreover, the preceding objective is impossible to solve, since you don't observe the post-intervention values of $\mathbf{Y}$. Still, let's keep it as an ideal and see if you can somehow approximate it.

If the preceding objective finds the cities that you can use as treatment, your second objective is to find another group of cities, different from the first, that will also approximate the market average:

$$\mathbf{Y}_{post}\mathbf{f} = \mathbf{Y}_{post}\mathbf{v}$$
$$\text{s.t } w_i v_i = 0 \ \forall \ i,$$

Combining both objectives, the nonzero elements in $\mathbf{w}$ and $\mathbf{v}$ would be the treatment and control cities, respectively. Also, this second objective introduces a constraint which states that you can't use the same city as a treatment and as a control. Once again, this objective is not feasible, as it looks at the post-treatment period.

Now, you just need to think a bit on how to swap those impossible objectives with one that you might be able to solve. The obvious first step is looking at the pre-intervention period. This means that you would find two disjoint groups of cities such that a weighted average of each approximates the market average. That alone would be enough, but, practically speaking, you probably want to add some extra constraints. For instance, since your goal is to first test a marketing campaign before rolling it out to the entire market, you probably don't want to choose a lot of treatment cities. A big treatment group would treat almost everyone and kind of defeat the purpose of the test.

Moreover, in many markets, the size of cities tends to follow an exponential distribution, with a small number of cities accounting for almost all of the market (see Figure 10-1). If you use the canonical synthetic control formulation for this, you would be forced to include the biggest cities, as you are not allowed to extrapolate.

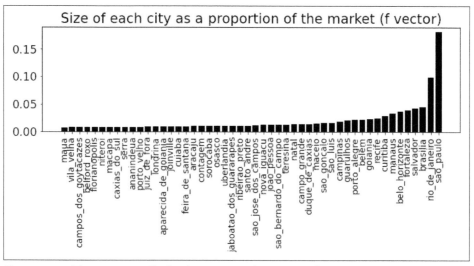

Figure 10-1. There are usually few big cities and many smaller ones

As a consequence, you probably want to allow for an intercept shift in the synthetic control model. Putting these extra requirements together, combining both objectives and adding the synthetic control constraints, you'll end up with the following objective:

$$\min_{w,\,v} \; \left\| \mathbf{Y}_{pre}\mathbf{f} - \mathbf{Y}_{pre}\mathbf{w}_{tr} - \alpha_0 \right\|^2 + \left\| \mathbf{Y}_{pre}\mathbf{f} - \mathbf{Y}_{pre}\mathbf{v}_{co} - \beta_0 \right\|^2$$

$$\text{s.t} \quad \sum w_i = 1 \text{ and } \sum v_i = 1,$$

$$w_i, v_i \geq 0 \;\; \forall \; i,$$

$$w_i v_i = 0 \;\; \forall \; i,$$

$$|\mathbf{w}|_0 \leq m$$

I know it seems complicated, but it really isn't. First, it adds intercept terms, α_0 and β_0, to both the synthetic treatment and synthetic control objectives. Then, it adds a bunch of constraints. The first two rows are simply the traditional synthetic control constraints, which states that the weights must sum up to 1 and be nonnegative. Next, you have the constraint which states that a city cannot be used for both treatment and control. Finally, you have a constraint on the maximum number of cities, m, you want on the treatment set.

Before you go running to implement this objective in cvxpy, I'm sorry to bring it to you, but it is not convex. But don't worry too much with it. Finding the *best* possible sets of treatment and control cities is not strictly necessary. In most cases, it's pretty easy to find sets that are just *good enough*. So, in favor of simplicity, let's see how to code a more modest optimization.

Trying a Random Set of Treated Units

First, let's try something incredibly simple, which is just selecting a random set of cities. In order to do that, let's first define some constants: $\mathbf{Y}_{pre}\mathbf{f}$, the market average you'll try to approximate, a list of all possible cities and m, the maximum number of treatment cities. I'm setting this last one to 5, but that depends on your business constraints. If your budget only allows for, say, three treatment cities, feel free to change that number:

```
In [5]: y_avg = df_piv.dot(f)
        geos = list(df_piv.columns)
        n_tr = 5
```

Next, let's select a random set of five cities and see how well they perform as a possible treatment set:

```
In [6]: np.random.seed(1)
        rand_geos = np.random.choice(geos, n_tr, replace=False)
        rand_geos
```

```
Out[6]: array(['manaus', 'recife', 'sao_bernardo_do_campo',
               'salvador', 'aracaju'], dtype='<U23')
```

These are the possible treatment cities, but you still need to find the weights for them. If some of those weights turns out to be zero, you won't need to use all five.

To get the weights, I'm using the SyntheticControl class that allows for an intercept shift, which was implemented in the previous chapter. The idea is to use the synthetic control to predict y_avg by using just these five cities:

```
In [7]: def get_sc(geos, df_sc, y_mean_pre):

            model = SyntheticControl(fit_intercept=True)
            model.fit(df_sc[geos], y_mean_pre)

            selected_geos = geos[np.abs(model.w_) > 1e-5]

            return {"geos": selected_geos, "loss": model.loss_ }
```

```
          get_sc(rand_geos, df_piv, y_avg)


Out[7]: {'geos': array(['salvador', 'aracaju'], dtype='<U23'),
          'loss': 1598616.80875266}
```

Once that is done, you can inspect the estimated weights and select the cities with weights that are not too close to zero. I'm wrapping all of that in a function that will allow you to try many different samples and see which one performs better. It is also worth storing the synthetic control loss, as minimizing it will be your objective.

When you fit a synthetic control model using those five cities, you can see that it chooses only two of them as treatment. The other three can be added back to the pool of possible cities and can compose the control group.

With that, you are ready to move to the next step, which is finding both the synthetic treatment and synthetic control:

```
In [8]: def get_sc_st_combination(treatment_geos, df_sc, y_mean_pre):

            treatment_result = get_sc(treatment_geos, df_sc, y_mean_pre)

            remaining_geos = df_sc.drop(
                columns=treatment_result["geos"]
            ).columns

            control_result = get_sc(remaining_geos, df_sc, y_mean_pre)

            return {"st_geos": treatment_result["geos"],
                    "sc_geos": control_result["geos"],
                    "loss": treatment_result["loss"] + control_result["loss"]}


        resulting_geos = get_sc_st_combination(rand_geos, df_piv, y_avg)
```

First, you need to call `get_sc` on the random sample of cities, just like before. This will give you the treatment cities and synthetic treatment loss. Next, you'll figure out what cities are not selected for the synthetic treatment units and call `get_sc` again, passing the remaining cities. This second call to `get_sc` will give you the control cities and the synthetic control loss. If you sum the two losses, you'll end up with the total loss you wish to minimize.

As expected, calling `get_sc_st_combination` with the same five cities will give you the same treatment units as before:

```
In [9]: resulting_geos.get("st_geos")
```

```
Out[9]: array(['salvador', 'aracaju'], dtype='<U23')
```

Interestingly, the sum of the treatment and control cities amount to the entire list of 50 cities. But that should not be surprising, especially when m is small:

```
In [10]: len(resulting_geos.get("st_geos")) + len(resulting_geos.get("sc_geos"))
```

```
Out[10]: 50
```

If $m = 0$ (no treatment units), the obvious solution would be to choose all the cities as a control and set $\mathbf{v} = \mathbf{f}$. For $m > 0$, but still pretty small, selecting all the cities and slightly adjusting the weights tends to be the optimal choice. This also means that the majority of the total loss will come from the synthetic treatment objective, since the synthetic control will tend to reconstruct the average market behavior pretty well when m is small. So much so that when plotting both synthetic treatment and control alongside the market average you can see that, while the synthetic treatment has a poor fit, the synthetic control matches the average almost exactly:

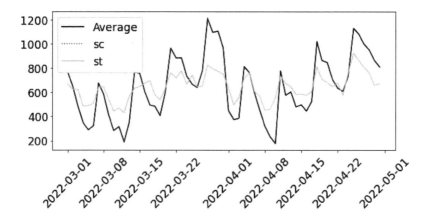

Random Search

Let's see how to improve upon the result you just got. Since you have a way to calculate the total loss given the number of cities, you can devise many fancy methods to minimize that loss. But since I'm very fond of simplicity, what I suggest is just randomly searching many combinations and picking one that performs OK. The following code does exactly that. It first generates 1,000 sets of 5 cities and stores everything in the geo_samples list. Then, it partially applies get_sc_st_combination to the data and average market outcome argument. Finally, it applies that function to the 1,000 sets of cities, all of that in parallel:

```
In [11]: from joblib import Parallel, delayed
         from toolz import partial

         np.random.seed(1)
         geo_samples = [np.random.choice(geos, n_tr, replace=False)
                        for _ in range(1000)]

         est_combination = partial(get_sc_st_combination,
                                   df_sc=df_piv,
                                   y_mean_pre=y_avg)

         results = Parallel(n_jobs=4)(delayed(est_combination)(geos)
                                      for geos in geo_samples)
```

It's worth mentioning that this approach is not optimal, but it does tend to produce reasonable sets of treatment cities.

Optimization

Formulating the treatment city selection problem like you just did is a simplification on top of the one presented in the paper "Synthetic Controls for Experimental Design," by Abadie and Zhao. The paper suggests using enumeration or converting the optimization to a constrained quadratic programming problem. Both approaches take a significant amount of time to run, which is why I recommend checking if a simple random search isn't enough to find good treatment cities.

I myself have also experimented with genetic algorithms for this problem and found that they tend to achieve a better result than simple random search while using the same number of iterations. Additionally, the paper "Designing Experiments with Synthetic Controls," by Doudchenko et al., proposes a simulated annealing procedure to select the best set of cities. If you find that a simple random search isn't good enough, I recommend you try those algorithms.

Inspecting the selected treatment cities, you can see that the model chooses only four cities. Not surprisingly, the biggest city, Sao Paulo, is among them. This tends to happen because the biggest cities compose a big chunk of the total market average, so including them in the treated group tends to reduce the loss a lot. If you wish to avoid this, you can always exclude the largest city from the possible control units:

```
In [12]: resulting_geos = min(results, key=lambda x: x.get("loss"))
         resulting_geos.get("st_geos")

Out[12]: array(['sao_paulo', 'florianopolis', 'recife', 'belem', 'sorocaba'],
               dtype='<U23')
```

Plotting the synthetic control and treatment once more, you can see how this approach, despite its simplicity, can give you a solution that works pretty well, with both synthetic treatment and control tracking the market average pretty closely:

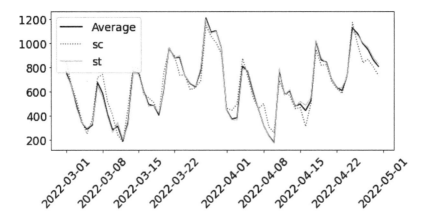

Other Experiment Objectives

The idea of minimizing the sum of the synthetic treatment and control objective is so that you can maximize the external validity of the experiment. By selecting a treatment group that closely resembles the market average, the hope is that, with a small experiment, you can learn what would happen if the treatment was implemented nationwide. This is not the only possible objective, though. The paper "Designing Experiments with Synthetic Controls," by Doudchenko et al., focuses on maximizing the power of the experiment by selecting a set of units with low out-of-sample error. A subsequent paper, "Synthetic Design: An Optimization Approach to Experimental Design with Synthetic Controls,"by Doudchenko et al., casts the treatment units selection into a mixed-integer programming formulation to find the units that minimize the root mean squared error of the effect estimate.

Finally, it is worth mentioning that, even though you designed an experiment using a synthetic control design, you don't necessarily need to read its result with synthetic control, although that is surely a reasonable idea. For instance, you could use synthetic diff-in-diff, as that tends to reduce the variance of the estimator. You do have to be careful on how to estimate the variance of the resulting estimator, though. Since the group of selected cities is not random, inference procedures based on reassignment of the treatment to different units are not valid. Fortunately, the t-test you learned in the previous chapter doesn't make an assumption on how the units were selected, so you can use it here.

Switchback Experiment

Synthetic control experiment designs are great for when you have a small number of units and you want to select the best set of them to compose a treatment group. However, to do that, you still need a somewhat reasonable amount of units. But what happens if you only have, say, four units or even one unit? To give an example, suppose you are a small food delivery marketplace that operates within a single city. This company uses dynamic pricing to regulate the supply and demand of the food delivery marketplace, and it wants to know how an increase in delivery fee can impact delivery time by attracting more drivers to the fleet while throttling or postponing customer demand. Notice that traditional A/B testing wouldn't work here. Increasing the price for 50% of the customers would also benefit those in the control group, since the overall demand would fall, increasing the number of available drivers. Also, synthetic control experiments wouldn't work either, because the company operates in just one city. But there is one type of experiment design that might just do in this situation.

If the effect of rising prices dissipates rather quickly once they go back to the normal level, the company can turn the price increases on and off multiple times and do a sequence of before-and-after comparisons. This approach is named *switchback experiments*, and it is great for when you have just one or a very small number of units. But for it to work, *the order of the carryover effect must be small.* That is, the effect of the treatment cannot propagate to many periods after the treatment. For instance, in the food delivery case, increasing prices tend to cause an increase in supply shortly after; when prices are back to normal, the excess supply dissipates in a few hours. Hence, the order of the carryover effect is small, so switchback experiments are an interesting proposition.

Before talking about designing a switchback experiment, since this is the first time they appear in this book, I think it's worth walking through one for you to grasp how they work. The following data frame contains data from a switchback experiment with 120 periods, where each period is 1 hour. In this experiment, *the treatment was randomized at every time period, with a 50% chance of selecting the treatment or control.* The d column tells you if the price increase (treatment) was on or off at that hour and the delivery_time is the outcome of interest. Additionally, I've added three columns that would not be observed in reality, but should help your understanding of what is going on. delivery_time_1 is the delivery time you would get if the treatment was always on and delivery_time_0, if it was always off. The difference between them, tau, is the total effect of the treatment and it is usually the causal quantity of interest in a switchback experiment. Since the treatment decreases delivery time, the effect is negative. Also, due to carryover, the effects on the first two periods are smaller:

```
In [13]: df = pd.read_csv("./data/sb_exp_every.csv")
         df.head()
```

	d	delivery_time	delivery_time_1	delivery_time_0	tau
0	1	2.84	2.84	5.84	-3.0
1	0	4.49	1.49	6.49	-5.0
2	0	7.27	2.27	8.27	-6.0
3	1	5.27	2.27	8.27	-6.0
4	1	5.59	4.59	10.59	-6.0

Figure 10-2 shows that the observed delivery time fluctuates between the delivery
time you would have with the treatment always on and always off. Moreover, after
three consecutive equal treatments, the observed outcome matches the one you
would have with the treatment always on or always off.

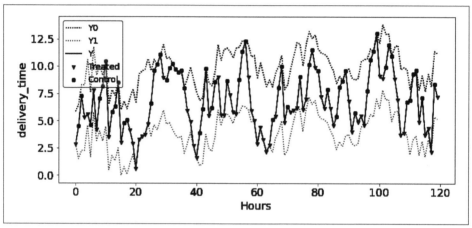

*Figure 10-2. In a switchback experiment, the observed outcome fluctuates between the
always treat and never treat potential outcomes*

Take $T = 20$ to $T = 23$, for example. At those points, due to chance, the treatment was
on for three or more consecutive periods and the delivery time matches the delivery
time you would have under the treatment being always on. Conversely, at around
$T = 32$, you can see a sequence where the treatment has been off (control) for three or
more consecutive periods. At that point, the outcome matches the outcome you
would have if the treatment was always off. If the treatment was on or off for less than
three consecutive periods, the observed outcome is somewhere in the middle. This
tells you that, in this case, the outcome depends on the treatment of three periods: the
immediate treatment and the treatment from two periods before:

$$Y_t = f\left(d_{t-2}, d_{t-1}, d_t\right)$$

In other words, the order of the carryover effect is 2.

Of course, in reality, you wouldn't know this, since you can only see the observed outcome. But don't worry about that too much. I'll show you how to estimate the size of the carryover period. For now, I just want you to get an intuitive understanding of switchback experiments. On top of that, you'll be able to develop a more formal language to describe what is going on.

Potential Outcomes of Sequences

Since the effect of the treatment carries over to subsequent time (2 in this case), when it comes to switchback experiments, the potential outcome has to be defined in terms of a vector of treatments, $Y_t(\mathbf{D}) = Y_t([d_0, d_1, d_2, \ldots, d_T])$. Fortunately, you can simplify this with two assumptions. First, if you assume no anticipation of the treatment, the potential outcome will only depend on current and past treatment, but not on future ones. As a result, you can write $Y_t(\mathbf{D}) = Y_t([d_0, d_1, d_2, \ldots, d_t])$. If you know the size of the carryover period m, you could write it as $Y_t(\mathbf{D}) = Y_t([d_{t-m}, \ldots, d_t])$. Since $m = 2$ here, the potential outcome simplifies to $Y_t(\mathbf{D}) = Y_t([d_{t-2}, d_{t-1}, d_t])$, which is a lot simpler than what you would have with no assumptions at all.

Having defined those potential outcomes, you can write the total effect of the treatment as:

$$\tau_m = E\left[Y_t(1_{t-m}, \ldots, 1_t) - Y_t(0_{t-m}, \ldots, 0_t)\right]$$

This is the effect of going from an always off treatment to an always on treatment. In the case where $m = 2$, this would be $E\left[Y_t(1, 1, 1) - Y_t(0, 0, 0)\right]$. Since all of that simplification requires you to know m, let's turn your attention to that now.

Estimating the Order of Carryover Effect

Let's say that you have some business expert knowledge that puts an upper bound on m. For instance, you know that the effect of price increases doesn't last for more than 6 hours. In that case, you can regression-estimate the model:

$$y_t = \alpha + d_t + d_{t-1}, \ldots, d_{t-K} + e_t$$

and read the parameter estimates' size and significance. The order of the carryover effect will depend on which parameters are statistically significant and also have a large impact on the outcome.

Notice that this imposes another assumption, which is that the effects of the lags are additive:

$$Y_t = f(d_t, d_{t-1}, d_{t-2}) = \alpha + d_t + d_{t-1} + d_{t-2} + e_t$$

To create lags of the treatment, you can use the `.shift(lag)` method from pandas. To programmatically create six lags, I'm taking advantage of the fact that the `.assign(...)` method takes as argument the name of the new column you want to create and that, in Python, you can pass named argument with `**` and a dictionary. So, for instance, `df.assign(a=1, b=1)` is the same as `df.assign(**{"a":1, "b": 2})`:

```
In [14]: df_lags = df.assign(**{
            f"d_l{l}" : df["d"].shift(l) for l in range(7)
         })

         df_lags[[f"d_l{l}" for l in range(7)]].head()
```

	d_l0	d_l1	d_l2	...	d_l4	d_l5	d_l6
0	1	NaN	NaN	...	NaN	NaN	NaN
1	0	1.0	NaN	...	NaN	NaN	NaN
2	0	0.0	1.0	...	NaN	NaN	NaN
3	1	0.0	0.0	...	NaN	NaN	NaN
4	1	1.0	0.0	...	1.0	NaN	NaN

Once you have the data with its lags, all you have to do is regress the outcome on the lags and the current treatment (which can be thought of as lag 0). Notice that stats-models will drop the rows with NaNs:

```
In [15]: import statsmodels.formula.api as smf

         model = smf.ols("delivery_time ~" + "+".join([f"d_l{l}"
                                             for l in range(7)]),
                         data=df_lags).fit()

         model.summary().tables[1]
```

	coef	std err	t	P>|t|	[0.025	0.975]
Intercept	9.3270	0.461	20.246	0.000	8.414	10.240
d_l0	-2.9645	0.335	-8.843	0.000	-3.629	-2.300
d_l1	-1.8861	0.339	-5.560	0.000	-2.559	-1.213
d_l2	-1.0013	0.340	-2.943	0.004	-1.676	-0.327
d_l3	0.2594	0.341	0.762	0.448	-0.416	0.935
d_l4	0.1431	0.340	0.421	0.675	-0.531	0.817
d_l5	0.1388	0.340	0.408	0.684	-0.536	0.813
d_l6	0.5588	0.336	1.662	0.099	-0.108	1.225

By looking at the lag parameters, you can see that they are significant up to lag 2, which indicates a carryover effect of 2. Interestingly, with the regression model, you don't need to know the correct order of the carryover effect m to estimate the total effect τ_m. As long as your regression contains more lags than the correct m, you can just sum up all the lag parameter estimates:

$$\hat{\tau}_m = \sum_{l=0}^{lags} \hat{d}_{t-l}.$$

To get the variance, you also have to sum up the variance of each individual lag:

```
In [16]: ## remember to remove the intercept
         tau_m_hat = model.params[1:].sum()
         se_tau_m_hat = np.sqrt((model.bse[1:]**2).sum())
         print("tau_m:", tau_m_hat)
         print("95% CI:", [tau_m_hat -1.96*se_tau_m_hat,
                           tau_m_hat +1.96*se_tau_m_hat])


Out[16]: tau_m: -4.751686115272022
         95% CI: [-6.5087183781545574, -2.9946538523894857]
```

Since you are using a bunch of lags, the total effect estimate will be rather imprecise. But if you settle for two lags, you can reduce the variance substantially:

```
In [17]: ## selecting lags 0, 1 and 2
         tau_m_hat = model.params[1:4].sum()
         se_tau_m_hat = np.sqrt((model.bse[1:4]**2).sum())
         print("tau_m:", tau_m_hat)
         print("95% CI:", [tau_m_hat -1.96*se_tau_m_hat,
                           tau_m_hat +1.96*se_tau_m_hat])


Out[17]: tau_m: -5.8518568954422925
         95% CI: [-7.000105171362163, -4.703608619522422]
```

Design-Based Estimation

The previous procedure depends on a correct specification of the model for the potential outcome $Y_t(\mathbf{D})$. Since it's a time series, this is not a trivial task. One alternative is to estimate τ_m with something like inverse propensity weighting (IPW), which would only require knowledge of how the treatment was assigned. Since that is controlled by the company designing the experiment, this second approach relies on more plausible assumptions. It will only require you to know the carryover effect order, m.

Remember that IPW reconstructs a potential outcome by scaling up the observed outcome by the inverse treatment probability $E[\hat{Y}_d] = N^{-1}\Sigma(Y_d \mathbb{1}(D = d)/P(D = d))$. You'll do the same thing, but now you have to take into account that the potential outcome is defined in terms of a vector of treatment. For instance, in the case that the effect carries over for two periods, $m = 2$, you want to reconstruct $Y_t(0, 0, 0)$ and $Y_t(1, 1, 1)$, which requires you to calculate the running probability of observing three equal treatments in a row. For $m = 2$, that would be $P(d_{t-2} = d, d_{t-1} = d, d_t = d)$, or, more generally:

$$P(\mathbf{D}_{t-m:t} = \mathbf{d}),$$

where $\mathbf{D}_{t-m:t}$ is the vector of the current and last m treatments and $\mathbf{d}$ is a vector of constant treatment d. Here, you can focus on the case where the randomization probability p is always 50%. That is, at each randomization point, the treatment has a 50% chance of staying the same or switching. In terms of experiment design, this will increase the power of the experiment, as it increases the treatment variance. From an estimation procedure, it makes it so that $P(\mathbf{D}_{t-m:t} = 1) = P(\mathbf{D}_{t-m:t} = 0)$. However, this does not mean that $P(\mathbf{D}_{t-m:t} = \mathbf{d})$ will be the same everywhere. In fact that probability depends on the randomization points and where you are on the sequence. In your food delivery example, $p = 50\%$ and the treatment was randomized at every time period. So, the running probability of observing three consecutive treatments, like in the sequence `[1,1,1,1,1,1]`, is `[na,na,.5^3,.5^3,.5^3,.5^3]`. However, if you randomize every three periods, the same sequence has a running probability of `[na,na,.5, .5^2,.5^2,.5]`. That's because, at $t = 4, 5$ the lag 2 window, which contains the current time period and the previous two, will contain two randomization points.

I hope that is easy to conceptualize, but, unfortunately, it is not as easy to code. I'll do my best to explain how it's done, but it does require some clever array manipulation. But maybe this will teach you some new NumPy tricks. To make things more tangible, let's try to compute the running probability of observing $m + 1$ equal consecutive treatments in the case where the randomization happens every three periods:

```
In [18]: rad_points_3 = np.array([True, False, False]*(2))
         rad_points_3
```

```
Out[18]: array([ True, False, False,  True, False, False])
```

The first step is identifying the randomization windows from the randomization points. You can take advantage of the fact that True is interpreted as 1 and False, as 0. If you compute the cumulative sum of the randomization points, the sum will increase by 1 at each randomization point:

```
In [19]: rad_points_3.cumsum()
```

```
Out[19]: array([1, 1, 1, 2, 2, 2])
```

Now, you can view each randomization window as the sequence of equal integer numbers. You have two randomization windows of size 3 each.

The next step is to compute the carryover window, which will be of size $m + 1$. Notice that, in this case, the randomization window is equal to the carryover window, but this is not generally the case, so the code has to work for different ms. One way to do that is to use the function sliding_window_view, from NumPy, which, as the name suggests, creates a running window array. Notice that this function discards the first m windows, as they would not be complete:

```
In [20]: from numpy.lib.stride_tricks import sliding_window_view

         m = 2
         sliding_window_view(rad_points_3.cumsum(), window_shape=m+1)
```

```
Out[20]: array([[1, 1, 1],
                [1, 1, 2],
                [1, 2, 2],
                [2, 2, 2]])
```

From these windows, you can calculate how many randomization windows are contained in each carryover window. It is simply the quantity of different numbers in each carryover window. Unfortunately, there isn't a NumPy function that counts the unique elements across an axis, so you'll have to build one on your own. To do that, you can use the function np.diff, which counts the difference of subsequent entries in an array:

```
In [21]: np.diff(sliding_window_view(rad_points_3.cumsum(), 3), axis=1)
```

```
Out[21]: array([[0, 0],
                [0, 1],
```

```
                    [1, 0],
                    [0, 0]])
```

Then, finally, summing up the columns and adding 1 returns the number of random-ization windows at each point of the original array. Notice that the result starts at index 2 ($T = 3$), since sliding_window_view discards the first m windows. In this example, at $T = 3$, the last three entries contain a single randomization window, at time $T = 4$, it contains two randomization windows, and so on. To avoid any confusion, you can prepend m np.nan at the beginning of the array:

```
In [22]: n_rand_windows = np.concatenate([
             [np.nan]*m,
             np.diff(sliding_window_view(rad_points_3.cumsum(), 3),
                     axis=1).sum(axis=1)+1
         ])

         n_rand_windows

Out[22]: array([nan, nan,  1.,  2.,  2.,  1.])
```

Now, to get the probability vector, all you have to do is take the probability of the experiment, in this case, 0.5, and exponentiate it by the preceding array:

```
In [23]: p=0.5
         p**n_rand_windows

Out[23]: array([ nan, nan, 0.5, 0.25, 0.25, 0.5 ])
```

Here is everything wrapped up in a function. You can also check that this logic works for other randomization frequencies, like randomizing every period:

```
In [24]: def compute_p(rand_points, m, p=0.5):
             n_windows_last_m = np.concatenate([
                 [np.nan]*m,
                 np.diff(sliding_window_view(rand_points.cumsum(), m+1),
                         axis=1).sum(axis=1)+1
             ])
             return p**n_windows_last_m

         compute_p(np.ones(6)==1, 2, 0.5)

Out[24]: array([ nan, nan, 0.125, 0.125, 0.125, 0.125])
```

and even for nonregular randomization intervals:

```
In [25]: rand_points = np.array([True, False, False, True, False, True, False])
         compute_p(rand_points, 2, 0.5)
```

```
Out[25]: array([ nan, nan, 0.5, 0.25, 0.25, 0.25, 0.25])
```

But all of that was just to compute $P(\mathbf{D}_{t-m:t} = \mathbf{d})$. You still have to take a look at the rest of the estimator for the potential outcome:

$$\hat{Y}(\mathbf{d}) = \frac{1}{T-m} \sum_{t=m+1}^{T} Y_t \frac{\mathbb{1}(\mathbf{D}_{t-m:t} = \mathbf{d})}{P(\mathbf{D}_{t-m:t} = \mathbf{d})}$$

In other words, this estimator will scale up the observed outcome by the running probability you just learned how to compute, whenever the last m treatment and the current one are all the same. Then, it will average those scaled-up outcomes.

To code this, the only missing piece is the indicator function in the numerator, which evaluates to true whenever the last $m + 1$ treatments are equal to d. Fortunately, now that you know about sliding_window_view, that is pretty easy to do. First, create the $m + 1$ window view of the treatment array. Then, check if all the elements in that window are equal to the treatment. Here is a function to do just that:

```
In [26]: def last_m_d_equal(d_vec, d, m):
             return np.concatenate([
                 [np.nan]*m,
                 (sliding_window_view(d_vec, m+1)==d).all(axis=1)
             ])

         print(last_m_d_equal([1, 1, 1, 0, 0, 0], 1, m=2))
         print(last_m_d_equal([1, 1, 1, 0, 0, 0], 0, m=2))
```

```
Out[26]: [nan nan  1.  0.  0.  0.]
         [nan nan  0.  0.  0.  1.]
```

Applying this function to the treatment vector $[1,1,1,0,0,0]$, using $m = 2$ and trying to find when the current and last two entries are treated ($d = 1$) returns a 1 only at the third entry, as it should be.

You are finally ready to join all those pieces into the IPW estimator for switchback experiments:

$$\hat{\tau} = \frac{1}{T-m} \sum_{t=m+1}^{T} \left\{ Y_t \left(\frac{\mathbb{1}(\mathbf{D}_{t-m:t} = \mathbf{1})}{P(\mathbf{D}_{t-m:t} = \mathbf{1})} - \frac{\mathbb{1}(\mathbf{D}_{t-m:t} = \mathbf{0})}{P(\mathbf{D}_{t-m:t} = \mathbf{0})} \right) \right\}$$

```
In [27]: def ipw_switchback(d, y, rand_points, m, p=0.5):

             p_last_m_equal_1 = compute_p(rand_points, m=m, p=p)
             p_last_m_equal_0 = compute_p(rand_points, m=m, p=1-p)

             last_m_is_1 = last_m_d_equal(d,1,m)
             last_m_is_0 = last_m_d_equal(d,0,m)

             y1_rec = y*last_m_is_1/p_last_m_equal_1
             y0_rec = y*last_m_is_0/p_last_m_equal_0

             return np.mean((y1_rec-y0_rec)[m:])
```

Let's now use this function to estimate τ from the price increase switchback experiment. Remember that the treatment was randomized at each time period, so you can pass a vector of Trues, np.ones(len(df))==1, to the rand_points arguments:

```
In [28]: ipw_switchback(df["d"],
                         df["delivery_time"],
                         np.ones(len(df))==1,
                         m=2, p=0.5)
```

```
Out[28]: -7.426440677966101
```

This estimated effect is a bit lower (meaning that prices decrease waiting time more) than the one you got with OLS. Also, it is worth mentioning that it has a much higher variance. In the following plot, I've simulated 500 switchback experiments just like the one you have and computed both the OLS and IPW estimates for the total effect. As you can see, both methods are unbiased, since the average of the estimated $\hat{\tau}$ matches τ in both cases. However, the IPW distribution is much more spread out:

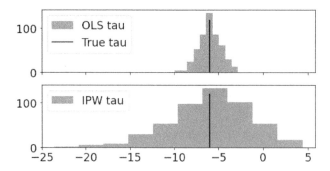

Optimal Switchback Design

I think we can all agree that more variance is undesirable from an estimation standpoint. However, if you plan to design a switchback experiment, you probably want to be conservative and look at the worst possible case. Also, you likely want to make the least amount of assumptions possible. For this reason, taking the IPW estimator and trying to come up with an experiment design that will reduce its variance is an attractive proposition. First, let's think on an intuitive level how you might go about doing that.

From the IPW estimator formula, you know that it only keeps the sequences with $m + 1$ consecutive equal treatments. This means it throws away any $m + 1$ sequence that has more than one treatment assignment. If you go back to the plot that shows the observed and potential outcomes of your experiment, it would mean throwing away all the data in between the upper and lower potential outcomes. Hence, if you want to use more data, all you have to do is make sure you have more consecutive equal treatments. At the limit, you would just set all the treatment sequences to either 0 or 1. This would maximize the usable data; however, it would decrease the variance of the treatment—and, in this extreme case, make estimation impossible. Since the variance of the estimator can be decreased by having both more useful data and higher treatment variance, you have to find a balance between the two.

Intuitively speaking, one way to do that is by randomizing every $m + 1$ period. So, in your example, if the order of the carryover effect is 2, you would randomize every three periods. This is indeed very close to the design that minimized variance, but it is not exactly it. Turns out you can improve it slightly if you instead randomize at every m periods and add a gap of size m at the beginning and end of the experiment horizon, when $m > 0$:

$$\mathbb{T}^* = \{1, 2m + 1, 3m + 1, \ldots, (n - 2)m + 1\},$$

where $\mathbb{T}^*$ are the optimal randomization points, m is the order of the carryover effect, and n is an integer ≥ 4 such that $T/m = n$. In practice, this means that the length of the experiment has to be divisible by the carryover order and long enough to contain at least four blocks of size m.

 When there is no carryover, $(m = 0)$, the optimal design is just randomizing at every period, which would maximize treatment variance while keeping all the data.

To consolidate your understanding about this, let's look at some examples. First, if $T = 12$ and $m = 2$, you would randomize at $t = 1$, leave a gap of size 2 at $t = 3$ then randomize again at $t = 5, 7, 9$, and leave a final gap of size 2 at $t = 11$:

```
In [29]: m = 2
         T = 12
         n = T/m
```

```
        np.isin(
            np.arange(1, T+1),
            [1] + [i*m+1 for i in range(2, int(n)-1)]
        )*1
```

```
Out[29]: array([1, 0, 0, 0, 1, 0, 1, 0, 1, 0, 0, 0])
```

When $m = 3$ and $T = 15$, you again randomize at $t = 1$, then leave a gap of size 3 at $t = 4$, randomize again at $t = 7, 10$, and leave a final gap of size 3 at $t = 13$:

```
In [30]: m = 3
        T = 15
        n = T/m
        np.isin(
            np.arange(1, T+1),
            [1] + [i*m+1 for i in range(2, int(n)-1)]
        )*1
```

```
Out[30]: array([1, 0, 0, 0, 0, 0, 1, 0, 0, 1, 0, 0, 0, 0, 0])
```

Now, as interesting as this is, it is worth mentioning that the variance decrease you'll probably get with this optimal design is nowhere as near as the one you would get by making a model assumption and using OLS. In the following plots, I've simulated 500 experiments with $T = 120$ and $m = 2$ using the optimal design, the intuitive design (randomizing every three periods), and randomizing every period. Then, I used the IPW estimator to estimate the effect in all of them. As you can see, there is a variance reduction, but it's nothing dramatic:

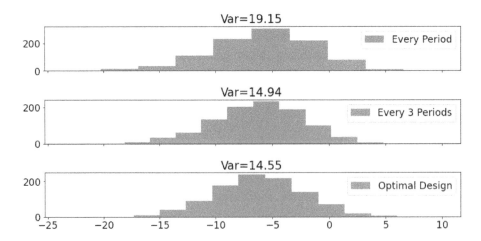

Still, since the optimal design is rather simple to implement, I don't see any reason not to.

Robust Variance

We talked a lot about reducing variance, but I haven't yet told you how to estimate the variance of the IPW estimator. That's because it actually depends on the design of your experiment. Now that we've set on an optimal design, you can compute the variance that it entails. So, for the sake of the example, let's say that the food delivery company ran a second experiment, a lot like the first one, with $T = 120$, p = 0.5, but now they decided the randomization points based on the optimal design. The data from that experiment is stored in the following data frame:

```
In [31]: df_opt = pd.read_csv("./data/sb_exp_opt.csv")
         df_opt.head(6)
```

	rand_points	d	delivery_time
0	True	0	5.84
1	False	0	5.40
2	False	0	8.86
3	False	0	8.79
4	True	0	10.93
5	False	0	7.02

The IPW function from before is pretty general, so you can use it here to estimate the treatment effect:

```
In [32]: tau_hat = ipw_switchback(df_opt["d"],
                                   df_opt["delivery_time"],
                                   df_opt["rand_points"],
                                   m=2, p=0.5)

         tau_hat


Out[32]: -9.921016949152545
```

Now, for the variance. The formula is a bit ugly, but you'll see it's not that complicated, once I parse it for you. First, let's partition your data into $K = T/m$ blocks such that each block has size m. Then, define the sum of the outcomes of a block k as $\bar{Y}_k = \sum Y_{km + 1 : (k + 1)m}$. For instance, if $Y = [1, 1, 1, 2, 2, 3]$, for $m = 2$, $k = \{1, 2\}$, $\bar{Y} = [\sum Y_{3:4}, \sum Y_{5:6}] = [3, 5]$. Notice that the first block is thrown away. Having defined the sum of those blocks, a conservative estimate to the variance is as follows:

$$\hat{\sigma}(\hat{\tau}) = \frac{1}{(T - m)^2}\left\{8\bar{Y}_1^2 + \sum_{k = 2}^{K - 1} 32\bar{Y}_k^2 \mathbb{1}\left(d_{km + 1} = d_{(k + 1)m + 1}\right) + 8\bar{Y}_K^2\right\}$$

Now, let me parse it for you. First, the denominator is the square of the sample size. But since you discarded the first m entries, you have to subtract m. The numerator is composed of three main terms. The first and the last term take into account the gap you left at the beginning and end of the optimal design. The term in the middle is a bit more complicated, because it has this indicator function. That function evaluates to 1 whenever two consecutive blocks have the same treatment. Notice that, because of the gap at the beginning and end, this is sure to happen for the first and last term, which is why you don't need the indicator function there.

To code this formula, you'll first need to make sure that T is divisible by m by a factor greater or equal to 4. Then, you'll make use of the functions hsplit and vstack. The first will partition the array into blocks and the second will pile up the blocks vertically. Here is an example:

```
In [33]: np.vstack(np.hsplit(np.array([1,1,1,2,2,3]), 3))
```

```
Out[33]: array([[1, 1],
                [1, 2],
                [2, 3]])
```

You can then sum the columns of that piled-up array to get $\bar{Y}$.

For the indicator function, you'll do the same thing, but with the treatment vector. Due to the nature of the experiment design, the entire block of treatment will be either 1 or 0, so you can take just the first column to know which treatment was assigned to that block. To know if two consecutive blocks have the same treatment, use the diff function. This will discard yet another block. Here is an example:

```
In [34]: np.diff(np.vstack(np.hsplit(np.array([1,1,0,0,0,0]), 3))[:, 0]) == 0
```

```
Out[34]: array([False,  True])
```

Now, for the entire variance function:

```
In [35]: def var_opt_design(d_opt, y_opt, T, m):

             assert ((T//m == T/m)
                     & (T//m >= 4)), "T must be divisible by m and T/m >= 4"

             # discard 1st block
             y_m_blocks = np.vstack(np.hsplit(y_opt, int(T/m))).sum(axis=1)[1:]

             # take 1st column
             d_m_blocks = np.vstack(np.split(d_opt, int(T/m))[1:])[:, 0]

             return (
                 8*y_m_blocks[0]**2
```

```
            + (32*y_m_blocks[1:-1]**2*(np.diff(d_m_blocks)==0)[:-1]).sum()
            + 8*y_m_blocks[-1]**2
    ) / (T-m)**2
```

Finally, with that function, you can estimate the variance and place a confidence interval around your effect estimate:

```
In [36]: se_hat = np.sqrt(var_opt_design(df_opt["d"],
                                          df_opt["delivery_time"],
                                          T=120, m=2))

         [tau_hat - 1.96*se_hat, tau_hat + 1.96*se_hat]


Out[36]: [-18.490627362048095, -1.351406536256997]
```

That is a pretty wide confidence interval—a lot wider than the earlier one, with OLS and the design that randomized every period. Still, sometimes this extra variance is a price worth paying, if you don't want to make further model assumptions. Moreover, even if you follow the optimized design, you can still analyze it with OLS. Even though this optimal design is not meant to minimize the OLS variance, I find that it still gives more precise estimates than randomizing at every period, for instance.

Finding M with Fewer Assumptions

The optimal switchback experiment design, the IPW estimator and the variance estimator presented in this chapter was taken from the paper "Design and Analysis of Switchback Experiments," by Bojinov, Simchi-Levi, and Zhao (yes, it's the same Zhao from the synthetic control design paper). That paper contains a more generic formula for the optimal design, which works when T is not divisible by m. Since that formula is a lot more complex and a company can easily make it so that T is divisible by m, I chose to omit it here.

Moreover, the paper proposes another procedure to find the order of the carryover effect m. The idea is based on running two optimal experiments, e_1 and e_2, each one with a candidate value for m, m_1, and m_2. Say that $m_1 < m_2$. If the effect estimates from both experiments are the same, you cannot reject the hypothesis $H_0 : m \leq m_1$. That's because, if $m > m_1$, e_1 would return a more biased estimate for the effect than e_2. Hence, you can search for m based on rejecting the hypothesis that the effect estimates from two experiments are the same, $H_0 : \widehat{\tau_1} = \widehat{\tau_2}$.

Honestly, I'm not sure I like that procedure. The high variance will make it very hard to reject that null hypothesis, unless the experiment is incredibly long (very high T). Still, that is an alternative to the OLS method I showed you, in case you don't want to make any model-based assumptions.

Key Ideas

This chapter looks at two alternative experiment designs for when the number of experimental units at your disposal is rather short. This can happen, for example, when you are forced to zoom out from treating customers to treating entire cities, as it is often the case in both online and offline marketing.

First, you learned about synthetic control design. Here, the goal is to find a small set of units which, when combined together, approximate the average behavior of all units. This can be done by maximizing the following objective:

$$\min_{w, v} \|\mathbf{Y}_{pre}\mathbf{f} - \mathbf{Y}_{pre}\mathbf{w}_{tr} - \alpha_0\|^2 + \|\mathbf{Y}_{pre}\mathbf{f} - \mathbf{Y}_{pre}\mathbf{v}_{co} - \beta_0\|^2$$

$$\text{s.t} \quad \sum w_i = 1 \text{ and } \sum v_i = 1,$$

$$w_i, v_i \geq 0 \ \forall \ i,$$

$$w_i v_i = 0 \ \forall \ i,$$

$$|\mathbf{w}|_0 \leq m$$

where $\mathbf{f}$ corresponds to the weight each unit contributes to the global average, $\mathbf{w}$ and $\mathbf{v}$ are the weights of the synthetic treatment and control units, and m is is a constraint on the maximum number of treatment units.

Synthetic control designs are great for when you have a relatively small number of experimental units, as it allows you to treat just the ones that are good at reproducing the average. Moreover, synthetic control design is well suited for when the order of the carryover effect is large, meaning that the treatment effect takes a long time to dissipate.

If that is not the case—that is, the order of carryover effect is small—then switchback experiments tend to offer a good alternative. Even if you have very few or only one experimentation unit, switchback experiments work by turning the treatment on and off for the same unit and then doing a bunch of before-and-after comparisons.

A switchback experiment is defined by the probability of treatment—which, if you want to maximize power, should be set to 50%—and the randomization points, or time periods when randomization happens. If you know the order of the carryover effect, m, and it is greater than 0, then the optimal design randomizes every $m + 1$ time periods:

$$\mathbb{T}^* = \{1, 2m + 1, 3m + 1, \ldots, (n - 2)m + 1\},$$

where $n = T/m$. For this to work, the length of the experiment T has to be divisible by m by more than 4. Also, if there is no carryover effect ($m = 0$), the optimal design is one that simply randomizes at each time period.

CHAPTER 11

Noncompliance and Instruments

It's not uncommon for companies to offer products or services to their existing customer base. For instance, a retailer can offer a subscription-based program where customers get free shipping. A streaming company can offer an ad-free version of its services for an additional fee. Or a bank can offer a prime credit card with lots of perks for customers who spend above a certain threshold.

In all of these examples, *the customer must opt in* for the additional service, which makes inferring its impact challenging. As the choice to participate lies with the customer, that choice often confounds the impact evaluation of the service; after all, customers who opt in and customers who don't will likely have different Y_0. Even if the company *randomizes the availability* of the service or product, it can't force customers to take it. This is called *noncompliance, where not everyone that gets assigned to the treatment takes it*. This chapter will walk you through how to think about this issue and what to consider when you want to design an experiment that suffers from noncompliance.

Noncompliance

Noncompliance comes from pharmaceutical science (although some of the tooling to deal with it comes from economics). Imagine you are conducting an experiment to test the effect of a new drug on some illness. Each subject gets assigned to a treatment: a drug or a placebo. But those subjects are imperfect human beings, who sometimes forget to take their medicine. As a result, not everyone assigned to the treatment gets it. Also, someone critically ill might figure out they were assigned the placebo and manage to find a way to get the treatment regardless. That is to say, if you *separate the treatment assignment from the treatment intake*, you'll end up with four groups:

Compliers
  Those who take the treatment that was assigned to them

Always takers
  Those who always take the treatment, regardless of the assignment

Never takers
  Those who never take the treatment, regardless of the assignment

Defiers
  Those who take the opposite treatment from the one assigned

The catch here is that you don't know who belongs to each group.

You can also represent noncompliance in a DAG (see Figure 11-1), where Z is the treatment assignment (random in this case), T is the treatment, Y is the outcome, and U is hidden factors that confound the treatment choice and the outcome. Z is what is called *an instrument*: a variable that (1) impacts the treatment in a nonconfounded way and (2) doesn't impact the outcome, unless through the treatment.

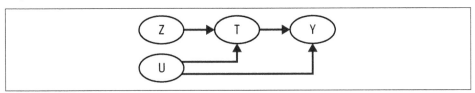

Figure 11-1. The canonical instrumental variable DAG

Since the compliance group and the treatment assignment deterministically cause the treatment intake, you can also think of U as unknown factors that cause the compliance group. As you can see from the DAG in Figure 11-1, without further assumptions, you can't identify the effect of the treatment on Y due to an open backdoor path through U. As you'll soon see, identification of that effect will involve clever usage of Z.

To make things more concrete, let's work with a typical industry setting where a bank wants to know the impact of offering a prime credit card to its customers. Since this prime service is costly, the bank charges a small fee, which is not enough to cover all its costs. But, if the purchase volume—the total amount spent on the card—of those prime customers increases by at least 500 USD, then it is worth it. Hence, the bank wants to know how much the prime card increases customers' purchase volume.

The bank managed to run an experiment where it randomized the availability of the prime credit card (prime_eligible) to 10,000 customers, with each customer having a 50% chance of being eligible and 50% of being in the control. Of course, the bank can't force customers to choose the card, making this an experiment with non-compliance.

If you map these variables to Figure 11-1, purchase volume would be Y, availability of the prime credit card would be Z, and having the prime card would be T. All this information is stored in the following data frame. The bank also has information on the customer's age, income, and credit score, but let's not worry about those variables for now. Additionally, I've added information on the true effect of the prime card on PV, τ (tau), and which group a customer belongs to. Keep in mind that the compliance category and τ are not available to you in real life. I'll only use them here to make some examples easier to understand:

```
In [1]: import pandas as pd
        import numpy as np

        df = pd.read_csv("./data/prime_card.csv")

        df.head()
```

	age	income	credit_score	prime_eligible	prime_card	pv	tau	categ
0	37.7	9687.0	822.0	0	0	4913.79	700.0	complier
1	46.0	13731.0	190.0	0	0	5637.66	200.0	never-taker
2	43.1	2839.0	214.0	1	1	2410.45	700.0	complier
3	36.0	1206.0	318.0	1	1	1363.06	700.0	complier
4	39.7	4095.0	430.0	0	0	2189.80	700.0	complier

Extending Potential Outcomes

To be more precise with noncompliance and to proceed with identification, you'll have to extend the potential outcome notation. Since Z causes T, you can now define a *potential treatment* T_z. Also, the potential outcome has new counterfactuals with respect to the instrument Z, $Y_{z,t}$.

In the prime credit card example, Z is randomized, which means that the effect of Z on Y—also called the *intention-to-treat effect* (ITTE)—is pretty easy to identify:

$$ITTE = E[Y|Z=1] - E[Y|Z=0] = E[Y_{1,t} - Y_{0,t}],$$

which you can estimate with a simple linear regression:

```
In [2]: m = smf.ols("pv~prime_eligible", data=df).fit()
        m.summary().tables[1]
```

	coef	std err	t	P>|t|	[0.025	0.975]
Intercept	2498.3618	24.327	102.701	0.000	2450.677	2546.047
prime_eligible	321.3880	34.321	9.364	0.000	254.113	388.663

The ITTE is a valuable metric in its own right as it measures the impact of assigning a treatment, such as offering the prime credit card in this scenario. For the bank, this number indicates the additional purchase volume (PV) per customer it can expect by having the prime credit card available as part of its product suite. However, it's crucial to note that the ITTE is not the same as the treatment effect. The bank's primary objective is to determine whether the benefits of the prime card outweigh its costs. Therefore, the bank needs to identify the treatment effect of choosing the card, rather than solely relying on the ITTE.

In this particular example, the bank has full control on who has the prime card available. As a result, you have *one-sided noncompliance*, since there is no way for customers who are not eligible for the prime card to get it, but customers who have the card available can still choose to not have it. This forces the always takers into compliance and the defiers into never takers, reducing the number of compliance groups from four to two.

Now that you understand the setting, let's think about identifying the effect of the prime card. An obvious idea is to use the ITTE as a proxy for the card effect. Maybe they are not so different after all. So, what is the ITTE anyway?

Due to randomization of treatment assignment, the ITTE can be obtained by comparing those assigned to the treatment to those assigned in the control. But you can quickly see that this comparison will give you a *biased toward zero estimate for the treatment effect* (see Figure 11-2). That's because some of those assigned to the treatment actually get the control, which decreases the perceived difference between the two groups.

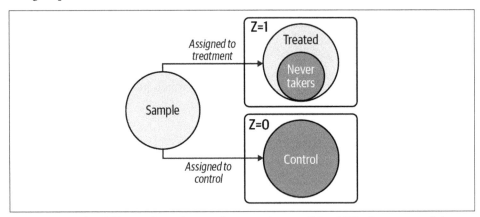

Figure 11-2. The ITTE is a biased toward zero estimate of the ATE, since some of the units assigned to one treatment actually get the other treatment

To prove that, you can take advantage of those taus I've added to the dataset. The average treatment effect is quite larger than the ITTE:

```
In [3]: df["tau"].mean()
```

```
Out[3]: 413.45
```

OK, so that turned out to be a dead end. But what about a simple average comparison between treated and control $E[Y|T=1] - E[Y|T=0]$? Maybe the randomization assignment will make that a good proxy for the effect estimate you care about. Well... let's estimate that and see:

```
In [4]: m = smf.ols("pv~prime_card", data=df).fit()
        m.summary().tables[1]
```

	coef	std err	t	P>|t|	[0.025	0.975]
Intercept	2534.4947	19.239	131.740	0.000	2496.783	2572.206
prime_card	588.1388	41.676	14.112	0.000	506.446	669.831

Now the measured effect is much larger than the true effect (see Figure 11-3). The reason is that, in this example the bias is upward, $E[Y_0|T=1] > E[Y_0|T=0]$, meaning that customers who choose the prime card spend more regardless of the prime card. In other words, the never takers have lower Y_0 than the compliers, which artificially lowers the average outcome of the untreated group.

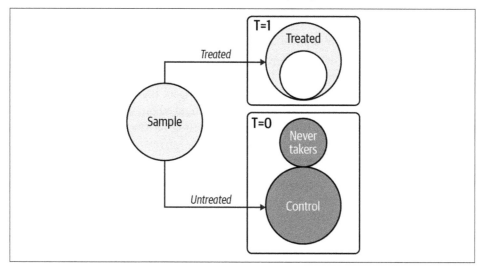

Figure 11-3. Under noncompliance, comparing treated and untreated will not recover the ATE, since treatment choice is not random

It seems that you are a bit stuck here. The ATE can't be identified and ITTE is a biased measure for it. As with much in causal inference, in order to make some progress, you'll need to make additional assumptions.

Instrument Identification Assumptions

Let's take the DAG I showed you earlier and reproduce it here for better readability. As you'll see, the first few assumptions you'll need for identification are already spelled out in that DAG:

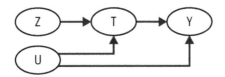

Here they are:

1. The first assumption you need is *independence*; the lack of unmeasured confounders between Z and T, $T_z \perp Z|X$, and between Z and Y, $Y(Z, T_z) \perp Z|X$. This assumption states that the instrument is as good as randomly assigned. This assumption is not testable, but it can be made more plausible by the experiment design. In your example, you can probably say this assumption is satisfied, since the bank randomized the availability of the prime card.

2. The second assumption is the *exclusion restriction*, $Y_{z,t} = Y_t$, which is the lack of a path from Z to Y that does not go through the treatment T. In words, it says that the instrument only affects the outcome through the treatment. This one is more tricky. Even if Z is randomized, it could impact the outcome through other channels. For example, let's say that customers figured out which group they were assigned to and those in the control got very mad at the bank and decided to close their accounts. In this case, randomization affects the outcome through a channel that is not the treatment.

3. The third assumption is *relevance*, $E[T_1 - T_0] \neq 0$, which is the existence of an arrow from Z to T. This assumption states that the instrument must have an influence on the treatment. Fortunately, this assumption is testable, since you can estimate the effect of the instrument on the treatment.

4. The fourth and final assumption is not stated in the DAG. It is mostly a functional from assumption imposed on the causal model: *monotonicity*, $T_{i1} \geq T_{i0}$ (or vice versa). It might look confusing, but it simply states that the instrument flips the treatment in only one direction. It either increases the chance of getting the treatment for everyone who got the instrument, which is equivalent to assuming that there are no defiers; or it decreases that chance, which is equivalent to

assuming that there are no compliers. In your example, this is also a plausible assumption, as customers in the control group can't force their way into getting the prime credit card. As a result, the defiers are collapsed into the never takers.

Now, let's see how to use those assumptions for identification. The goal here is to start with the ITTE and see if we can get something like an average treatment effect. First, let's expand the outcome into the potential outcomes. Recall that you can do this using the treatment as a switch—$Y = Y_1 T + Y_0(1 - T)$:

$$E[Y|Z = 1] - E[Y|Z = 0] = E\left[Y_{1,1}T_1 + Y_{1,0}(1 - T_1)\big|Z = 1\right]$$
$$-E\left[Y_{0,1}T_0 + Y_{0,0}(1 - T_0)\big|Z = 0\right]$$

Now, because of the exclusion restriction, you can remove the instrument subscript of $Y_{z,t}$:

$$E\left[Y_1 T_1 + Y_0(1 - T_1)\big|Z = 1\right] - E\left[Y_1 T_0 + Y_0(1 - T_0)\big|Z = 0\right]$$

Next, using the independence assumption, you can merge both expectations:

$$E\left[Y_1 T_1 + Y_0(1 - T_1) - Y_1 T_0 - Y_0(1 - T_0)\right]$$

which you can simplify to

$$E\left[(Y_1 - Y_0)(T_1 - T_0)\right].$$

Next, let's use the monotonicity assumption and expand this expectation into the possible cases, $T_1 > T_0$ and $T_1 = T_0$:

$$E\left[(Y_1 - Y_0)(T_1 - T_0)\big|T_1 > T_0\right] * P(T_1 > T_0)$$
$$+ \ E\left[(Y_1 - Y_0)(T_1 - T_0)\big|T_1 = T_0\right] * P(T_1 = T_0)$$

And since $T_1 - T_0$ would be 0 if $T_1 = T_0$, you are left with only the first term. Since Z is binary, $T_1 - T_0 = 1$ and:

$$E[Y|Z = 1] - E[Y|Z = 0] = E\left[Y_1 - Y_0\big|T_1 > T_0\right] * P(T_1 > T_0).$$

This is a good time to pause and see what you've accomplished. First, notice that $T_1 > T_0$ are the compliers, the population where the instrument shifts the treatment from 0 to 1. This means that this last equation tells you that *the effect of the instrument on the outcome is the treatment effect of the compliers times the compliance rate*. This explains why the ITTE is a biased-toward-zero estimate for this effect: you are multiplying it by a rate, which is between 0 and 1. If you could only estimate $P(T_1 > T_0)$, then you would be able to correct the previous estimator…

But wait a second! Since the instrument is randomized, you can estimate its impact on the treatment, $E[T_1 - T_0]$. And since $T_1 - T_0 = 1$ for the compliers and 0 otherwise (due to the monotonicity assumption), this effect is the compliance rate:

$$E[T_1 - T_0] = P(T_1 > T_0)$$

Putting it all together, this means that you can *identify the average treatment effect on the compliers by scaling up the effect of the instrument on the outcome by the compliance rate*, which is the effect of the instrument on the treatment:

$$E[Y_1 - Y_0 | T_1 > T_0] = \frac{E[Y|Z=1] - E[Y|Z=0]}{E[T|Z=1] - E[T|Z=0]}$$

This is how you can use instruments to identify the effect in noncompliance settings. The good news is that you can identify that effect. The bad news is that it is not the ATE, but only the effect on the compliers, which is usually called the *local average treatment effect* (LATE). Unfortunately, you can't identify the ATE. But this might not be a problem. In your credit card example, the LATE would be the effect on those who choose the prime card when it is available to them. Now, the bank wants to know if the effect in terms of extra *PV* compensate for the cost of the prime card, both of which only occur for those who choose the prime card. In this situation, it's enough to know the LATE. The bank doesn't care about the effect of those who will never opt in for the prime card.

Having gone through the theory about instrument identification, it is now time to check how to apply it in practice.

First Stage

The first step in instrumental variables analysis is to run what is conveniently called a *first stage* regression, where you regress the treatment on the instrument. During this step, you can check the relevance assumption—if the parameter estimate associated with the instrument is large and statistically significant, you have good reason to believe that assumption holds:

```
In [5]: first_stage = smf.ols("prime_card ~ prime_eligible", data=df).fit()
        first_stage.summary().tables[1]
```

	coef	std err	t	P>|t|	[0.025	0.975]
Intercept	6.729e−15	0.005	1.35e−12	1.000	−0.010	0.010
prime_eligible	0.4242	0.007	60.536	0.000	0.410	0.438

In this example, the compliance rate is estimated to be about 42%, which is also statistically significant (the 95% CI is [0.410, 0.438]). Since I've included the true group to which each customer belongs, you can even check if that is indeed the actual compliance rate:

```
In [6]: df.groupby("categ").size()/len(df)
```

```
Out[6]: categ
        complier      0.4269
        never-taker   0.5731
        dtype: float64
```

Reduced Form

The second step is called the *reduced form*. At this stage, you regress the outcome on the instrument to obtain the intention to treat the effect:

```
In [7]: red_form = smf.ols("pv ~ prime_eligible", data=df).fit()
        red_form.summary().tables[1]
```

	coef	std err	t	P>|t|	[0.025	0.975]
Intercept	2498.3618	24.327	102.701	0.000	2450.677	2546.047
prime_eligible	321.3880	34.321	9.364	0.000	254.113	388.663

Once you've run the first stage and the reduced form, you can divide the parameter estimate from the first by the parameter estimate on the latter to obtain the estimate for the local average treatment effect:

```
In [8]: late = (red_form.params["prime_eligible"] /
               first_stage.params["prime_eligible"])
        late
```

```
Out[8]: 757.6973795343938
```

As you can see, this effect is more than twice the ITTE. This is expected, since the compliance rate is lower than 50%. It is also larger than the ATE, but that is because the compliers have a higher than average effect. In fact, if you compute the effect for the compliers, you can see that your LATE estimate is pretty close to it:

```
In [9]: df.groupby("categ")["tau"].mean()
```

```
Out[9]: categ
        complier      700.0
        never-taker   200.0
        Name: tau, dtype: float64
```

There is still some difference, though. It's hard to tell if this is right or not if you don't wrap that point estimate in a confidence interval. You could do that using bootstrap, but I think it is worth looking into the actual formula for the standard error of instrumental variable (IV) estimates. To do that, you have to learn an alternate way to estimate the LATE.

Two-Stage Least Squares

If you zoom in the treatment part of the DAG, you can see that it is caused by two components: first, there is a random component, which is the randomized instrument. Second, there is the U component, which is where the confounding bias comes from:

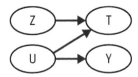

Recall how the first stage is a regression of the treatment on the instrument, which essentially means you are estimating the path $Z \rightarrow T$. But there is more to it. Since that is what the first stage is estimating, you can think of its predicted values, $\hat{T}$, as an unbiased version of the treatment. Which in turn means that if you regress the outcome on those predicted values, you'll get the same IV estimate as before:

```
In [10]: iv_regr = smf.ols(
             "pv ~ prime_card",
             data=df.assign(prime_card=first_stage.fittedvalues)).fit()

         iv_regr.summary().tables[1]
```

	coef	std err	t	P>|t|	[0.025	0.975]
Intercept	2498.3618	24.327	102.701	0.000	2450.677	2546.047
prime_card	757.6974	80.914	9.364	0.000	599.091	916.304

This approach is called two-stage least squares (2SLS). OK, but why is it useful? First, because it will allow you to properly compute standard errors; second, because it makes adding more instruments and covariates as easy as adding variables in a regression model. Let's now talk about each of those in turn.

Standard Error

The residuals from the second stage's prediction can be defined as follows:

$$\hat{e}_{IV} = Y - \hat{\beta}_{IV}T$$

Notice that this is *not* the same residuals you would get with the .resid method from the second stage, since those would be $Y - \hat{\beta}_{IV}\hat{T}$. The residual you want uses the raw version of the treatment, not the predicted one.

With that residual, you can compute the standard error for the IV estimates:

$$SE(\hat{\beta}_{IV}) = \frac{\sigma(\hat{e}_{IV})}{\hat{\beta}_{z,1st}\sigma(Z)\sqrt{n}},$$

where $\sigma(.)$ stands for the standard deviation function and $\hat{\beta}_{z,1st}$ is the estimated compliance rate, which you got from the first stage:

```
In [11]: Z = df["prime_eligible"]
         T = df["prime_card"]
         n = len(df)

         # not the same as iv_regr.resid!
         e_iv = df["pv"] - iv_regr.predict(df)
         compliance = np.cov(T, Z)[0, 1]/Z.var()

         se = np.std(e_iv)/(compliance*np.std(Z)*np.sqrt(n))

         print("SE IV:", se)
         print("95% CI:", [late - 2*se, late + 2*se])


Out[11]: SE IV: 80.52861026141942
         95% CI: [596.6401590115549, 918.7546000572327]
```

Just to double-check your results, you can use the 2SLS module from the linearmo dels' Python package. With it, you can wrap the first stage, as in [T~Z], inside the model's formula and fit an IV model. As you can see, using this package gives not only the same LATE estimate as the one you got earlier, but also the same standard error as the one you've just calculated:

```
In [12]: from linearmodels import IV2SLS

         formula = 'pv ~ 1 + [prime_card ~ prime_eligible]'
         iv_model = IV2SLS.from_formula(formula, df).fit(cov_type="unadjusted")

         iv_model.summary.tables[1]
```

	Parameter	Std. Err.	T-stat	P-value	Lower CI	Upper CI
Intercept	2498.4	24.211	103.19	0.0000	2450.9	2545.8
prime_card	757.70	80.529	9.4090	0.0000	599.86	915.53

Regardless of the method you use, you can see that this is a pretty huge confidence interval, even if it does contain the true ATE for the compliers, which is 700. More importantly, I think that the standard error formula can shed some light on the challenges of noncompliance experiments. First, notice $\sigma(Z)$ in the denominator. Since Z is a binary variable, the maximum value for $\sigma(Z)$ is 0.5. This is not much different from OLS with a binary treatment. (Recall that then, the standard error was $\sigma(\hat{e})/(\sigma(T)\sqrt{n})$). It simply states that you can maximize the power of a test by randomizing the treatment in a 50%-50% fashion.

But now you have an extra term in the denominator: the compliance rate, $\hat{\beta}_{z,1st}$. Not surprisingly, if compliance is 100%, then $Z = T$, $\hat{\beta}_{z,1st} = 1$ and you get back the OLS standard error. But with noncompliance, the standard error increases, since $\hat{\beta}_{z,1st} < 1$. For instance, with 50% compliance, the IV standard error will be twice as large as the OLS standard error. As a result, the required sample size for an experiment with 50% compliance is 4x the sample you would need if you had 100% compliance.

 ### Bias of IV

It turns out that the IV estimates are consistent, but not unbiased. That is, $E[\beta_{IV}] \neq \beta$. This is mostly due to sampling error in the first stage. Since you don't have infinite data, the fitted value for the treatment, $\hat{T}$, will be a function of both Z and U, meaning that not all the bias will go away. As you gather more data $\hat{T}$ will become less and less a function of U. This is why the estimator is consistent, meaning that $\operatorname*{plim}_{n \to \infty} \beta_{IV} = \beta$.

The following plot compares the size of the confidence interval for your LATE parameter estimate assuming different estimated compliance rates (first image). It also shows how many more samples you would need for a test with noncompliance, considering multiple compliance rates:

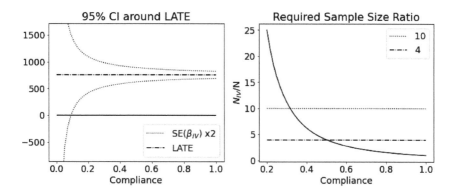

Fifty percent compliance is still a lot. In most applications, only a small fraction of customers opt in for the prime service or product, which makes it even harder to estimate the LATE. For instance, if compliance is as low as 30%, you'll need a sample 10x larger than the one you would need if compliance weren't an issue. Gathering a sample that big tends to be impractical, if not impossible. But if you run into a problem like this, not all is lost. There are still some tricks you can use to lower the IV standard error. In order to do that, you'll have to include extra covariates in your analysis.

Additional Controls and Instruments

Remember how the prime credit card data had three additional covariates, besides the treatment, the instrument, and the outcome? They were the customer's income, age, and credit score. Now, suppose that the causal graph that describes their relationship with T, Z, and Y is as follows:

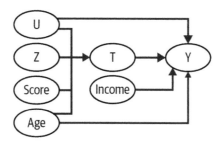

That is, income is highly predictive of the outcome, but doesn't predict compliance; credit score predicts compliance, but not the outcome, and age predicts both of them (is a confounder). If you are smart about how you use those variables, you can decrease the standard error by using all of them.

First, let's look at credit score. Credit score causes compliance, but does not cause the outcome. This means that it can be treated as an additional instrumental variable. From the DAG, you can see that it satisfies the first three IV assumptions, just like Z. You only have to assume positivity. Including that variable as an extra IV in your 2SLS model will significantly reduce the standard error of the LATE parameter:

```
In [13]: formula = 'pv ~ 1 + [prime_card ~ prime_eligible + credit_score]'
         iv_model = IV2SLS.from_formula(formula, df).fit()

         iv_model.summary.tables[1]
```

	Parameter	Std. Err.	T-stat	P-value	Lower CI	Upper CI
Intercept	2519.4	21.168	119.02	0.0000	2477.9	2560.9
prime_card	659.04	58.089	11.345	0.0000	545.19	772.90

Now, you have to be careful here. If instead of treating it as an instrument, you condition on it, adding it to the second stage too, the error will increase. But you know this already, from Chapter 4, where you learned that conditioning on variables that cause the treatment, but not the outcome, will increase variance. The bigger issue here is that, unless you know the instrument assignment mechanism (as you do with Z), it is hard to know if the exclusion restriction holds. For instance, you are assuming that credit score doesn't cause the outcome mostly because I told you so and you trust me since I was the one who generated the data. But in real life, it's hard to find instruments like that. Most likely, a covariate affects both compliance and the outcome, which is the case of age here. For this reason, a much more promising approach to reducing variance of the IV estimate is to include controls that are highly predictive of the outcome. For instance, in this example, customer income is very predictive of purchase volume, so including it as an additional control will lower the standard error quite substantially:

```
In [14]: formula = '''pv ~ 1
         + [prime_card ~ prime_eligible + credit_score]
         + income + age'''

         iv_model = IV2SLS.from_formula(formula, df).fit(cov_type="unadjusted")

         iv_model.summary.tables[1]
```

	Parameter	Std. Err.	T-stat	P-value	Lower CI	Upper CI
Intercept	210.62	37.605	5.6008	0.0000	136.91	284.32
age	9.7444	0.8873	10.982	0.0000	8.0053	11.483

income	0.3998	0.0008	471.04	0.0000	0.3981	0.4014
prime_card	693.12	12.165	56.978	0.0000	669.28	716.96

As for variables like age, which affect both the outcome and compliance, the effect on the standard error will be more nuanced. Like with the regression case, if it explains the treatment a lot more than the outcome, it might end up increasing the variance.

2SLS by Hand

Since you won't always have instrumental variable software at your disposal, I think it is worth learning how to implement 2SLS by hand, especially since it is not at all complicated. If you have more than one instrument and additional covariates, you can include them in your model by:

1. Running the first stage, regressing the treatment on instruments and the additional covariates, T ~ Z + X.

2. Running the second stage by regressing the outcome on the treated fitted values (from the first stage) and the additional covariates, Y ~ T_hat + X:

```
In [15]: formula_1st = "prime_card ~ prime_eligible + credit_score + income+age"
         first_stage = smf.ols(formula_1st, data=df).fit()

         iv_model = smf.ols(
             "pv ~ prime_card + income + age",
             data=df.assign(prime_card=first_stage.fittedvalues)).fit()

         iv_model.summary().tables[1]
```

	coef	std err	t	P>|t|	[0.025	0.975]
Intercept	210.6177	40.832	5.158	0.000	130.578	290.657
prime_card	693.1207	13.209	52.474	0.000	667.229	719.013
income	0.3998	0.001	433.806	0.000	0.398	0.402
age	9.7444	0.963	10.114	0.000	7.856	11.633

Matrix Implementation

This will give you the exact same IV estimate as the one you got with linearmodels, but the standard errors will be off. If you want those, you are probably better off with the matrix implementation of 2SLS. To do that, you have to append the additional covariates into both the treatment and the instrument matrix. Then, you can find the IV parameters as follows:

$$\hat{X} = Z(Z'Z)^{-1}Z'X$$

$$\beta_{IV} = \left(\hat{X}'\hat{X}\right)^{-1}\hat{X}Y$$

When coding it up, you just have to be careful with large N. $Z(Z'Z)^{-1}Z'$ will be an huge $N \times N$ matrix, which can be avoided if you just first multiply $(Z'Z)^{-1}Z'X$ and then pre-multiply Z:

```
In [16]: Z = df[["prime_eligible", "credit_score", "income", "age"]].values
         X = df[["prime_card", "income", "age"]].values
         Y = df[["pv"]].values

         def add_intercept(x):
             return np.concatenate([np.ones((x.shape[0], 1)), x], axis=1)

         Z_ = add_intercept(Z)
         X_ = add_intercept(X)

         # pre-multiplying Z_.dot(...) last is important to avoid
         # creating a huge NxN matrix
         X_hat = Z_.dot(np.linalg.inv(Z_.T.dot(Z_))).dot(Z_.T).dot(X_))

         b_iv = np.linalg.inv(X_hat.T.dot(X_hat)).dot(X_hat.T).dot(Y)
         b_iv[1]
```

```
Out[16]: array([693.12072518])
```

Once more, you have the exact same coefficient as before. Once you have that, you can compute the IV residuals and the variance:

$$\widehat{Var}\left(\hat{\beta}_{IV}\right) = \sigma^2\left(\hat{e}_{iv}\right)diag\left(\left(\hat{X}'\hat{X}\right)^{-1}\right)$$

```
In [17]: e_hat_iv = (Y - X_.dot(b_iv))

         var = e_hat_iv.var()*np.diag(np.linalg.inv(X_hat.T.dot(X_hat)))

         np.sqrt(var[1])
```

```
Out[17]: 12.164694395033125
```

This variance formula is a bit harder to interpret, due to the matrix notation, but you can approximate something that is more in line with what you had before, in the case without additional covariates:

$$SE\left(\widehat{\beta_{IV}}\right) \approx \frac{\sigma\left(\hat{e}_{IV}\right)}{\sigma\left(\tilde{T}\right)\sqrt{nR_{1st}^2}}$$

Here, $\tilde{T}$ is the residuals of the treatment regressed on the additional covariates, but not the instrument, and R_{1st}^2 is the R^2 from the first stage:

```
In [18]: t_tilde = smf.ols("prime_card ~ income + age", data=df).fit().resid

         e_hat_iv.std()/(t_tilde.std()*np.sqrt(n*first_stage.rsquared))
```

```
Out[18]: 12.156252763192523
```

With this formula, you can see that, aside from increasing the sample size, you have three levers to decrease the standard error:

1. Increasing the first stage R^2. This can be done by finding strong instruments, which are variables that are good at predicting compliance, but satisfy the exclusion restriction (do not cause the outcome).

2. Removing variables that are highly predictive of T in order to increase $\sigma\left(\tilde{T}\right)$.

3. Decreasing the size of the second stage residuals, which can be done by finding variables that are highly predictive of the outcome.

Of those three levers, I confess I only like the last one. As I said before, it is very hard to find IVs in the wild. Also, there is only so much you can remove in order to decrease $\sigma\left(\tilde{T}\right)$. Which leaves you with the only reliable way to decrease the variance: finding variables that are good at predicting the outcome.

Discontinuity Design

Regression discontinuity design (RDD) is another design worth mentioning in addition to the traditional instrumental variable and noncompliance designs. Although RDD is widely used in academia, its application in industry may be more limited. RDD leverages artificial discontinuities in the treatment assignment to identify the treatment effect. For example, suppose a government implements a money transfer program that offers poor families a monthly check of 200 USD in the local currency, but only families earning less than 50 USD are eligible. This creates a discontinuity in the program's assignment at 50 USD, allowing researchers to compare families just above and just below the threshold to measure the program's effectiveness, provided that the two groups are similar.

RDD can be applied to many other situations besides the money transfer program example. Discontinuities are pervasive, making RDD very attractive to researchers.

For instance, to understand the impact of college, researchers can compare people who scored just above and just below a passing threshold in an admission exam. To assess the impact of women on politics, researchers can compare cities where a female candidate lost by a small margin to those where a female candidate won by a small margin. The applications are endless.

RDD can also be useful in industry, but to a lesser extent. For example, suppose a bank offers a credit card to all its customers, but charges a fee to those with an account balance below 5,000 USD. This creates a discontinuity in the way the card is offered, where customers with balances above the threshold are more likely to choose the prime card, while those with balances below the threshold are not. Thus, RDD can be applied to compare the effects of having a prime card versus a regular card, provided that customers above and below the threshold are similar in other respects.

Regarding the relevance of discontinuity designs in the industry, I believe that it is less applicable since firms could easily conduct experiments to randomize eligibility, as we have discussed earlier. However, let us suppose, for the sake of this example, that running such experiments would be time-consuming. Maybe because the required sample is too big, due to low compliance.

In contrast, the bank in question already has data following the discontinuity design described previously. Therefore, the bank can leverage this data to determine the effect of the prime credit card. How can the bank use the discontinuity for this purpose? The basic idea is to recognize that the threshold can be understood as an instrument since crossing it increases the likelihood of receiving the treatment.

In the following image, you can see how the discontinuity design relates to instrumental variables. The bottom part shows the counterfactual treatment by account balance. Since the instrument is crossing the 5,000 USD threshold, you can observe T_0 when *balance* < 5,000 and T_1 otherwise. Moreover, since the instrument increases the chance of getting the treatment (the prime card), there is a jump in $P(T = 1)$ once you cross the threshold. The upper part of the plot reflects how those changes in treatment probability impact the outcome.

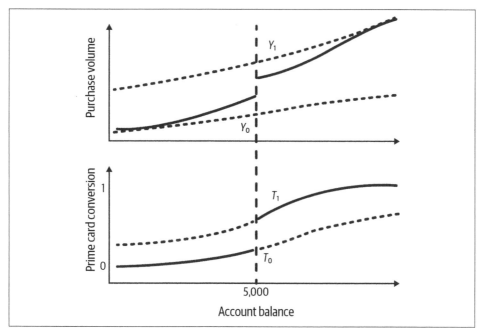

Figure 11-4. Potential outcomes and potential treatment in a discontinuity design

The probability of treatment being less than one, even above the threshold, makes the outcome you observe less than the true potential outcome Y_1. By the same token, the outcome you observe below the threshold is higher than the true potential outcome Y_0. This makes it look like the treatment effect at the threshold is smaller than it actually is and you will have to use IV to correct for that.

Discontinuity Design Assumptions

Besides the IV assumptions, the discontinuity design requires one further assumption about the smoothness of the potential outcomes and potential treatment functions. Let's define a running variable R such that the treatment probability is a discontinuous function of that variable at a threshold $R = c$. In your banking example, R would be the account balance and $c = 5,000$.

Now, you need to assume that:

$$\lim_{r \to c^-} E[Y_t|R = r] = \lim_{r \to c^+} E[Y_t|R = r]$$

$$\lim_{r \to c^-} E[T_z|R = r] = \lim_{r \to c^+} E[T_z|R = r]$$

In other words, the potential outcome Y_t and potential treatment T_z at the discontinuity $R = c$ are the same if you approach them from the left or from the right.

With those assumptions at hand, you can derive the local average treatment effect estimator for a discontinuity design:

$$LATE = \frac{\lim_{r \to c^+} E[Y|R = r] - \lim_{r \to c^-} E[Y|R = r]}{\lim_{r \to c^+} E[T|R = r] - \lim_{r \to c^-} E[T|R = r]}$$

$$= E[Y_1 - Y_0 | T_1 > T_0, R = c]$$

Importantly, this estimator is local in two senses. First, it is local because it only gives the treatment effect at the threshold $R = c$. This is the discontinuity design locality. Second, it is local because it only estimates the treatment effect for the compliers. This is the IV locality.

Intention to Treat Effect

In the top part of Figure 11-4, the jump in the observed outcome at the threshold is the intention-to-treat effect, since it measures how the outcome changes as you change the instrument. Let's now see how you can estimate it, since this will be the numerator of your final IV estimate. To do so, let's first read the data containing information on the customer's account balance, whether or not they choose the prime card, and what their purchase volume is:

```
In [19]: df_dd = pd.read_csv("./data/prime_card_discontinuity.csv")
         df_dd.head()
```

	balance	prime_card	pv	tau	categ
0	12100.0	1	356.472	300.0	always-takers
1	4400.0	1	268.172	300.0	always-takers
2	4600.0	1	668.896	300.0	always-takers
3	3500.0	1	428.094	300.0	always-takers
4	12700.0	1	1619.793	700.0	complier

Next, you need to regress the outcome variable on the running variable R (balance) interacted with a dummy for being above the threshold ($R > c$):

$$y_i = \beta_0 + \beta_1 r_i + \beta_2 \mathbb{1}(r_i > c) + \beta_3 \mathbb{1}(r_i > c) r_i$$

The parameter estimate associated with crossing the threshold, $\widehat{\beta_2}$, can be interpreted as the intention-to-treat effect:

```
In [20]: m = smf.ols(f"pv~balance*I(balance>5000)", df_dd).fit()
         m.summary().tables[1]
```

	coef	std err	t	P>|t|	[0.025	0.975]
Intercept	251.1350	19.632	12.792	0.000	212.655	289.615
I(balance > 5000)[T.True]	354.7539	22.992	15.430	0.000	309.688	399.820
balance	0.0616	0.005	11.892	0.000	0.051	0.072
balance:I(balance > 5000)[T.True]	−0.0187	0.005	−3.488	0.000	−0.029	−0.008

Notice that this is essentially running two regression lines: one above and one below the threshold. If compliance was not an issue, meaning that everyone above the threshold would get the treatment and everyone below the threshold would get the control, you could still use this approach. If that where the case, compliance would be 100%, the ITTE would already be the ATE:

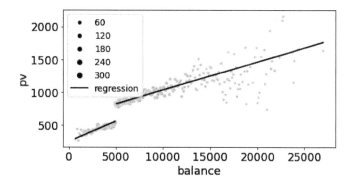

The IV Estimate

Since compliance is not 100%, you need to divide the intention-to-treat effect by the compliance rate. In the context of a discontinuity design, that would be how much the treatment probability changes as you cross the threshold. To estimate this number, you can simply repeat the previous procedure, replacing the outcome variable, pv, with the treatment, prime_card. Here is a simple function to compute the IV estimate in a discontinuity design. It estimates the ITTE and the compliance rate and divides one by the other:

```
In [21]: def rdd_iv(data, y, t, r, cutoff):
             compliance = smf.ols(f"{t}~{r}*I({r}>{cutoff})", data).fit()
             itte = smf.ols(f"{y}~{r}*I({r}>{cutoff})", data).fit()

             param = f"I({r} > {cutoff})[T.True]"
             return itte.params[param]/compliance.params[param]
```

```
        rdd_iv(df_dd, y="pv", t="prime_card", r="balance", cutoff=10000)
```

Out[21]: 654.3917626767736

Applying this function to your data yields an estimate that is pretty close to the true LATE. Remember that you can check this since this dataset contains the individual level treatment effect stored in the `tau` column and the compliance category:

```
In [22]: (df_dd
          .round({"balance":-2}) # round to nearest hundred
          .query("balance==5000 & categ=='complier'")["tau"].mean())
```

Out[22]: 700.0

Finally, although you could derive a formula to calculate the confidence interval of that estimator, the easiest way is to simply wrap the entire function in a bootstrap procedure. I'll hide the code for this since it is fairly repetitive, but you can see the resulting interval here:

```
        array([535.49935691, 781.24156232])
```

Bunching

Before closing this chapter, I just wanted to mention a potential issue to the discontinuity design identification. If the units (customers in your example) can manipulate the running variable, they can also self-select into the treatment group. In the prime credit card example, customers could decide to increase their deposits until it reached just 5,000 so that they would get the prime credit card for free. This would violate the assumption about the smoothness in the potential outcomes, since those just above the threshold would no longer be comparable to those just below it.

A simple and visual way to check if this is happening is to plot the density around the threshold. If units are self-selecting into the treatment, you would expect a huge spike in the density at the threshold. Fortunately, it does not appear to be the case with this data:

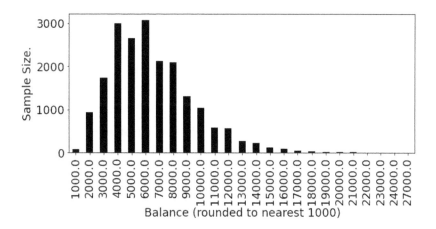

Key Ideas

In this chapter you learned that noncompliance becomes an issue when people can choose not to take a treatment. This is fairly common in the industry, as companies tend to have a pool of optional products or services. In those situations, the customer choice confounds the effect of the product or service, even if the company can randomize their availability.

You also learned about the compliance groups or types:

Compliers
    Those who take the treatment that was assigned to them.

Always takers
    Those who always take the treatment, regardless of the assignment.

Never takers
    Those who never take the treatment, regardless of the assignment.

Defiers
    Those who take the opposite treatment from the one assigned.

And you learned how to use instruments to deal with noncompliance. Namely, an instrument Z is a variable that (1) impacts the treatment in a nonconfounded way and (2) doesn't impact the outcome, unless through the treatment:

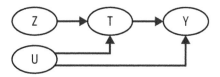

On top of that, if you assume that the instrument flips the treatment in a single direction (monotonicity assumption), you can use it to identify the average treatment effect on the compliers:

$$E[Y_1 - Y_0 | T_1 > T_0] = \frac{E[Y|Z=1] - E[Y|Z=0]}{E[T|Z=1] - E[T|Z=0]}$$

In other words, all you have to do is to normalize the intention to treat the effect by the compliance rate, both of which are easy to identify if the instrument is randomized.

However, there is still a price to pay in terms of variance. If compliance is low, the variance of the instrumental variable estimate will be substantially larger than that of OLS. Particularly, if compliance is 50%, you would need 4x more samples to achieve the same standard errors as if compliance was not an issue (100% compliance). There are some additional tricks to decrease the variance, but the most promising one seems to be finding variables that are good at predicting the outcome, pretty much as it was the case with OLS.

Additionally, you learned that discontinuities in your data could also be treated as instruments. In general, you probably won't need to rely on them, since deploying experiments is fairly common and easy in the industry. Still, in the case that experiments are not available, you can leverage those discontinuities to identify the local average treatment effect.

PRACTICAL EXAMPLE

Quarter of Birth Instrument

As I said earlier, it is pretty hard to find valid instrumental variables in the wild, but quarter of birth might be one of those. In the US, being born in the last quarter means you'll probably have more school years, since you'll join school earlier in your life. If quarter of birth doesn't affect income (unless through schooling) and is as good as random, economists can use it to identify the effect of school on income.

By doing that, economists estimated that we should expect one extra year of education to increase wages by 8.5%, on average:

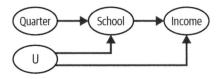

CHAPTER 12

Next Steps

It has been a long way since you were first introduced to counterfactuals. This book has taken you on a journey through the world of causal inference, starting with the basics and gradually building up to more advanced concepts and techniques. You should now have a solid understanding of how to reason about causation and how to use various methods to untangle causation from correlation in your data.

You have learned about the importance of A/B testing as the gold standard for causal inference, the power of graphical models for causal identification, and the use of linear regression and propensity weighting for bias removal. You have explored the intersection between machine learning and causal inference and how to use these tools for personalized decision making.

Furthermore, you have learned how to incorporate the time dimension into your causal inference analyses using panel datasets and methods like difference-in-differences and synthetic control. Finally, you have gained an understanding of alternative experiment designs for when randomization is not possible, such as geo and switchback experiments, instrumental variables, and discontinuities.

With the knowledge and tools presented in this book, you are equipped to tackle real-world problems and make informed decisions based on causation rather than correlation. I hope you enjoyed it and that it keeps being useful to you throughout your career.

This being an introductory book, I intentionally left out some of the causal inference topics that are active areas of research, but have not yet become widespread in the industry. This doesn't mean they aren't useful. Sometimes they are simply complicated, with no easy-to-use software that wraps them. If you enjoyed this book and you are craving something more, I suggest you explore one of the following topics.

Causal Discovery

Throughout this book, you used causal graphs as a starting point for your causal inference analysis. But what if you don't know the causal graph and, instead, have to learn it from data? Causal discovery is a field of study that focuses on finding causal relationships between variables in a given system by using data generated from that system. Causal discovery is the process of going from data to causal knowledge. If you want to learn more about it, a good place to start is the paper "Causal Discovery Toolbox: Uncover Causal Relationships in Python," by Diviyan Kalainathan and Olivier Goudet.

Sequential Decision Making

Although this book covered panel data structures, it did it mostly in the context of staggered adoption, which (among other things) means that there is no treatment-confounder feedback, which can typically arise when the treatment assignment is decided at each period in a sequence. To provide a concrete example, suppose you want to study the effect of a medical procedure (T) on hospital discharge rates (Y). However, the decision to perform the procedure depends on patient symptoms, and this decision is made on a daily basis. Therefore, the probability of a patient receiving the treatment on a particular day depends on whether they were treated on previous days and their symptoms over those days:

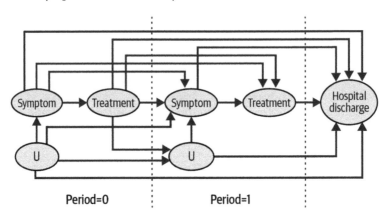

Although all the variables used to determine whether to treat or not are observable, traditional methods like regression may not be suitable for estimating the treatment effect due to the complex time dynamics and treatment-confounder feedback. Adjusting for confounders, such as patient symptoms, leads to noncausal paths, such as $T_0 \rightarrow Symptom_1 \leftarrow U_1 \rightarrow Y$.

Causal inference with sequential decision making has many applications in the industry. However, it is an incredibly intricate topic, which is why I left it out of this book. Still, if you are faced with a situation like the one I just described, I suggest you check out the book *Causal Inference: What If*, by Hernán and Robins. The last part of the book is dedicated to sequential decision making.

Causal Reinforcement Learning

Causal reinforcement learning (CRL) is an area of machine learning that combines the principles of causal inference and reinforcement learning. The goal of CRL is to automate the treatment allocation process with the objective of optimizing the outcome that the treatment influences. To achieve this goal, the automated decision-making system needs to balance exploiting promising treatments with exploring new treatments or applying the same treatment to different types of individuals. However, the use of observable variables in the decision-making process can lead to confounding, as there may be factors that affect both the treatment allocation and the observed outcome. Therefore, the system must adjust for these confounders to better understand the optimal treatments, which is a key challenge in CRL.

A simple example of where CRL could be applied is in the medical setting described earlier. However, instead of understanding the impact of a medical procedure, the objective would be to craft an agent that can recommend the procedure to physicians in a way that optimizes the patient outcomes. The agent would need to consider factors such as patient symptoms and medical history to make treatment recommendations that are tailored to each patient's individual needs while accounting for the causal relationships between the treatment and the observed outcomes.

Much of the literature in causal reinforcement learning gets entangled with that of contextual bandits. The two are, in fact, closely related. If you want a good place to start, I recommend the paper "Contextual Bandits in a Survey Experiment on Charitable Giving: Within-Experiment Outcomes Versus Policy Learning," by Athey et al., and the American Economic Association Continuing Education Webcast on "Modern Sampling Methods," by Keisuke Hirano and Jack Porter.

Causal Forecasting

Causal forecasting is a methodology that seeks to forecast future outcomes by taking into account the causal relationships between variables. Unlike traditional forecasting methods that rely solely on statistical associations between variables, causal forecasting aims to identify and model the underlying causal mechanisms that drive the relationships between variables. This approach can lead to more accurate and reliable forecasts, especially in complex systems where traditional statistical models may fail to capture the true causal relationships.

Causal forecasting typically involves a bit of causal discovery, since an important step in causal forecasting is figuring out if a correlation between X and Y is due to $X \rightarrow Y$, $Y \rightarrow X$, or $Y \leftarrow U \rightarrow X$. However, causal forecasting also requires dealing with the additional complexity of traditional time-series modeling, like nonstationarity and the data not being independent and identically distributed. A good place to learn more about this topic is the American Economic Association 2019 Continuing Education Webcast on Time-Series Econometrics, by James H. Stock and Mark W. Watson.

Domain Adaptation

Causal inference is the process of understanding what would happen from what did happen. This involves moving from a factual distribution, such as $Y \mid T = 1$, to a counterfactual one, like Y_1. The problem of inferring something about a distribution while having data from another one is known as *domain adaptation*, and it has many applications beyond causal inference. For instance, consider a financial services company that wants to detect fraudulent transactions. At first glance, this may appear to be a purely predictive task, where the company can train a machine learning model on its past transactions and use it to classify future transactions. However, the data the company has is fundamentally different from the data it needs to classify. Specifically, the company only has transactions that were authorized by its previous fraud-detection system. If that system was effective, then *P(fraud)* in the training data will be lower than *P(fraud)* for the future transactions the company model has to classify. In other words, the company has data on *Y|filtered* but wants to build a model that is good at predicting Y without the filter. The company wants its model to act as the filter.

This is just one example, but there are many others. For instance, a company that is expanding into new countries may want to use its existing data from other countries to train predictive models that will perform well in the new country. Alternatively, a company's past data may behave differently from its current and future data, indicating that the distributions are shifting over time. In fact, since data is rarely stationary, most businesses will have to deal with distribution shifts in some way or another. This will require them to learn from one distribution to apply their insights to another. Although this problem is not strictly in the realm of causal inference, many of the techniques used in causal inference can be applied here. A good review on the literature on concept drift is given by the paper "Learning Under Concept Drift: A Review," by Lu et al.

Closing Thoughts

I hope I have sparked your interest in continuing your journey in causal inference. The nice thing about research is that it never ends. I myself intend to keep writing about causal inference for the foreseeable future and I would like to invite you to join me. You can find me on GitHub (*https://github.com/matheusfacure*), Twitter (*https://twitter.com/MatheusFacure*), and LinkedIn (*https://www.linkedin.com/in/matheus-facure-7b0099117/*), where I post regularly about causal inference. But most of all, my wish is that I have sparked in you an interest in this very fascinating topic. Although this book has come to an end, your learning journey on causal inference has just begun. I wish you all the best on the path ahead!

Index

Symbols
* operator, 185
$1 - \beta$ for power, 56
2SLS (see two-stage least squares)
: operator, 185
@curry decorator, 189
^ (hat) denoting sample estimates, 42
α for significance level, 52
β and β-hat, 98
δ as detectable difference between parameter
    estimate and null hypothesis, 56
    sample size calculation, 57
$\hat{e}(x)$ for propensity score model, 159
μ for mean, 36
$\hat{\mu}$ for sample mean, 36
$\hat{m}(x)$ for outcome model, 162
σ as standard deviation, 38
σ-squared for variance, 36
$\hat{\sigma}$ as estimate of standard deviation, 42
$\hat{\sigma}$-squared for estimate of variance, 36
$\bar{x}$ as mean of x, 42
← for causal model nonreversibility, 9

A
"A/B Testing Intuition Busters: Common Mis-
    understandings in Online Controlled
    Experiments" (Kohavi et al.), 58
A/B tests
    linear regression, 97-100
    randomized treatment example, 33-37
    randomizing treatment and confounders, 82
Abadie, Alberto, 248, 287, 317
Abraham, Sarah, 270
adjustment formula, 77

curse of dimensionality, 97
positivity assumption, 78
advanced topics
    causal discovery, 362
    causal forecasting, 363
    causal reinforcement learning, 363
    domain adaptation, 364
    sequential decision making, 362
Agrawal, Ajay, 5
American Economic Association Continuing
    Education Webcast, 363, 364
Angrist, Joshua D., 115
area under the curve (AUC), 195
Arkhangelsky, Dmitry, 304
association
    causation and
        about, 6
        association equal to causation, 24, 31
        bias making association different from
            causation, 18
        causal models, 9
        causal quantities of interest, 14-16
        causal quantities of interest example,
            16-18
        do(.) operator, 11
        fundamental problem of causal infer-
            ence, 8, 14
        graphing, 74
        (see also graphical causal models)
        individual treatment effect, 12
        interventions, 10-12
        potential outcomes, 12
        treatment and outcome, 7
        untangling association and causation, 65

null hypothesis, 51-52

I

identification
    as eliminating bias, 24, 27
    as eliminating do(.) operator, 12
    first step in causal inference analysis, 23, 25, 61
    graphical causal models for, 61, 75
        example with data, 78-79
    identifying the treatment effect, 23
        independence assumption, 25
    model-based versus design-based, 161
        doubly robust estimation for both, 162-164
        doubly robust outcome model example, 167-169
        doubly robust treatment model example, 164-167
    partial identification, 82
    randomization with, 25-28
    selection bias and, 84
ignorability (see conditional independence assumption)
Imbens, Guido W., 248
immorality between variables, 70
    conditioning on collider, 70
        conditioning on effect of collider, 70
impact estimation (see causal inference)
importance sampling and inverse propensity weighting, 155
income affected by school, 360
independence assumption, 25
independent variables, 67
    immorality and colliders, 70
    querying a graph in Python, 72-75
indicator function, 114
individual treatment effect (ITE), 12
    conditional average treatment effects versus, 183
inference, 38-41
    difference-in-differences, 246-248
    panel data, 246-248
    synthetic control, 295-297
instrumental variables (IV)
    analysis
        first stage regression, 344
        reduced form second step, 345
        standard error, 347-348

standard error additional controls, 349-351
        two-stage least squares, 346
        two-stage least squares by hand, 351
        two-stage least squares matrix implementation, 351
    bias, 348
    definition of instrument, 338
    estimate in discontinuity design, 357
    noncompliance definition, 142
        DAG representation, 338
    quarter of birth example, 360
"Intelligent Credit Limit Management in Consumer Loans Based on Causal Inference" (Miao et al.), 198
intention-to-treat effect (ITTE), 339, 356
"Interpreting OLS Estimands When Treatment Effects Are Heterogeneous" (Słoczyński), 95
interventions
    causal models, 10-12
    definition, 10
    do(.) operator, 11
        individual treatment effect, 12
        potential outcomes, 12
inverse propensity weighting (IPW), 149-151
    as application of importance sampling, 155
    estimator variance, 159
    positivity assumption, 159-161
        IPW estimator versus linear regression, 161
    pseudo-population creation, 149
        bias removed by IPW, 156
    regression and, 151
    when to use IPW versus regression, 161
IPW (see inverse propensity weighting)

K

K folds, 224, 296
K-Nearest-Neighbors (KNN) algorithm, 146
    suspicious of, 148
Kalainathan, Diviyan, 362
King, Gary, 148
KNN (see K-Nearest-Neighbors)
Kohavi, Ron, 58
Krueger, Alan, 240
Künzel, S. R., 212

About the Author

Matheus Facure is an economist and senior data scientist at Nubank, the biggest Fin-Tech company outside Asia. He has successfully applied causal inference in a wide range of business scenarios, from automated and real-time interest and credit decision making, to cross-sell emails and optimizing marketing budgets. He is also the author of *Causal Inference for the Brave and True*, a popular book that aims to make causal inference mainstream in a lighthearted, yet rigorous way.

Colophon

The animal on the cover of *Causal Inference in Python* is a green forest lizard (*Calotes calotes*). The Latin name comes from the Greek word *kalos*, which means pretty or gracile. Calotes, the genus, is characterized by the ability to change color in certain conditions. For example, the male green forest lizard's head and throat turn bright red during the breeding season. They are usually a slightly yellow or brown shade of green with stripes of white or dark green across their backs.

Green forest lizards are considered medium to large among lizards with an average length of 19.5 to 25.5 inches. This estimate includes the tail, which is notably long and slender.

These lizards are found only in the biodiverse forests of Sri Lanka and of India's Western Ghats mountain range and Shevaroy Hills. Parts of their habitat are protected, and hundreds of their neighboring species are threatened. Green forest lizard populations are stable in this pocket of the world. Many of the animals on O'Reilly's covers are endangered; all of them are important to the world.

The cover illustration is by Karen Montgomery, based on a black and white engraving from *Natural History of Ceylon*. The cover fonts are Gilroy Semibold and Guardian Sans. The text font is Adobe Minion Pro; the heading font is Adobe Myriad Condensed; and the code font is Dalton Maag's Ubuntu Mono.

O'REILLY®

Learn from experts.
Become one yourself.

Books | Live online courses
Instant answers | Virtual events
Videos | Interactive learning

Get started at oreilly.com.

Ingram Content Group UK Ltd.
Milton Keynes UK
UKHW031943170723
425286UK00003B/6